Richard Twiss

**Travels through Portugal and Spain**

In 1772-1773

Richard Twiss

**Travels through Portugal and Spain**
*In 1772-1773*

ISBN/EAN: 9783744757447

Printed in Europe, USA, Canada, Australia, Japan

Cover: Foto ©Andreas Hilbeck / pixelio.de

More available books at **www.hansebooks.com**

# TRAVELS

THROUGH

PORTUGAL AND SPAIN,

IN 1772 AND 1773.

Entered in the Hall-Book of the Company of Stationers.

# TRAVELS

THROUGH

# PORTUGAL and SPAIN,

IN 1772 AND 1773.

BY

RICHARD TWISS, Esq. F.R.S.

WITH COPPER-PLATES;

AND

AN APPENDIX.

───── he puesto en la certidumbre de lo que refiero mi principal cuidado.
Pref. à la Hist. de Mexico, de Solis.

LONDON,
Printed for the AUTHOR,
And Sold by G. ROBINSON, T. BECKET, and J. ROBSON.
MDCCLXXV.

# PREFACE.

*Una de las cosas en que se vee la grandeza del animo del hombre, y la parte imortal adonde aspira, es el no hallarse contento, ni satisfecho en un lugar, procurando hartar su deseo, inclinado a diversidad de cosas, rodeando el mundo, y tentando diferentes lugares para hurtar el cuerpo à los fastidios de la vida.* Disc. prelim. à la *Araucana*.

The meaning of which is, " Nothing perhaps more evidently proves the greatness of the mind of man, and the immortality to which it aspires, than not finding ourselves contented or satisfied in one place, but procuring the gratification of our desires, which are inclined to a diversity of objects, by rambling about the world, and visiting different places, to steal (as it were) ourselves from the cares of life."

AFTER having spent several years in travelling through England, Scotland, Holland, Flanders, France, Switzerland, Italy, Germany, Bohemia, &c. the love of variety, or curiosity of seeing new things, was still so prevalent, that I determined to visit Spain and Portugal; and I was the more eager, as I had never seen any satisfactory account of those two kingdoms,

doms, promising to myself the enjoyment of objects entirely novel, in countries which were imagined to be far behind the rest of Europe in arts and literature. The following sheets contain the observations made in that tour; they are published as my first attempt, and the strictest truth has been inviolably adhered to throughout the whole work.

In regard to the few levities upon the subject of superstition, I have not endeavoured to ridicule the persons believing, but the objects of their belief; for we cannot with reason condemn mankind for differing in their opinions: we all seek for truth, but God only knows who has found it.

If those parts of the work relative to painting be thought too prolix, all I have to offer in excuse is my attachment to that science. Almost all the plates were executed after my own sketches; and I have selected such subjects as have never before been published.

I cannot conclude this preface with more propriety than with the following quotation from the best book

that

# PREFACE.

that exists in the Spanish language: " Es grandísimo el
" riesgo a que se pone el que imprime un libro, siendo
" de toda imposibilidad imposible componerle tal que
" satisfaga y contente à todos los que le leyeren."

Don Quixote, tom. iii. cap. lv.

Great Russel-Street, Bloomsbury,
March 26, 1775.

# DESCRIPTION of the PLATES,.

TO face the title. A Map of Spain and Portugal. In this map the provinces have their proper titles and boundaries, the names are rightly fpelt, the latitude and longitude (from London) of thofe cities, where aftronomical obfervations have been made, are exact: no names are inferted but fuch as belong to fome remarkable city, town, village, cape, mountain, or river. The places are marked where the cities of *Numancia, Saguntum, Illiberia,* and *Italica* exifted. My route is traced with parallel lines. The ornamental part reprefents a fhield with the arms of Portugal, wind-mills, &c.

P. 38. The fecond plate contains views of three of the moft remarkable Moorifh caftles: that of *Alcobaça* in Portugal, and thofe of *Almanfa* and *Sax*, with a profpect of the town of *Ronda* in Spain.

P. 82. The third plate reprefents the aqueduct of Segovia (engraven from a large print which I procured at Madrid.)

P. 112. The fourth is a copy of the picture known by the name of *our Lady of the Fifh*, which is preferved in the *Efcorial*.

P. 156. The fifth contains the notes of the *Fandango*, or national dance.

P. 240. The fixth plate is a profpect of the *Alhambra*, or palace of the ancient Moorifh kings in *Granada*. At one corner of the plate are two infcriptions faid to be Phœnician, and three in Arabic (one of which is on a round tile), all copied from thofe in this palace; and three capitals of columns, according to the Moorifh architecture; the laft column reprefents one of thofe which are in the *Mefquita* at *Cordova*. At the other corner is one of the gate-ways of the *Alhambra*.

P. 288. The feventh is the reprefentation of a bull-fight in the amphitheatre of *Cadiz*, and fhews all the principal actions of the bulls and. combatants.

The tail-piece reprefents the arms of Spain,.

# TRAVELS

THROUGH

## PORTUGAL AND SPAIN.

AFTER having waited eighteen days at Falmouth for a favourable wind, I embarked on board one of the packets, on the 12th of November, 1772, at four in the afternoon; and, on the 17th, early in the morning, we saw the Rock; at one in the afternoon anchored in the Tagus, and landed at Lisbon at six in the evening. This speedy passage made amends for the tedious delay in Falmouth.

On landing, I was conducted to an English inn, kept by one De War, on the hill of Buenos Ayres, where there is an ordinary every day, frequented by Englishmen, who reside in Lisbon for their health, and by members of the factory.

Lisbon is pretty nearly in the same ruinous state it was the day after the earthquake in 1755. Indeed there are many new buildings

ings carrying on, but the streets are yet in various places stopped up by the ruins occasioned by that devastation; which recalled to my mind the similar situation in which I had seen the city of Dresden, caused by war and fire. This city is built on seven steep hills, and the streets are very badly paved with small sharp stones, which renders walking almost impracticable; and at night, as there is no kind of light in those streets, it would not be prudent for a stranger to walk about alone. A few days after my arrival, an Italian was murdered and robbed among some of the ruins.

About one fifth of the inhabitants of Lisbon consists of blacks, mulattoes, or of some intermediate tint of black and white.

The houses are generally two stories high, sometimes three, with no other chimney but that of the kitchen; they are built of a kind of half marble *, with iron balconies, and wooden lattices to the ground-floor, but are not remarkable for architecture.

Here is a theatre for Italian operas; la Signora Anna Zamperini, who was some time in London, and whom I had before known in Turin, was the chief singer in the comic opera, and appeared daily on the stage, ornamented with three or four thousand pounds worth of jewels.

* Presque Marbre.

The other theatre is for Portuguese plays; there are four rows of boxes, twenty-seven boxes in each row. The Italian house is nearly of the same size. I saw the tragedy of Doña Ignes de Castro acted, with a farce called O Naō, or the Dwarf. The seats in the pit are appropriated solely to the men. The admittance money to the opera is a crusado novo, or two shillings and eight pence half-penny.

There are two long rooms, where the British factory assemble twice a week, during the winter, to dance and play at cards. The minuets composed by Don Pedro Antonio Avondano, who lives here, are much esteemed. Any British stranger who does not intend to reside six months in Lisbon is admitted gratis to these assemblies; but the subscription for the inhabitants is seven moidores for each room. I am informed that since my departure both these societies are united, and that a very large room is built for that purpose. During the course of the winter there are four grand balls, with suppers; to which many of the Portuguese nobility are invited.

Immediately after my arrival I waited on his excellency the honourable Mr. Walpole, his majesty's envoy extraordinary to the Portuguese court. I am happy in thus publicly acknowledging the very great politeness and kindness which I experienced from this gentleman, who does honour to his station, and every obliging service in his power to all. I had the pleasure of being present at several magnificent entertainments he gave to the factory during my stay in Lisbon.

In the church of St. Rocco, is a chapel with three pieces in mosaic, made at Rome. The altar-piece represents the Baptism by St. John, in which are seven figures as large as the life: on one side is the Annunciation, which of course consists of only two figures, and on the other side the Gift of Tongues. The pavement of this chapel is likewise in mosaic, being a sphere, which is the arms of the Brasils. The altar itself is of silver, with figures in alto relievo.

On and about the spot where the royal palace stood, before it was demolished by the earthquake, there are many new streets building, intersecting each other at right angles, parallel and straight, especially that called the Rua Augusta. On each side of these new streets is a foot-path, elevated somewhat above the pavement, and defended from carriages by stone posts. The houses are four and five stories in height. The exchange is finished, and is near the river, with porticos, under which the merchants assemble. This building forms one side of an intended square, in the midst of which is to be placed an equestrian statue of the present king. The pedestal is, as I was told, of a single stone, that required eighty yoke of oxen to drag it from the quarry, about two miles from the spot where it now is.

The

PORTUGAL.

The arfenal is a very large building, though not quite finifhed. Slaves are employed in carrying the ftones, morter, &c. They are condemned criminals, and are chained by the leg in pairs.

Near the arfenal is the fifh-market, which is a very commodious one, even fuperior to thofe in Holland. It is plentifully fupplied with fifh, moft of them unknown in England; but with neither falmon nor cod: the former of which, however, the inhabitants procure from Oporto, by men employed for the purpofe, who perform the journey in four days on foot, taking the fhorteft route, without regarding the common roads, and deliver each fifh at Lifbon for a moidore. The john dory is to be met with larger here than any on the weftern coaft of England; as, likewife, are red mullets. I faw fome very large conger eels, and a fcate that meafured near feven feet from the head to the extremity of the tail. Near this market, are alfo fold vegetables, fruits, tortoifes, monkies, parrots, and Brafil birds.

As in a late publication of a journey through Portugal, the author has inadvertently erred in the account of his fearch after the weftern Lifbon, I fhall here quote a paffage from a book printed at Amfterdam in 1730, in French, entitled, *a Defcription of Lifbon*.

" Lifbon was divided, about the year 1716, in two, under the
" names of the Oriental part, and Occidental part. This divifion
" was

" was made on occasion of the creation of the patriarch, whose
" diocese consists of the occidental part, and the archbishop
" has retained the oriental. Since this partition, the inhabi-
" tants are obliged, under pain of nullity, to express in all acts
" the part of the town in which they have passed; exact
" merchants also distinguish it in their bills of exchange, and
" in their letters."

There has never yet been a plan of Lisbon published. But four very finely engraved views of Lisbon and Bellem, were published in London in 1756, by George Hawkins, on as many large sheets.

The new books which describe Portugal are the following:

*Mappa de Portugal Antigo e Moderno*, in three volumes, small quarto, written by Father de Castro, in Portuguese, and printed at Lisbon in 1762. At the end is a table of the roads, with the distances from place to place.

In 1762, Don Pedro Rodriguez Campomanès, wrote a book in Spanish, in one volume octavo, which he dedicated to Mr. Wall, entitled, *Noticia Geografica del Reyno y Caminos de Portugal*.

I have also a thin folio, written by Father do Prado, and printed at Lisbon in 1751, containing a description of the

Royal

Royal Convent near Mafra, illuftrated with an elevation and two plans. This book treats chiefly of the ceremony of bleffing the relics, and of the confecration of the church and altars, with a lift of the ornaments, plate, and veftments there made ufe of; in fhort, of every thing one does not defire to know.

There is no news-paper or gazette in the Portuguefe language: they were prohibited in 1763. The Englifh, French, and Spanifh papers are in the coffee-houfes, of which two are extremely elegant, efpecially that of Cafaco, which is pannelled with looking-glaffes.

The country about Lifbon is agreeably diverfified with groves of orange and lemon trees, intermixed with olive and vine-yards. The roads are bordered with aloes, which make an uncommon appearance to a native of a colder climate when they are in flower, the ftem being then twelve or fourteen feet in height. Thefe aloes blow the fixth or feventh year. What Mr. Brydone fays of thofe of Sicily, is likewife juft in refpect to thefe. " As the whole " fubftance of the plant is carried into the ftem and flowers, the " leaves begin to decay as foon as the blow is completed, and " numerous young plants are produced round the root of the " old ones," which wither and die.

Moft of the roads in the environs are paved with large ftones. Near the city, in the valley of Alcantara, is fituated the celebrated aqueduct

aqueduct which joins two hills; the arches in this part are thirty-five in number, fourteen large ones, and twenty-one smaller, the largest of which is three hundred and thirty-two feet in height, and two hundred and forty-nine feet in width; so that St. Paul's church in London is only seventy-two feet higher. There are ten smaller arches nearer to the city, and many still smaller near the source of the water which supplies this aqueduct. This water is emptied into a great reservoir at one of the extremities of Lisbon. The whole pile was erected in 1748; and happily received no damage from the earthquake in 1755. It is built of a kind of white marble. The pillars which support the arches are square, the largest measure thirty-three feet at each side of the base; so that the breadth of this aqueduct is but a tenth part of its height, and consequently makes that height appear much more considerable than it really is to a spectator who stands under the great arch [*].

The patriarchal church stands on the top of one of the seven hills on which Lisbon is built; the great altar is placed under the dome, and has a baldachino, or canopy over it, supported by four spirally twisted columns of wood gilt, like that in St. Peter's at Rome. There is a very large organ with horizontal pipes in this church. Indeed all the organs I afterwards saw in this peninsula (as the natives call Portugal and Spain) are built in the same manner.

[*] In 1750, T. Bowles published a view of this aqueduct.

The 26th of November, being St. Cecilia's day, I went in the morning to the church of St. Rocco, to hear the mufical *funçaõ*, which lafted three hours. The mufic performed was of Jomelli's compofition, and the band was placed as follows.

The organ over the church door; and in the organ-gallery were ten eunuchs from the king's chapel: on one fide were fixteen violins, fix baffes, three double baffes, four tenors, two hautboys, a French horn, and a trumpet; and underneath them, about fixty voices for the choruffes; and, on the other fide, were the fame number of vocal and inftrumental performers. The firft violin was played by Mr. Groeneman, a German, who was engaged to go with lord Clive to the Eaft Indies fome time ago, but left him at the Brafils, and came to Lifbon, where he now is firft violin to the king. The whole concert was under the direction of the celebrated Mr. David Perez; fome of whofe compofitions have been lately publifhed in London. The church was extremely crowded by perfons of each fex. High mafs was celebrated; during which the women remained fquatted on the ground, having all white muflin veils, and black filk cloaks.

As I am on the fubject of mufic, I muft mention the talents on the harpfichord of the lady of Mr. May, an Englifh merchant here. This lady equals any performer I ever heard on that inftrument, for the rapidity of execution, and the delicacy and tafte with which fhe plays the moft difficult pieces: fhe is
likewife

likewife well verfed in the theory of mufic. The harpfichord under her hands, was literally

"By flying fingers touch'd into a voice."

I had likewife the pleafure of hearing Mr. Rodill, a Spaniard, whofe fkill on the German flute and hautboy is now well known in London. I alfo heard a Portuguefe young lady's performance on the mufical glaffes, which were empty, but her fingers were occafionally dipped in water.

I went on the 17th of November to the king's palace at Bellem, about five miles from Lifbon, and heard the Italian opera of Ezio performed there. The orcheftra confifted of very accurate players. No ladies are ever admitted to this opera, neither are there any actreffes; but, inftead of women, they have eunuchs dreffed exactly as women are; fo that, from the ftage, they appear to be really what they reprefent. But the dancing between the acts being likewife by men with great black beards and broad fhoulders, dreffed in female apparel, was a difgufting fight. The jealoufy of the queen is faid to be the caufe of this uncommon exhibition.

Many of the priefts here are eunuchs. Miffon, who travelled in Italy in 1688, and there faw two priefts of the fame kind, gives the following account of them, which being tranflated, runs thus: "You know that a prieft muft be a complete man: "it is a law without any exception. However, as it has been re-
"marked,

"  marked, that that perfection of the body sometimes causes a
"  disagreeable voice; and that, on the other hand, sweetness
"  of voice is very necessary to infinuate things into the mind,
"  whether at church or at the opera, there has been found
"  a means of conciliating these difficulties; and it has been re-
"  folved, that a priest cut out for music, may exercise the sacer-
"  dotal functions, provided he has his necessities, or, if you
"  please, superfluities, in his pocket."

This theatre is small, and without any side-boxes; in the pit are ten benches without backs, behind which is the king's box. All the royal family were present that evening. The king himself, Don Joseph I. is a well looking man, and is now (in 1772) fifty-eight years of age. The queen is fifty-four years. The king's brother, Don Pedro, who is fifty-five years old, married his majesty's eldest daughter, who has the title of princess of Brasil, and is thirty-eight. They have a son of eleven years, who is heir-apparent to the crown of Portugal, his title is prince of Beira; and another son and daughter. The king's other two daughters, the infantas Dona Maria Anna of thirty-six, and Dona Maria Francisca Benedicta, of twenty-six years, were also there, as that day was the anniversary of the birth of the princess of Brasil.

These ladies were without caps, neither were they painted, but were ornamented with a great number of jewels. The opera began at seven, and ended at ten, and during the whole performance

formance the most strict silence was observed by the audience; who between the acts rose and stood with their faces towards the royal family.

The cardinal-patriarch sat in a small box appropriated to him on the right hand of the king's box.

Any well dressed men are admitted gratis to this spectacle.

The palace of Bellem is a very mean wooden edifice, and has nothing worthy of remark neither on the outside nor in the inside. There is not so much as a single picture from any of the Italian schools in the whole kingdom of Portugal. What few pictures there were formerly in Lisbon, were destroyed by the earthquake.

At the house of Messrs. Purry and De Vismes, is a picture painted by Van Loo, representing the marquis of Pombal (who is prime minister) sitting, of the natural size, at a table covered with plans and elevations of buildings intended for Lisbon. The back ground shows the Tagus down to Bellem, with ships, in which Jesuits are embarking, and is painted by Vernet; the whole piece was executed in Paris two or three years ago. The proprietors have caused a very fine copper-plate of it to be engraven; and this is the only picture I ever heard of at Lisbon, worth any notice.

Neither

PORTUGAL. 13

Neither have I been able to find any ſtatues in Portugal, except two groupes in the royal garden at Bellem, expoſed to the air very injudiciouſly; I could get no information about the name of the ſtatuary, but was told they were ſent from Rome: probably they are by il Cavalier Bernini, or perhaps by Algardi, being equal to any of the ſtatues I ſaw at Rome of thoſe two great ſculptors. Theſe groups are of two figures each, as large as the life, and of white marble. One is the daughter giving ſuck to her father, and the other is a woman fainting and reclining within the arms of another woman. Theſe ſtatues

"ſeemed to breathe,
"And ſoften into fleſh beneath the touch
"Of forming art, imagination fluſh'd." THOMSON.

They are indeed perfectly beautiful, and hitherto in good preſervation; poſſibly in ſuch a fine climate as this is, they may remain unhurt for ages; as the Farneſian Hercules, the Perſius of Cellini, and many other invaluable ſtatues, both at Rome and at Florence, have done.

In this garden I ſaw a very large elephant, being no leſs than twenty-two feet in height; it is kept in a yard, partly covered, and partly expoſed to the air, and is viewed from the top of the wall. The reſt of the menagerie conſiſts of two lions, a leopard, and ten fine zebras, or wild aſſes; theſe latter are in one ſtable: ſome of them were brought from Angola, the others are natives of this place. They can never be ſufficiently broke to endure a
bit

bit or a rein, though it was attempted, to enable fix of them to draw the prince of Beira's chariot.

Near the palace of Bellem is a pillar erected with an inscription, importing that this is the spot whereon the late duke of Aveiro's palace stood; he was executed for having shot at the king in 1759, and the palace was erased.

The building of the church, of which the king laid the first stone, on the spot where his majesty was shot at, is discontinued; the walls are carried only to a few feet in height; indeed there are churches enough already.

On the 6th of January, 1773, I rode on horseback to the castle of St. Julian, at the mouth of the Tagus, about fifteen miles from Lisbon. The road is paved the whole way, and extends along the banks of this noble river. The weather was extremely fine and warm. To the left the grand view of the ships sailing various ways, the castle of Bellem, the castle of St. Julian, the immense rock called Cape Roque, and at last the ocean; and to the right, groves of orange and lemon trees loaden with blossoms as well as fruit, aloe and Indian fig-hedges, interspersed with convents, churches, and olive yards, with the distant prospect of the opposite shore, contributed to render this one of the most agreeable rides I ever enjoyed. Unfortunately there is no inn nor house of any kind to put up at, so that I left my horse to the care of one of the soldiers, whilst I was ob-

serving

serving the castle, and returned to Lisbon with a keen appetite, which I imagine was likewise the case with my poor beast, after trotting thirty miles on a paved, rugged, and hilly road without baiting.

The castle of St. Julian is an irregular pentagon, and is founded on the solid rock, the base of which is washed by the sea. It is garrisoned with two thousand and eighty men, as the officer who accompanied me informed me; but I much doubt the truth of this assertion. It is planted with two hundred and five large brass cannon, one of which is eighteen feet in length, and was made at Diu. Opposite to this castle is a smaller one on an island, which, together with St. Julian's defends the entrance of this river.

Another excursion which I made was to the royal convent and palace of Mafra, about thirty miles from Lisbon. I set out early in the morning, with a servant, in a two-wheeled chaise drawn by a pair of mules: we stopped about half way to refresh ourselves, for we all messed together, mules, driver, servant, and self, on provisions brought with us from Lisbon, as there was nothing at all to be had in this hotel. The road thus far is through a romantic country, producing orange, lemon, olive, mulberry, cypress, and palm trees, hedges of wild pomegranate, rosemary, jessamines, aloes, prickly pear, bays, laurel, and myrtle. The country is well cultivated. I observed eight oxen drawing one plough. Afterward the country " assumes a
Highland

Highland appearance," and the inclofures are of loofe ftones piled on each other, as in Derbyfhire. To the left is the view of Cape Roque, and to the right the royal park, three leagues in circumference, environed by a wall of fifteen feet in height. The building itfelf is fituated near the fmall village of Mafra, and is conftructed of a kind of white marble. It contains thirty-feven windows in front, and is nearly a fquare of feven hundred and twenty-eight feet. The church is placed in the center of this fabric, having the palace on one fide, and the convent on the other.

There is a grand flight of ftairs which projects one hundred and fifty-two feet into the fquare before the building. Under the portico, at the entrance, are twelve gigantic Italian marble ftatues of faints, of tolerable workmanfhip. That of St. Sebaftian is extremely well executed. This portico is of two orders of architecture, each of fix columns, the firft ionic, the other compofite. The ingrefs to the church is by five doors.

The architect of the whole fabric was a German, John Fredcrics. It was begun during the reign of John V in 1717, and finifhed in 1731. There are three hundred cells in the convent, each of twenty palms, or feet, by eighteen; the kitchen is ninety-fix palms by forty-two: the new library is three hundred and eighty-one palms in length, and forty-three in breadth. In the whole building the printed account affures, that there are eight hundred and feventy rooms, and five thoufand two hundred

hundred windows. The floors are of bricks, nicely laid. The palace is not furnished, as the king seldom resides here. Three or four of the rooms have chimnies; and the late duke of York was lodged in these apartments for a few days.

On each side of the church is a tower, or belfry, having each forty-eight bells, which form chimes, or what the French call *carillon*, and the Spaniards *organo de las campanas*. The ascent to these towers is by one hundred and sixty-two steps: and at each end of the *façade*, the three last windows are decorated with a small cupola. The church has a cupola of the Corinthian order, with a gallery round the inside of it. There are six altars, over each of which is a marble basso relievo; and there are no less than six organs in this temple. Some few paintings are dispersed here, but they are only by obscure Italian masters. The whole building is covered with a flat roof, which forms an agreeable terrace for walking. There are several handsome courtyards with porticos; and behind the edifice is a pretty large garden.

The inn at Mafra is the best I met with in Portugal, out of Lisbon. After having been to see the chime-player, and examined his *musical bricks*, which are nothing but the *staccato pastorale*, I was agreeably entertained with seeing my landlord and landlady dance the *fandango*, to the music of the guitar. The person who played on it struck merely a few chords in triple time, and beat time with the same hand on the belly of the instrument.

D The

The dance itself is for two perfons, and much like the Dutch *plugge danfen*. I imagine the Dutch, by having been fo long under the Spanifh dominion, have retained this dance, as well as many other cuftoms. For inftance, the veils; which are large fquare pieces of black filk, that the women, when walking throw over their heads, and keep nearly clofed over their faces. The Spanifh name is *velo*, the Dutch call it *faly*. The cuftom of fmoking tobacco the inhabitants of the Netherlands have probably alfo derived from the Spaniards. The pronunciation of the two languages in the harfh and guttural G, is exactly the fame.

But to return to the *fandango*. Every part of the body is in motion, and is thrown into all poftures, frequently into very indecent ones. Stamping the time with the feet, and playing all the while with the *caftañetas*, which are a kind of fmall fhells of ivory, or hard wood, of which two are rattled together in each hand. When they have not thefe inftruments, they fnap with their fingers and thumbs. The dancers approach, turn, retire, and approach again; the man with his hat on. I afterwards faw this dance to greater perfection on the ftage, to the mufic of the whole orcheftra. It feems the tune is always identically the fame. When thefe dancers were tired, and in a profufe fweat with the violence of the exercife, their place was immediately fupplied by another couple, as the room was by this time filled with moft of the decent people of the village, who having danced in their turns, I difcharged the mufician, and paffed the remainder of the evening in playing a rubber at whift with my landlady, her hufband, and her fifter. I muft not omit, that before the dancing I had for fupper an excellent roafted fowl with bacon and fallad, pickled *fardinhas* (a kind of fprats), with eggs, cheftnuts, apples, and oranges; and afterward flept comfortably on a feather-bed. Thefe good accommodations are owing to the members of the Englifh factory making frequent excurfions to Mafra on parties of pleafure, during their fummer refidence at Cintra.

The next day I returned to Lifbon by the fame road, fo well pleafed with this jaunt, that a few days after I made another to Cintra on horfeback. The road is paved all the way from Lifbon, being about eighteen miles. I went to the Englifh inn, as it is called, though kept by a Turinefe; and it is a very good one. I immediately mounted a jack-afs, of which numbers are to be hired here, and after three quarters of an hour's continual winding afcent, I found myfelf on the top of a high mountain, called *Cabo de Penha*; on the fummit of which is a fmall convent, which was at that time inhabited by eleven poor Jeronymite monks. I had no barometer to compute the height of this mountain, neither could I get any information from thefe ignorant wretches. This place is inacceffible but by the road the *burro*\* carried me. The profpect is boundlefs, comprehending the beautiful *quintas* (or country houfes) at the foot of the mountain, the palace of Mafra at a great diftance, the expanded ocean, the Tagus, and the continent as far as the eye can carry.

\* Jack-afs

Udal ap Rhys in his account of this place fays, " Here was " an ancient temple called *Templum Lunæ*, and there being fome " fimilitude between the name *Cintra* and *Cynthia*, it is imagin- " ed that the firft is only a corruption of the fecond," &c. He farther fays, " The height and romantic form of this moun- " tain, the prodigious breaks and cavities, and the vaft maffes " of projecting and impending rocks, enriched with fhrubs, or " ennobled by tall and luxuriant trees, render it one of the moft " furprifing and agreeable objects in the world." And fo it cer- tainly is.

" Here Nature's quiet wonders fill the mind."

I defcended this mountain on foot near half way down, then mounted my afs, and was carried in an hour and a half to the adjacent mountain, called Cape Roque, or the Rock of Lifbon, which is the moft weftern point of the European continent, and bears latitude 38° 45′. On the top of it is fituated a convent, wherein, at that time, twenty-two monks lived. It is commonly called the Cork convent by the Englifh, this place being fo damp, that every part in it is covered with cork, which grows here in great abundance. Mr. Baretti has given an accurate de- fcription of it. The hermits were as fociable as when he was with them, " and helped us to our glaffes very brifkly." I re- mained with them till late in the evening and by moon-light re- turned in two hours to the inn at Cintra, being carried with the greateft fafety over loofe pieces of rock, and on the brink of pre- cipices and fteep defcents, by my afs, which was fo fure-footed, that

that it never made a falfe ftep. The cold this night was intenfe; it was on the 10th of January, the moon was full, and not a fingle cloud was to be feen; the fhallow waters were frozen, the ice being near an inch in thicknefs, but it melted the next day as foon as the fun had been a few hours above the horizon. Mr. Baretti gives a fhort account of the remains of the Moorifh palace in Cintra, but I did not fee the infide of that building.

The next day, after two hours and a half riding on the road to Lifbon, I ftruck out about a mile to the right, to fee the palace called Caluz, belonging to Don Pedro, the king's brother and fon-in-law. It is built of wood, and is two ftories high. The furniture is extremely elegant, and quite new, in the French tafte. The audience faloon is floored with marble, and pannelled with looking-glaffes. Seven very large china vafes are placed on each fide of it.

The concert-room is two hundred feet in length, and its ceiling is very magnificent, being of white ftucco, with a profufion of gilding.

In one room, the hiftory of Don Quixote is reprefented in eighteen compartments. In another, are various pieces, whimfically reprefenting young children quite naked, except fome ornament which they have got on. One of them has a bag to his hair, and a fword girt about his naked loins, with a cane in his hand: he gallants his companion, who wears a muff and tippet,

tippet, and a pair of high-heeled shoes; her hair is powdered, she is decorated with a necklace and ear-rings, but is in other respects naked. All these ludicrous pieces are intended only as furniture, and as such, greatly enliven the apartments.

There is a large garden behind this palace, with a labyrinth, and orange and lemon groves. After having refreshed myself with some of these fruits, just plucked from the trees, I remounted my horse, and returned to Lisbon, amply satisfied with what I had seen.

Strolling one day about Lisbon in search of new objects, I was witness to an uncommon scene, which was of two men sitting in the street, having each of them a large baboon on his shoulders, freeing his head from vermin, with which it swarmed. The baboons were very dexterous, and are the property of a man who gains his livelihood by thus employing them, exacting a *vinten*, or about three halfpence per head, for cleansing it. It is very common to see numbers of people sitting in the sun, with their heads in each other's laps alternately, having their " retinue abridged.' They seem indeed to be the lousiest people I know of, especially the women, who have an enormous quantity of hair. This dirtiness, however, is only to be imputed to the lower class of people.

I made enquiry about the state of the Portuguese navy and army, and was informed that the latter consisted of thirty-eight regiments

regiments of foot, of eight hundred and twenty-one men each, including officers; and of twelve regiments of cavalry, of four hundred horse to each. The horses are of different sizes and colours, and make a very uncouth appearance. The navy consists of eleven men of war, and four frigates. Four of these vessels are commanded by British captains; in the army are likewise a great number of British officers, who are mostly protestants and Scotchmen.

The chief order of knighthood here, is called *the order of Christ*. It was instituted by Denis their sixth king, in 1283. This order is given to almost any one, provided he be a Roman catholic, and is so very common, that it is almost a disgrace to accept of it, though his Portuguese majesty wears the *insignia* of it himself. I have seen a valet de chambre, the keeper of a billiard table, and a musician, decorated with those *insignia*; which are, a star on the left breast, and a small enamelled red cross, charged with another white one, hanging by a ribbon at the button-hole.

The other order, is that of *Avis*, instituted in 1147, by Alfonso, their first king. The knights wear a small enamelled green cross fleuric, at the button-hole.

Nobility is not hereditary in this kingdom; the king confers the titles of earl, marquis, duke, &c. in the same manner as knighthood is conferred in England. Frequently the son
has

has a title, and the father none. The only duke at present, excepting the king's brother, who is duke of Braganza, is the duke of Cadaval.

The Portuguese money consists of twelve golden coins, seven silver, and three copper. Accompts are kept in reis, which is an imaginary denomination. The par is $67\frac{1}{4}$ d. sterling for a thousand reis: according to which the sterling value of their coins is nearly as follows.

Gold Coins,

| | | | |
|---|---|---|---|
| A five moidore piece, which is | 24000 reis is | £.6 15 0 | |
| A two and a half moidore piece | 12000 | 3 7 6 | |
| A double Johannes — — | 12800 | 3 12 0 | |
| These three pieces were prohibited being coined anew in 1732, by king John V. | | | |
| A Johannes, as it is commonly called, | 6400 | 1 16 0 | |
| A half ditto — — — — | 3200 | 0 18 0 | |
| A quarter ditto — — — | 1600 | 0 9 0 | |
| An eighth ditto — — — | 800 | 0 4 6 | |
| A *moeda de ouro*, which means literally a coin of gold, and is commonly called a moidore, — — | 4800 | 1 7 0 | |
| A half ditto — — — | 2400 | 0 13 6 | |
| A quarter ditto — — — | 1200 | 0 6 9 | |
| A *cruzado novo*, or new crown, | 480 | 0 2 $8\frac{1}{4}$ | |
| $\frac{1}{16}$ of a Johannes, or an old crown, | 400 | 0 2 3 | |

PORTUGAL.

Most of these coins are well known in England, as they were there current till very lately.

|  |  | s. | d. |
|---|---|---|---|
| The seven Silver Coins are, |  |  |  |
| A new crown of | 480 reis is | 2 | 8½ |
| A half ditto, or twelve *vintens*, which is twelve times twenty reis | 240 | 1 | 4¼ |
| A quarter ditto, or six *vintens* | 120 | 0 | 8¼ |
| An eighth ditto, or three *vintens* | 60 | 0 | 4⅛ |
| A *tostaō*, or testoon | 100 | 0 | 6¾ |
| A half ditto | 50 | 0 | 3½ |
| A *vinten*. This is a Brasil coin, and is as scarce as our penny | 20 | 0 | 1½ |

The copper coins are a piece of 10 reis, a piece of 5, and a piece of 3 reis. The Portuguese book, called *Mappa de Portugal*, mentions the existence of another small piece, half the value of the last mentioned coin, but they are so scarce that I was not able to procure even the sight of one of them.

An English guinea passes in Lisbon for 3600 reis, which is 134 reis, or nine pence, less than the value; a crown passes for 800 reis, which is 89 reis, or six pence, less; and a shilling for 160 reis, which is 18 reis, or five farthings, less than the worth. Thus £.100 sterling is 355,556 reis, and 100,000 reis is £.28 2s. 6d. In cloth measure, a *vara* is 43½ inches English, and a *covedo* is 26¼ inches.

It

It is very difficult to ascertain the number of inhabitants in Lisbon. The different foreign factories are not numbered with the natives. The English factory alone is computed at six hundred souls. The Dutch and German factories consist also of a very great number of persons.

In 1716, pope Clement XI. declared, in a consistory, that the attestations sent to him from Lisbon, asserted, that only the western part of that city contained near three hundred thousand inhabitants.

The French book before mentioned, printed in 1730, gives two hundred and fifty thousand souls for the number.

In 1739, Antonio de Oliveria Freire, in his Chorographical Description of Portugal, attributes no less than eight hundred thousand inhabitants to Lisbon.

In 1754, the attestations sent to Rome, in order to procure *bulls*, assigned six hundred thousand inhabitants to the metropolis.

The earthquake, which happened the following year, is said by some to have destroyed fifteen thousand persons, by others twenty-four thousand, and by others seventy thousand; indeed, it is impossible to calculate this loss exactly, which, however great, is at present not sensibly perceived; so that I should imagine, Lisbon may with propriety be classed among the first rate cities

cities in Europe for fize and populoufnefs, and poffibly may be ranked as the fourth, the other three being London, Paris, and Naples.

The Englifh factory has a burying-ground in one of the fkirts of the city, planted with walks of cyprefs trees, under which are the graves, where I had the mortification to fee many marble monuments with long, pompous, flattering infcriptions, erected to the memory of fome of the merchants, their wives, and their children; whilft the great author of Tom Jones is here interred, without even a ftone to indicate, that " *Here lies* " *Henry Fielding.*"

The garden of the convent *Das Neceffidades*, immediately under the hill of Buenos Ayres, is a very fine one, and is open to the decent part of the public. The king's hot-houfes in his garden of *Noffa Senhora de Ajuda*, or our Lady of Help, near Bellem, are alfo well worth notice. The ceilings are very neatly painted in frefco. The chief gardener is an Italian. In another neighbouring royal garden is an exceeding large mandrake tree.

The Portuguefe nobility is divided into three claffes. When the *Ecuyer* on horfeback rides before a carriage, the Lifbon *Etiquette* denotes it to belong to the firft rank; the *Ecuyer*'s riding on one fide fhows the fecond rank; and when he rides behind he belongs to the third clafs of nobility. Moft of the carriages

riages are two-wheeled, though on gala days there are many four-wheeled coaches and chariots used, especially by the ambassadors and ministers. It is also customary for the gentlemen to sit uncovered in their carriages, but a servant returning in one is obliged to sit covered, by which means the persons sitting in other carriages which meet or pass it, are betrayed into no improper salutation.

The saddles used here are like our *manége demi-piques*, the stirrups are wooden boxes, which appear very aukward.

Swords are only worn by well-dressed people, and all ornaments of gold or silver lace, or embroidery, are prohibited to be worn on the clothes of the Portuguese of both sexes. Their silk clothes are sometimes elegantly embroidered with silk of a different colour, and many jewels are displayed on gala days. Topazes are very plentiful here, and are extremely well set; but their silversmiths' workmanship is very clumsy.

The kingdom of Portugal produces corn, oil, wine, oranges sour and sweet, lemons, citrons, pears, apples, cherries, figs, damascenes, peaches, apricots, grapes, melons, chesnuts, almonds, nuts, medlars, walnuts, haselnuts, filberds, *alferrobas (filiqua\*), medronhos (arbutus†)*, mulberries, truffles, cab-

---

\* A kind of sweet acorn.      † Strawberry-trees.

bages,

# PORTUGAL.

bages, turnips, cauliflowers, &c. with various medicinal and aromatic herbs and flowers. The quadrupeds are the fame as in England. The birds are, cocks and hens, pigeons, geefe and turkies. Thefe laft are called *Perù* in Portuguefe, as the birds were originally imported from the country of the fame name. The fifh are falmon, foles, tench, lampreys, *dorados*, tunny, mullet, john doric, *fardinhas*, fturgeon, trout, barbel, whiting, roach, congers, eels, carp, lobfters, oyfters, and a great variety of other forts.

There are fome few iron mines in this kingdom. It is faid that in 1528, a filver mine was difcovered near Bragança, but it was never worked. The ancients celebrated the golden fands of the Tagus; and the Portuguefe affirm, that king John III. had a fceptre made of the gold found in that river: Duarte Nunez, in his Defcription of Portugal, fays, that this fceptre is yet preferved in the royal treafury. Several copper-mines were likewife difcovered in the laft century, but I could never hear of any being worked at prefent. Some magnets are found near Cintra: amber is fometimes met with on the coaft, near Setubal. Turquoifes, amethyfts, hyacinths, cryftals, talc, and mercury are alfo produced in Portugal. Here are many ftone and marble quarries; and the fabric of falt is very confiderable.

The Tagus is navigable but a little way above Lifbon, occafioned by its running between inacceffible rocks, and its current is broke by many rapid cataracts. A company of Dutchmen,

men, in the reign of Charles II. offered to trace roads over the rocks, and to make dikes and fluices which would facilitate the paſſage of boats from Liſbon quite to Madrid, as they propoſed to render the river Mançanarès, which empties itſelf into the Tagus, alſo navigable. They required the revenue which was to amount from the taxes to be levied on goods thus conveyed by water. Several councils were accordingly called in Madrid and Liſbon : the concluſion of their deliberations (according to Colmenares) was this :

"If God had been willing to have thoſe two rivers navigable,
"he did not want the aſſiſtance of men to render them ſo, be-
"cauſe he was able to produce that great effect by a ſingle *fiat*.
"Now, as he has not done it, it follows, that he did not think
"proper to do it, ſo that it would be contradicting his provi-
"dence to endeavour to rectify what he appears to have left im-
"perfect, for reaſons known to himſelf."

Thus vaniſhed this uſeful project in conſequence of this philoſophical determination.

A ſimilar method of reaſoning ſeems to be uſed by the Minorquins; who, as Mr. Armſtrong writes, "never prune a tree
"(the vine excepted), thinking it irreligious in ſome degree to
"preſume to direct its growth; and if you expreſs your won-
"der that they forbear this uſeful practice, and inform them of
"the advantages that attend it in other countries, their
"anſwer

"answer is ever ready, *God knows best how a tree should grow.*"

Tobacco is not allowed to be cultivated in any part of Portugal or Spain under pain of death. All kinds of it, as well as snuffs, excepting those which come from the Brasils, are strictly prohibited. The tobacco is of two sorts, the one in dry leaves, the price is 4 s. 6 d. or 800 reis per pound; the other rolled up in pieces of an inch thick, and five or six inches long. This sort is very black, wet, and stinking, and sells at about half the price of the other sort. The snuff is of the fine dust, known in England by the names of Spanish and Brasil snuffs: these are sold only at the royal tobacco office. Since my departure from Lisbon, I am informed that there is a royal fabric for *rappé* erected.

Saint Anthony of Padua was formerly the generalissimo of the Portuguese army; his appointments were three hundred thousand reis, or £ 84. 7 s. 6 d. per annum; but lately the Count de la Lippe supplied the saint's place, and a year ago, as the count is retired to his estate in Germany, a Scotch gentleman of the name of Maclean, was appointed general in chief and governor of Lisbon. This gentleman, who has been in the Portuguese service since the year 1763, was formerly governor of Almeida, and of the whole province of Beira, and is in every respect worthy of the high dignity to which he is raised. The British officers here have the same pay as in the English service, which is double that of the Portuguese.

I paid

I paid a visit one evening to the English nunnery of St. Bridget, in Lisbon, and found the ladies, who were at that time twenty-two in number, very *chatty* and entertaining. The reader will please to observe that the grate was between them and me. There is another English nunnery at Bellem near Lisbon, which I did not visit.

The windmills in this kingdom, as well as those of Spain, are about seven feet in height, and of a very simple construction. The mill-stone lies horizontally, and the sails almost touch the ground. An excellent convenience for Don Quixote, who would have found it a difficult matter to have encountered a Dutch windmill, the sails of which are sometimes forty or fifty feet above the ground.

The ladies here ride on *burros*, or jack-asses, with a pack-saddle. A servant attends them with a sharp stick, to make the beast go faster when necessary: if it goes too fast, he stops it by pulling it by the tail. Gentlemen ride on horses, servants on mules, as likewise do those physicians who have no carriages.

There was a wooden theatre, or circus, erected for the bull-fights when I was at Lisbon, but as I did not see any there, I shall defer the account of them till I describe those which I saw in Spain. I was informed that here they place wooden knobs on the horns of the bulls on those occasions.

In one of the suburbs of Lisbon is a convent, over the door of which the arms of England and Portugal are hewn in stone, party per pale, the lion and unicorn for supporters, with the royal crown on the top. I could get no information on what occasion this ornament was placed there.

A new public walk is now planting at Lisbon; at one end is a fine prospect of the gallows, and at the other end is the *hôtel* of the inquisition. I am happy in informing my readers that the power of this infernal tribunal is very much diminished, and that no person has suffered death on a religious account during these last fourteen years, either in this kingdom or that of Spain, *autos da fé* being quite abolished, though the inquisition may possibly be yet used as a state-trap, in order to squeeze some of the over-rich.

The dress of the men, among the common people, is a large cloak and slouched hat; under the cloak they commonly wear a dagger, though that treacherous weapon is prohibited: the blades of some of these will strike through a crown piece. The women wear no caps, but tie a kind of net-work silk purse over their hair, with a long tassel behind, and a ribbon tied in a bow-knot over their forehead. This head-dress they call *redecilla*, and it is worn indiscriminately by both sexes. The London caricatures of *Macaroni* hair-clubs are not at all exaggerated when applied to the Portuguese. The gentry dress entirely in the French fashion.

The ladies wear very large and heavy pendants in their ears: the sleeves of their gowns are wide enough to admit their waist, which, however, seldom exceeds a span in diameter.

Large nosegays are much in fashion with the fair sex among the Portuguese. A very erroneous notion concerning them and the Spanish ladies prevails in England: we are apt to imagine that they are inclined to gravity and reserve; whereas, in reality, one ought to adopt Voltaire's opinion of the ladies of the southern countries. He says, those of the northern climates have milk in their veins, whereas these have quicksilver in theirs. By this expression mercury, in a medical light, is not to be understood, but that they are as volatile as that mineral. I never met with women more lively in any part of Europe; they are perpetually dancing, singing, laughing, and talking, and are sprightly and vivacious in the highest degree.

*Cortejos* here are synonimous with the Italian *Cicisbei*, but I do not mean to assert that *all* their ladies have such attendants; and to the honour of the British factory be it said, the conduct of the ladies who belong to it, has exempted them from any censure on that account.

Towards the latter end of January I had determined to set out for Oporto, but I deferred my journey a few days, in order to be present at a singular execution, which was that of a man to be burnt alive. He was condemned for stealing the plate and vestments

ments out of a church, and afterwards firing it, to conceal the theft. He had been a year in prifon, and was dragged from thence to the church he had burnt, tied by the legs to the tails of two horfes; but the friars of the *Mifericordia* had placed him on an ox's hide, fo that he did not fuffer much. Before the church was fixed a ftake with a feat, on a fcaffold elevated about fix feet, under which faggots, torches, pitch-barrels, and other combuftible materials were placed. The fcaffold was environed by a regiment of cavalry, behind which ftood moft of the monks of Lifbon, who had joined in the proceffion. He was faftened to the ftake at half an hour paft five, and fire was immediately put underneath the fcaffold. In five-and-twenty minutes all was reduced to afhes. The rope which tied his neck to the ftake was foon burnt, and then his body fell into the fire. He was probably ftifled with the fmoke before the flames reached him: the fire afterward penetrated between his ribs, which were fhortly confumed. This fpectacle was very tremendous and awful. It was dark before the fire was put to the fcaffold. Each of the cavalry had a torch in his hand; and the multitude of fpectators was innumerable.

The months of November and December are ufually rainy in this country, when travelling is impracticable, becaufe the waters gather together in the valleys to fuch a depth, that they cannot be forded. After the rains have fubfided, it is neceffary to wait about a month till the waters are retired to their proper channels. Sometimes thefe heavy rains, which

" Unbroken

"Unbroken floods, and folid torrents pour,"
laſt till February, after which there hardly falls a drop for five or ſix months.

About four leagues from Liſbon is ſituated the convent of Odivelas, where it is ſaid that three hundred beautiful nuns formed a ſeraglio for the late king; had each one or more lovers, and were the moſt attracting miſtreſſes of the Portugueſe nobility. At preſent but a very few of theſe nuns are living, and they are become old and ugly; ſo that this convent is no longer a ſcene of debauchery. A French author ſpeaking of it, ſays, " I was aſſured that the famous *Portugueſe Letters*, of which we have a French tranſlation, came out of this tender, gallant, and voluptuous monaſtery. That theſe letters which breathe the moſt ardent and moſt generous love, which paint it with all its ſhades, in all its details, wherein are found its ſtorms, its inquietudes, its returns, its momentary reſolves, the delicacy of its apprehenſions, and the heroiſm of its ſacrifices, were really written by an impaſſioned nun, and an unfaithful lover."

I bought here ſeveral work-bags made in the Braſils, of the fibres of aloë leaves. They coſt about a crown a-piece; and when ſoiled are cleaned by waſhing them in lemon juice and water. Laces, gloves, reins for horſes, &c. are likewiſe made of the ſame materials.

Their majeſties go a hunting every day, eſpecially after wolves and wild boars. The queen is very courageous on horſeback;

## PORTUGAL.

and, as I was informed, rides in boots and leather-breeches, and is moreover extremely expert at her gun.

I now began to prepare for my departure; firſt applying to Mr. Walpole for a paſſport, which he gave me written in French, and was ſo obliging as to procure another for me from the Spaniſh ambaſſador. This laſt was the only one that ever was of any ſervice; for, by ſhewing it (as it was written in Spaniſh) to the ſearchers of baggage, at the gates of the cities in Spain, and giving them the value of a ſhilling or two, the cloaths, &c. remained untouched. The trunks, however, were always opened for form ſake.

I purchaſed a Portugueſe paſs from the governor of the ward in which I lived in Liſbon. Theſe paſſes ſpecified my name, the number of ſervants, mules, and horſes, and likewiſe that I had leave to carry piſtols, and other fire-arms.

I then hired a chaiſe drawn by a pair of mules, and agreed with the driver that he ſhould drag me to Oporto in nine days, and likewiſe furniſh a ſaddle-horſe for my Engliſh ſervant. It was alſo agreed, that I ſhould pay for his maintenance, and that of the owner of the horſe who accompanied us on foot, but not for that of the beaſts. I choſe to go by way of Alcobaça and Batalha, which is not the direct road. The diſtance from Liſ-bon to Oporto, on this road, is about two hundred and eighty Engliſh miles.

I likewiſe

I likewise hired Jean Baptiste Pecquèt, the same servant who had, in 1760, travelled with Mr. Baretti. He was to serve as purveyor and cook. The whole travelling expence was, for myself, two servants, the mule-driver, the horse-driver, two mules and a horse, about three pounds sterling per day.

I moreover purchased a pair of blankets and sheets, knives, forks, spoons, drinking-glasses, candlesticks, snuffers, wax-candles, a pepper and salt box, a gun, a pair of pistols, powder, shot, and bullets.

Thus equipped, I set out from Lisbon, on the 30th of January, at eight in the morning; at eleven we crossed a small branch of the Tagus in a ferry-boat, and at two we stopped to bait at Alverca, which is four leagues from Lisbon; and after resting there three hours, we proceeded four leagues farther to Castanhera, passing through Villafranca, and leaving the Tagus to the right. This road lies chiefly through olive grounds, bordered with aloës. Having wrapped myself in a large cloak, I passed the night on a mattress of straw placed on the ground, laying a sheet over it. The muleteer slept in the stable near his beasts.

January 31. This morning, after four hours journey, we dined at Otta, the road to which lies over a sandy heath, producing many *prickly pears*. Four hours more brought us to Tagarro, where we found nothing to eat but a few eggs. We
passed

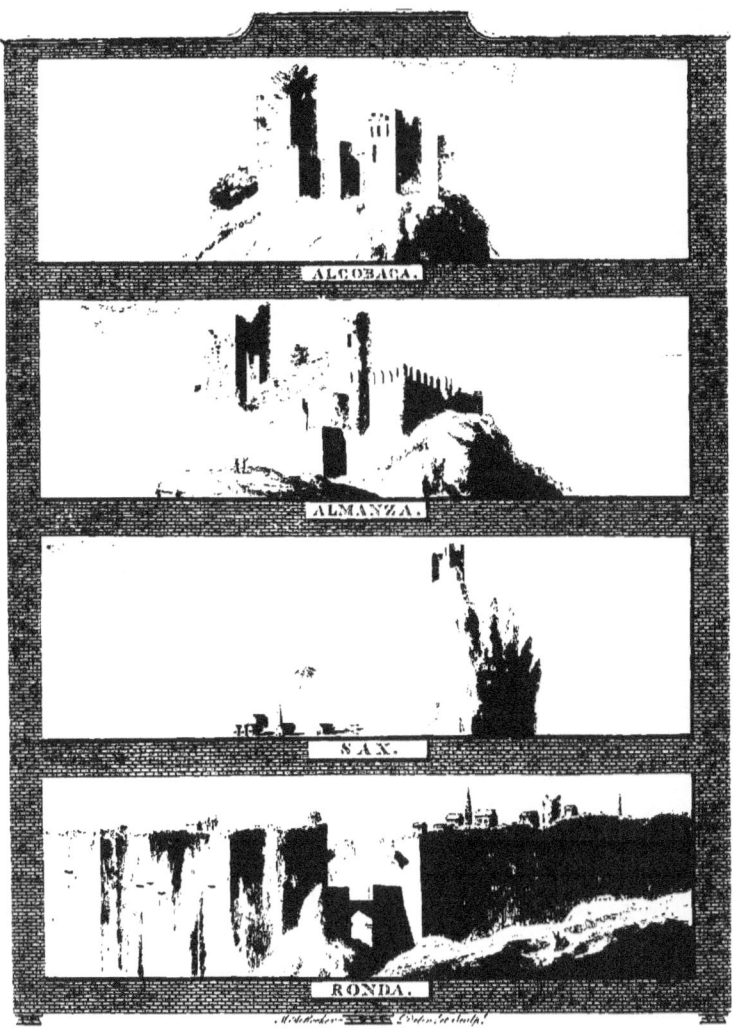

paſſed the night here, and in the morning breakfaſted on hot wine, boiled with ſugar and a dozen yolks of eggs. This food is very nouriſhing, and I continued to uſe it till the hot weather came on.

February 1. This morning Baptiſte bought half a dozen live fowls, which he killed immediately, and ſtripped off the feathers in the chaiſe. We proceeded for five hours till we came to a *venta* \*. The weather was exceſſively cold and windy. Five hours more brought us to Alcobaça. The roads were ſo bad, that the chaiſe was ſupported by a man on each ſide, though we had alighted, and walked moſt part of the way. The mules go at the rate of three and a half, or four Engliſh miles an hour, ſo that one may walk till tired, and then get into the chaiſe again. I amuſed myſelf daily with my gun, though there is very little game near the roads. On a hill near this village, is an old Mooriſh caſtle, now ruined, built of large rough ſtones, with very thick morter, a view of which is given in one of the plates in this work.

\* A *venta* is a lone houſe, eſtabliſhed by public authority, for the convenience of travellers. Theſe hovels are frequently ſituated at the diſtance of eighteen or twenty miles not only from each other, but from any other houſes. In them the prices of the accommodations are regulated monthly by government. The landlord is obliged to fix the paper with the taxation in ſome conſpicuous part of his houſe; accordingly, he paſtes it on the higheſt part of the roof, ſo that it cannot be read without the aſſiſtance of a teleſcope.

Feb. 2. I here visited the royal convent, delivering a letter to the superior, which I had brought from Lisbon. This convent is of the order of St. Bernard, and was founded in 1151, by Don Alfonso Henriques, king of Portugal. The front consists of the church, which is situated in the middle of the convent. The latter has eighteen windows on each side, and is two stories in height. A noble flight of steps leads up to the church, which is two hundred and thirty-eight feet in length. The roof is supported by twenty-six marble pillars. Here is a fine organ, with one hundred and seventy-three horizontal pipes: two sepulchres of marble, with bad basso relievos, contain the bodies of Don Pedro I. and his queen; Sancho I. and Alfonso II. and III. are likewise buried here. Behind the great altar are eight small chapels. Here are at present one hundred and thirty monks, who are all noblemen, and have each a servant, which, with the cooks and gardeners, amount to above three hundred persons to be maintained; so that it is not to be wondered at that it is as difficult to procure an egg or an onion for many miles round, as it would be if one travelled by land from Petersburgh to Peking; for this great gulph swallows up every thing.

The revenue of this convent amounts to 180,000 crusados per annum, or £. 24,373. Round the cornice of a large hall are the statues of twenty of the kings of Portugal as large as the life, made of plaister, and painted with the natural colours: and there is room for six more. In the garden of the cloister are four very large orange trees, with lemons grafted in them. The sacristy was

was thrown down by the great earthquake, but is now rebuilt. I was here shewn a golden chalice, very curiously carved and inlaid with precious stones; and in the library I saw *Baskerville*'s *Virgil*, and *Foulis*'s *Homer*, both which books were presented by *George Pitt*, esq.

The kitchen is very large, and all tiled: the chimney stands in the center, the funnel of which is thirty-four feet long and thirteen feet broad, and is supported by eight iron pillars. Under this funnel are a great number of caldrons of different sizes. A small rivulet is made to run through this kitchen, the conveniencce of which need not be pointed out: and seven cooks are constantly employed.

The rabbit-warren is adjacent to the kitchen, and is a very singular one. It is a large area, paved with square marble slabs, and walled in; several rows of low sheds are built, in parallel lines, from one end to the other; and under these are placed five thousand earthen pots, with lids, and furnished with straw, having a hole in one side to admit the conies, which consequently are all tame. At one end of the area is an inclosure to separate the young from the bucks occasionally. They are readily caught by the hand, on lifting off the lid of the pot.

Adjoining to the warren, stands the pigeon-house, which is circular. A round column supports the roof; the inside is full of earthen pots, in which the pigeons build their nests.

There

There are twenty-four rows of these pots, one hundred and twenty in each row; and round the column, in the middle, are likewise twenty-four rows, each containing twenty-four pots: the total number of which is three thousand four hundred and fifty-six.

Behind the convent are the gardens, which produce all kinds of fruits and kitchen stuff: and round these are olive and vine yards, and groves,

> " Where the lemon and the piercing lime,
> " With the deep orange, glowing thro' the green,
> " Their lighter glories blend."
>
> THOMSON'S SUMMER.

The vaults under the convent are very large, and filled with various kinds of wines: and in their stables are several hundreds of mules, for these worthy fathers to take the diversion of riding. I dined and supped with about twenty of the superior friars, in a private room; the others all dined in the refectory; and in the evening the bottle went as briskly about as ever I saw it do in *Scotland*; so that with the aid of some musical instruments, we spent a very agreeable day. Soon after midnight I retired to my inn, though much pressed to take a bed in the convent. If I had accepted it, I should probably have passed a week with these jovial companions,—from whom I parted with great regret, but shall always retain a grateful sense of their unaffected politeness and frankness. This convent is the most magnificent

nificent and the richeft I know; and its inhabitants compofe the moſt agreeable body of ecclefiaftics I ever had the pleaſure of being acquainted with.

Feb. 3. Early in the morning I fet out for Batalha, through olive grounds and cork forefts, the road being pretty good. We paffed by a Moorifh caftle to the right, at fome diftance.

I immediately waited on the fuperior of the monaftery here, with a letter given to me by the gentlemen of Alcobaça. It is alfo a royal convent, founded in 1426, by Don John I. The church is a very fine Gothic building, much like King's College chapel in Cambridge, and is feventy-one paces in length. The roof is fuftained by fixteen columns of marble. In a circular chapel is interred king John I. with his queen Philippa, (who was eldeft daughter to the duke of Lancafter, uncle to king Richard II. of England, and was given in marriage to king John I. in 1386, at Oporto) in a marble fepulchre, his right hand locked in her's. Their arms are engraven at one end of the tomb. Her's are quarterly the royal arms of England, charged with a label of three points, and *argent* a crofs *fable*, encircled with the Garter. Four of their fons are interred in as many fmall tombs placed in the wall. In this chapel are eight fmall pieces of painting on wood, much in the ftyle of Albert Durer. King Edward and his queen are buried near the great altar. Their figures are very clumfily cut in ftone, and lie hand in hand.

The corpse of king John II. is preserved in a wooden cheft, to which there is an afcent by feveral fteps.

In another chapel, which is a cube of twenty-three paces, are buried, in two chefts, Alfonfo V. and his fon who died 1481. The roof of this chapel is vaulted in the fhape of a ftar, with eight points, and is without fupport.

In another chapel is a very handfome monument, erected to the count of Miranda, in 1740; and made in Italy. It is a fquare tomb of black marble, with yellow veins, fupported on the backs of three lions of yellow marble, *couchant* on three black marble cufhions. On each fide is a death's head, with a naked weeping boy of white marble; and on the top is his coronet lying on a cufhion.

The cloifters form a fquare, confifting of feven arches on each fide. In the center is a well, and at each corner a large orange tree.

Behind the church is a fpacious octagon chapel without a roof, as it was left unfinifhed. The carving in ftone is very fine, and in the Gothic manner. The walls are ornamented with fmall baffo relievos of two branches intertwined, in the midft of which are the following Gothic characters $\binom{\text{tāyas}}{\text{c rey}}$ this is repeated thoufands of times, though in some parts the characters are placed thus $\begin{pmatrix} \text{tāyā} \\ \text{fcrey} \end{pmatrix}$ the meaning of which is unknown.

This convent is of the Dominican order, and contained formerly one hundred and eighty monks, though at present no more than forty-eight reside here: they are all noblemen. The revenues are only eight thousand crusados per annum, i. e. about a thousand guineas. I declined passing the night in this convent, as I saw they had little or nothing to eat, and less to drink, because they are but three leagues distant from the Alcobaçan monks, who are in possession of all the good things, and seem to have divided the circumjacent lands according to the Montgomery equity, " *tout d'un coté & rien de l'autre.*" There is no inn nor *venta* here, so that I proceeded to Leyria, which is only two leagues farther. The roads were very muddy. I procured an ass and a guide, and rode over a small hill, leaving the chaise to follow at leisure. Leyria is a pretty large town, and possesses a Moorish castle on a hill, but nothing else worthy of observation. Near this town is a glass manufactory carried on by an Englishman.

Feb. 4. We proceeded five leagues to Pombal, a small village which gives title of marquis to the present prime minister of Portugal. The inhabitants are chiefly hatters.

We dined this day by the side of the road, turning the mules and horse loose to graze; and spreading our provisions on the ground

ground. These consisted of cold fowls, hard eggs, ham, cheese, and bread, together with water-cresses, of which we had " stript the brook" on our way. The *boracha*, which is a leathern bag, and was filled with wine, went merrily about. Mine held four gallons. It was regularly filled every morning, and as regularly emptied. The wine is chiefly white, and costs about four pence a quart. I climbed up a high hill near Pombal, to inspect a Moorish castle, the walls only are standing; the inside was full of rue, which had grown to a very great height. The country we went through this day was chiefly olive-grounds and corn-fields.

Feb. 5. Seven leagues march this day brought us to Coimbra, having dined at the village of Pondès. For the last two leagues the road is paved, and bordered by olive and pine trees. Coimbra is an university, and is situated on a hill, near the river Mondego, over which is a very long and low bridge, with a great number of arches of different sizes. Five English families reside here, one of them is that of a physician. This city is celebrated for its curious cups and boxes of turned horn.

Feb. 6. On a hill in Coimbra, is a church with a cupola, of very good architecture, plain and simple. In the church of Santa Cruz is a painting over the great altar representing the assumption of a female saint. It is here attributed to Raphael; it appeared to me to be a very good Italian picture, but it was so dark that I could not ascertain the truth of the above assertion.

PORTUGAL. 47

tion. I obferved alfo a large organ with horizontal pipes in this church. Here is an aqueduct of twenty arches, which conveys water to the caftle, both built about the middle of the fixteenth century by king Sebaftian. " As I now difcovered that there was nothing farther to difcover," I proceeded three leagues to Amolhada. The road is good, and lies through plantations of olive-tees, vine-yards, and corn-fields.

Feb. 7. We proceeded through forefts of pine and cork, dined at Sardon, and fhortly after croffed the little river Agueda, over a bridge of three arches; afterwards ferried over the river Vouga, which is broad, fhallow, and exceedingly tranfparent. Near the ferry is a ftone bridge, which had fifteen arches; but the two firft are broken. We then afcended a fteep rugged rock on foot, and arrived at Albergaria.

Feb. 8. All this day there was a thick fog. The road was very bad, over loofe pieces of rock, through pine and cork woods. We dined at Sant-Antonio. On each fide of the road I faw a pole with a man's head upon it: they were thofe of two banditti, who had been lately executed. We paffed the night in a *venta*.

Feb. 9. It rained violently all this day. We travelled eight hours on a very clayey road, and arrived at Villanova, which is a long ftreet of fmiths' fhops. We then defcended a fteep hill to the edge of the river Douro, which we ferried over, and entered

tered Oporto, where there being no tolerable inn, I took lodgings on the quay, at an English house.

This city, which is the second in the kingdom, is said to contain thirty thousand inhabitants. Thirty English families reside here, who are chiefly concerned in the wine trade: this factory maintains a clergyman, who performs service on Sundays at each house alternately. Their burying ground is only a field, at some distance from the town. A British consul also resides here.

I was present at an assembly in the factory-house, where there were about twenty British ladies.

Oporto, and its suburb Villanova, are each built on a hill, with the Douro between them: a situation much resembling Newcastle-upon-Tyne and its suburb Gateshead. There is no bridge over the Douro, because, when the snows melt on the mountains, that river overflows its banks, and lays the lower part of the city under water, sometimes twelve or fourteen feet, running at the amazing rate of sixteen miles an hour, and carrying all the vessels to sea, many of which are lost on the sands, or beat to pieces against the shores.

The theatre here is the vilest in the two kingdoms, very old and shabby. It serves for Portuguese plays and for Italian operas. I saw the opera of Demofoonte *done*, suitably to the place it was *done* in.
The

The church of San Francifco is full of wooden ornaments, profufely carved, and entirely gilt, which has a very difgufting effect. I obferved many letters directed to the moft glorious Saint Francis, hanging by threads of the walls. As they were all open, I took the liberty of reading fome of them, and found they were only complimentary cards and letters of thanks, for cures which the writers thought they had received by means of that faint's intereft with the Virgin Mary, &c.

The church dos Clerigos, fituated on the higheft part of the city, has a fteeple, much like that of the New Church in the Strand, which ferves for a land-mark to mariners.

They were at that time building a new gate and prifon, of free-ftone, in a very good ftyle: after the completion of which, it will be neceffary to widen the ftreet in which that prifon ftands, "if only to let a man have the fatisfaction of knowing on which fide of the ftreet he walks." There are few carriages here, as the ftreets are fteep and narrow: thefe are all paved with broad ftones, as thofe in Florence are.

Chairs and horfe-litters are ufed here in bad weather: thefe litters are fedans, fupported between two horfes or mules. The boats on the river have an awning like the Venetian gondolas, and are rowed by men ftanding forward, after the fame manner as the Barcaruoli of Venice row, and fometimes by one man with a fingle oar.

The merchants assemble daily in the chief street, to transact business; and are protected from the sun by sail-cloths hung across from the opposite houses.

Mr. Wood, to whom I was recommended, took me to his *quinta*, or country-house, about a mile off. The gardens are on the slope of a high hill; ten terraces rise gradually one above the other, each of them ornamented with a fountain, and various shady walks of orange and lemon trees, some of them remarkably large. The owner assured me he had gathered from a single orange tree, no less than *sixteen thousand* oranges in one season! From the upper terrace is one of the finest prospects imaginable, equalling that from Mount Edgecumbe, near Plymouth. To the east is the city of Oporto, with Villanova, which, by being so near, are very distinctly discovered. To the west, the sea, distant about two miles, with the mouth of the river, and ships continually entering into and sailing out of the harbour, form " a moving picture," the river itself running in a serpentine course, not far from the foot of the hill on which the garden stands; the opposite shores being mountains covered with vines, and numbers of the like small country-houses, in the environs (though inferior in point of situation to this inexpressibly pleasing retreat) enliven the scene.

The chief article of commerce in this city is wine. Twenty thousand pipes are yearly exported. The cost is about £. 10. or £. 12 each. Eighty thousand are the usual annual produce, so that three fourths are confumed in the country. The merchants here have very fpacious wine vaults, fome of which are capable of holding fix or feven thoufand pipes. The inhabitants of half the fhops in the city are coopers, who fell their cafks at about a moidore each.

Here I agreed with the fame *caleſſeiro* who had brought me from Lifbon, that I fhould have the whole difpofal of the carriage and beafts to go where I pleafed, not to exceed ten leagues per day. The fhaft-mule, which coft forty moidores, or £. 54, was one of the ftrongeft and fineft I ever faw.

Accordingly I fet out from Oporto on the 15th of February, early in the morning, ferried over the Douro, and afcended the hill on foot in an hour. My largeft trunk, which weighed above three hundred pounds, was carried on the back of a porter, which fhows the great ftrength of thefe fellows. We dined afterwards in the fhade of fome vaft cork-trees, and then proceeded to St. Antonio, having all the way the profpect of the fea to the right; and at that time two Portuguefe men of war under fail; and to the north-eaft two very high mountains covered with fnow. On the road we met about twenty criminals, chained together with one chain, by means of iron collars faftened round their necks, having each a fhort chain connected with the great one, one end of which was held by a foldier on horfeback; feveral other armed foldiers guarded thefe wretches, and who were alfo hand-cuffed and bare-headed, and were going to be shipped from Oporto to the Brasils, to work in the mines.

Feb. 16. We dined at Albergaria, ferried over the Vouga, and passed the night at Sardon. The roads were become so bad by the rains, that we did not arrive till late at night, causing the horse-driver to walk before the chaise with a torch. Thus far we returned on the same road we came, as there is no other carriage road from Oporto to Almeida, whither we were going.

Feb. 17. We proceeded through olive-grounds to the foot of the mountain of Bossaco, or Mariana. Here I hired a cart drawn by two oxen, by means of which my baggage was dragged up this mountain in two hours. I ascended it on horseback, and the chaise followed us empty. On the top is a convent of Carthusians, in which I was told are confined two illegitimate sons of the late king John V. Another natural son of that king is at present archbishop of Braga.

Here we saw the still higher mountains Sierras de Estrella, whose summits are always covered with snow.

> Stiff with eternal ice, and hid in snow
> That fell a thousand centuries ago,
> These mountains stand, nor can the rising sun
> Unfix their frosts, and teach 'em how to run.
> ADDISON.

In going down the mountain we had juſt afcended, the chaife overfet, and one of the wheels was broken to pieces. The neareſt houfe was eight miles off, fo that I left Baptiſte with the caleſſeiro and his man on the road, where they remained all night, and procuring a guide, walked with my Engliſh fervant to the fmall village of Barilhe, in about two hours and a half, taking the fire-arms with me. The next morning the baggage arrived in a cart drawn by oxen. The chaife remained on the road, and a new wheel was befpoke at a village near fourteen miles off. This accident detained us two days in Barilhe. I amufed myfelf by fhooting. The country is very mountainous and barren, like Weſtmoreland. The ſtones here appear to be of the fame nature as the Corniſh granite. I hired a whole houfe to myfelf, which indeed was only one room, the floor of which was of the fame materials as the highway, with no furniture, except a table, a bench, and a trufs of ſtraw full of fleas. The roof admitted the rain through large crevices, which ſerved for the contemplation of the ſtars.

Feb. 20. This morning we paſſed over a ſtrong ſtone bridge of four arches, under which rolls a torrent of very clear water; and immediately after afcended a ſteep and rugged mountain, in half an hour; then we paſſed through the village of Santo Combo, and croſſed the fame torrent on a ſtone bridge of fix arches, of which two are pretty large. From this fpot is a very romantic view. The road from hence to Cargal is good, chiefly through olive grounds, with vaſt numbers both of black and white fheep

feeding

feeding under the trees. In this village is no inn, but I procured a lodging in a carpenter's shop.

Feb. 21. We passed the river Mondego over a bridge of three arches, and then ascended a mountain. Two oxen were added to the chaise to assist the mules in dragging it up. When we arrived at the top, we let the mules rest an hour, and afterwards passed over a bridge of a single arch: then the road became excessively dangerous, over loose rocks, deep clay, and slippery precipices. The mules frequently fell down, the traces broke, it rained hard, and was quite dark when we arrived at Vinhofa, where we put up at the worst inn I ever entered before or since. There was only one room, which was full of people. They had kindled a large fire of wet wood in the middle of it; and, as there was no chimney, the smoke was left to find its way out of the windows and door. I got some straw, placed it on the top of a large chest, and rolling myself up in my cloak, fell directly asleep with all my cloaths on, my head being half out of a window to avoid suffocation.

Feb. 22. We travelled this day over barren mountains, with a few cork trees, chesnuts, and pines, scattered here and there, then passed over a bridge of two arches, through some fields of *maize*: over another bridge of a single arch, and dined at Celorico, where we were regaled by a *new Christian*, who had lately been a Jew, with the finest red wine I ever drank, resembling Burgundy in colour and flavour, but superior in goodness. We
went

went on to the village of Cavaçal, where there is no inn, but we procured a miferable lodging at a fruit-fhop; however, the Jew's wine made it appear like a palace, as we had drank pretty freely of it. At Celorico is a Moorifh caftle, with two towers, fituated on a mountain, down the declivity of which, to the village, is a wall of nine feet thick, built of large rough ftones, without any morter or cement. This morning I obferved on the fide of the road five ftones ftanding upright, of eight feet each in height, and four others of the fame dimenfions lying by them, refembling a little ftone-henge. And among thefe mountains many enormous ftones are feen in very unaccountable fituations.

Feb. 23. This day's journey was very fatiguing, as we travelled during eleven hours on a very bad road, covered with loofe pieces of rock, with chefnut trees growing between the interftices. We came at laft to the river Coa, which we croffed over a high and dangerous bridge of three arches: the parapets were broken down, and the bridge itfelf was juft broad enough to admit the paffage of the chaife. We then afcended a very high mountain, on the top of which is the town of Almeida. The diftance of this town from Oporto, by the road we came, I imagine to be about two hundred and twenty-eight miles, or fixty-five hours. There is no inn in this town; but Colonel Calder, who was Governor in the abfence of General Maclean, very politely offered me his houfe, where I fpent two nights, being received with the hofpitality peculiar to his nation, and which I had had the happinefs of experiencing

encing the year before in Scotland. At that time seven or eight other British officers, in the Portuguese service resided here.

Feb. 24. Almeida is on the frontiers of the province of Beira, and but a league and a half distant from the Spanish castle, in the kingdom of Leon.

The town is well fortified; one hundred and ten guns, chiefly of brass, are planted on six bastions. There are two gates, a quadrangular castle in the middle of the town, and handsome barracks. I walked round Almeida in a quarter of an hour. Here I shewed my passports.

Feb. 25. This morning, having proceeded a league and a half, we crossed a rivulet which divides the kingdom of Portugal from that of Spain, and were stopped at the village of el Obispo, where we were detained all day, by reason of the driver's having neglected to take a pass for the mules, and to sign a bond that they should return into Portugal, as the importation of horses, mules, and asses, is not allowed in either of the kingdoms, without the payment of a very considerable tax. I therefore sent back to Almeida, and procured the necessary papers.

Feb. 26. We proceeded through an exceeding fertile country, consisting of immense corn-fields, on gentle risings. Every inch of ground is cultivated, but not a tree to be seen. We dined

dined at the village of Gallego, where I obferved two ftorks, which had built their nefts on the church fteeple: thefe were the firft birds of the kind I had yet feen in thefe kingdoms, but I afterwards found them in every part of Spain, and likewife in Barbary.

We croffed the river Agueda on a temporary bridge; (a very fine ftone one is now building; it is to have feven arches, three of which are already finifhed;) and immediately entered the city of Ciudad-Rodrigo, where I faw many ftorks nefts on the fteeples and chimnies. This city is very neat, has three gates, and a pleafant public walk of five rows of trees, along the fide of the river.

The inns here are much better than thofe in Portugal. We were provided with good beds, elevated from the ground, and clean fheets, though without curtains, which none of the beds in Spain have.

The cathedral is a Gothic building; the front ornamented with feventeen ftatues of faints, the fteeple is modern, and the entrance is under a porch, fupported by four Corinthian columns.

Here is alfo an old caftle. The houfes are chiefly built of ftone, and made a much cleaner appearance than thofe in Portugal.

Feb. 27. The country we travelled over this day was a fine plain, and corn-fields intermixed with woods of dwarf and evergreen oaks, under one of which we dined, and passed the night in a *venta*. There were no locks to the doors, but the landlord told me, that he himself was the lock to his house, and that every thing was perfectly safe, which I had the pleasure of finding to be true, both here and in every other part of Spain through which I afterwards travelled.

Feb. 28. Passing through a forest of green oaks, and over a fine plain of corn-fields, leaving a long chain of mountains covered with snow to the right, at three in the afternoon I arrived at Salamanca, and put up at the Sun inn, in the great square. This is the best inn I ever entered that was kept by a Spaniard, for all the great inns in Madrid, Cadiz, Seville, &c. are kept either by Italians or Frenchmen.

This city is built on three small hills; the streets are very narrow and dirty, and the whole has a melancholy aspect. The university is much on the decline: it was founded in 1200, by Alphonsus IX. and is the most ancient in Spain. Here are sixteen schools, and about four thousand scholars. The number of professors in this city is seventy. Here is a college for Irish students: the rector, Mr. Philip Haffett, and his assistant Mr. Michael Broders, were so obliging as to accompany me to see every thing remarkable in Salamanca. They have about thirty young men under their care.

The

The lower clafs of men wear large hats uncocked, fome black and fome white, flit fleeves, broad leather belts, and fandals made of cords: and here I faw for the firft time in Spain, huge clumfy coaches drawn by fix mules, with very long traces.

We paid a vifit to the Profeffor of Aftronomy, who informed me, that Salamanca is fituated in 41° 5′ latitude, and 12° 50′ longitude from the ifle of Ferro.

The moft beautiful part of this city is the great fquare, built about thirty years ago. The houfes are of three ftories, and all of equal height and exact fymmetry, with iron balconies, and a ftone balluftrade on the top of them: the lower part is arched, which forms a piazza all round the fquare, of two hundred and ninety-three feet to each fide. Over fome of the arches are medallions, with bad bufts of the kings of Spain, and of feveral eminent men, in ftone baffo-relievo, among which are thofe of Fernand Cortez, Francis Pizarro, Davila, and Cid Ruy. In this fquare the bull-fights are exhibited for three days only, in the month of June. The river Tormes runs by this city, and has a bridge over it of twenty-five arches, built by the Romans, and yet entire.

The cathedral is a Gothic building, with a fuperfluity of carving in ftone on the outfide, and has a fine organ with horizontal pipes.

Here are four royal, and four military colleges. That of Calatrava has a very handsome modern stone stair-case. That of St. Bartholomew is a new building; the entrance is under a porch, supported by four Corinthian columns, each three feet and a half in diameter. The cloisters are two stories in height, one of which is of the Doric, and the other of the Composite order. The grand stair-case has a double flight of steps. The library is placed in the upper story, and commands a fine prospect over the adjacent country. This building is the handsomest in Salamanca.

St. Stephen's church and convent, wherein one hundred and fifty monks reside, is of the Dominican order. The front of the church is Gothic, with many stone basso-relievos, by Cerloni, a Milanese sculptor, in 1612. The picture over the great altar, which represents the stoning of St. Stephen, was begun by Claudio Cœlio, and finished by Luca Giordano.

The wall which extends from the choir to the roof, is semicircular, and was painted in fresco by Palomino, in 1705: it represents Religion with a tiara on her head, drawn in a car by four horses abreast, trampling on and riding over heretics. The *Three Persons* are in the clouds, attended by the Virgin Mary and many saints. All these figures are as large as the life.

In the sacristy are many pictures; the best are the following. A *Pietà*, extremely well painted by John Bapt. Mayno, who was born at Toledo, and died in 1640.

A large Flagellation, in the manner of Rubens.

A small *Ecce Homo*, with many figures, in the style of Albert Durer. This picture is over the altar, and the Annunciation is represented by the angel on the one side, and the Virgin on the other.

A small picture of St. Peter dictating to St. Dominic, who is writing.

In the church of the Minor Clerks, I observed the picture over the great altar, which represents the Assumption of St. Charles Boromeo, a good piece, by Francis Camillo: he was born at Madrid, and died in 1671.

The church which formerly belonged to the Jesuits, is now shut up, and their convent converted into a royal college. In the cloisters is the History of the Life of St. Ignatius, in thirty pictures, by Sebastian Concha: the figures are rather less than the natural size, and are painted on canvass. One of the monks has added another piece, daubed by himself. It may easily be distinguished from the others, among which it has so unworthily usurped a place.

Opposite to this church, I observed a palace, of which the front is quite covered with cockle shells, in stone basso relievo, which has as whimsical an effect as I have seen caused by the front of a palace in Ferrara, and of another in Naples, being in like manner covered with lozenges, vulgarly called diamonds.

In the Capuchin convent, which ſtands juſt without the elegant gate of Zamora, over the great altar, is a very large and fine piece by Vincent Carducci, but a little damaged: it repreſents the Aſſumption of St. Francis; the *Three Perſons* are in the upper part of the picture, environed with angels.

The celebrated profeſſor of mathematics, Don Diego de Torres, died two years ago, and is buried in this convent.

In the church of the Auguſtinian nuns, is a very good picture of the Aſſumption of the Virgin Mary, by Joſeph Ribera. Here is a curious inlaid marble pulpit, ſupported on the extended wings of an eagle, of bronze, of excellent workmanſhip. The church itſelf is very beautiful.

I waited on the *Cavalleras de Santiago*, in their convent; theſe are all noble ladies, who are knights of St. James, and wear the *inſignia* of the order on their breaſts. There were at that time no more than eight ladies, all old and ugly, ſo that I made my viſit as ſhort as poſſible, eſpecially as there is nothing worthy of attention either in the church or in the convent.

I afterwards ſaw the library of the univerſity, in which the books are *not* chained, as is reported by writers who have copied from one another. Two large Engliſh globes ſtand on a table in the middle of the room.

Here is a theatre for Spanish plays, which is a very ordinary building.

The students are dressed in black like priests, and have their crowns shorn.

Salamanca has ten gates, and contains twenty-five churches, twenty-five convents of friars, and the same number of nunneries. I compute this city to be about ninety-four miles distant from Almeida. I was at this time not sufficiently versed in the Spanish language to form any acquaintance with the natives; so that having gratified my curiosity in this city, I left it on the third of March, and travelled all day through a very fruitful country, producing corn, but no other trees than a few straggling green oaks and cork-trees. During this journey we met and overtook thousands of asses. The larks here are of an extraordinary size. The largest which I shot measured seventeen inches when the wings were extended: they were crested, had a black semicircle upon their necks, and proved very delicate eating. We passed this night in a *venta*, which had a stork's nest on the roof.

March 4. We proceeded to Zamora, traversing a wood of pine-trees, and some corn-fields. Close to this city we crossed the river Duero, over an ancient and clumsy stone bridge, with sixteen arches of unequal sizes. The cathedral has a handsome modern porch. As it was the time of the fair, the chief street was filled with booths; and the end of it was appropriated for the sale of mules

mules and asses. I saw a jack-ass sold here for three thousand reals, or one hundred and fifty piastres, which is £. 33. 15*s*. So that £. 100 which was paid by a gentleman of my acquaintance in Norfolk for a Spanish jack-ass, will appear to be no exorbitant price, when we consider the first cost, the danger of being detected in exporting them, the punishment of which is death, and the charge of freight, with the risque of the animals dying on their passage. The above mentioned gentleman has bred many fine mules by means of this ass. There is a ruined Moorish castle near this city.

March 5. We arrived this day at the city of Toro, which has the same coat of arms as the city of Turin, i. e. a bull, as the names imply. The road was very good, chiefly along the banks of the Duero, with continued vine-yards and corn-fields. I here observed great numbers of hoopoes, which birds I afterwards found were very common all over Spain. This city is one of the most ancient in the whole kingdom. It is situated on the summit of a high hill, at the foot of which runs the Duero, crossed by a narrow stone bridge of twenty-two arches. The descent of the hill is by a winding road, which forms thirteen zig-zags: the prospect from the top is very romantic over a fine plain, embellished by the river and bridge. Here are also the walls of a Moorish castle, which form a square of one hundred and forty-three feet, with a round tower at each angle; the roof is fallen in.

Over

Over the door of the cathedral are several very ancient basso relievos in stone; among which I observed one of two angels, playing on a musical instrument, somewhat like that called by the French *Vielle*, *Leyer* by the Germans, and Beggar's Lyre by Dr. Burney; one of the angels plays with his fingers on the keys, of which there are ten, and the other turns the handle. The length of the instrument is about five feet.

March 6. This day we arrived at Tordesillas, travelling over a sandy plain producing corn and vines. I observed many eagles *planing* over head. The city stands on a hill, and has a bridge of ten pointed arches over the Duero.

March 7. We proceeded three leagues to Simanca, which city stands on an eminence, and has a stone bridge of seventeen arches over the river Pisuerga, and a large Moorish castle, on the remains of which is built a modern one, surrounded by a dry ditch, over which are two bridges. The archives of the kingdom were deposited here by Philip II. in 1566, where they are still kept. Travelling two leagues farther, we entered into Old Castile, and arrived at Valladolid; the road was through corn-fields, sandy and level, exactly answering the lines in Thomson's Autumn,

" A gaily chequer'd heart-expanding view,
" Far as the circling eye can shoot around,
" Unbounded tossing in a flood of corn *."

* " Y los creci dos trigos y cebadas,
" Hacen como del mar sus oleadas." Obs. Rust.
And the grown wheat and barley form waves like those of the sea.

Near the gate at which we entered, I saw the head of a man stuck on a pole, and one of his quarters, confisting of an arm, shoulder, and part of the ribs, nailed underneath: they were close to the road, and quite fresh; and the beard continued to grow, which formed altogether a ghastly spectacle. It was part of the body of an assassin.

Valladolid is situated on a plain, near the river Pisuerga, which has a handsome stone bridge over it of ten arches. The banks are ornamented with walks, planted with a double row of trees.

This city is one of the largest in Spain, and has an university, founded in 1471, by Cardinal Ximenes.

I observed that the names of the streets were painted on tiles fixed in the walls of the corner houses; and that the houses were numbered.

I waited on Dr. John Geddes, who is rector of the Scotch college, and on Dr. Perry, rector of the English college: these gentlemen have each two assistants, and fifteen or sixteen young men under their tuition. Dr. Geddes was so obliging as to show me every thing remarkable in Valladolid: we went first to the library of the university, where there are theological

 Unwieldy volumes, and in number great;
 And long it is since any reader's hand
 Has reach'd them from their unfrequented seat;

For a deep duſt, which time does ſoftly ſhed
Where only time does come, their covers beare,
On which grave ſpyders ſtreets of webs have ſpread,
Subtle and ſlight as the grave writers were.
D'Avenant's Gondibert, Canto V. v. 48, 49.

Here are about one thouſand five hundred ſtudents, who are habited in the ſame manner as thoſe at Salamanca. The chief ſtudy here is that of the law. Father Caimo, ſpeaking of this univerſity ſays, " From hence, as out of a vaſt ſtore-houſe of " civil law, iſſue all the judges, advocates, lawyers, procurators, " proctors, doctors, attornies, notaries, ſollicitors, and other " ſuch harpies, who fill the cities in Spain, and prey on poor " men, &c." The building has a handſome modern front.

The palace in which Philip II. and III. were born, and which was afterwards inhabited by Charles V. is now quite decayed, and nothing left but the bare walls; though all the modern compilers, ſuch as Salmon, la Martiniere, &c. continue to deſcribe the furniture, pictures, plate, &c. ſuppoſed to be contained in it.

As I have mentioned Charles V. I ſhall add a ſhort quotation from the Abbé de la Porte: he ſays, he was in 1755 in the monaſtery of St. Juſt, which is ſituated between the cities of Talavera la Reyna and Placentia; and that one of the monks ſhewed him the place where that emperor had lodged. " There, ſaid he ſneeringly, there is the melancholy ſolitude "where that monarch, become imbecile and devout; paſſed his days in winding up clocks, in teazing the friars, in giving himſelf the diſcipline, in daubing the walls of his cell with ſcraps on predeſtination and grace, in ſtunning himſelf with reflecting on the abandonment of all his crowns, and in re‑penting. There he performed the farce of his own burial, put himſelf in a coffin, ſung for himſelf the *de profundis*, and ſhewed all the follies of a diſtempered brain. One day when he went in his turn to wake the novices, at the hour of mat‑tins, one of them, whom he ſhook too violently, becauſe he ſtill ſlept, ſaid to him, haſt thou not troubled the repoſe of the world long enough, without coming to diſturb that of peaceable men who have forſaken it!"

I ſaw in ſeveral libraries in Spain, a work in two large folio volumes, printed in 1614, entitled, *Hiſtoria de la vida y hechos del Emperador Carlos V.* by Sandoval; but I was not able to purchaſe it, as it is not to be met with in the bookſellers ſhops.

The large field called *El Campo Grande*, is within the walls, and round it are fifteen churches. On this ſpot many thouſands of heretics have been burnt alive, by order of the Inquiſition; among the reſt, the famous Dr. Auguſtin Caçalla, preacher to Charles V. ſuffered that death here in 1559. But, as I have before obſerved, none of theſe execrable executions have been *committed* for theſe laſt fourteen years in either of theſe kingdoms.

The

The names of the criminals who have been burnt are hung up in the inside of most of the cathedrals in Spain.

Here are in all eighty churches.

The Plaça Mayor is arched round; the houses are of three stories, and of equal height, but make a very shabby appearance.

The Royal Chancery is a very large and beautiful building, of the Tuscan order. The other Royal Chancery is at Granada.

In the cathedral here, the communion table has at each end a wooden statue of an angel as large as the life, and dressed with clothes, such as the eunuchs wear when they represent serious operas!—This church is embellished with a magnificent organ, with horizontal pipes.

In the church of St. Paul, of the Dominicans, are two good pictures over the great altar, by Barthol. Cardenas, a Portuguese painter; there is likewise a large piece in the choir, representing the Assumption, by the same artist. Near this altar are two statues of the duke and duchess of Lerma kneeling, in bronze gilt, by Pompey Leoni.

In the Chapter-house is a St. James, well painted by El Mudo.

In the Sacristy are the portraits of all the popes, including his late holiness Clement XIV. They are but indifferently done.

Here are moreover twenty-two large pictures of various saints suffering martyrdom, painted by different masters: they are in general well executed, though the subjects are disagreeable. I was also shewn a coloured wax head of St. Paul, very finely formed by John Alfonso Abrille. The other good pictures are two Madonnas, a St. Sebastian, and a dead Christ with two apostles: this last appears to have been painted by Bassano. The outside of this church is Gothic, loaded with carvings in stone. I shall never mention any thing regarding jewels, gold and silver lamps, candlesticks, vases, caskets for relics, vestments for the priests, &c. which are kept in custody in immense quantities in most of the chief churches in Spain, as I always declined seeing them. As to the relics, the priests who shew them, perceiving that I despised such vile trumpery, honestly joined me in laughing at them, and forbore shewing me any more; neither did they attempt to tell me any lies about miracles, &c. &c.

I visited many other churches, but found none of them worthy of notice, except that of St. Benedict, wherein are some of the works in painting, sculpture, and architecture of Alonso Berruguete, who was born near this city, and died at Madrid in 1545. About half a league out of the city, on the other side of the river, is a very large convent of Jeronymites, divided into three cloisters, of two stories each; the one of the Doric, and the other of the Corinthian order.

In the Sacrifty is an altar, of which the painting, sculpture, and architecture, are all by the above mentioned Berruguete. Here are twelve small pictures on copper, representing the History of the Life of Christ, by Luca Giordano.

Valladolid is a very still, lonely, and melancholy city. I left it on the 9th of March, and travelled to Olmedo: having dined at Valdestillas, we passed over three stone bridges, one of three arches, one of a single arch, and one of five. The road was flat and sandy; on each side are corn-fields, vines, and pine forests. Here I observed several bustards, and a great number of hawks, blue jays, and magpies. Olmedo is a walled town, but nearly ruined.

March 10. This morning we passed over a bridge, and soon after I caused the carriage to stop, and went on horseback to see the castle of Coca, which is a very large square edifice, of two stories in height, entirely built of bricks, the masonry of which is extremely neat: it belongs to the counts of Alcalà, and is encompassed with a dry ditch: the walls are embattled, and a turret rises from the center. It is built near the town of the same name, which is walled, and as much ruined as Olmedo. Coca was anciently a considerable place, but was destroyed, with twenty thousand inhabitants, after a long siege, by Lucullus. It is said the emperor Theodosius the Great was born here.

I returned to the chaise, and entered into a forest of pines, and afterwards travelled along the banks of a small lake, on which thousands of wild ducks were swimming. I also observed several herons near the edges. We dined at a small village, where there are many caves dug in the sand for preserving of wine, and passed the night at the village of St. Mary. All this day we had before us the prospect of the long chain of mountains then covered with snow, which divide the two Castiles.

March 11. The road over which we travelled this day, was somewhat hilly. We arrived at noon at the city of Segovia, which stands on a hill, at the foot of which runs the small river Eresma. Segovia is walled, and is about eighty-eight miles distant from Valladolid. Between Olmedo and this city we saw vast numbers of sheep, the wool of which is accounted the finest in Spain. I made enquiry about the sheep-walks, and concerning the method of managing those animals, of which a very just account is given by the Abbé de la Porte, in the sixteenth volume of his *Voyageur François*, printed in Paris in 1772: it is as follows.

" Numberless flocks of sheep cover the plains of Segovia, and
" produce that excellent wool, which makes such an important
" branch of the commerce of Spain. The kings were anciently
" the proprietors of the greatest part of those flocks: they have
" been successively alienated for state exigencies. Philip I. was
" obliged to sell the last fourteen thousand sheep which belonged
" to the crown, to defray the expences of war. They are, how-
" ever, still the object of the government's particular attention:
" in

" in effect, there is a considerable exportation of wool, which is
" used all over Europe. Does its superiority depend only on the
" climate, or on a particular method of managing the sheep?
" Those that embrace the latter opinion say, that there are in
" Spain two sorts of sheep, very different in their fleece, though
" they appear to be of the same breed. The sheep with coarse
" fleeces remain all the year in the same place, and in the win-
" ter nights they are shut up in a fold. On the contrary, the
" others live always in the open air, and travel twice a year.
" During the summer they stray on the mountains of Leon, of
" Old Castile, of Cuença, and of Arragon: they pass the win-
" ter on the temperate plains of la Mancha, Estramadura, and
" Andalusia. According to very exact calculations, there are
" reckoned in Spain more than five millions of those travelling
" sheep with fine wool. It may easily be imagined how much
" care, intelligence, and activity is requisite from those who have
" the charge of conducting those vast flocks.

" They must take particular heed not to let them want salt,
" especially after their return from the south to their summer
" pasturages. That commodity keeps them in health, and
" hardens their constitution, which contributes infinitely to the
" beauty of the wool. After having passed the winter in a tem-
" perate climate, they set out in the month of April for the
" mountains.

" The sheep themselves show their desire of changing their
" place, by many unquiet motions; and that desire is so

" strong

" strong, that the shepherds must be very watchful to prevent
" their escaping.

" They begin to shear them in the month of May, either on
" the road, or after their arrival. It is necessary to wait for fine
" weather, for if their wool was not dry enough, the fleeces be-
" ing piled on each other would ferment and spoil. Towards
" the end of July, the number of rams necessary for propaga-
" tion are mixed with the sheep. Six or seven rams are suffici-
" ent for a hundred sheep: out of a numerous flock of rams the
" strongest and handsomest are chosen for that purpose. There
" are in general very few sheep in these travelling flocks, though
" their wool is finer, and their flesh better than that of the rams,
" but the fleece of these is heavier, they live longer, and by
" that means their total product is more considerable. It is
" esteemed very essential to besmear these animals in the month
" of September, from the neck to the root of the tail, with a
" ferruginous earth mixed with water. It is said that this un-
" guent, mixing with the grease of the wool, becomes impene-
" trable to rain and to cold, and that it absorbs part of the transf-
" piration, which would otherwise render the fleece rough and
" coarse. At the end of September, the sheep begin their march
" towards the lower plains. They travel one hundred and fifty
" leagues in forty days, and the time comes when the sheep drop
" their lambs. The shepherds first separate those which are steril
" from those which are fruitful: these are guided to the best places
" of shelter, and those to the coldest parts of the district. The spots
" which

"which produce the best and most abundant herbs, are also allotted
"to the youngest lambs; that, by being fortified with good
"food, they may be able to depart with the others. Their tail
"is cut off within five inches of the rump, to keep them the
"cleaner. It is an error to believe that sheep prefer aromatic
"plants to others, and that they are more beneficial to them.
"It is the tender herbs that grow between those plants, that af-
"ford the most wholesome nourishment for them, and that gives
"a good taste to their flesh. They must never be led to feed till
"the sun has dissipated the morning dew, and must not be allow-
"ed to drink immediately after a hail storm; because *that* wa-
"ter, or wet grafs, renders them melancholy, and makes them
"languish and die.

"It appears then to be certain, that the superiority of the
"wool in this country is not to be attributed to the climate only;
"and that it depends in a great measure on the precautions above
"mentioned; because, in the same climate, the sheep of Anda-
"lusia, which are of the same breed, but which are not taken
"the like care of, have their wool much coarser. Would it be
"advantageous in other countries to allot large tracts of land for
"the pasturage of these animals; and would it be as much so
"to the proprietor as if he had made those lands serve for other
"purposes? In those countries where lands are successfully cul-
"cultivated, flocks of sheep must be considered more for the
"use they are of to agriculture, than for their fleeces. Dung
"is there much more necessary than wool. The travelling sheep
"furnish

"furnish no manure when they wander in the mountains, so that they must be confined together on lands which require cultivation *."

In the Gentleman's Magazines for May and June 1764, is an account of these sheep-walks, addressed to Mr. Peter Collinson, which is very accurate, and from which the following extracts are a necessary addition.

" From computations made with the utmost accuracy, it has appeared, that there are five millions of fine woolled sheep in Spain, and that the wool and flesh of a flock of ten thousand sheep, produce yearly about twenty-four reals a head, which we will suppose to be nearly the value of twelve English sixpences; of these but one goes to the owner, three to the king, and the other eight to the expences of pasture, tythes, shepherds, dogs, shearing, &c.

" Thus the annual product of the five millions of sheep, amounts to thirty-seven millions and a half of six-pences, a little more or less, of which there is about three millions and a half for the owners, above fifteen millions enter into the treasury, and seventeen millions and a half go to the benefit of the public.

* In the book entitled *Secretss de Agricultura*, by Fr. Mig. Augustin, 1617, are the methods of curing the infirmities of sheep, &c. This book has been very often reprinted. It is a large quarto volume.

" Ten

"  Ten thousand sheep compose a flock, which is divided in-
" to ten tribes: one man has the conduct of all. He must be
" the owner of four or five hundred sheep, strong, active, vigi-
" lant, intelligent in pasture, in the weather, and in the diseases
" of sheep. He has absolute dominion over fifty shepherds, and
" fifty dogs, five of each to a tribe. He chuses them, he
" chastises them, or discharges them at will; he is the *præpo-*
" *situs*, or chief shepherd of the whole flock. One may judge
" of his importance by his salary; he has forty pounds a year
" and a horse; whereas the first shepherd of a tribe has but
" forty shillings a year, the second thirty-four, the third twen-
" ty-five, the fourth fifteen, and a boy ten shillings a year. All
" their allowance is two pounds of bread a day each. They may
" keep a few goats and sheep in the flock, but the wool is for
" the master; they have only the lambs and the flesh.

"  The chief shepherds give them three shillings in April, and
" three in October, by way of regale for the road. They are ex-
" posed every day to all weathers, and every night lie in a hut.
" Thus fare, and thus live, generally to old age, five-and-twen-
" ty thousand men, with the same number of dogs of the
" large mastiff kind, who are allowed two pounds of bread a-
" piece a day.

"  The first thing the shepherd does when the flocks return
" from the South to their summer downs, is to give them as
" much salt as they will eat. Every owner allows his flock of a
                                                    " thousand

" thoufand, one hundred *arrobas*, or twenty-five quintals of
" falt, which the flock eats in about five months. They eat none
" in their journey, nor in their winter walk. This has ever
" been the cuftom, and is the true reafon why the kings of
" Spain cannot raife the price of falt to the height it is in France,
" for it would tempt the fhepherds to ftint the fheep; which, it
" is believed, would weaken their conftitutions, and degrade
" the wool. The fhepherd places fifty or fixty flat ftones, at
" about five paces diftant from each other, he ftrews falt upon
" each ftone; he leads the flock flowly among the ftones, and
" each fheep eats to its liking.

" The fleeces of three rams generally weigh twenty-five
" pounds: there muft be the wool of four wethers, or of five
" ewes, to equal that weight.

" The latter end of September the fheep begin their march
" towards the low plains: the itinerary is marked out by im-
" memorial cuftom, and is *better* regulated than the march of
" troops. They feed freely in all the wilds and commons they
" pafs through, but as they muft neceffarily traverfe many cul-
" tivated fpots, the proprietors of them are obliged by law, to
" leave a paffage open for the fheep, through vine-yards, olive-
" yards, corn-fields, and pafture-lands common to towns; and
" thefe paffages muft be at leaft ninety yards wide, that they
" may not be too crowded in a narrow lane. Thefe paffages are
" often fo long, that the fheep march fix or feven leagues a day

" to get into the open wilds, where the shepherd walks slowly,
" to let them feed at ease, and rest; they never stop, but
" march two leagues a day at least, without any intervening day
" of repose, ever following the shepherd, always feeding, or
" seeking with their heads to the ground, till they get to the end
" of their journey.

" The chief shepherd's first care is to see that each tribe is
" conducted to the same district it fed in the year before, and
" where the sheep were yeaned, which they think prevents a
" variation in the wool, though indeed this requires but little
" care, for the sheep would go to that very spot of their own
" accord. His next care is to fix the toils where the sheep pass
" the night, lest they should stray and become a prey to wolves."

These toils are made of *esparto*, *gramen sparterum*, or *genista Hispanica*, in Latin. Mr. Ray calls it mat-weed: it is a soft rushy shrub, which grows to the height of about a yard, chiefly about Murcia and Carthagena. Sandals, mats, baskets, and ropes are made of it: it floats, whereas hemp sinks: it is called *Bass* by the English sailors.

The meshes are a foot wide, and of the thickness of a finger, so that they serve instead of hurdles.

" The shepherds make their own huts with stakes, branches,
" and brambles; for which end, and for firing, they are allowed
" by

"by the law to cut off one branch from every foreſt-tree. In the
"month of March they pay the twentieth lamb; the other half
"tythe is paid in the winter-walk. They ſaw off part of their
"horns, that the rams may neither hurt one another, nor the
"ewes. They render impotent the lambs doomed for docile
"bell-wethers, to walk at the head of the tribe: they make no
"inciſion, the ſhepherd turns the teſticles many times about
"in the *ſcrotum*, till he twiſts the ſpermatic veſſels as a rope,
"and they wither away without any danger.

"As ſoon as the month of April comes about, the ſhepherds
"muſt exert all their vigilance leſt the ſheep ſhould eſcape; it
"has often happened, that a tribe has ſtolen a forced march of
"three or four leagues upon a ſleepy ſhepherd; but he is ſure to
"find them; and there are many examples of three or four ſtray-
"ed ſheep walking a hundred leagues to the very place they fed
"the year before.

"Some of the ſhearing houſes are capable of containing twenty
"thouſand ſheep; the ewes are ſo tender, that if they were ex-
"poſed immediately after ſhearing to the air of a bleak night,
"they would all periſh.

"There are one hundred and twenty-five ſhearers employed
"to ſhear a flock of ten thouſand ſheep: a man ſhears twelve
"ewes a day, and but eight rams; the reaſon of this difference
"is, not only becauſe the rams have larger bodies, ſtronger, and

more

" more wool, but becaufe the fhearers dare not tie their feet, as
" they do thofe of the unrefifting ewes. Experience has taught,
" that the bold rebellious ram would ftruggle even to fuffocation
" in captivity under the fhears: they gently lay him down, they
" ftroke his belly, and beguile him of his fleece. A certain
" number of fheep are led into the great fhelter-houfe, which
" is a parallelogram of four or five hundred feet long, and one
" hundred feet wide, where they remain all day. As many as
" the fhearers judge they can difpatch next day, are driven from
" the fhelter-houfe into a long, narrow, and low place, where
" they remain all night, crowded together as clofe as poffible,
" that they may fweat plentifully, which foftens the wool for
" the fhears, and oils their edges. They are led by degrees in
" the morning to the fpacious fhearing hall, adjoining to the
" fweating-room. The fhepherd carries them off, as faft as they
" are fheared, to be marked with tar; and as this operation can
" only be performed upon one at a time, it gives an opportunity
" to the fhepherds to cull out for the butchery all the fheep of
" the flock which have outlived their teeth. The fheared
" fheep go to the fields to feed a little, if it be fine weather, and
" they return in the evening to pafs the night in the yard before
" the houfe, within the fhelter of the walls; but if it be cold
" and cloudy they go into the houfe: they are thus brought by
" degrees to bear the open air, and their firft days journies from
" the fhearing-houfe are fhort.

" The wool is divided into three forts: the back and belly
" give the fuperfine, the neck and fides give the fine, and the
breaft,

"breaſt, ſhoulders, and thighs the coarſe wool. It is ſold af-
"ter it is waſhed; for, as it never loſes leſs than half its weight
"in waſhing, and often more, when the ſweating is violent,
"half the carriage is ſaved."

The firſt object of my attention in Segovia was the famous aqueduct, the building of which is attributed to the Goths, to Hercules, to the emperor Trajan, &c. Diego Colmenares, ſeems to make it cotemporary with the pyramids of Egypt, as he ſays there is much ſimilitude between them and this aqueduct; and adds, that this is of a very different order of architecture from any of the five uſed by the Romans: but it is moſt generally believed to have been erected by Trajan *. There is a range of one hundred and eighteen arches, over forty-three of which there is an equal number of others; the total is one hundred and ſixty-one: the greateſt height of this building is one hundred and two feet. The whole is built with ſtones of about three feet long, and two feet thick, without any morter or cement; but thoſe on the top of all are joined by cramp-irons. There are many houſes built about this aqueduct, which prevent a complete and general view of it †: the two largeſt arches ſerve as paſſages, which lead to the *Plaza del Azoguejo*. An Engliſh gentleman of my acquaintance, with two of his companions, walked over the top of the aqueduct, which is but eight feet broad, and without any parapet. On the whole, it is one of

---
* See Clarke, p. 182. Caimo, tom. ii, p. 156. Florez, Montfaucon, &c.
† See the annexed plate.

the nobleſt and moſt perfect monuments of antiquity now exiſting, and is at preſent as entire as when it was firſt erected. The Spaniards call it *el Puente*, or *the Bridge*, which is a very improper name *.

I afterwards went to the *Alcaçar*, or royal palace, ſituated on a rock, detached by a deep dry ditch from the city, with which it communicates by a ſtrong ſtone bridge. It was built by the Moors in the eighth century; was afterwards inhabited by the kings of Caſtile, and is now uſed for a ſtate priſon: there were thirteen Turkiſh corſair captains confined in it at the time I was there. Part of the palace is converted into a military ſchool, in which eighty cadets are educated, who alſo reſide here. This is the caſtle of Segovia mentioned in Gil Blas, which is an original French work of Mr. le Sage, and not a tranſlation from the Spaniſh, as has been imagined.

The caſtle is built of white ſtone, a tower riſes from the center, environed with many turrets; the roof of the whole is covered with lead. In the royal ſaloon, round the wall, are fifty-two ſtatues of painted wood; they repreſent a ſeries of the kings and queens of Spain, ſitting on thrones, and of ſeveral eminent perſons, all as large as the life, with an inſcription under each. The ceiling of this room, and of ſeveral others, is ſo well gilt,

* I ſaw the Pont du Gard near Nimes in 1768, and found it to be one hundred and forty-four feet in height, but it has three rows of arches, one above another: it was built by Agrippa.

that though it probably was done seven centuries ago, it appears quite fresh and new.

I was shewn the cabinet where Alfonso X. surnamed the Impious and the Wise, composed his Astronomical Tables, in 1260: he was here struck by lightning, the marks of which still appear in the wall.

The cathedral is an old Gothic building, with a high square tower, but contains nothing worth notice, except the old clothes of some Jews, who had the misfortune to be burnt by order of the *most holy* Inquisition in the last century.

The mint is situated at the bottom of the city, upon the small river Eresma: the whole machinery for coining is moved by water-wheels, by means of which the metal is weighed, cut, beaten, stamped, and milled, as it were in a moment. This is the most ancient of the three mints in Spain; the other two are at Seville and at Madrid. I here obtained specimens in gold, silver, and copper, of the new coinage; the smallest piece in copper is called a *maravedi*, one hundred and fifty-three of which are of equal value with our shilling: the *real de plata* is a silver piece, and the *peso de oro* a gold piece, of the same size and stamp as the *maravedi*; nine of the first are equal to two shillings, and the value of the latter is two ninths of our pound sterling. There has been an universal new coinage of all the Spanish gold, silver, and copper money, though the old coins

coins still retain their value, and are equally current with the new. The impression on one side of the copper coins represents the profile of his majesty, the inscription is *Carolus III. D. G. Hisp. Rex*, 1773, and on the reverse quarterly a castle and a lion, being the arms of Castile and Leon, with the arms of France in the center, without any inscription : the milling represents a wreath of leaves. The impressions upon the new silver and gold coins differ very little from those in copper; the inscription on one side is *Carolus III. Dei G.* 1772, and on the reverse, *Hispaniarum Rex* : the arms are stamped on these pieces, crowned with a regal crown, and at the bottom have a pomegranate, which is the arms of the kingdom of Granada. Those which are struck at Segovia have a small stamp of four of the arches of the aqueduct on one side of the head : those coined at Madrid have a capital *M*, with a crown over it; and those that are fabricated in Seville have an *S*.

There are four new copper coins ; a piece of one maravedi ; an ochavo, or one of two ; a quarto, or one of four ; and a piece called dos quartos, consisting of eight. Five new silver pieces, one of a single real, one of two, one of four, one of ten, and one of twenty reals, which last is called a hard dollar, *peso duro*, piastre, or piece-of-eight. The four new gold coins are, the piece of twenty reals, that of seventy-five reals ten maravedis, that of one hundred and fifty reals and twenty maravedis, and that of three hundred reals and six maravedis. But, in common currency, when a single piece is exchanged for smaller money, the

the odd maravedis are not accounted : ninety reals are equal to a pound sterling when at par.

Some of the coins prior to these have whimsical combinations of the letters composing the words CAROLVS and PHILIPPVS, which at first view appear more like the arbitrary *marks* of merchants upon their bales of goods, than as cyphers, for which the inventor probably designed them. The milling on the silver coins is a circle between two oblique lines, thus //o//o//o//o; that on the gold coins nearly resembles that on our guineas *.

March 12. I left Segovia this day, and travelled to the royal seat of St. Ildefonso, which is also called la Grange and Balsain. The distance is but two leagues : the road is very stony, and on each side we saw vast herds of deer, many hares, and very numerous covies of partridges, which live here in perfect security,
 " And, undisturb'd by guns, in quiet sleep,"
because hunting and shooting in the proper season are free to every body all over Spain, excepting four leagues round Madrid, or round any of the royal seats, the game being there reserved for his majesty alone, who daily amuses himself with shooting.

The weather was cold, and the puddles on the road were covered with a skim of ice as thick as a halfpenny. The town, which

* See Clarke's account of the old coins, p. 267.

contains about six thousand inhabitants, is built at the bottom of a long ridge of mountains, which were then wholly covered with snow. I called on Mr. John Dowling, an Irishman, who has erected a large building, in which he carries on a manufacture of knives, scissors, razors, sword-blades, and other steel wares: his workmen are chiefly from Birmingham. This gentleman was so kind as to accompany me during my stay here. We first visited the royal fabric for plate-glass, where I saw glasses of one hundred and twenty French inches by seventy-two, which are the largest that were ever made *. These plates are not made for sale, but only for the king's use; his palaces are furnished with them, and he presents some of them to his nobility. There are also six glass-houses, for the fabric of bottles, drinking-glasses, &c. for sale. Mr. Dowling has likewise erected a machine which polishes forty-eight plates of glass at a time.

I dined this day at Dr. Matthew Lawler's, an Irish ecclesiastic who resides here.

The inns here are detestable; and during the time that the court resides here, which is annually from the 21st of July to the 8th of October, the expence of living is to the highest degree extravagant.

* I saw a looking-glass in Burleigh-house, the seat of the earl of Exeter, near Stamford, which was made in London, and was seven feet by four; and one at the fabric in the Fauxbourg St. Antoine in Paris, of eight feet ten, by six feet two inches.

The court pafs the reft of the year as follows: from the 9th of October to the 10th of December, in the Efcurial; then at Madrid till the 5th of January, from which time they are at the Pardo till the Holy-week, which is fpent at Madrid, and the remainder at Aranjuez. The ambaffadors and foreign minifters all accompany the king to thefe four feats, where they are obliged to keep houfes at a great expence, excepting at the Pardo, which is but about fix miles from Madrid.

The royal palace of St. Ildefonfo is built of brick, plaiftered and painted; it is two ftories high, and the garden-front has thirty-one windows, and twelve rooms in a fuite. In the middle is fituated the church. The gardens are on a flope, on the top of which is the great refervoir of water, called here *el Mar*, the fea, which fupplies the fountains: this refervoir is furnifhed from the torrents which pour down the mountains. The great entry is fomewhat fimilar to that of Verfailles, and with a large iron palifade. In the gardens are twenty-feven fountains; the bafons are of white marble, and the ftatues, which are all excellent, and equal to any thing of the kind I ever faw, even in Italy, are of lead, bronzed and gilt: thofe of Fame, Andromeda, Latona, Neptune, Diana, and the Fruit-Bafket, are the moft confpicuous. Here are two noble cafcades, of ten falls each Thefe gardens are alfo ornamented with fixty-one very fine marble ftatues as large as the life, with twenty-eight marble vafes, and with twenty leaden vafes gilt. For the diverfion of the younger branches of the royal family, here is a mall of five hundred and

and eighty paces in length. Near which is a large labyrinth. The gardens were laid out by a Frenchman, named Bouteleux. The fountain of Fame, which is the lowest in situation, spouts water to the height of one hundred and thirty-three feet eleven lines, French measure, which is exactly that of the weather-cock on the top of the church steeple.

The best statues in the garden are the following:
The Four Elements. Juno, Neptune, Saturn, and a Nymph.
Four allegorical figures, representing Pastoral, Lyric, Heroic, and Satiric Poesy.
Four Fames and two Satyrs; a Cleopatra; two Lions; the Four Seasons; the Four Quarters of the World; Apollo and the Nine Muses; four Huntresses.
Four groups of Cephalus and Procris; Endymion and Diana; Zephyrus and Flora; and Bacchus and Ariadne.
Apollo, Daphne, Mercury, Pandora, Ceres, Bacchus, Atalanta, Lucretia, Faith, Glory, Munificence.

The upper part of the palace contains many valuable paintings, and the lower part antique statues, busts, and basso relievos. All the rooms have their ceilings painted in fresco, and are decorated with large looking-glasses made here. The floors are all of chequered marble, and the tables of the finest Spanish marbles of various sorts. The windows, which reach from the ceiling to the floor, consist of large plates of glass set in lead gilt.

The paintings that are moſt remarkable are the following *:

A ſmall piece by Mieris.

Four by Teniers, which repreſent dancing.

A large St. Sebaſtian.

Chriſt and the Money-Tellers, n. ſ.

A ſleeping Cupid, with a ſhell.  Guido.

A St. John, like that at Bologna by Raphael.

Charles V. on horſeback, a ſmall copy of that by Vandyke, which is in the poſſeſſion of lady Leiceſter, at her ſeat at Holkam, in Norfolk.

A Lucretia, n. ſ.

The Marriage of St. Catherine, n. ſ.

Two pieces by Baſſano, repreſenting Suppers.

Two large pictures of Fowls, by Hondekoter.

A St. Suaire with four Angels.  Amiconi.

The Marriage of St. Catherine, ½ l. n. ſ.  P. Veroneſe.

A Boy and Girl with a Bird's Neſt.  Mieris.

A copy of Guido's Madonna, which is engraven by Mr. Strange.

A Man and Woman telling of Money, by Reinier Marinus, 1538, much in the ſtyle of Quintin Matſys, the celebrated blackſmith.

Two by Watteau.

Four naked Cupids by Rubens, within a garland of flowers and fruits, by another hand.

---

* n. ſ. ſtands for the natural ſize; w. l. for whole length; ½ and ¾ l. for half and three quarter length.

The infide of a church. P. Nef.

A Copperfmith's Shop, by Baffano.

A Whimfical Temptation of St. Anthony.

The portrait of a Pope fitting, ½ l. n. f.

Four large Views of Meffina, Baya, the Grotto of Paufilipo, and the Strada Chiaya in Naples.

Two Views of St. Mark's Square in Venice, by Canaletti.

Six very large and fine Landfcapes by Claude Lorraine.

A Man with his Wife, Maid, and Child, w. l. n. f. L. Jordaans.

A portrait of Erafmus.

Two Madonnas, by Titian.

Two Buftards.

Four very large pictures, with cattle, &c. by Snyders.

A Roman Charity, w. l. n. f.

Twelve Heads in Crayons, by the late Queen-mother in 1721: their chief merit confifts in being painted by a queen.

A large and good picture, reprefenting a Pope, fix Cardinals, and many Doctors affembled in council; the figures are about fix inches in fize.

A picture thirty feet in length, containing upwards of fixty figures as large as the life, by Solimene: it reprefents the Supper of Herod, when the head of St. John was brought in after the Decollation.

The Twelve Apoftles, by Rubens.

Four fmall Baffanos.

A Bacchanal, a Satyr, and two Cupids, w. l. n. f.

An extraordinary reprefentation of men and women fuppofed to be ftarved.

A copy of the Venus of Titian, which is in the Medicis Collection at Florence.

A fmall piece, Sufan and the two *chafte* Elders. P. Veronefe.

In a room pannelled with feven very large looking-glaffes, are four paintings reprefenting defigns in architecture.

Three very fine pieces of tapeftry, by P. Ferloni, reprefenting pope Benedict XIV. St. John, and St. Cecilia.

Two figures of Women's Heads, in mofaic ovals.

In the apartments of the prince of Afturias, I faw the Hiftory of Don Quixote in feventy-two pieces, cut out in paper, by Pedro Lazo de la Vega. I afterwards faw this man in Malaga, and employed him in cutting a piece for me: he is now in London.

A very good Italian Madonna.

A picture by Baffano. A large Teniers.

A fmall bronze model of the Toro Farnefe, and two bronzes of Marcus Aurelius.

In this palace is a fmall theatre, the roof of which is fuftained by ten *verde antico* marble, and alabafter columns. There is another theatre in the town, but not worth feeing.

The greateft part of the ground-floor of the palace, confifting of twelve rooms, ferves for a repofitory of ftatues, bufts, and baffo relievos; they are chiefly antique, and of white marble, the principal of which are here enumerated.

## SPAIN.

### In the First Room.
Leda; two statues; five modern busts.
Ganymede; three busts.

### In the Second.
Two colossal statues of Jupiter and Apollo.
Three statues; two termini; twelve heads: a head of Homer, modern.

### In the Third.
A woman veiled, by Corradini.
Hercules; two statues; a very fine small Seneca, sitting.

### In the Fourth.
Two Cupids with palm-branches, modern.
Six statues; a small statue; two busts of black marble.

### In the Gallery.
Neptune in a reclining posture, larger than the life: this is a capital statue.

Ten Egyptian Idols standing, and one sitting of *black basaltes:* these represent Isis, Osiris, Semiramis, Priests and Priestesses, with uncommon Symbols.

Two large statues, and a smaller one.

Fifty-six busts: thirty-four basso relievos of heads, &c.

A small Laocoon in basso relievo.

A basso

A baſſo relievo of alabaſter; the heads of the figures are of porphyry.

A very fine and large baſſo relievo of Olimpia.

Four columns, each a ſingle block, ten feet high, two of which are of *verde antico*, and the other two of Grecian alabaſter.

### In the Fifth Room.

A circular altar of Bacchus, with ſeven figures, fifteen inches each, in baſſo relievo.

Four heads; a modern Cupid; and a modern head.

### In the Sixth.

A coloſſal Cleopatra, " recumbent:" this is a very fine ſtatue.

Two bulls in alto relievo.

Four ſtatues; four buſts; two modern buſts.

### The Seventh Room,

Which is decorated with ſix very large looking-glaſſes, contains two buſts, ſeven porphyry vaſes, and twelve modern buſts of coloured marble.

### In the Eighth.

A modern fountain of Apollo.

Two ſtatues; ten buſts.

Eight ſtatues of the Muſes ſitting: the ninth is in Rome: theſe are of Grecian workmanſhip, and belonged formerly to the

the queen of Sweden. Figures of thefe ftatues are engraven in Montfaucon's work, and alfo in that of Francifo Aquila.

In the Ninth Room.

Two ftatues; ten bufts.

In the Tenth.

Two very fine Grecian ftatues, which reprefent two young men quite naked, crowned with laurel, one of whom holds a *patera* in his right hand, and has his left on the fhoulder of the other, who has a torch in each hand, with the one he fets fire to an altar fuppofed to be placed before an idol; the other arm and torch are behind his back. Thefe ftatues have been defcribed by many antiquaries, and are thought to reprefent Caftor and Pollux: they were once in the poffeffion of the queen of Sweden.

The celebrated Venus Aphrodite, kneeling with one knee on a large fhell, called by the French *la Venus aux belles feffes*; nine ftatues; fix bufts.

In the Eleventh.

Daphne: the upper half is modern.

A faun, with a kid on his fhoulders, and the paftoral crook *(pedum)* in his right hand: this ftatue is attributed to Praxiteles, and has been often defcribed.

Two wild boars in alto relievo; two ftatues; three of Venus.

A modern copy of the Venus de Medicis, but with a veil on her body.

The Twelfth, or laſt Room contains

A circular altar, with many figures in baſſo relievo, of the ſame ſize as that above mentioned.

A coloſſal Venus; a ſtatue; ſix modern buſts.

Two gigantic ſtatues of Cæſar and Pompey, of Grecian alabaſter, but the heads, arms, and feet are of gilt bronze.

St. Ildefonſo has been deſcribed by no other author than Father Caimo, who was here in 1755, becauſe the palace, gardens, and fountains were all begun and finiſhed within theſe laſt thirty years. His work is very ſcarce, being prohibited in all Catholic countries.

I had the pleaſure of being acquainted with him in Rome in 1769, when he was ſo kind as to preſent me with his book, which is in four octavo volumes, in the Italian language, containing an account of his travels. He embarked at Genoa for Spain, and landed at Barcelona, near which city he viſited the convent, which is ſituated on the top of the mountain of Monferrato, from thence he proceeded to Madrid through Saragoça.

The deſcription of theſe places conſtitutes the firſt volume of his work.

Half the ſecond volume is a deſcription of the Eſcurial; the other half is an account of St. Ildefonſo, Segovia, Valladolid, and Salamanca.

The

SPAIN.

The third volume contains an account of the author's travels to Toledo, Aranjuez, Seville, and Cadiz; from whence, in 1756, he embarked for Lisbon.

The last volume begins with a narrative of his voyage from Lisbon to London, of which last city he gives a very curious account: he afterwards embarked at Harwich for Helvoetsluys, and travelled through Rotterdam, Delft, the Hague, Leyden, Amsterdam, Utrecht, Dort, Antwerp, Brussels, Ghent, Lisle, and Arras to Paris; and from thence he proceeded through Lyons to Turin, where he concludes his work.

On the 13th of March I set out from St. Ildefonso, and saw at a distance a grand cascade of melted snow tumbling from a mountain. We then passed the spring which supplies the aqueduct of Segovia with water. Two leagues farther, I saw the large palace which is now building for the accommodation of part of the royal family: it is of brick, and forms an exact square, of three stories in height, seventeen windows in length to each front, with a stone balustrade on the attic story, ornamented with a vase, answering to each window. I passed the night in a *venta*.

March 14. We now travelled on the royal road, which is continued quite to Madrid: it is broad enough for five carriages a-breast, and very good, though carried over mountains. It snowed all this day. At noon we had attained to the summit of a mountain, where I obferved a lion couchant, extremely well carved in ftone, holding a fhield between his paws, with a Latin infcription, importing that Ferdinand VI. had caufed this road to be made in 1749.

At the bottom of this mountain, which is called the pafs of Guadarama, is a turnpike, the firft I faw in Spain: I here paid about three fhillings, and having paffed through it, entered into New Caftille. We dined at the village of Guadarama; and, in the evening, arrived at the Efcorial, which is about fifty-fix miles diftant from St. Ildefonfo. The mountains we paffed over this day produce great quantities of pine and fir-trees, and are inhabited by numbers of eagles and vultures.

The Efcorial is fix leagues and a half diftant from Madrid, and is fituated in 40° 34' latitude: every half league along the road has a ftone to mark the diftance. There are three pofthoufes, where, within thefe four years, the king has eftablifhed four-wheeled poft-chaifes, with relays of mules. If a fingle perfon travels in one of thefe chaifes, it muft be drawn by two mules; if two perfons, they muft take three; which regulation is after the method of travelling in France. Thefe mules trot as faft as our poft-horfes, and thus the thirty miles are performed in four hours. Poft-chaifes are in like manner inftituted on the roads to the other three royal feats, but as yet no where elfe in Spain.

The village which gave name to this palace, is called *el Efco-rial*, derived from the Spanifh word *Efcoria*, which fignifies the fcum of melted metal, becaufe formerly fome iron mines were worked here.

The whole building confifts of a palace, a church, a convent, and a burial-place for the fovereigns of Spain. It was begun in 1563, by Philip II. in confequence of a vow he made, if he fhould vanquifh the French army near St. Quintin's, which he did in 1557, on St. Laurence's day. The architects were John Bat. Monegro of Toledo, and John de Herrera, who finifhed it in 1586. It is dedicated to St. Laurence: and as this faint is faid to have been broiled alive on a gridiron, in the third century, the founder chofe to have the building on the plan of that culinary inftrument, the bars of which form feveral courts, and the handle is the royal apartments.

Gridirons are met with in every part of this building; there are fculptured gridirons, painted gridirons, iron gridirons, marble gridirons, wooden gridirons, and ftucco gridirons: there are gridirons over the doors, gridirons in the yards, gridirons in the windows, gridirons in the galleries. Never was inftrument of martyrdom fo multiplied, fo honoured, fo celebrated: and thus much for gridirons. I never fee a broiled beef-ftake without thinking of the Efcorial. St. Jerom is the fecond patron of this place. The monks who inhabit this convent, to the number of two hundred, are Jeronymites.

At the firſt ſight of the Eſcorial, it conveys the idea of a ſquare quarry of ſtone above ground; for it is indeed the largeſt, though not the moſt elegant palace in Europe. The Doric architecture prevails in it. It is wholly built of a grey ſtone, called *Beroqueña*, reſembling a kind of granite, though not ſo hard. It is ſituated in a dry ſoil, environed with barren mountains; which ſituation was choſen, becauſe the quarries which ſupply the ſtone made uſe of for building it, were near at hand.

The Spaniſh deſcription ſays, that the chief front is ſeven hundred and forty feet broad, and ſeventy feet high to the cornice, which goes round the whole fabric. I meaſured it myſelf, and found the breadth to be no more than ſix hundred and fifty-ſeven feet: the ſides, which I likewiſe meaſured, are four hundred and ninety-four feet in depth; the Spaniſh book ſays five hundred and eighty.

There is a ſquare tower at each end of the four corners, ſaid to be two hundred feet in height.

The chief front, which has thirty-five windows in breadth, is turned towards the mountains, which are only a hundred paces diſtant; and, conſequently, it is dark there half an hour before it is ſo at the back front, which commands a fine proſpect, that reaches quite to Madrid.

It is ſaid, that there are four thouſand windows, and eight thouſand doors in this building; one thouſand one hundred and ten of these windows are on the outside of the four fronts. This number is falsely augmented by almost all the describers of it, to eleven thousand windows, and fourteen thousand doors.

There are three doors in the chief front. Over the principal entrance are the arms of Spain, carved in stone; and a little higher, in a nich, a statue of St. Laurence in a deacon's habit, a gilt gridiron in his right hand, and a book in his left: this statue, which is fifteen feet in height, was executed by John Bat. Monegro, and is of the *Beroqueña* stone, except the head, feet, and hands, which are of marble.

Directly over the door are two enormous gridirons in stone basso relievo.

Through this door I entered into a large court, at the bottom of which is the church, which has five doors; over them are placed six statues, each of seventeen feet in height: they were made by Monegro, and are of stone, but with heads, hands, and feet of marble: they represent six kings of Judah, their crowns, and other *insignia*, are of bronze gilt.

The church is built with a cupola, after the model of St. Peter's at Rome; and on each side is a tower with chimes. The choir is so ill placed, that it renders the church very obscure: here are two hundred and sixteen choral books in folio, written

written on parchment, with exceeding fine miniatures. Behind the choir is an altar, over which is a reprefentation, as large as the life, of Chrift on the Crofs: the body is of white, and the crofs of black marble. This is the celebrated crucifix, fculptured by the no lefs celebrated Benvenuto Cellini: this artift publifhed a book on fculpture, dedicated to Cardinal de Medicis, printed in Florence in 1568. In p. 56, he fays, " Though I " have made many ftatues of marble, yet I fhall only mention " one, it being one of the moft difficult parts of the art to repre- " fent dead bodies; this is the image of Chrift crucified, in carv- " ing of which I took great pains, working with all the atten- " tion and care which fuch a fubject requires, and I knew that " I was the firft who had ever carved a crucifix in marble. I " finifhed it in a manner that gave great fatisfaction to thofe " who faw it: it is now in the poffeffion of the duke of Florence, " my mafter and benefactor. I placed the body of Chrift on a " crofs of black Carrara marble, which is a ftone fo extremely " hard, that it is very difficult to cut it."

Cellini mentions this crucifix likewife in his Life, which was lately tranflated into Englifh by Dr. Nugent; in p. 389, of the fecond volume, he fays, " Having completely finifhed my " marble crucifix, I thought that if I raifed it a few cubits above " the ground, it would appear to much greater advantage than " if it were placed immediately upon it; fo I began to fhew it " to whoever had a mind to fee fuch an exhibition. The duke " and duchefs being informed of this, one day, upon their return
" from

"from Pisa, came unexpectedly with a grand retinue to my "workshop, in order to see this image of Christ upon the Cross: "it pleased them so highly, that their excellencies, as well as "all the nobility and gentry present, bestowed the highest enco- "miums on me. When I found that it gave them such satis- "faction, by their extolling it to the skies, I with pleasure "made them a present of it, thinking none more worthy of that "fine piece of work than their excellencies."

Vasari, in his Lives of Painters and Sculptors, vol. II. p. 283, says, "Cellini likewise made a Christ upon the Cross, as big as "the life, a most exquisite and extraordinary performance: the "duke keeps it as a piece upon which he sets a very great value, "in the palace of Pitti, in order to place it in the little chapel, "which he is erecting there, and which could contain nothing "more grand, nor more worthy of so illustrious a prince: in a "word, this work cannot be sufficiently commended."

The grand duke Cosimo sent it as a present to Philip II. It was landed at Barcelona, and was carried from thence to where it now is, on men's shoulders. At the foot of the cross is in- scribed, "*Benvenutus Zelinus, civis Florentinus, faciebat* 1562." It is certainly the finest crucifix extant, and I have been so par- ticular in describing it, because it is the work of so extraordi- nary a man, "whose life is certainly a phænomenon in bio- "graphy; as to the man himself, there is not perhaps a more "singular character among the race of Adam[*]."

---

[*] Miscell. by Dr. Johnson, and others, vol. III. p. 297.

If Cellini were yet living, what imprecations would he not utter, if he knew that the priefts have, by way of ornament, tied a purple velvet gold laced petticoat round the waift of the ftatue, and which defcends below the knees!

Near to this altar, in a nich, is a marble ftatue of St. Laurence, in a deacon's habit, as large as the life, with a gilt bronze gridiron in one hand, and a palm-branch in the other: it was found in the ruins of Rome, and fent to Philip II. by his ambaffador then refiding there. This ftatue is in the ancient tafte, and is of good workmanfhip.

The church contains forty-eight altars, in forty chapels. The great altar is decorated with fifteen bronze ftatues, to which is an afcent by feventeen red jafper fteps: on one fide is the monument of Charles V. whofe effigies, together with thofe of his emprefs, daughter, and two fifters, are reprefented kneeling, as large as the life, in gilt bronze: on the other fide is the monument of Philip II. who, together with two of his queens, are reprefented in like manner. All by Pompey Leoni.

Here are eight organs, one of which is of filver, which are all performed on together, on folemn feftivals.

There are eleven thoufand reliques preferved here, which I fhall not attempt to defcribe, as I did not fee one of them; but in the Spanifh account of the Efcorial, in folio, printed in 1764, the defcription of them is fo curious, that I cannot refrain from making the following literal extract, which will ferve to fhow of what *immenfe value* they are.

"We will firft begin with the reliques of our Saviour, who, as he gave himfelf to us, left us fome of his precious jewels, which are incomparable and divine.

"A facred hair of his moft holy head or bread, is preferved here with the utmoft veneration in a precious vafe; and opportunity can never offer us a better hair to obtain glory by. Several pieces of his moft holy crofs, all admirably garnifhed with gold, filver, and jewels, efpecially that which is *adored* on Good-Friday.

"Thirteen thorns out of his crown, which pierce the foul with their points, when we confider them as in the delicate temples of that moft loving king of glory.

"Some pieces of the column to which he was bound, and of the manger in which he was born to die for us; which invite hearts to break in pieces through compaffion and gratitude.

"All thefe are placed in very rich vafes; but it is not much that kings fhould fignalize themfelves in beftowing riches on him, who left fuch precious reliques to them; even the whole prodigious edifice of the Efcorial is too fmall for the eftimation and reverence due to them.

"In

"In the second place, are the reliques of his most holy mo-
"ther, which gladden the heart of those who seriously consider
"their incomparable value. Three or four pieces of the habit
"which adorned that most pure and virginal body, in which
"was formed that of Jesus Christ our Lord, her son, are placed
"in one case. Also a piece of the handkerchief with which she
"wiped her eyes, at the foot of the Cross, when those tears,
"as precious as the gems of Aurora, joining with the rubies of
"the western sun, incorporated themselves with the treasure of
"our redemption.

"Besides these, we possess a hair, which may be suspected to
"be that which flowing down her neck, enamoured her spouse.
"The vase which contains these reliques is of crystal, with a
"golden cover and ornaments: two kneeling angels support it,
"denoting the veneration due to these remains of their queen
"and our lady, who is elevated above all the angelical choirs
"in heaven.

"Eleven entire bodies of saints; among which is that of a
"very little saint, who was one of the innocent children mur-
"dered by order of Herod.

"One hundred and three heads, above twelve hundred arms
"and legs; the shoulder-blade of St. Laurence, in a silver case,
"which is of such ancient workmanship, as sufficiently demon-
"strates the bone to be his: we may safely leave to these arms
"the dispatch of the most arduous negociations of our salvation,
"which

"which ought always to be present with us; many of these
"arms and legs belonged to the two squadrons of saints who
"combatted under the banners of St. Maurice and St. Ursula.

"We possess also a thigh of the glorious martyr St. Lau-
"rence; it is entire, but the hair is toasted (singed), the holes
"which were made in it by the prongs which turned him on
"the gridiron, are very visible. One of this saint's feet; the
"toes are entire, though contracted: between two of them is a
"finall cinder, which in the eye of piety shines like a carbuncle.

"A silver statue of St. Laurence, which weighs eighteen
"arrobas (of twenty-five pounds each) ornamented with gold,
"to the weight of eighteen pounds: he holds in his hand one
"of the very bars of the gridiron on which he was broiled.

"The smaller relics are innumerable.

"In order to protect the edifice from lightning, there are se-
"veral reliques, especially some of St. Laurence, its patron, in
"metal cases, inserted in the balls and crosses which are on the
"tops of the towers; so that if the ancients, for the same
"effect, placed laurels on the summits of their towers and other
"edifices, which beautified and protected them, because they
"thought that lightning would never strike those plants; how
„much better is this defended by such superior laurels?"

I shall leave the reader to make his own reflections on the foregoing, and proceed with the description of the building; but in justice, I inform him, that a Spanish account in octavo of the Escorial, printed in 1773, says, " As to the reliques " which are kept here, it is better and more concise to venerate " them, than to form a catalogue of them ;" which is all that is therein said about them.

The tabernacle, on the great altar, is of porphyry, gold, and jewels, sixteen feet high; it may be seen, but not touched by laymen. *Odit profanum vulgus & arcet.*

Immediately under this altar is the Pantheon, designed as a repository for the remains of the kings and queens of Spain: the descent to it is by fifty-eight marble steps, chiefly of jasper. This mausoleum is circular, and was built in 1654, according to the design of John Bat. Crescenzio. It is thirty-six feet in diameter, and thirty-eight in height, and is entirely constructed of the most valuable marbles, highly polished, intermixed with ornaments of gilt bronze: round the wall are eight double columns of the Corinthian order, with their bases and capitals of bronze gilt: between these are placed twenty-four urns, or sepulchral chests of marble, of seven feet in length, in as many niches, four over each other: two more urns are placed over the door which fronts the great altar. These chests are placed on four lions paws of gilt bronze, and are farther adorned with the same metal: on each of them is a shield, containing the name

name of the king or queen whofe body is contained within. There are at prefent thirteen depofited here, which are thofe of Charles V. Philip II. III. and IV. Charles II. and Lewis I. The emprefs Elizabeth; the queens Anne, Margaret of Auftria, Elizabeth of Bourbon, Marianne of Auftria, Louifa of Savoy, and Mary Amelia of Saxony. The bodies of the royal children, and of thofe queens who left no iffue, are buried in a chapel near the Pantheon. There are fifty-one niches, forty of which are occupied.

Over the altar is a crucifix; the crofs is of black marble, and the body of gilt bronze, as large as the life, made in Rome by Julian Fineli of Carrara, a difciple of Algardi; but fome attribute it to Pedro Taca: the back ground is of porphyry. The cupola of the Pantheon is of marble, with foliages of gilt bronze: from the middle is fufpended a curious luftre of bronze gilt, of feven feet and a half in height, made in Genoa; there are eight other branches for lamps, held by bronze angels, as the daylight only appears through a fingle window.

The arms of Spain are reprefented over the door, in a kind of mofaic of different coloured marbles, gold, filver, and lapis lazuli.

In the Sacrifty is kept a pectoral crofs, worn about the neck of the prior on folemn days: it confifts of five diamonds, eight emeralds, four rubies, and five pearls, of which the

the largest is of the size of a pigeon's egg, and the other four are as big as filberds.

Here I was likewise shewn a book called *el Capitularo*, being nineteen sheets of parchment, on which are represented various festivals of the year in miniature, by the delicate pencil of father Andrew Leone, and the other painters of the choral books.

In the small chapel *de la Santa Forma*, is a very fine *custodia d'ostia*, of silver *filagrana*, which was made in China, and presented to Charles II. by the emperor Leopold.

In the palace are two meridian lines by John Wendlingen, a German Jesuit.

The library, which consists of two rooms, contains twenty-one thousand volumes : about four thousand three hundred of these are in manuscript; of which, five hundred and seventy-seven are Greek, sixty-seven Hebrew, one thousand eight hundred Arabic, and one thousand eight hundred and twenty Latin and vulgar. The fire in 1661 burnt many MSS. among which were one thousand two hundred in Arabic [*].

The largest room is one hundred and ninety-four feet long ; five marble tables are placed in it. On one of them stands an

[*] See Clarke, p. 131, and 155, for a further account of these MSS.

equestrian statue of Philip II. four feet in height, with a slave at each of the four corners of the pedestal; the whole is of silver. Some other silver statues decorate the other tables. I saw a load-stone here that weighs seven pounds, and suspends an iron weight of twenty-six pounds; but if it were properly mounted, it might be made to suspend one of seven hundred and fifty pounds. This magnet is said to have been extracted from one of the neighbouring mountains.

In a small room called *el Camerino*, is a portable golden altar, which was made use of by Charles V. the cross of its crucifix is ornamented with a topaz as big as a hen's egg, and with a diamond and ruby, each of the size of a common bean; the diamond may possibly be some kind of sapphire.

Behind two sides of the Escorial is a small garden, with a great number of fountains. The royal apartments contain nothing worthy of notice; the kitchen and fruit-garden, with the park, are about a league in circumference.

I shall now give some account of the pictures which are preserved here, of which there are upwards of one thousand six hundred in oil colours, exclusive of the paintings in fresco, in which manner ten ceilings are painted by Luca Giordano.

The best picture here is that which is preserved in the old church; it was painted by Raphael, and as the following ac-
coun-

count of it has never appeared in the English language, and contains many very judicious remarks, not only on the picture, but also on painting, I shall here insert a translation of it from the Spanish paper published in Madrid in 1773, by Don Pedro Antonio de la Puente. Attention to these observations will enable the intelligent spectator to discover the merits of the other pictures he may see here, for which reason I have placed the ensuing reflections at the head of the catalogue of pictures.

In the year 1754, John Henry, Esq. an Irish gentleman, travelled through Spain, and having seen the famous picture called the Madonna, or our Lady of the Fish, in the Escorial, wrote the following reflections on it, as he had heard that James Amiconi, one of the king's painters, had said that it was not an original by Raphael Urbino. He wrote them in English, and gave a copy of them to a relation of his, father James Henry, of the order of St. Francis, in Seville, who translated them into Spanish.

>Volet hæc sub luce videri,
>Judicis argutum, quæ non formidat acumen.
>
>HOR. ART. POET. v. 363.

"Whoever desires to form a right judgment of a painting, must
" first determine the subject of it exactly, because a historical
" picture is only a portrait, and for a man to despise or to praise a
" portrait when he has no just idea of the original, is rash and
" absurd.

" But

" But as portraits vary innumerably, according to the point of
" view in which they are examined, so the same object will ap-
" pear very different, according to the instant of time in which it
" is beheld. For example, the Resurrection of Lazarus, at the
" instant that Christ commands him to come forth from the
" sepulchre, would be in many circumstances the reverse of that
" same resurrection, considered in the point of time immediately
" following it. In the first case, few would appear disposed to
" believe, many to doubt the event, and many more to laugh
" at and ridicule the undertaking of the Saviour; but in the
" second, the greater number would appear believing, many con-
" vinced, and few or none incredulous. Hope, fear, suspicion,
" doubt, and incredulity, would be the predominating passions
" in the first representation; and those of astonishment, confi-
" dence, joy, and tumultuous confusion, in the second.

" When the subject of the picture is ambiguous or defective,
" in that case the imagination is at liberty to determine or to
" suppose it. But in actions like the above, the picture must
" be adjusted to the subject, and not the subject to the picture.

" The subject once determined, we must examine whether
" the painter has treated it judiciously or not; that is, whether
" he has chosen the properest moment, and whether he has dis-
" posed his figures in the most advantageous order and manner:
" if not, we may say that the artist has taken a bad likeness; but
" if he has selected the most happy moment, and disposed the
                                                    " figures

"figures in the best manner possible, that advantage alone,
"which is but little prized by many pretended connoisseurs, and
"never by ignorant persons, screens him from all censure from
"those who understand the rules of the art. Of all the great
"painters I at present recollect, Tintoret is the most defective in
"this particular: he appears to have studied to select the most
"improper time he could have chosen: his heads are always
"low and mean; his attitudes likewise low, and often ridicu-
"lous. As the greater number of his works are evident proofs,
"of this, it will suffice to name one, which is the *Washing of*
"*the Feet*, placed in the sacristy of the Escorial; where, among
"many other enormities, he represents one of the disciples
"stretched on the ground, when another disciple is exerting his
"strength by pulling off one of his stockings.

"In the composition of a picture, three things are chiefly to
"be attended to: first, that the principal action be the chief ob-
"ject; that is, the figures must be so placed that one may at the
"first glance distinguish which are the persons interested in the
"occasion, and which not, otherwise the composition would be
"confused, and the embarrassed eye would remain in an uneasy
"suspence, because each figure, or group, being equally attract-
"ing, it finds no principal object to rest and fix upon. Very
"few artists have composed correctly. Even Raphael has his
"defects; for in his famous picture of the Transfiguration, he
"has painted two subjects which so equally distract the sight,
"that one knows not where to fix, whether on the mi-
                                            "racle

"racle above, or on the disciples and the lunatic at the foot of
"the mountain.

"Secondly, in a good picture there must be an exact propriety
"in the *contrast*, by which is meant, that the figures or groups
"must not be much like each other, either in their attitudes,
"faces, or habits. The Heaven which is painted in the chief
"choir of the Escorial, by Luca Cambiaso, proves what I say,
"for by want of a due contrast, it looks more like a regiment
"of militia in battle array, than a choir of angels and happy
"spirits praising their Creator.

"Lastly, each of the figures and groups must balance one
"another exactly; if they do not, one side of the picture will
"appear to preponderate over the other, which will necessarily
"hurt the eye. This rule is likewise extended to portraits, be-
"cause an exact equilibrium is as necessary in a single figure as
"in a group. The picture by Velasquez, of the count-duke of
"Olivares on horseback, may be called a model of perfect equi-
"poise, and I prefer it to any thing of the kind I have ever
"seen: it is at present in the king's palace at Madrid.

"Many strange anachronisms are found in pictures, for in-
"stance, the Marriage of St. Catherine with the Child Jesus,
"St. Anthony of Padua, St. Ignatius Loyola, and many others
"with the same child in their arms. The first time I saw the
"picture of the Transfiguration, by Raphael, I was surprised to
"see

" see two Franciscan monks on the top of Mount Tabor, not
" far from Christ, Moses, and Elias, and I could not have
" thought that a painter who possessed so much true taste and
" erudition as Raphael did, could commit such glaring absurdi-
" ties; but my astonishment ceased, when I was informed that he
" painted that picture by order of a community of Capu-
" chin friars.

" Du Piles reduces the art of painting to four parts, composi-
" tion, design, colouring, and expression. That division is de-
" fective, because it omits gracefulness, which is much more
" essential to good painting than any of the others\*. Grace-
" fulness is the art of inspiring an air of dignity and ease in the
" figures represented, so that it may appear to be naturally be-
" longing to them, and not the effect of the painter's ability;
" which noble facility places Raphael in such a superior light to
" most other painters. Gracefulness in Raphael is an inherent ex-
" cellency, whereas, in others, it appears to be a mere casualty.
" Some have drawn as well as he, many are superior to him in
" colouring, others composed with equal judgment; but there
" never was a painter so graceful: that is the reason why the
" paintings of Raphael please the more, the more they are
" examined, and that intelligent persons are as it were forced to
" examine them every time with renewed care and attention, and
" that they quit them with greater reluctance.

\* Senza le grazie ogni fatica è vana, as Lord Chesterfield says.

" We

"We must here take notice that gracefulness must not be
"confounded with what is called genteelness; the former con-
"sists of dignity and ease, and the latter of ease and delicacy.
"The one is noble, the other beautiful: in this last I esteem
"Guido to have gone beyond any other painter. Correggio
"united both in a degree peculiar to himself; his attitudes are
"usually graceful; however his heads, though never mean or
"plebeian, have very seldom that dignity necessary to consti-
"tute what is called nobleness. Thus, in his School of Love,
"which is in the collection of the duke of Alva, the attitude of
"his Venus is perfectly graceful; but her head, though beau-
"tiful beyond expression, is no more than a copy from nature.

"Some persons set about examining pictures only to find out
"their defects, as if all their knowledge of the art consisted in
"making such discoveries: they are often heard to say, what a
"bad leg that is! and that foot, how crooked! that arm ap-
"pears to be one of those of Artaxerxes Longimanus! and
"other equally just and sensible remarks, wherewith they so
"lightly censure the picture and the painter. Such critics ought
"to remember three things: first, that it is much easier to dis-
"cover the defects of a picture than its beauties, because all
"pictures have defects, and but very few have perfections: se-
"condly, that those inadvertencies, though they are granted to
"be faults, are not always to be attributed to the painter's want
"of ability: and, finally, that the greatest masters have fallen
"into some errors. Nevertheless, when we see a leg, an arm,
"or

" or any other member ill drawn, the painter is doubly reprehen-
" fible ; for not knowing the laws of defign, and for not en-
" deavouring to hide his want of fkill. Baffano, for example,
" feldom ventured to draw naked arms or legs, through a con-
" fcioufnefs of his incapacity.

"If, on the contrary, we fee the fame members correctly
" drawn in other pieces by the fame painter, we are to believe
" that thofe defects, which we now cenfure, did not arife from
" want of fkill or power, but from fome accident or inadver-
" tency, hafte, &c. If we are to cenfure great painters for fuch
" trifling faults, which are to be found in all their works, we
" muft fuppofe that Raphael did not know in what pofition a
" man's leg fhould be placed to fuftain his body, becaufe in his
" fchool of Athens, painted in frefco in the Vatican, one of the
" legs of Alcibiades is reverfed : nor that Leonard da Vinci
" knew how many fingers were on a hand, becaufe in his *Laſt*
" *Supper*, which is his mafter-piece, and is preferved at Milan, he
" has painted the hand of one of the apoftles with fix fingers.
" With equal reafon might we fay that Virgil knew not the rules
" of poetry, becaufe he has admitted a falfe quantity in fome of
" his verfes.

" Thofe who criticife paintings, would do well to learn firft
" of what fchool the painter was: for as every nation has its
" own particular idiom, fo each fchool has its particular manner
" which diftinguifhes it from all others; and farther, that it is
" not

"  not possible that it should attain, in any degree of perfection,
" to a beauty peculiar to another different school; so that it is
" as unjust to censure a disciple of the German school for not
" composing as correctly as a Roman, as to find fault with a
" German because he cannot speak Italian: and to say as many
" do, what a pity it is that Raphael did not give to his works
" such beautiful and lasting colours as Titian did to his, is the
" same thing as if we said, what a pity it is that Raphael is not
" a Roman and a Lombard; that is, of the Roman school and of
" that of Lombardy at the same time.

" As Felibien, Fresnoy, and du Piles, have treated at large on
" the rules and precepts of painting, I refer the reader to their
" works with regard to those rules, and shall examine partly ac-
" cording to the rules established by those masters, and partly
" according to the observations hitherto made, a picture which
" is in the Escorial, whose merit I cannot express better than by
" saying, that it is a master-piece of Raphael Urbino: it is paint-
" ed on five tables of wood, and is about eight feet high,
" celebrated under the name of *la Madonna del Pesce*, our Lady
" of the Fish.

" Vasari informs us, that Raphael painted this picture by
" desire of a community of nuns in Naples. Marc Antonio has
" engraven it. The order given to Raphael was probably that
" he should paint a picture in which the following personages
" were to concur: Christ, the Virgin Mary, St. Jerom, St.
" Raphael

" Raphael the archangel, and his young pupil Tobit; happily
" leaving him to contrive, as he was beft able, how to join in
" one picture perfonages who were fo diftant from each other
" in point of time. I fay happily, becaufe certainly none but
" Raphael could have formed fo extraordinary and fo beautiful
" a picture from a fubject fo fteril and fo unconnected.

" To execute this intent, Raphael formed in his mind the
" fictitious idea, which ferved him for an example, in the fol-
" lowing order and manner.

" The Virgin is fuppofed to be fitting in a chair, with the
" child Jefus in her lap, attentively liftening to St. Jerom, who
" is reading the prophecies of the Old Teftament relative to the
" birth, preaching, and miracles of the Meffiah. St Jerom is
" interrupted in his lecture by the entry of the Archangel, who
" introduces the young Tobit, whom he prefents to the Virgin,
" and in an attitude which only Raphael could have drawn, im-
" plores her favour and interceffion with God, that the elder To-
" bit might be reftored to his fight.

" During the pathetic harangue of the archangel, the painter
" pitched on his inftant of time, and, in confequence, has drawn
" him actually fpeaking to the Virgin. She, as the mother of
" Piety and Clemency, is liftening to the archangel with great
" attention, directing her compaffionate looks to the young To-
" bit, who, full of reverential awe, raifes his eyes to the child,

" or

" or rather towards it, because Tobit appears to be too much
" embarrassed and confused to fix them on any determinate
" object.

" As the child and St. Jerom have a share in the principal
" action, the painter, in order to preserve the unity of his sub-
" ject, introduces them by way of episodes, but in such a judi-
" cious and natural manner, that they neither distract the sight,
" nor fatigue the eye of those who examine the whole of the
" work. The child, anxious to get at the fish, which hangs to
" a string in the right hand of Tobit, bends gently towards it,
" looking, in the mean time, at the archangel, as if desiring his
" assistance to obtain it; meanwhile, St. Jerom, who since the
" entrance of the angel had been reading to himself, and had
" finished the leaf, is ready to turn over another, and appears
" only to wait till the child lifts its little arm from the book,
" whereon it had carelessly rested it.

" Thus we see that the whole piece is composed of one prin-
" cipal, and two minor or subaltern actions; or, as the painters
" express themselves, of one action and two accidents. The ac-
" tion is the intercession of Raphael with the Virgin; the
" accidents are, the anxiety of the child for the fish, and the
" silent attention with which St. Jerom waits till it should take
" its arm from the book, in order to turn over the leaf. The
" accidents, besides being distinct from each other, are so much
" inferior to the principal action, that they do not in any man-
" ner

" ner mix with it, but on the contrary ferve to refrefh the fight
" as often as it is wearied with the examination of the principal
" action. This and the firft accident are extremely natural and
" obvious; however, the manner of uniting St. Jerom with the
" other figures, by making the child's arm reft on his book,
" was a thought certainly worthy of Raphael; becaufe, if he had
" painted the faint farther off, and detached him entirely from
" the other figures, he would have been a fuperfluous and unne-
" ceffary perfonage; and if he had reprefented him, as many
" painters would have done, near to the angel who is fupplicat-
" ing the Virgin in Tobit's favour, he would have been an in-
" truding and troublefome perfonage.

" I do not remember ever to have feen a piece in which all
" the laws of a perfect contraft are better obferved: there is not
" one thing in it which refembles another; the child appears to
" be a year old, Tobit ten or twelve, the angel fifteen, the Vir-
" gin eighteen or twenty, and St. Jerom upwards of fixty.

" The child appears as if defirous to ftand up, Tobit kneels
" on one knee, the angel is ftanding, the Virgin fitting, and
" St. Jerom kneels on both knees. The child's face is three
" quarters, that of Tobit an exact profile, that of the angel fore-
" fhortened, that of the Virgin nearly full, and that of St. Jerom
" fomewhat more than a profile.

" The child's hair is of a clear chefnut colour, Tobit's inclin-
" ing to red, the angel's brown, the Virgin's rather darker, and

" St. Jerom's grey, and the crown of his head bald. In a word,
" the whole piece is diversified in the most judicious and agree-
" able manner imaginable. The equilibrium, as well of the whole,
" as of each part, is as perfect as the contrast, and is managed
" with exquisite industry and art; more especially the body of
" the angel, which is an exact balance.

" As the painter had no room for the Lion of St. Jerom, and
" knew that without this, or an equivalent help, the saint would
" not be a sufficient counterpoise for the angel and Tobit, he
" placed the child on the left arm of the Virgin's chair, with
" only one of its feet bearing on her lap; thus preserving an
" exact counterpoise, and at the same time adding beauty to the
" picture: the lion is discovered to lie behind the saint, the
" paws and part of the head appearing. Having thus described
" the plan which Raphael formed for this piece, I shall now dis-
" cover in what manner he executed it, and examine the diffe-
" rent parts of which it is composed; that is, the design, the
" colouring, and the expression.

" As to the drawing or design, it is far superior to any I have
" seen. All the heads are noble and majestic, except that of
" Tobit, which the painter lowered a little on purpose, and for a
" reason which shall be given hereafter. The head of the Virgin
" is perfectly Grecian or Attic; that of the angel is a mixture
" of the antique and of the natural, in a supreme degree of per-
" fection; the oval face of the Virgin, and the exterior linea-
" ments

"ments of the neck of Raphael, are exquisitely beautiful,
"and extremely difficult to execute: the face of the child is
"correct and delicate. In short, the whole drawing is absolute-
"ly complete; because, as to what regards Tobit's right leg,
"(which is the only objection I ever heard made to this picture)
"if the constrained position in which he is represented be not
"a sufficient excuse, I say, that it is such a slight mistake, that
"it will always pass with intelligent persons for the effect of
"haste, or inadvertency in the painter, very pardonable accord-
"ing to the rule of Horace, which is as applicable to painting,
"as to poetry.

> Verum ubi plura nitent in carmine, non ego paucis
> Offendar maculis, quas aut incuria fudit
> Aut humana parum cavit natura.
> HOR. ART. POET.

"The colouring is in the last and best manner of Raphael,
"with this singular excellency, that there is not a single tint
"but what is mixed. Of three different greens, two of which
"are seen in the drapery of the Virgin, and the third in the
"curtain behind her, not one is either grass-green or sea-green:
"the Virgin's head-dress and tunic, as well as the angel's wings,
"are not quite white, but whitish: the habit of St. Jerom is
"scarlet, but not pure scarlet. In short, there is not one original
"or primitive colour in the whole piece; notwithstanding which,
"the painter has shewn exquisite judgment and fine taste, and
"what in any other hands would have been the means of spoil-
"ing

"ing the whole picture, has in those of Raphael produced a soft
"sweet colour, a tenderness and a delicacy which almost equals
"Correggio. To be convinced of this, we need only examine
"the apotheosis of Charles V. by Titian, which hangs to the
"right of our picture \*. It is certainly a very fine piece; but
"notwithstanding its innumerable pure tints, it appears harsh and
"faded, by being placed so near to our Madonna.

"In regard to expression, the action of this piece admits but
"very little: the angel, who is speaking, is properly the only
"person from whom much is required, and is effectively the
"most expressive figure I ever saw, without even excepting the
"father of the lunatic at the foot of Mount Tabor, in the
"famous picture of the Transfiguration. It is true, that Tobit
"testifies a reverential awe and dread, which, though admirably
"expressed, is no more than a passion of an inferior species, or
"a character which the painter introduced merely to animate
"the figure, and the more to set off the angel by means of
"this contrast.

"Let us now take a general idea or view of this work, and
"remark the beauties which arise from the harmony of its parts:
"but as pilots, in computing the ship's way, make allowances
"for tides, currents, and variations; so, in order to examine
"this picture rigorously and without partiality, we must reckon

\* This picture is at present placed in the Old Church.

"among

" among its merits, the difficulties which the painter overcame
" in its execution.

" The first difficulty is in the subject, which, besides being full
" of anachronisms, is not by any means picturesque. A pic-
" turesque subject consists of a true and real action, which being
" an object of vision, can be represented by colours. But the ac-
" tion of the Madonna is a speech or discourse, which belongs
" to hearing, and can no more be expressed by colours, than
" sight can be by sounds; so that though the painter has select-
" ed the most proper moment, the action is nevertheless no
" more than what painters call inert, or still-life. All that
" Raphael could intend, or pretend to express, was how the
" company looked whilst the angel was speaking to the Virgin.

" Now follows the cardinal's habit of St. Jerom, which is
" neither antique, graceful, nor picturesque. Raphael did
" what he could to diminish and deaden that excessive mass of
" scarlet, in order to prevent its vanquishing or drowning the
" other colours, and to divert the eye from fixing upon it. It
" cannot be denied but that he has obtained his end; but the
" Gothic shape of the habit still remains without any possible re-
" medy, forming an antinomy in the draperies of the figures, a
" fault into which it was impossible for Raphael to fall, if he
" had not been compelled to it by inevitable necessity.

" The third difficulty is the fish, which, according to the ac-
" count given of it in Scripture, was at least eight feet long,

"which deftroys proportion, and much exceeeds the limits of
"the picture, fo that Raphael with great judgment reduced it to
"a picturefque fize.

"Thefe I think are the chief difficulties which Raphael had
"to overcome; but I could mention fome others, which I fhall
"leave to be difcovered by the fpectators; and fhall enumerate
"fome of the mafterly ftrokes which fo much diftinguifh
"Raphael from other painters, and our Lady of the Fifh from
"other pictures.

"The attitude of the Virgin is perfectly graceful. The child,
"who is anxious to get at Tobit's fifh, inclines itfelf towards it,
"as was before-mentioned: that motion is fo fudden that the
"child is in danger of falling off the arm of the chair. To pre-
"vent which, the Virgin, without interrupting the angel, or
"taking her eyes off Tobit, inclines herfelf gently, placing her
"right hand againft the breaft of the child, the right fide of
"whofe head almoft touches the left cheek of its affectionate
"mother, which adds to her beautiful face a kind of celeftial
"tendernefs, which may be felt, but is impoffible to be defcribed;
"caufing, at the fame time, a flight turn of her neck, which
"incomparably exceeds whatever I have feen of grace and de-
"licacy in painting.

"The angel and Tobit are likewife perfect in their kind: the
"angel's head is noble, his figure full of grace, his attitude eafy
"and

" and difengaged. Tobit's head is ruftic, his figure is *cham-*
" *pêtre* and heavy, his attitude is harfh. In the angel's face we
" difcover innocence, fweetnefs, and compaffion: in that of
" Tobit, timidity and diffidence. The angel, confcious of his
" own dignity, appears to afk with the confidence that his peti-
" tion is granted the moment he makes it; whilft Tobit, fen-
" fible of his own unworthinefs, trembles even though an angel
" pleads for him.

" But there is hardly a circumftance in the whole piece which
" fhows Raphael's confummate judgment fo much, as his hav-
" ing omitted Tobit's dog; which, by having been twice men-
" tioned in Scripture, is become one of his attributes, as the keys
" are thofe of St. Peter, and the fword and book of St. Paul;
" for which reafon, according to rigour, Raphael ought to have
" introduced it. But it is with painters as with poets

> Great wits fometimes may glorioufly offend,
> And rife to faults true critics dare not mend;
> From vulgar bounds with brave diforder part,
> And fnatch a grace beyond the reach of art.
> 
> POPE'S ESSAY ON CRITICISM.

" In the prefent cafe we muft firft confider that every domeftic
" animal is a thing belonging to plebeian or vulgar life, and is
" confequently unworthy of a place in this picture. Secondly,
" according to the difpofition of the figures, the dog muft necef-
" farily have been painted on the fore-ground, which is the moft
" confpicuous

" conspicuous and honourable place; and lastly, the action of
" the dog would have disturbed the subject: so that if Raphael
" had not broken this precept, he must infallibly have spoiled
" the picture.

" I should never have done, were I to point out all the beau-
" ties in this piece; the uniformity of the lights, the Virgin's
" foot, the oblique position of her garment, the equilibrium of
" the angel's body maintained by the extension of his wings,
" the position of his right foot, that of Tobit's left arm, the
" grand taste of the draperies; in short, every stroke of the
" pencil is of such extreme beauty, that, notwithstanding all
" the difficulties which Raphael had to surmount in its execu-
" tion, it far surpasses every picture in the Escorial, or in
" any other collection of paintings, and is the most precious
" jewel that his catholic majesty possesses: in this I am under
" no apprehension of being contradicted. To conclude, all the
" figures represented in it appear to be thinking and dis-
" coursing."

Omnia sub correctione sapientium [*].

---

[*] " Many strange anachronisms are found in pictures; for instance, the
" marriage of St. Catherine with the child Jesus, St. Anthony of Padua,
" St. Ignatius Loyola, and many others with the same child in their arms."

After this passage (see p. 115.), the Spanish original goes on with the following paragraph, which I have omitted in the text, where it was not worthy
of a place.

" However, these are not properly anachronisms, but rather pious repre-
" sentations of some favours which the Lord chose to bestow upon those his
" servants,

The other principal pictures are the following:

### In the Church.

Eight pictures, each representing a pair of saints; by Juan Hernandez Ximenez Navarrete, surnamed *el Mudo*, the Dumb. He was born in Biscay, and died about the year 1577. He is esteemed one of the best Spanish painters: his style is much in the manner of Titian, whose disciple he was.

### In the Choir.

The large heaven, painted in fresco, on the ceiling, is by Luca Cambiaso. He has here represented *himself* in heaven. The figures are disposed in as exact symmetry as the seats in the choir, which has a disgusting effect.

Christ carrying the Cross, by Sebastian del Piombo.

### Over the great Altar.

The Martyrdom of St. Laurence, by Pellegrino Tibaldi.

The ceiling of the whole church is painted in fresco, in ten compartments, by Luca Giordano. This painter died in 1705.

---

" servants, as it is certain that *his majesty* can communicate himself to his
" chosen, when, and how he pleases; because, as St. Paul says, *Jesu Christus,*
" *heri & hodie ipse & in sæcula:* and he who could after the resurrection present
" himself before Magdalen in the habit of a gardener, and in the habit of a
" pilgrim to the disciples of Emaus, can likewise in the shape of a child
" collocate himself in the arms of any one of his chosen, even in this mor-
" tal life." !

In the Anti-Sacrifty.

The Flight into Egypt, by Titian. The child is eating cherries, given to him by St. John: an angel pulls them for him. This picture is much celebrated.

The Adoration of the Wife Men.

The Crucifixion.

And Prefentation in the Temple. All by Paul Veronefe: the figures are half length.

The Sepulchre of Chrift, by Tintoret.

A Madonna, Bambino[*], and Saints, by Van Dyke.

Chrift and his difciples at fupper in the caftle of Emaus, by Rubens.

St. John preaching in the defert. P. Veronefe.

St. Peter and St. Paul, half length, by Spagnoletto.

In the Sacrifty, which is one hundred and eight feet long, and thirty-three feet wide.

Over the great altar is a very fine picture by Claudio Coello, reprefenting a proceffion in which Charles II. marches: there are a very great number of figures in it, fomewhat lefs than the life. The painter was born at Madrid, and died about the year 1693.

A Holy Family, by Raphael. This picture is called the Pearl. It was bought, for two thoufand pounds, out of our king Charles I's. collection.

[*] Whenever *il Bambino* is written in Italian, or *el Niño* in Spanifh, it means the child Jefus.

The Virgin is reprefented fitting, fhe embraces the child with her right arm. It refts one foot on her knee, and the other on a fmall cradle. The Virgin's left hand is feen on the fhoulder of St. Anne, who kneels by the fide of her daughter, placing one hand in her lap, and reclining her head on the other. St. John (a child) offers fome fruits which he has in his apron of camel's hair. The child appears to reach at the fruit, and at the fame time turns its head to look at its mother, laughing with the fimplicity and grace peculiar to its age: the back ground reprefents a very beautiful landfcape, with a diftant city and river.

The Wafhing of Feet, by Tintoretto. The poftures of the difciples are ridiculous and extravagant, but it is notwithftanding a very fine picture.

A Madonna, Child, St. John, and an Angel; by Andrew del Sarto. Thefe two pictures were purchafed out of king Charles. I's. collection.

Chrift tied to the column: one of the beft works of Luca Cambiafi.

An Ecce Homo. Paul Veronefe.

A Madonna.

Chrift in the Garden. This picture is decayed: it is a night piece, but the colours are much obfcured.

Chrift interrogated about Cæfar's tribute, $\frac{1}{4}$ l. n. f.

The celebrated Magdalen, of which there are fuch an infinite number of copies, $\frac{1}{4}$ l. n. f.

## SPAIN.

St. Margaret and the Dragon.

St. Sebastian, his hands tied behind him, and his body with several arrows shot into it.

The Virgin, Child, St. John, and St. Catherine.

Christ crucified. Christ shown to the people. St. John in the desart. All by Titian.

Magdalen dressing herself before a looking-glass.

A penitent Magdalen. Both by Tintoret.

> Here twice was drawn the am'rous Magdaline,
> Whilst beauty was her care, then her neglect,
> And brightest thro' her tears she seem'd to shine.
> 
> GONDIB. book ii. canto vi.

St. Jerom.

The Adulteress. Both by Van Dyke. This last piece is somewhat damaged.

St. Margaret raising a boy from the dead. Caravaggio

A *noli me tangere*, or Christ appearing to Magdalen. Correggio.

Mary giving suck to the Child. Guido Rheni.

The Sacrifice of Isaac. P. Veronese.

The Assumption of the Virgin. Annibal Carraccio.

Joseph with the Child in his arms. Guido Rheni.

Mary visiting St. Elizabeth.

Mary, Child, and St. John. Both by Raphael.

Christ bearing the Cross. Sebastian del Piombo,

### In the Refectory.

The famous Supper, by Titian, fo well known by the print called the Table Cloth, engraven by Maffon.

The figures are nearly as large as the life. The painter was feven years employed about this picture, and received two thoufand golden crowns for it from Philip II. There is a picture exactly like this preferved in the Royal Collection at Paris.

### In the Old Church.

The Madonna of the Fifh, already defcribed.

The Martyrdom of St. Laurence, by Titian. This appears to be the fame defign as that which I faw in the Jefuits church in Venice, which is painted by the fame hand. A very old print of this picture is extant, but I know not by whom it was engraven.

The Adoration of the Wife Men.

The Sepulchre of Chrift.

An Ecce Homo, and a dolorous Virgin. All by Titian.

A Madonna, by Andrew del Sarto.

Two fmall pictures of the two tombs that are in the church.

The ceiling of the grand ftair-cafe is painted in frefco, by Luca Giordano; and reprefents the battle of St. Quintin.

There are feveral paintings in frefco in the great Cloifter by Pellegrini; and in the great upper Cloifter are five pictures by *el Mudo*.

SPAIN. 135

In the Capitulo Prioral, which is a room of eighty feet long, and twenty feet wide.

St. John embracing a lamb. Spagnoletto.

Christ with a globe in his hand. ½ l. n f. Titian.

A Madonna and Child. Van Dyke.

Christ at the wedding of Cana. P. Veronese.

A Madonna, by Frederic Barocci.

Christ in the garden, by Titian. This picture is over the altar.

The Martyrdom of St. Justina, by Luca Giordano.

Four flower pieces, by Daniel Seegers.

St. Paul falling from his horse.

David triumphing over Goliah. Both by Palma the elder.

The Crowning with Thorns. Van Dyke.

The Centurion. P. Veronese. Many figures, and noble architecture, w. l. n. f. rather damaged.

A picture by Rubens, representing the dead body of Christ lying across the lap of Mary, St. John wiping away his tears, and Mary Magdalen kissing the dead hand: the painting is very fine and natural, which only makes it the more disgusting.

Another picture by Rubens, which is one of the finest in this whole collection. I esteem it be next in value after Raphael's Madonna of the Fish. It represents the Virgin sitting, the naked child stands in her lap, resting its little hand on the uncovered breast of the mother; Joseph and St. Anne are standing by them.

" Here life came out, and met the painter's thought."

St.

St. Sebaſtian, with two men who are tying his feet to a tree, and a boy with bows and arrows, by Van Dyke.

A very large head of St. Peter, and one of St. Paul, by Guido.

Mary ſwathing the infant; St. John, and two women, by Paul Veroneſe. Injured by time.

The Conception of the Virgin. Rubens. n. f. This picture repreſents Mary ſtanding on a globe, with a creſcent and ſerpent at her feet, and ſeveral angels flying about her.

St. James, or Santiago, the patron of Spain, by Spagnoletto; as large as the life.

A Madonna ſitting on a throne, the child ſits on her lap, and is crowned by two angels, who hover over it, by Guido Rheni. This is one of the moſt capital pictures that is preſerved here. Over the door are two baſſo relievos in porphyry; one is a head of Chriſt, the other is a Madonna and Child.

In the Capitulo Vicarial, which is a room of the ſame ſize as the laſt, are likewiſe two baſſo relievos in porphyry of Chriſt and the Madonna.

It contains moreover the following pictures.

St. Jerom penitent in the deſert, over the altar, by Titian, who alſo painted the allegorical picture next to it, which repreſents Faith, Juſtice, Religion, the Spaniſh monarchy, &c. with a diſtant view of ſhips at ſea.

The ſons of Jacob, ſhewing him Joſeph's bloody garment. One of the beſt pictures that Velaſquez ever painted. All the figures are as large as the life.

Don

## SPAIN.

Don Diego Velasquez de Silva was born in 1594, at Seville, and died in 1660 at Madrid: he travelled in Italy for improvement; his style is much like that of Caravaggio, and he is esteemed to have been one of the best Spanish painters.

Esther before Ahasuerus; a very large picture, by Tintoret. Esther is here represented as a languishing beauty.

The Madonna and Bambino, St. John and St. Elizabeth: the figures about half as large as the life. Leonard da Vinci.

St. Rosalia penitent, by Van Dyke. She looks up to heaven, one hand rests on a skull, the other presses her breast, and a little flying angel crowns her with roses.

Christ at the table of the Pharisee, with the weeping Magdalen. Tintoretto.

St. Sebastian: Irene and another woman are extracting the arrows out of his body; angels are represented flying above, and bearing a crown of martyrdom. By Spagnoletto.

The Flight into Egypt. Titian. In this picture is a boy holding a horse.

### In the Sala Aulilla.

The famous picture known by the name of the Glory of Titian. I am informed there are prints extant of this picture, but I never saw one of them. It was painted for the monastery of St. Juste, and was brought here together with the body of Charles V. It represents the three persons and the Virgin in heaven: a damsel allegorically representing the Church, offers to them Charles V. his wife, and Philip II. who are introduced by by angels between the clouds: feveral faints of the Old Teftament are alfo painted in heaven. The figures are about half as large as the life.

A large Annunciation, by Paul Veronefe.

The Sepulchre of Chrift. Titian.

St. Margaret, as large as the life, with the dragon at her feet, by Titian. One of her thighs, which was naked, is daubed over by a common painter, out of an imaginary regard to decency; and thus one of the moft capital pictures in the Efcorial is fpoiled.

This indifcreet zeal prevails even in Italy; the famous painting in frefco, of the laft Judgment, by Michael Angelo, in the Sixtine chapel in the Vatican at Rome, has all the nudities daubed over with blue paint, though, it muft be owned, that according to the print, decency appears to have been grofsly violated: a devil is reprefented pulling a man down, *fcroto*; and a ferpent is twifted round the waift of another figure, *mordet pencm*.

In the Villa Pamphili near Rome, all the antique marble ftatues have their nudities covered with plaifter, which eats into the marble, and can never be got off. At la Veneric, which is a feat of the king of Sardinia, near Turin, all the nudities of the ftatues are in like manner plaiftered. And in St. Peter's church at Rome, the great maufoleum of pope Paul III. is decorated with two ftatues of Prudence and Juftice; the latter is a large and beautiful woman of white marble, which was quite naked; but a

fucceeding

succeeding pope caused it to be partly covered with a bronze drapery, as he was informed that a Spaniard had been sensible of its beauties in a very unphilosophical manner.

There are various other good pictures preserved in the Escorial, painted by Bassano, Jerom Bosco, Carduccio, Herrera, Caravajal, Pantoja, Peregrino, Romulo Cincinnato, Giorgione, Zucaro, and Massacio.

I departed from the Escorial on the 16th of March, and proceeded on the royal road. There are stones at every half league to mark the distance: the first league traverses the royal park, which is walled in; coming out of this park I discovered Madrid, at five leagues distance: we then passed over a handsome stone bridge of seven arches, and soon after we stopped an hour and a half at a venta to let the mules rest: we afterwards passed over a small stone bridge of two arches, on one side of which is a statue of king-saint Ferdinand III. and on the other side, one representing Spain in the figure of a woman, both of marble: they were erected in 1750. We then entered the *corso*, or mall, which is on the banks of the little river Mançanarez, and has a double row of trees on each side, with lamps between them: it was at that time full of coaches, each drawn by six mules, slowly following each other, and then returning. We entered Madrid at five in the evening, through the gate of Toledo, which is opposite to the magnificent bridge of the same name, and put up at the inn called the Crofs of Malta, kept by Italians, in as elegant a manner both as to the apartments and entertainment as any inn in England : it is fituated in the *Calle de Alcalà*, which is the chief ftreet in Madrid, and is broad enough for twenty coaches a-breaft, and of a very confiderable length. My firft care was to difmifs the chaife, mules, horfe, and drivers, who had brought me from Lifbon.

I then walked about the town, and obferved that the names of the ftreets were painted on the corner houfes ; that the houfes were all numbered ; that there were as many lamps as there are in the ftreets of London; that the paving was as regular and neat as can be imagined; and that, moreover, the ftreets were kept fo clean, that I never faw any neater, not even in the cities in Holland; whereas, ten years ago, Madrid might have vied with Edinburgh in its former ftate, for filthinefs.

I next day waited on his excellency lord Grantham, his majefty's ambaffador to this court, and was received with great politenefs by that nobleman.

I gladly embrace this opportunity of acknowledging the many favours conferred on me during my ftay in Madrid by Alexander Munro, Efq. his majefty's conful-general.

As it was Lent, all public diverfions were fufpended. I firft vifited the new royal palace, begun in 1756, which is perhaps

the

the grandeft and moft fumptuous of any in Europe[*]: it is fquare, and built of white ftone, on the moft elevated extremity of the town: the front is four hundred feet in length, as I meafured it myfelf, and is of three ftories in height, each of twenty-one windows; one the top is a baluftrade, ornamented with ftone vafes. There are five doors in front; over the middle door is a gallery fupported by four columns. At the back front is a grand flight of fteps. The architect of this palace is Signor Sacchetti, an Italian, who ftill lives in Madrid, though very old and infirm. The grand cortile is a fquare of one hundred and ninety-five feet. The dome of the chapel is fupported by fixteen marble columns. The grand faloon of ftate is one hundred and twenty feet in length, and has five windows in front; it is entirely hung with crimfon velvet, richly embroidered with gold, and farther ornamented with twelve of the looking-glaffes made at St. Ildefonfo, each ten feet high, and in magnificent frames, and with twelve tables of the fineft Spanifh marbles. The ceiling was painted in frefco, in 1764, by Tiepolo the Venetian, who died here lately.

I had before feen all the palaces of the kings of England, France, Sardinia, Naples, Pruffia, and Portugal; thofe of the pope, the emperor, and of feveral German princes; and I give the preference to this; but it may poffibly be equalled by the

[*] The old palace was burnt down in 1734, and two years were employed in excavating the ruins.

palace which the king of Naples is now building at Caserta, and of which I saw part in 1769.

In the sixteenth volume of *le Voyageur François*, published in Paris in 1772, is the following ill-natured passage concerning this palace, which will serve to shew how the French in general despise every thing out of France, unless it should happen to be the performance of a French artist. Indeed there are no nations which so cordially hate each other as the Spanish and the French: these are in Spain called Gavachos. My French servant, Baptiste, has many times had a suite of boys and women ridiculing him, and crying out, *wik, wik, Gavacho*, &c. In p. 288. we read,

"I know not whether I ought to mention the new palace, which, though more than fifty millions of livres have been spent upon it, is not yet finished, and perhaps never will, for want of money. It is a great square building, situated on a mountain, near the edge of the river, and looks more like a Benedictine convent than a royal house. The interior parts are, however, pretty well distributed, though they have a very melancholy aspect, because the edifice is close and massive. It does not appear that it can have large gardens: I was told that some were intended to be constructed amphitheatrewise, which will be the more singular, as the descent is very rapid. They will be seen terminated by the Mançanarez, and by the bald hills which rise in heaps on the white and stony soil of the environs of Madrid."

How much more juftly could a Spaniard criticife on the wonderful palace of Verfailles, as the French ftyle it. When I was there in 1768, the ftatues in the gardens were broken and tumbled down, the water-works were incapable of being played: grafs grew between the crevices of the grand marble fteps: the paintings in the palace were mouldering away; the looking-glaffes were broken, and fpiders fpun undifturbed by hoftile brooms.

I fpent a whole day in viewing the pictures, of which the beft are fpecified in the following catalogue, not one of them are mentioned in any defcription of Spain, though there are upwards of a hundred volumes in various languages which treat of Spain and Portugal; indeed none of their authors, or compilers, were ever in this palace, except Mr. Baretti. The enfuing account I wrote on the fpot, having previoufly procured a Spanifh painter to accompany and affift me. I mention feveral pictures which are very fine, though I could not come at the knowledge of the painter's name, nor was able to diftinguifh any characteriftics of the more celebrated painters in them, but they all appear to be Italian; fome future curious traveller may poffibly be more fuccefsful in his enquiries.

The firft room I went into has its ceiling painted in frefco, by Tiepolo, reprefenting Apollo, and many other figures; the compofition and execution almoft equal Luca Giordano, and the colouring is fuperior to his.

Four:

Four porphyry busts are placed in the corners of this room, and two antique marble busts on a table.

The chief pictures are: Sixteen portraits by Titian.
Six large and four small pictures by Baffano.
A Madonna and three Saints; half length; natural size.
A Man and Woman, ditto, ditto.
Two pictures representing Prometheus and Sisyphus; whole length; as large as the life.
Venus in her shift, Cupid holding a looking-glass to her.
Adam and Eve, the tree between them, round the trunk is twisted the serpent, with a handsome young man's head, an ingenious way of accounting for Eve's frailty. This picture is near eight feet square *.

* I remember to have seen a marble basso relievo on the outside of the celebrated Carthusian convent, between Pavia and Milan, which likewise represents the serpent with the head of a young man, with long flowing hair. And behind the great altar of the cathedral of Pisa, are two very bad marble statues of Adam and Eve, as large as the life, with the serpent represented in the same manner.
In the church of St. Mary Impertica, in Pavia, I saw a painting representing the Virgin Mary standing on a cloud, squeezing milk out of her breasts into the mouths of the souls in purgatory at her feet.
Another painting which is in the Carthusian convent between Pavia and Milan, represents Christ standing on the bason of a fountain, spouting blood from the five wounds in his hands, feet, and side, and underneath is this inscription:

"Si quis sitit veniat ad me et bibat."

In the Cloister, near the church of the Holy Ghost in Florence, I saw a painting in fresco, representing St Nicholas in bed, a servant holds a plate on which is a roasted partridge; another of these birds is seen flying away: it
seems

# SPAIN.

A Venus, two Cupids, and two Nymphs, h. l. n. f.

A Madonna and Child, with an old Man and five Girls; ¼ l. n. f.

A head of Chrift, and another of the Virgin.

All thefe pictures were painted by Titian.

An exact copy of the above-mentioned picture of Adam and Eve, by Rubens.

Judith and Holofernes; w. l. n. f. Tintoretto.

A Woman fitting, another Woman and a Boy ftanding by her. P. Veronefe.

Four pictures reprefenting Morning, Noon, Evening, and Night, by Mengs, the Saxon painter, who, as I was lately informed, returned to Madrid in July 1775.

feems, that the faint would not eat them, as it was a meagre day, but chofe rather to raife them from the dead, furnifhing them at once with life and feathers; and, in recompenfe, the Madonna and her Bambino are feen reaching a loaf of bread to the confcientious faint from the clouds. The infcription underneath is,

"San Nicola col fegno della croce rifufcita due pernice arroftite."

This fubject is again reprefented in a very fine picture by Luca Giordano, which is in the Corfini palace in Florence.

The next painting in the above mentioned Cloifters, is St. Auguftin in a carpenter's fhop; the bungling workman, who notwithftanding was a monk, had made a beam too fhort, fo the faint takes hold of one end, and the carpenter of the other, and pull it till it becomes of the length required. The infcription is,

"Una trave ftirata da S. Agoftino e da un fuo religiofo fi ftunga."

For an account of twn other remarkable pictures, I refer the reader to Mr. Wright's Travels in Italy, in p. 436, of the quarto edition, he has given a plate of one he faw at Bologna; and to the fifteenth volume of *le Voyageur François*, p 288.

An Angel's head, as large as the life, in Roman mosaic.

In the next room the ceiling is circular, and is painted in fresco by Mengs, who has there represented Apollo and Venus, with the Four Seasons, in as many compartments. The pictures here are,

An Executioner flaying St. Bartholomew; half length, n. f. by Spagnoletto. He might have chosen a more pleasing subject.

Two pictures, Women with baskets of flowers, by Carlo Maratti.

Six small pictures by Breughel.

A Painter's Shop. Teniers.

Eight very large historical pieces, by Luca Giordano.

St. Laurence, by ditto.

The Annunciation; n. f. w. l.

The Nativity, with several shepherds. Both by Murillo [*]..

Four pictures of saints, as large as the life. Spagnoletto.

A Magdalen.

A larger Magdalen. Both by Titian.

### The next Room contains

A picture which occupies nearly the whole of one end of that room: it represents an Army marching, and is painted by Velasquez. The principal figures are as large as the life.

---

[*] Bartholomew Stephen Murillo, was born near Seville, in 1613, and never was out of Spain: he died in 1685. His style is in the manner of Paul Veronese, whom he has sometimes nearly equalled.

At.

At the other end of the room is a very large picture: a Painter is reprefented fitting at work. Luca Giordano has in this piece endeavoured to imitate Rubens's manner, and has fucceeded admirably well.

Four fmall fketches by Rubens.

A Quack drawing a peafant's tooth: half length, natural fize. Murillo.

Tarquin and Lucretia, n. f. w. l. Titian.
Two Amazons fighting, n. f. w. l. Spagnoletto.
A Madonna and Bambino. Julio Romano.
Two portraits of Women. Leonard da Vinci.
Cephalus and Procris, n. f. w. l. Paul Veronefe.

The Count-duke of Olivares on horfeback. This picture is allowed to be the fineft in its kind of any extant.

Bacchus with fix of his companions.

Two pictures reprefenting two Kings of Spain on horfeback.

Two others, with two Queens of Spain on horfeback. Thefe fix laft pictures are by Velafquez. All the figures are as large as the life.

The Spanifh Prince Ferdinand on horfeback, n. f. Rubens.

Venus and Adonis, n. f. Paul Veronefe.

A large hiftorical piece: the figures are ½ l. and n. f. Rubens.

Judith carrying Holofernes's head, n. f. Murillo. The bloody head ferves as a foil to the pretty face of the lady.

A fmall picture by Rubens, reprefenting two Priefts on horfeback, with two Guides on foot.

A head

A head, by Albert Durer.

Charles V. on horfeback, n. f. by Titian. There are prints of this picture extant.

Chrift feized in the Garden, n. f. w. l. Van Dyke.

Ifaac and Jacob.

Two pictures with faints. Both by Spagnoletto. w. l n. f.

Chrift among the Doctors in the Temple. P. Veronefe. The architecture painted in this piece is very noble.

One fide of another room is covered by a picture reprefenting the Adoration of the Three Kings: there are upwards of twenty figures as large as the life in this picture: it was painted by Rubens; and Luca Giordano added a piece to it to make it of the fize of the room.

Apollo, Pan, Midas, and another figure.

Saturn devouring one of his children.

The Rape of Ganymede.

Mercury and Argus.

Atalanta and another woman running.

Ulyffes. Thefe fix pictures are by Rubens: the figures as large as the life.

A fmall Chrift and St. John. Rubens.

Four very large hiftorical pictures. Luca Giordano.

A Martyrdom. w. l. n. f. Spagnoletto.

Chrift bearing the Crofs. This picture is painted on wood, and confifts of upwards of twelve figures, of the natural fize, by Raphael.

Judith,

Judith, with a fervant maid carrying Holofernes's head. w. l. n. f. Tintoretto.

A very fine Magdalen. n. f. half length. Van Dyke.

A copy, by Mengs, of the celebrated Nativity of Correggio, which is at Drefden, in the elector's collection. There are two different prints of this picture extant.

A very large picture by the Dutch Jordaans, with dead game, fwans, greens, two old men, and an old woman.

Centaurs carrying off women. n. f. w. l.

Mercury and Cadmus fowing men. n. f. w. l. Both by Rubens.

St. Paul with a Monk in a defart; a raven brings them a loaf of bread. The figures are two feet in height. This is one of the moft capital paintings of Velafquez.

Venus and Adonis with four dogs. n. f. Titian.

A very large and pleafing picture by Rubens, reprefenting Orpheus in a foreft playing to a numerous audience of all kinds of birds and beafts, painted as large as the life.

A General and three Soldiers. w. l. n. f. Titian.

A St. Sebaftian, half length, n. f.

A Man and Boy, half length, n. f. Both by Spagnoletto.

Abfalom. This is a very large picture. By Luca Giordano.

A Woman fitting by a well. n. f. P. Veronefe.

Two pictures reprefenting Nymphs, Satyrs, and Cupids. The figures two feet in height. By Titian.

Two copies of the fame, by Rubens; who has alfo painted the next picture, being

St.

St. George on horseback, flaying the dragon. Larger than the life.

Susannah and the Elders. P. Veronese. ½ l. n. f.

A small picture by Titian, representing a concert of music. ½ l.

The Brazen Serpent. Rubens.
Diana hunting. Ditto. The figures are of six inches.
The Bull carrying off Europa. Titian.

Five large historical pictures, by Lanfranchi.

A ditto, by Coypel. The figures two feet high. I only mention this picture, because it is one of the worst here.

A Landscape, by Claude Lorraine.

Three Children playing with a Dwarf. n. f. Velasquez.

Philip III. offering his infant son upon an altar. w. l. n. f. Titian.

Barbarossa. w. l. n. f. Velasquez.

A Madonna and Child.

St. John with his Lamb. Both by Murillo.

Portrait of a Woman. Rembrandt. h. l.

Cupid on the back of a swimming Dolphin. Rubens.

The fresco ceiling of this saloon was painted by Mengs, and represents the assembly of all the gods and goddesses.

In the king's bed-chamber, are six pictures by Mengs: the subjects of them are taken from Scripture.

Near his majesty's bed, over the holy-water pot, is a large head of Chrift in Roman mofaic.

In the fmall chapel adjoining, are two pictures by Mengs; one reprefenting the Nativity, and the other the Holy Family; and in a clofet are two other Nativities, by the fame hand; one in oil colours, and the other in frefco.

In the laft room I faw, are twenty-four pictures, by Teniers.
St. Jerom, by Spagnoletto.
And the Sepulchre of Chrift, by Alexis Cano. This painter was born in Granada in 1600, and died there in 1676.

The ceilings of many rooms in this palace are of ftucco, gilt and painted, and feveral rooms are hung with tapeftry, made at Madrid, which equals that made at the Gobelins in Paris.

A few days after, I went to fee the old palace, called *El Buen Retiro*, i. e. The Good Retreat: it is fituated juft without the gate of Alcalà. The king never refides here. It is very large. In the grand court is an equeftrian ftatue of Philip IV. The extenfive gardens behind it are open to the public: in them is an ample fquare lake.

The royal theatre in this palace is very capacious, and has five rows of boxes, fixteen to each row. The king's box is decorated with four pictures, by James Amiconi, a Venetian painter, who

who died here in 1752. Here is likewife a good picture of the marquis of Santa Cruz, fuccouring the city of Geneva, by Anthony Pereda. This painter was born in Valladolid, and died in Madrid in 1669, aged feventy: he could neither read nor write. The end of the ftage opens to the gardens, fo that the profpect may be varied and extended at pleafure. This theatre is now no more made ufe of. It was here that Farinelli ufed to perform in the Italian operas during the late reign.

There are a vaft number of the large St. Ildefonfo looking-glaffes in the rooms of this palace, and many fine pictures, of which the following are the moft remarkable: I could not learn the names of the painters of all of them.

The ceiling of the grand faloon is painted in frefco by Luca Giordano, and reprefents the inftitution of the order of the Golden Fleece, in 1429, by Philip the Good, duke of Burgundy, with a variety of allegorical figures. The cornices are painted by Corrado. This faloon is fquare; one end opens into an octangular room entirely pannelled with fmall bits of looking-glafs, which reflect images thoufands of times, fo that a fingle foldier when here appears to form whole a regiment. At the other end is an oval room, the ceiling of which is painted in frefco, by Luca Giordano.

In one of the galleries here, is a very large picture reprefenting the late king and queen of Spain, with twelve other perfonages sonages of the royal family; whole length, and as large as the life, by Amiconi. The other pictures are,

Twelve small pieces, and two large, by Bassano.

Five with game, dogs, &c. Snyders.

A very large picture with four Shepherds, three Shepherdesses, and two Satyrs, by Rubens. The fruit, which is represented in this piece, is by Daniel Seegers.

Five large historical pieces.

An allegorical picture representing Spain triumphant.

Orpheus and Eurydice.

Cephalus and Procris. All by Luca Giordano. The figures as large as the life.

A Holy Family. n. f. w. l. I conjecture by Titian.

A Madonna standing, with the child in her arms; by Jordaans, in the manner of Rembrandt.

A Lion entangled in a net. Snyders.

Adam and Eve driven out of Eden by the angel. n. f. w. l. Probably by Titian.

Portrait of an old Cardinal in 1521. I think by Quintin Matsys, the blacksmith.

Three Women and a Man laughing and eating pap. ½ l. n. f. This is a very fine picture, but I know not by whom it was painted.

A Madonna and Bambino; which appeared to me to have been painted by Leonardo da Vinci.

A King in his royal robes, and a General in armour, both sitting. w. l. n. f.

A small

A small piece designed for an altar; the Three Persons are represented above, and various subjects are painted in eight compartments, by Bassano.

St. Jerom in the desart. ⎱ Figures of three feet. By Nicholas.
The Samaritan. ⎰ Poussin.

Portrait of a man writing.

Orpheus and the beasts. Titian. w. l. n. s.

Two flower pieces.

The Judgment of Paris.

Mercury and Argus. w. l. n. s. Rubens. This last is a copy of that which is in the new palace.

The Death of Dido; copied from the picture painted by Guido, which is preserved in Houghton-hall.

A Resurrection, by Francis Collantes, 1630. This is a very fine, but horrible picture: many bodies appear to rise out of their tombs, some have only a little flesh on their bones, some are represented as rotten, others with a livid paleness, and wild looks of horror and fear. The painter was born at Madrid, and died in 1656, aged fifty-seven.

Twelve very large historical pictures, four of which represent the wars of Granada, the others are subjects from the Old Testament, by Luca Giordano.

Seneca expiring in the bath.

Two or three pictures by Velasquez.

The pope celebrating mass in the Sixtine chapel. Small figures.

In one of the rooms I saw a table of Florentine mosaic.

This

This palace was built by the count-duke of Olivares, in the reign of Philip IV. and is situated near the *Prado,* or public Mall, which has lately been embellished, by planting young trees on each side of it, and by stone benches and fountains.

In the church of the Salesan nuns, over the great altar, is a fine copy of Raphael's Transfiguration.

In the Sacristy of the church *de los Recoletos,* are the following pictures.

A dead Christ supported by two angels. As large as the life. This is one of the best pictures Correggio ever painted.

A Madonna, Bambino, St. Anne, and St. John. Half length, n. f. Raphael.

A Magdalen's head. n. f. w. l. Spagnoletto.

St. John, n f. w. l. El Mudo.

A head of Christ, by Morales, in the manner of Albert Durer. Morales was born at Badajoz, and died there in 1586, aged seventy-seven. He was surnamed the Divine, because he painted nothing but holy subjects.

Christ and the Samaritan Woman. n. f. By Murillo.

The Royal Library is open to the public, and consists of two long rooms, forming a right angle.

The amphitheatre, conftructed in 1767, is a plain oval building, with three rows of galleries over each other. During the carnival here are fixteen mafquerades exhibited. The other evenings of that feafon of difiipation, are allotted to dancing fandangos, minuets, and Englifh country-dances. Mr. Baretti gives an account of this edifice, and the fandango, which, though I had no opportunity of feeing in public here, by reafon of its being Lent, yet I faw danced in various private affemblies in Madrid, and afterwards in every place I was in. The fury and ardour for dancing with which the Spaniards are poffeffed on hearing the fandango played, recall to my mind the impatience of the Italian race-horfes ftanding behind the rope, which being fixed acrofs the ftreet breaft-high reftrains them; and the velocity and eagernefs with which they fet off, and run without riders the inftant that that barrier is removed.

There are two kinds of fandangos, though they are danced to the fame tune : the one is the decent dance ; the other is gallant, full of expreffion, and, as a late French author energetically expreffes it, " eft mêlée de certaines attitudes qui offrent un tableau " continuel de jouiffance."

In the dictionary, entitled, *Sobrino Aumentado por F. Cormon* printed at Antwerp in 1769, the Fandango is thus defcribed :

" It is a kind of very lively dance, which the Spaniards have " learnt from the Indians."

I know.

# EL FANDANGO.

I know not what foundation there is for this assertion.

The celebrated air, known by the name of *la follia di Spagna*, which, with its variations, is at the end of the set of solos by Corelli, was probably composed to gratify the desire of some Spaniard, who wished to have the favourite national dance of his country immortalized by that great musician. The modulation of the *follia* is exactly similar to that of the *fandango*, and the name farther demonstrates the truth of this assertion [*].

The circular amphitheatre for the bull-fights, is built of wood, and was erected in 1749. Formerly these exhibitions were in the Great Square, where there have been none since that in 1760, on the present king's accession. The inner circle, or area of this amphitheatre, is one hundred and sixty feet in diameter: there are two rows of covered boxes, one hundred and ten in each row: the other seats are without any covering. The profits arising from the hire of the places, are appropriated to the benefit of the royal hospitals.

The first bull-fight I saw was in Andalusia, which I shall describe hereafter.

There are no hackney coaches in Madrid; but *carosses de remise* may be had at about half a guinea per day.

---

[*] This remark was suggested to me by Mr. Giardini, who has likewise been so obliging as to set a bass to the *fandango*, of which the notes are inserted in the annexed plate.

Three weeks before my arrival in Madrid, two criminals had been hanged; their heads and arms had been cut off, and stuck on posts on the highway: they were now brought again to Madrid, and exposed on an altar in the open street, with a box to receive alms, in order to pay for their burial, and for having masses said for their souls. This sight was highly disgusting, the heads and arms being rotten, and emitting a very offensive smell.

Just without the gate, at the end of the street of Atocha, I observed some very fine madder growing wild on one side of the road: I gathered a few of these plants, and afterwards, on making enquiry how they came to grow here, I was informed, that a few years ago a Dutchman had endeavoured to cultivate madder, but had broke and left Spain, and that these were some of the plants which he had reared.

I afterwards saw more madder growing wild in the garden of the governor of Alicant, about two leagues from that city. Nobody there knew even what plant it was: it appeared to me to be as fine and thriving as any I had seen in Zealand. I never found it in any other places in Spain.

Miller, in his Gardener's Dictionary, v. *Rubia*, says, that he received some from Gibraltar and Minorca, where the plants grew out of the crevices of the rocks.

The Great Square in Madrid is built around with houses of an equal height, on porticos. On one side is an edifice appropriated to the use of the Royal Academy of Painting, Sculpture, and Architecture: some of the members were at that time sent to Granada, to take plans and drawings of the Alhambra, or Moorish palace of that city, which I shall describe hereafter. There are three other Royal Academies in Madrid, that of the Spanish Language, that of History, and that of Physic.

A printing-press for music was lately established here: I purchased some of this music very neatly engraven.

Don Manuele Salvador Carmona is the chief Spanish engraver; his prints are well known in England and in France: he studied the art in Paris, at the expence of his sovereign.

Don Thomas Lopez is the king's geographer, and is now publishing a set of large maps of each of the provinces of Spain and Portugal: they are defective in point of longitude and latitude, but carefully mark every village and *venta*. A plan of Madrid was published in four large sheets in 1761.

Don Lewis Boccherini, the celebrated violoncello player and composer, resides here: he is an Italian.

There are two theatres in Madrid for the performance of Spanish plays: I saw rope-dancing in one of them, which was

*El theatro de la Cruz,* where there are three rows of boxes, fifteen in each row. Part of the pit has benches, with arms dividing them into distinct seats. It may not be thought improper to give the plot of a Spanish comedy, and afterwards that of an *entremés,* or interlude: this latter will match that of which Mr. Baretti has given an account.

The comedy is called *Disdain with Disdain,* was written by Don Augustin Moreto, and is esteemed one of the best Spanish plays: it is in three acts (as they all are), in a kind of measured prose, and sometimes in verse. The actors are,

The Earl of Urgel,  
The Prince of Bearne, } three suitors of Diana.  
Don Gaston Earl of Foix,  
The Earl of Barcelona, father of Diana.  
Polilla, a Buffoon; servant to the Earl of Urgel,  
Diana, daughter to the Earl of Barcelona.  
Cinthia,  
Phenisa, } three Ladies of the court of Diana.  
Laura,  
Musicians.

The scene is in the Earl's palace in Barcelona during the whole play, excepting that, for a short time, in the second act it is in the garden of the palace.

The play begins with a dialogue between the earl of Urgel and his servant, in which the earl acquaints him with his passion for Diana, and gives a long account of the uncommon disposition of that princess, who professes an unconquerable aversion to love, and had rather suffer death than be married, though she is the only heiress to the sovereignty: Polilla comforts him, and encourages him to hope for an alteration in the princess's opinions.

To them enter the earl of Barcelona, the prince of Bearne, and Don Gaston. The three suitors ask the father's leave to try to gain the affections of his daughter, by feasts, assiduities, &c. Urgel pretends that his trial is only out of complaisance. They all retire, and then Diana, the three ladies, and their attendants enter. Her musicians are singing songs against love, professing an utter aversion to that weakness.

Polilla enters, and by dint of buffoonery, gets received into the house as Diana's buffoon, concealing his belonging to Urgel. Then the earl of Barcelona, and the three princes enter. Diana explains to them her reasons against marriage; Urgel alone feigns to approve of them, and tells her, that he not only hates to love, but moreover hates to be beloved. She, surprised to be outdone at her own weapons, disputes with him, and, by contradicting her, he artfully draws her to a confession, that though she does not, nor cannot love, nevertheless she likes to be beloved. The count pretending it impossible for all the charms of woman to move him; this piques Diana, who is resolved to use

Y every

every method to enamour him: she retires, which concludes the first act.

The second act begins with a dialogue between Urgel and Polilla: the servant assures his master, that if he can but continue to diffemble a little longer, she will love him, and even court him herself. They retire, and Diana enters with her ladies. Diana complains to Cinthia of Urgel's infenfibility; and, as at an entertainment, to be given by the princes, each lady was to have a different coloured riband hidden, and each gentleman was to chufe his colour, fo that the lady who had that colour became his partner for the day, Diana puts ribands of all colours in her pocket, in order to be provided with any which Urgel might chufe.

To them enters Urgel. She, after fome converfation, afks him, whether if he were to be beloved by her he would love her? he flatly anfwers in the negative: she burfts into a paffion, and he retires. Afterwards the ftage fills with ladies and gentlemen, who chufe colours, and the ladies fhow their ribands. Diana is matched with Urgel, and is handed by him: he, moved by her touch, is unable to conceal his paffion any longer, and makes a declaration of it. She triumphs over him, and is going to difcard him; upon which he immediately turns the tables, and pretends that he was only in jeft: she is so vexed that she feigns ficknefs to avoid being prefent at the ball, and difcharges

him:

him: he shews great joy at being difmiffed, thanks her, and leaves her, as he perceives fhe is in a rage.

The fcene then changes to a garden, in which Diana and her ladies, in an undrefs, (it being evening), fits finging, in order to endeavour to conquer the earl by mufic.

The earl and Polilla enter, the ladies fing, and the earl fhows a great defire to join them; but Polilla humoroufly holds a dagger at his face, to prevent him from looking round at them, forcing him to praife the beauty of the gardens, to admire the ftatues, fountains, &c. not taking the leaft notice of poor Diana; who, vexed to find herfelf fo grofsly flighted, queftions the earl how he dares enter the garden and intrude on her privacy, though fhe herfelf had employed Polilla, (who all along has been her go-between), little fufpecting his deceit, to entice the earl into the garden: he excufes himfelf, pretending not to have known that fhe had been there, and retires. Polilla then politely tells her, that the earl grofsly defpifed her fqualling; which concludes the fecond act.

The third and laft act begins with a converfation between the three princes. Bearne and Don Gafton tell Urgel that they will take Cinthia and Phenifa, pretending to be in love with them, being convinced of the impoffibility of fucceeding with Diana; which accordingly they do, and court them in Diana's prefence, who can hardly contain herfelf, at feeing others thus preferred to her, and endeavours to recall the two princes to her obedience, by feeming to defpife the weak charms of their *belles*, and by granting them fome flight favours.

Being left alone with Urgel, fhe, as her laft refource, acquaints him, that having maturely confidered her being an only child, fhe is at laft become fenfible of the folly of her antipathy to marriage, is determined to acquiefce in her father's defire, and has accordingly chofen the prince of Bearne, attempting to excite Urgel's jealoufy, and awaken his love, by a long fpeech in praife of Bearne. Urgel approves her refolution greatly, tells her he will fly to acquaint Bearne with his good fortune, and that himfelf is become a votary to the charms of Laura, and leaves Diana in a flate of defpair.

In the laft fcene all the actors being affembled, the princefs, unable to conceal her love any longer, and fearing to lofe Urgel, openly avows her paffion for him: he then difcovers his artifice, and they are united, which concludes the piece; wherein the author has fhown great judgment and knowledge of women: many ftrokes of humour are difperfed throughout Polilla's fpeeches; the arguments pro and con about love are very ingenious. Though the dramatic unities are little regarded, the time being ten or twelve days, this comedy is ftill acted on moft of the Spanifh theatres, and is a ftanding play. The proper title would be *Difdain for Difdain*. The incidents are all natural and fimple, which makes the plot the more beautiful,

tiful, and capable of being imitated in any language, because women being nearly alike in all countries, this is not a mere characteriftical Spanifh play.

The *Entremès*, which now follows, is of a different nature: it is entitled *the Hog of St. Anthony*. The dramatis perſonæ are, a Hufband, his Wife, a Conftable, a Sacriftan, and a Sow-gelder.

The hufband enters penfively, and in a foliloquy declares, that he fufpects his wife's having a criminal intercourfe with the Sacriftan.

He furprifes them converfing together; the facriftan walks off, and the hufband beats his wife till fhe confeffes, that the facriftan told her he loved her. The hufband tells her he is obliged to go to a diftant village, where he will remain all night, but intends to go only to his neighbour's houfe, in order to watch her.

Soon after his departure fhe apprifes the facriftan of it, who comes for admittance, counterfeiting the mewing of a cat. He tells her, that he is at her feet attending her commands, " From age to age, for ever and ever, amen."

She advifes him to act cautioufly, becaufe her hufband was but juft gone, and might foon return. He anfwers, that his
head-

head-piece will find a remedy for every thing, and that she may make him pafs for St. Anthony's hog. In the mean time, the hufband knocks at the door, and the wife orders the facriftan to get into the hog-fty. The hufband calls to his wife to open the door, and fhe tells him to wait till fhe has put on her fhift: fhe then lets him in. He accufes her of changing colour, faftens the door, and declares he will fearch the houfe. The wife implores the affiftance of the Virgin Mary, and vows to offer her a little filver facriftan, if fhe delivers her out of this fcrape. The hufband fearches every where, and fees fomething move in the hog-fty. His wife tells him it is St. Anthony's hog that was brought there the day before, becaufe it fpoiled the garden, and that fhe had faftened it with a rope. The facriftan runs on all-four, with a hog's head faftened over his own. The hufband, who feigns to miftake him for a real hog, afks his wife whether it is gelt? She anfwers, that to her certain knowledge it is not. The fow-gelder paffes by, and the hufband goes out to call him in. The facriftan fays, "thou "devil of a woman, what fhall I do, if they take away my ap- "pendages?" She anfwers, "Heaven will provide againft it." The hufband goes to fetch a cord to tie its feet: in the mean time, the facriftan fwears, that he will drink the blood of the fow-gelder if he ftirs. This poor fellow cries out, "libera me "domine." The hufband returns, and fays, "I will difarm "this hog that wanted to arm me:" he throws a noofe over him; the facriftan ftruggles, and they fight. The conftable hearing the noife, breaks open the door, and feparates them,

them, which concludes this ingenious and elegant entertainment *.

Between the comedy and the farce, tonadillas are fung: thefe are cantatas for two, three, or four voices, the mufic of which is national and uncommon, and confifts of three or four airs, fet in different keys, and different movements. After this performance there is ufually a fandango danced on the ftage. A feguedilla is only a part of a tonadilla.

Next door to the inn where I lodged, lived la Signora Belluomini, daughter to the late Signor Amiconi, the painter: that lady poffeffes many pictures painted by her father. Her fifter, la Signora Caftellini, paints portraits in Crayons extremely well, and both thefe ladies are perfectly fkilled in vocal and inftrumental mufic. I generally fpent the evenings with them, or at the houfe of the countefs of Benevento with Mr. Munro, where moft of the Spanifh nobility reforted, but no ladies, excepting her daughter, who is married to a fon of the duke of Offuna. On Saturdays there was a *tertulia*, or rout, at the houfe of the Chevalier Touffaint, where I had the pleafure of meeting with a great number of Spanifh ladies.

I went one Sunday to the church of Atocha, juft without the gates, and there faw his catholic majefty, king Charles III. He

* See le Voyageur François, vol. xvi. p. 216, on the fubject of the Spanifh theatre.

is of a very brown complexion, and the portraits of him which are difperfed throughout Europe are very like him. He was at that time fifty-feven years of age; his brother, Don Lewis, was with him: he was forty-fix. The prince of Afturias, Don Carlos, heir to the crown, was likewife there, with his two brothers, the infante Don Gabriel, aged twenty, and the infante Don Antonio, aged fixteen. The prince of Afturias, who is one of the talleft and ftrongeft men in the kingdom, is twenty-five years of age, and is married to the princefs Louifa of Parma, who is twenty-one, by whom he has two children; the eldeft fon was born in 1771. I afterwards faw the king's daughter, the infanta Donna Maria, who is twenty-nine years of age, and ftill unmarried.

The king's eldeft fon, Don Philip, refides in Naples, and was declared incapable of fucceeding to the crown, by reafon of an invincible weaknefs of underftanding.

His majefty's third fon is the prefent king of Naples, Ferdinand IV. and his fecond daughter is the prefent grand-duchefs of Tufcany.

All the royal family, when on the road, order their carriages to be driven as faft as the mules can poffibly gallop: many of thefe poor beafts are daily killed by this means, but there are always relays on the road.

One of the moſt conſpicuous buildings in Madrid, is the cuſtom-houſe, which was built in 1769, in the ſtreet of Alcalà: it is of white ſtone, has ſeventeen windows and five doors in in front, and is four ſtories in height.

The poſt-office is a very large and handſome brick building. Letters cannot be franked from this kingdom to any place whatſoever.

I did not go to *the Pardo*, which is one of the king's ſeats, about ſix miles from Madrid, as I was informed that there were no pictures preſerved there, nor any thing worthy of obſervation.

Four leagues from Madrid, near the road to Alcalà, is the village of Mejorada, where there is a very elegant chapel in the church, and two curious holy-water vaſes, one of which is of marble, and repreſents a group of three boys holding a baſon. The other is a vaſe ſupported by a ſingle figure as large as the life, ſitting aſtride on a winged monſter, which ſerves for a pedeſtal. They were probably made in Italy.

In the ſacriſty, is a large picture repreſenting the Flight into Egypt, by Luca Giordano.

About a league further is the village of Loeches.

This village contains a nunnery of the Dominican order, founded by Don Gaspar de Guzman, count-duke of Olivares, and prime minister of Philip IV. which monarch generously contributed to its embellishment. The church is celebrated for being the repository of the following capital pictures. Four small landscapes on the front of the great altar, in which are represented the Virgin and Child resting themselves; several angels hovering about them: the Nativity: the Adoration of the Three Kings: and a Holy Family, in which the child is asleep in its mother's arms.

Over these are two pictures, each of about twelve feet square: the first is called the Triumph of Religion, and is composed of the following figures; four angels drawing a car, in which Religion is sitting, clothed in scarlet, with a white veil, which, however, does not cover her face; whereas, Faith is represented with her face veiled, she holds a chalice in her hand; an angel precedes bearing a cross in his hand, with a sphere at his feet, and another angel accompanies him with a lighted torch: four figures follow the car, chained like slaves; one of them is a woman with many breasts, representing Heresy: many small angels fly before with different triumphal crowns. The other picture represents Abraham, and Melchisedech who is offering him loaves of bread, and receiving the tythe of the spoils; the sacerdotal habits of the two chief figures, and the armour of the soldiers, manifest the vast fecundity of the painter's ideas, though he has not much attended to the habits supposed to be used at that time.

Over

Over the rails of the choir, are two pictures as large as these last; one of which represents four Doctors of the Church, with St. Thomas, St. Clara, and St. Buenaventura. In the other are painted the four Evangelists, with their attributes: all these figures are standing, and as large as the life. This picture will soon be spoiled, if the frame be not repaired, as it now hangs in folds.

In another part of the church are two pictures equally large. One is Elias in the Desart; an angel appears to him and comforts him. The other is a representation of the Israelites receiving manna from heaven: this subject is feigned to be painted on a distinct piece of canvas, which is held by boys.

*All these ten pictures are by Rubens*; and, for expression and colouring, are equal to any of that great painter's works.

There are several very good copies from Titian, Van Dyke, and Veronese, in the sacristy; and one large picture of St. Dominic raising a man from the dead, by Tintoretto. In the Spanish account of Loeches, which was printed in 1772, are the following judicious reflections; but no attention has been paid to them. Describing the altar, the author says,

" Upon the altar is a tabernacle of the Corinthian order, made
" of ebony, lapis lazuli, and various metals; it is ornamented
" with columns in a good taste: but that there might not want
" a blot

"a blot to efface the beauty of this curious altar, they have
"placed on it a number of candlesticks on steps, and several
"saints of wood, very badly carved: these serve to hide the
"pictures, and the lights to blacken, and possibly to burn them.
"Many altars in Madrid are in like manner covered with com-
"bustible materials, so that the pictures cannot be discovered,
"and which every person of taste and judgment laughs at. I,
"who cannot contain myself on seeing such inconsistencies,
"complained highly of these, but in vain, as I had invincible
"ignorance to combat with. What shall we say of that foolish
"custom, of transforming the altars on festivals into a cupboard
"of all sorts of plate, as if it were the side-board of a great en-
"tertainment? Another custom still more ridiculous and despi-
"cable, is that of substituting pasteboard pasted over with silver-
"ed paper, instead of the real plate, which was usually stolen
"among the crowd. Many of our altars are also ornamented
"with carved festoons of grapes, melons, cucumbers, &c. one
"might imagine them to be offerings from the Scythians to the
"divinities who protected their plants."

I myself remember to have seen in the church of our Lady of the Stairs, or Ladder (Madonna della Scala), in Parma, a picture of the Virgin and Child by Correggio, and one of his best works in fresco, over the heads of which the priests had nailed two large silver crowns. *Risum teneatis amici!*

A custom peculiar to the Spaniards is that of affixing a paper on certain days to a church door, on which is written,

*Oy fe faca Anima*, meaning, To-day a foul is extracted out of purgatory. Mr. Baretti likewife takes notice of this peculiarity. According to the Madrid Almanac for 1773, I find that the days appointed for this humane action, performed by celebrating particular maffes, were the 7th of February, which was St. Richard king of England's day * : 2d, 13th, and 14th of March ; 2d, 3d, and 14th of April ; 3d, 5th, and 13th of June; which is no more than ten fouls refcued in a year. During the winter months they are left in purgatory, probably to keep themfelves warm, though the delivering them all at once would be as practicable as one at a time. Thefe maffes are only efficacious when celebrated in the chapel of the new royal palace in Madrid ; in any other place they lofe their virtue. For the truth of a foul's being delivered, we have the teftimony of the prieft and the Almanac, which are as valid as that of the waterman, who affirmed that he had ferried St. Peter over from Lambeth to Weftminfter, when he came to confecrate the Abbey. In the church of the convent of the Incarnation in Madrid, there is every year expofed to the public, on the 27th of July, a phial with fome of the blood of St. Pantaleon, which on that day liquifies, and afterwards remains coagulated, as the Spanifh book fays †.

* In the church of St. Frediano, in Lucca, I obferved a monument, with this infcription :
 Hic jacet corpus
 S. Ricardi, regis Angliæ.

† See Mr. Addifon's Remarks on Italy, p. 122, where he quotes a few lines from Horace relative to a fimilar trick.

When I was at Naples, I saw the annual miracle (as it is called) of the liquefaction of the blood of St. January; I respectfully kissed the two bottles which contain this precious blood, but could perceive no difference in it before nor after the miracle: this was on the 6th of May, 1769, at seven in the evening. There are two bottles inclosed in a large one, though very black and scarcely transparent; an altar was erected in the middle of the street in a temporary chapel, and the priest shook the bottle for eleven minutes and a half, he then rang a bell, and cried out that the miracle was done, " *il miracolo é fatto.*" For which the mob and I took his word, and returned quietly to our homes, much edified by this exhibition. This blood has likewise an inherent power of stilling the raging eruptions of Mount Vesuvius, but is never made use of upon those occasions, through fear of wearing it out. Thirty-six silver busts of saints, as large as the life, were carried in procession to see the miracle; some of them had live sparrows and goldfinches tied by a thread to their hands to play with; several *live* children were also ornamented with pasteboard wings; these represented angels *.

Madrid is the Mantua Carpetanorum of the ancients, and is situated in 13° 49′ 30″ longitude from the isle of Ferro, and 40° 26′ latitude. In 1563, Philip II. removed his court from

* Voltaire says Naples is,
——— Un sjo ur fertile
Qui fait plus cas du sang de St. Janvier,
Que de la cendre de Virgile.

Toledo

Toledo hither, and since that time it has been chosen by the Spanish monarchs for their residence. It is very populous, being said to contain three hundred thousand inhabitants, and about one hundred and forty churches: the number of coaches is said to be between four and five thousand. This town, which the natives call *Villa*, is environed by mountains covered with snow during the greatest part of the year, and has no fortifications, ditches, nor even walls, though there are gates; among which the only remarkable one is that of Alcalà. There are thirty public fountains in it, though the water is not of equal goodness, so that here are many carriers, who sell the best water, which they put into earthen vases, carried on the backs of asses. Most of the houses are of brick, and the windows are guarded by lattices, which are not so punctually kept shut as they were formerly, as jealousy is no longer a distinguishing characteristic of a Spaniard. The Mançanarès runs on the side of the town; in summer it is almost dry, but in winter is much swollen by the melting of the snows. Over this river are two stone bridges, one of which was built by Philip II. in 1584, has nine arches, and is called the bridge of Segovìa: it is six hundred and ninety-five feet long, and thirty-two broad. The other, Puente de Toledo, which is the finest, also consists of nine arches, and was erected by Philip V. in 1718, being three hundred and eighty-five feet long, and thirty-six broad. The prison for persons of quality is one of the handsomest buildings in Madrid: over the portico are the arms of Spain in stone basso relievo, and on the top are three statues, the middlemost of which represents justice.

The

The grandees, about ninety in number, are of three classes; those of the first class cover themselves before they speak to the king; those of the second, when they have spoken, and before he has answered; and those of the last, when they have received his answer: but none are to cover themselves till the king orders them to do so. This dignity is either for life, or perpetual; in the last case it is hereditary, and when the male line fails, descends even to females, who give it to their husbands. Not only the grandees have the privilege of wearing their hats in the king's presence, but also cardinals, nuncios, archbishops, ambassadors from crowned heads, the grand prior of Castile of the order of Malta, the generals of the Dominican and Franciscan orders, the knights of the Golden Fleece, of Calatrava, Santiago, and Alcantara, when they are in their habits, and when the king as grand-master assists at their chapter: titled noblemen of Portugal and France: and even the counsellors of the royal council, and of that of Castille, when they go in a body to confer with his majesty about the business of their ministry, are covered in his presence. There are several noble families, who, by their antiquity, have a right to the honour of grandee; but, as the king has never ordered them to be covered, they are styled *casas agraviadas*, injured houses. The king styles the grandees *prime*, (cousin) when he writes them. When they receive audience of the pope they are allowed to sit: they alone may drive with four mules to their carriage within Madrid, while the king is there: they cannot be arrested for any crime whatsoever, without an express order from his majesty.

Among

Among them all titles are equal; dukes, marquisses, or counts, have no precedence the one before the other, so that the father may be a count, and the son a duke, as in Portugal. The grandees, both in conversation and in writing to each other, always use *thee* and *thou*, but to their inferiors they make use of the ordinary style.

In the folio book, entitled, *Creacion y privilegios de los titulos de Castilla*, printed in Madrid 1769, I find forty-three privileges annexed to the dignity of grandee, among which, besides those above mentioned, are the following: They may never be put to the torture; they may have four footmen and four torches behind their carriage, as may also dukes; earls and marquisses are allowed but two; they are permitted to have a throne under a canopy in one room in their houses; this privilege is however granted to various other dignities which are specified in the book.

Besides the Spanish military orders of Calatrava, Santiago, Alcantara, and Montesa, which were instituted in the twelfth and thirteenth centuries, are the orders of the Golden Fleece, and of Charles the Third. This last was instituted on the 19th of September, 1771, in honour of the birth of his majesty's grandson, the infante, first-born of the prince of Asturias: the king has already created forty-six grand-cross knights of this order. The smaller cross of which has been given to a very great number of persons: these do not wear a riband; the grand crosses wear a broad sky-blue riband over the right shoulder, and have a silver star of eight points, in the shape of a cross of Malta, on the left breast; in the midst of the star is an oval in enamel, representing the Virgin Mary standing on a crescent, and underneath is inscribed, *virtuti et merito*, and the king's cypher. The king of Naples, and the infante-duke of Parma, are knights of this order; the other forty-four are all Spaniards, and their number is not limited.

The order of the Golden Fleece was instituted in 1429, by Philip duke of Burgundy; and the king of Spain is sovereign of the order, by being the head of the house of Burgundy. The number of knights is limited to fifty: four collars are at present vacant. This order is honoured by having among its members the king of France, the duke of Orleans, the king of Naples, the Elector of Bavaria, the infante-duke of Parma, the count de Provence, the duke of Choiseul, &c. The collar of the order is a gold chain representing flints and steels, to which is affixed a fleece, which the Spanish book *(Theatro universal de España, por Don Fran. de Garma,* vol. ii. p. 100.) says, alludes to the fleece offered in sacrifice to God by Gideon, and not, as I had irreligiously imagined, to Jason's Golden Fleece. The flints and steels were the arms of the institutor, with this device, *ante ferit quam flamma micet.*

Many Spanish gentlemen are also knights of Malta.

Perez, Cervantes, Lope de Vega, Calderon, and Quevedo were born here.

It may not be improper to mention the gypsies, who are very numerous throughout Spain, especially about and in Murcia, Cordova, Cadiz, and Ronda. The race of these vagabonds is found in every part of Europe: the French call them *Bohemiens*, the Italians *Zingari*, the Germans *Ziegenners*, the Dutch *Heydenen*, (pagans), the Portuguese *Siganos*, and the Spaniards *Gitanos*, in Latin *Cingari*. Their language, which is peculiar to themselves, is every where so similar, that they undoubtedly are all derived from the same source. They began to appear in Europe in the fifteenth century, and are probably a mixture of Egyptians and Ethiopians. The men are all thieves, and the women libertines: they follow no certain trade, and have no fixed religion: they do not enter into the order of society, wherein they are only tolerated. It is supposed that there are upwards of forty thousand of them in Spain; great numbers of whom are inn-keepers in the villages and small towns: they are every where fortune-tellers. In Spain they are not allowed to possess any lands, nor even to serve as soldiers. They marry among themselves: they stroll in troops about the country, and bury their dead under a tree. Their ignorance prevents their employing themselves in any thing but in providing for the immediate wants of nature, beyond which even their roguishness does not extend, and only endeavouring to save themselves the trouble of labour: they are contented if they can procure food by showing feats of dexterity, and only pilfer to supply themselves with the trifles they want; so that they never render themselves liable to any severer chastisement than whipping, for having stolen chickens, linen, &c.

Moſt of the men have a ſmattering of phyſic and ſurgery, and are ſkilled in tricks performed by ſlight of hand. The foregoing account is partly extracted from *le Voyageur François*, vol. xvi. but the aſſertion that they are *all* ſo abandoned as that author ſays, is too general; I have lodged many times in their houſes, and never miſſed the moſt trifling thing, though I have left my knives, forks, candleſticks, ſpoons, and linen at their mercy; and I have more than once known unſucceſsful attempts made for a private interview with ſome of their young females, who virtuouſly rejected both the courtſhip and the money.

I now began to prepare for my departure from Madrid: I ſent a cheſt of books to Bilboa by the mule-carriers, to be forwarded to England, it being previouſly examined and ſealed at the cuſtom-houſe: I bought a ſaddle-horſe, and agreed with a *caleſſeiro* to take his two-wheeled chaiſe, drawn by a ſingle horſe. I was to maintain him, and he was to accompany the chaiſe on foot. Accordingly we ſet out on the 6th of April for Toledo, which is twelve leagues diſtant from Madrid. We firſt paſſed through the long town of Getafe; four leagues farther, through Illeſcas, and ſpent the night in the village of Cabañas, which is three leagues diſtant from the laſt mentioned town. The road was very good, though ſandy, through a plain of corn-fields, intermixed with olive trees, among which a vaſt number of hoopoes were flying.

The next day, after travelling three leagues, we arrived at the ancient city of Toledo, the firſt and richeſt archbiſhoprick of all Spain, the revenues of which amount to thirty thousand pounds per annum. It is situated on the confluence of the rivers Tagus and Xarama, in forty-one degrees of latitude, and in the center of Spain; over the Tagus are two stone bridges: that of St. Martin has four arches, and that of Alcantara two; this was built by the Moors, and repaired, in 1259, by king Alfonso the Wise. The river at this time ran only under one arch of each bridge. I put up at the inn called the Blood of Christ, the same which Mr. Baretti was in: he appears to have been surprised at such a name being given to it; but I was not, as in Paris I have been at an inn, the sign of which was the Holy Ghost, at the coffee-house of the Prophet Elijah, and in several others with similar names.

Toledo is situated on a very steep hill, which the Tagus nearly environs, and is encompassed with a wall, flanked with near one hundred and fifty small towers, built by the Moors. This river takes its source among the mountains of Albaracin, somewhat above the city of Cuença, near forty leagues south-east from Toledo, and, after a course of about one hundred and twenty leagues, discharges itself into the Atlantic, a league beyond Lisbon. A Spanish author, mentioning the decayed grandeur of this city, says that its chief splendor at present is derived from the river, and quotes the following lines from a verse of Quevedo on Rome, only changing the Tiber for the Tagus.

Solo el Tajo quedò, cuya corriente
Si Ciudàd la regò, ya sepultado
La mira con confùso fón doliente.

The sense of which is, the Tagus alone remains, and its current, formerly ruled by the decayed city, runs through it, making a confused plaintive sound.

Indeed all the streets are narrow, crooked, and badly paved, and, excepting the cathedral and alcazar, there is hardly a good building in the whole city: half the streets are choaked up with heaps of ruined houses of brick; and the environs of the city are naked and bare of trees, which cause the heats in summer to be excessive, and the wood for fuel in winter very dear: without doubt there were more trees here when Martial wrote :

Æstus serenos aureo franges Tago,
Obscurus umbris arborum.

The ancient aqueducts, which were here, are destroyed, and water is sold about the streets, carried in small barrels on the backs of asses. Most of the floors in the houses are of brick, which fills the rooms with dust. In the fifteenth century this city contained above two hundred thousand inhabitants, but at present it hardly contains twenty-five thousand.

The cathedral was built in 587; and, in 714, together with the city, fell into the possession of the Moors, in whose hands it remained three hundred and seventy-six years, when king
Alphonso

Alphonso VI. re-conquered it. It is one of the largest Gothic buildings in Europe, and much in the same style of architecture as the dome of Milan, that of Sienna, St. Petronius's church in Bologna, and the cathedrals of Burgos and Seville. It is three hundred and eighty-four feet in length, one hundred and ninety-one in breadth, and one hundred and seven in height: the roof is sustained by eighty-five columns, which divide the church into five isles. It has a tower with a spire. The pope and the king of Spain are always canons of this cathedral. Every Christmas before the first vespers, their names are called aloud at the door of the choir: if they do not appear, as always happens, they are mulcted two thousand maravedis each, about sixteen shillings and nine pence. Andrew Navagiero, who was a Venetian writer, and ambassador from his republic to the emperor Charles V. speaking of Toledo, in his Itinerary of Spain, which was published in Venice in 1563, says, " The patrons of " this city, and of its principal women, are the priests, who have " very good houses, and triumphantly lead the best lives in the " world, without being reprehended by any body;" which they have probably continued to do to this day *. A modern Spanish author

* Mr. Armstrong, in his History of Minorca, says, in p. 201,
" The priests live well, and drink wine freely, taking care to be well
" provided with the best of the growth of the island: they make no scruple
" to indulge themselves in the conversation of the other sex; and have every
" opportunity they can wish for, in an unsuspected access to the houses of
" all their neighbours."

In a book, entitled, " An Account of Spain by a French Gentleman," in one volume octavo, 1695, is the following passage:

" And

fills two hundred and thirteen pages with a description of Toledo, in which every trifle is minutely described with the tediousness of a German.

The ceiling of the sacristy is painted in fresco, by Luca Giordano. Here is also preserved a picture, representing the Assumption of the Virgin, by Carlo Maratti. The library contains, among other books, seven hundred and fourteen manuscripts. Father Caimo says, he heard the famous question discussed, *utrum angelus peccaverit in primo instanti*, in the Archiepiscopal palace: the question is as important as that proposed by Father Sanchez in his book *de Matrimonio*, book ii. chap. xxi. beginning " Utrum Virgo Maria semen, &c."

The alcazar, or royal palace, was built by Charles V. in 1551: it is situated on a steep hill, near five hundred feet above the Tagus, and commands a very fine prospect over the city and all round the country: it has eleven windows in front, and is three stories in height, with a stone balustrade on the top, forming a square of two hundred and fifty-six feet, as I measured it. The Cortile is built with porticos, consisting of thirty-two arches, of the Corinthian and Composite orders, and was two stories in height: the grand stair-case is of very fine architecture: after a strait ascent on a flight of steps fifty feet broad, they are divid-

" And though the two excellencies of pimping and intriguing chiefly pre-
" vail among the Spanish laity, yet, to give the church its due, the clergy
" are very dexterous at any thing wherein a woman is concerned."

ed to the right and to the left. In one corner of the building is a geometrical ſtair-caſe. The whole edifice is of the Beroqueña ſtone, of the ſame kind of which the Eſcorial is built. The grand entrance is by an arched door, having two Ionic columns on each ſide. Under the frize is this inſcription, in large capitals, Car. V. Ro. imp. hiſ. rex. MDLI. Over each window is a large head carved in ſtone: they are all different. The chapel is of the Corinthian order, but almoſt ruined. The offices under-ground are very convenient; and the ſtables, which are likewiſe under-ground, are capable of containing five thouſand horſes. It was burnt in 1710, ſo that the roof and the galleries are deſtroyed, as likewiſe moſt of the rooms, of which only two or three are habitable, and in them the keeper and his family live. In one of theſe rooms is the moſt remarkable echo I ever heard, excepting that of the Simonetti palace near Milan: I amuſed myſelf two hours in this room with a muſical inſtrument. Here was formerly a machine to ſupply this palace with water, but it has lain in ruins for this century paſt.

Againſt the walls of the Franciſcan convent, called San Juan de los Reyes, are faſtened a great number of large iron chains, with which the Moors chained their Chriſtian ſlaves. The archbiſhop poſſeſſes a great number of houſes in this city: they are diſtinguiſhed by a tile placed over the door, on which is painted, " *Maria fue concebida ſin pecado original*;" that is, " Mary " was conceived without original ſin:" a nice diſtinction truly!

The manufactory of sword-blades, which were formerly so celebrated for the goodness of the steel, no longer exists; though another manufactory was lately erected for the king's account only, in which all the sword, hanger, and dagger blades for the Spanish army are made; but they are far from being so well tempered as those of former times; a true old Toledo sword-blade sells even in Spain for six or seven guineas, and can only be purchased by chance. I have seen daggers that were made here, which will strike through a crown-piece. All sword-blades made for the soldiers have the king's name engraven on one side, and some device on the other: I saw many of them with this; *No me saques sin razon, no me embaines sin honor.* Draw me not without reason, sheath me not without honour.

The small church of St. Mary the White, was formerly a synagogue; and just without one of the city gates, are the ruins of a Roman *Circus Maximus*. I only mention these to spare any other person the trouble of searching for them, as there is nothing worth notice about them.

In order to shew the more veneration for the relics and riches which are preserved in the cathedral, I shall follow the Spaniard's advice, which was before mentioned, and say nothing about them; neither about the Mozarabic rite, which is only a method of celebrating mass somewhat different from the common one, and both are equally absurd. I was informed that the next day there was to be a very grand procession of all the silver statues

statues and monks in the city; but as these exhibitions were never my hobby-horse, so I left Toledo early in the morning, much to the regret of my calesseiro, who thus missed, or escaped the archbishop's blessing: as to myself, I had already had that of the late pope, and after such a blessing I did not care to receive that of any inferior ecclesiastic.

We this day travelled seven leagues on a good level road, through corn-fields, and in the evening arrived at Aranjuez, dining on the side of the road, as there is no inn nor venta. In proportion as we approached this royal seat, the number of stags, wild-boars, and rabbits; partridges, hoopoes, starlings, and small birds increased:

> Here merrily they fed,
> As if their hearts were lighter than their wings.
> 
> GONDIB. p. 191.

The wild boars, with their sows and their litter, are so tame that they feed about the streets of the town: they are royal property, and are reserved for the king's table alone. We put up at a very good inn, kept by an Italian, but the most expensive one in Spain.

The town of Aranjuez is situated on the Tagus, and was chiefly built within these twelve years; whoever chuses to build houses here, may have a free-gift of the ground from the king, on condition of conforming to the general plan: the streets are broad and parallel, and interfect each other at right angles: one of them is called Stuart's street. The houses are of two stories in height, and are all painted white, with green doors and shutters. There are at present about five thousand inhabitants, who live by letting their houses to persons who come with the court, and who reside here annually from the middle of April to the end of July, during which time the number of inhabitants is increased to fifteen thousand. The whole town has much the resemblance of Potsdam, near Berlin, and is well illuminated at night. The principal church, which has a convex colonnade, is built in the Great Square: Sabatini was the architect This square is surrounded by porticos; four large arched gates form the entrance, and in the middle is a handsome fountain, which copiously supplies the town with water. There are two other churches in Aranjuez. Besides the wild-boars before mentioned, I saw several camels carrying wood about the streets: they belong to the king, and are twenty-one in number\*. The king possesses also a great number of buffaloes, brought from Naples, which are used to draw carts, and are governed by iron rings thrust through their nostrils. These animals abound in Rome, Naples, and Loretto, and are there put to the same service. Here is a new amphitheatre for the bull-fights, like that of Madrid: it is built of brick, with wooden seats: the inner circle, or area, is one hundred and sixty-eight feet in diameter: there are two rows of boxes, one

---

\* In a village near Pisa, in Tuscany, I saw, in 1769, sixty-four camels which were the property of the grand-duke.

above the other, each row containing one hundred and two; under thefe are ten circular rows of benches, which are expofed to the air: the whole building is capable of containing fix thoufand fpectators. All the amphitheatres in Spain are circular, and nearly of the fame fize and architecture. I know of only four, which are lafting edifices; thofe are at Madrid, Aranjuez, Granada, and Seville: at Cadiz and Port St. Mary, they are temporary wooden buildings, as is alfo that of Lifbon: and in the other Spanifh towns the great fquare is the place of combat. The beft places are about a crown each, and the loweft place fix pence: the perfons who fit in thefe, are perpetually expofed to the bull's leaping among them over the baluftrades, which are but four feet high: the places which are on the fhady-fide are fomewhat dearer than the others: it would be very neceffary to have a canvas drawn over the top of the whole area, in the fame manner as was practifed by the ancient Romans.

Neither the king, nor any of the royal family, are ever prefent at the bull-fights.

The royal palace is a fquare, and has twenty-one windows in front, and a turret at each end; but there is nothing remarkable either in its exterior or interior parts, except that in the chapel is a picture reprefenting the Annunciation, by Titian; and in one of the rooms fix portraits by Mengs; being thofe of the grand duke and duchefs of Tufcany, and their four children; and the

the king and queen of Naples, by one Bonito. In the church are fix pictures by Tiepolo. Before the palace are three very large walks, each planted with four rows of tall elms: fmall canals run between each row, which keep the roots conftantly fupplied with water, and make the trees grow to a very great fize: various other walks have been lately planted with young elms on the fame plan. I walked round the gardens in an hour: they are quite flat; the Tagus runs through them. This river is not very broad here, fo that there are eight or ten wooden bridges, and one of ftone, built over it. In the work, entitled, *El Parnaffo Efpañol,* vol. iii. p. 246 to 268, are two very fine poetical defcriptions of Aranjuez; the one by Don Gomez de Tarpia, and the other by Lupercio de Argenfola. Thefe gardens fo much beautify the Tagus, that Don Gomez juftly writes:

——— Defde allì à fu fuente,
Ni hafta el océano Lufitano
No fe halla en otra parte mas ufano *.

The gardens are ornamented with feven fountains, of all which there are very accurate views in the book called *Les Delices de l'Espagne et du Portugal.* That of the Tritons is decorated with feveral marble ftatues, which are thought to be the

* Neither from hence to its fource, nor to the Lufitanic ocean, is it to be found more beautiful.

work of Alonfo Berruguete. The fountain of Bacchus confifts principally in a ftatue of that god beftriding a cafk : both the god and the cafk are of bronze; the firft is reprefented extremely fat, and larger than the life. The largeft fountain is that of Hercules : the ftatues that accompany it have no merit ; but the fountain of Neptune, which has feven groups round it, in bronze, is the beft here : the ftatues being all by Algardi, the Roman fculptor, in 1621 : they are nearly as large as the life, and reprefent Jupiter and Juno launching thunder-bolts at the giants ; Ceres, in a car drawn by lions; and Neptune, with his trident, in a fhell drawn by Tritons. The other three fountains are thofe of the Harpies, of the Dolphins, and of Don John of Auftria, but they are not any way remarkable. Here are alfo two ftatues in bronze, of Venus and Antinous, as large as the life, caft from the antique. Thefe the gardener called Adam and Eve. Under the ftatue of Venus is this infcription :

*A Poblicius. d. l. Antioc. t. Barbius. q. p. l. Tiber.*

There is a new theatre for the performance of operas and plays, during the refidence of the court here : over the door is this infcription,

*Ruris deliciis adjecta urbana voluptas.*

I fpent a day in making fome excurfions on horfeback : I firft rode through the Queen's Alley, which is a road of forty feet broad, and four miles long, quite ftrait, with a double row of tall elms on each fide, at the end of which I entered into the
foreft,

forest, which abounds with deer and game. Three miles farther I saw a very pretty cascade, formed by the waters of the Tagus falling down a precipice of about fourteen feet high. I then returned to Aranjuez, and, riding two miles on another road, saw a small lake, in the midst of which is an island, with a summer-house built on it. In the afternoon I rode six miles on the road leading to Madrid, which city is seven leagues distant from Aranjuez, through very broad avenues, with a double row of elms on each side *, to see the stone-bridge of seventeen arches, which was finished in 1761, by Marcos de Vierna. At both ends are two lions of stone, each holding a shield, on which are engraven the names of the king and the architect, with the date. Near this bridge is a turnpike where I paid toll for my horse.

April 11. I set out this day for Valencia, which city is eight days journey from Aranjuez, sixty-two leagues, or about two hundred and eighty miles. I first arrived at the small ancient town of Ocaña, two leagues off, travelling on the royal road, which is very broad and strait, and in some parts planted with young trees on each side. The country is quite flat, and produces corn, wine, and oil. I remained here an hour to examine the celebrated fountain, which, at first view, appears to be a

* The grand Berceau walk in the gardens belonging to the earl of Breadalbane, at Taymouth, in the Highlands of Scotland, is as beautiful as these avenues, though not so long: it is planted in like manner with elms of an uncommon size.

work

work of the Romans, but a Spanish author rather suspects it to have been built by Philip II. about the year 1580, at the time he founded Aranjuez: the source of the fountain is discovered at the end of a long subterraneous passage, which admits a man standing upright: the water, which is very transparent, is conducted in two canals from thence to a large reservoir, which supplies the whole town. I then proceeded two leagues farther to the village of Villatobas; which, as the road is perfectly horizontal and strait, is seen at the end of it, immediately on leaving Ocaña. At every quarter of a league is a stone to mark the distance. This day being Easter-Sunday, I saw in several streets of the villages and towns I passed through, many artificial figures of men made of wood, straw, &c. and dressed in old cloaths, hanging by a rope fixed across the street from the opposite houses, in the same manner as the lamps are suspended in Paris: this is an universal custom throughout Spain and Portugal: the figures are intended to represent Judas: the boys amuse themselves with pelting them with stones, and burning them in the evening, which is similar to our rational custom of annually burning the figures of the devil and the pope. In the afternoon I proceeded three leagues to Coral, where I passed the night. The people were at that time at work in making the new road, which is perfectly strait, and as fine as any road in England. The quarter league stones were continued as far as the road was finished. The country is quite flat, and produces much corn, but no trees.

April 12. After travelling three leagues, I stopped to dine at Quintanar, in the province of la Mancha, where Don Quixote is feigned to have been born. A league farther, near to the south-side of the road, is the village of El Tobofo, which gave birth to his Dulcinea. I afterwards paffed by fifteen windmills, which I miftook for thofe which had been attacked by the knight, two centuries ago; but, on having recourfe to his hiftory, I learned that his antagonifts were built in the plains of Montiel, which are ten or twelve leagues more to the fouth. I proceeded five leagues to Pedronofa, where I paffed the night: the road is good and flat; fome few vine-yards and olives on each fide. The weather began to be hot and fultry, and, I was informed, that the night before three fmart fhocks of an earthquake had been felt in this village, and feveral leagues round it.

April 13. We dined at Provençor, and flept at Minaya. This day's journey was feven leagues, over a flat fandy road, and through a fmall wood of dwarf pines.

April 14. We travelled three leagues to la Roda, and afterwards three more to la Gineta, which is the firft village we arrived at in the kingdom of Murcia: the road is in a ftrait line for two or three leagues; fo that immediately on going out of one village, the church fteeple of the next is feen at the end of it. In this whole day's journey there was not a tree nor a hedge to be feen, only continued corn-fields. The foil is fandy: and the heat became fo great, as to prevent my walking even after fun-fet,

fet, as the ground burnt the foles of my feet; fo that the only agreeable time for that exercife was early in morning, when the earth had had a night to cool in.

April 15. Three leagues journey brought us to Albacete: this is a pretty large town, containing two churches, and five thoufand inhabitants, who are chiefly maintained by the profits arifing from the fale of clumfy knives and fciffors, for the manufacturing of which there are eighteen fhops. Two leagues farther we croffed over fome hills, wooded with pines and green oaks, and abounding with juniper, rofemary, and thyme; and paffed the night in the fmall village of Villar, which contains only fixty inhabitants.

April 16. We dined this day at Bonete, and lay at Almanfa, having travelled feven leagues. The road is hilly and fandy; a few green oaks and fhrubs are fcattered here and there.

Almanfa contains one thoufand fix hundred inhabitants; one church, of which the front is of ftone, and of tolerable architecture, and eight convents.

About half a mile eaft of the town, in the midft of a plain, is a fquare obelifk of ftone, thirty feet high: the pedeftal is furrounded by three fteps: on it are engraven infcriptions in Latin and Spanifh, importing, that on that fpot, on the 25th day of April, 1707, was gained the victory over the rebel Catalonians,

of

of whom the number killed and taken prisoners was sixteen thousand. The conquering army, which consisted of the troops of Philip V. aided by those of Lewis XIV. was commanded by James duke of Berwick. Philip caused fifty thousand masses to be said for the repose of the souls of the illustrious persons who were slain in this battle.

On the top of a steep rock, which is as much insulated as that on which the castle of Dunbarton, in Scotland, is built, are the ruins of a very large Moorish castle: the stair-case is yet entire, and of stone. A view of this castle is inserted in one of the plates in this work.

This day we met several four-wheeled carriages, some drawn by four, and some by six mules, with long traces of cords, going to Madrid. This method of travelling is near treble the expence of that which I pursued, and not so satisfactory; the only difference is, that the mules which draw the coaches always trot, so that they set out later from, and arrive sooner at the inns, but travel no more leagues a day than the chaises, by which means all the pleasure of walking is prevented, and the time is consumed in idleness in the ventas. These coaches have two men to attend them, one of whom sits on the box and drives, and the other runs by the side of the mules, whipping them; and this they do alternately. Women and children travel in this manner, which would likewise be the best way for a company of four or five persons having much baggage. A single traveller ought.

ought to be very careful in chufing a proper calefſeiro: fome of thefe people have fpent the greateſt part of their lives in traverſing every part of Spain, and being known in all the inns and ventas, are the greateſt protection a traveller can have againſt being murdered, for they would be immediately miſſed, and the moſt diligent fearch would be made after them, and the perfons who had employed them; but if a young and obfcure muleteer ſhould be chofen, he, as well as his fare, might be affaſſinated with impunity *.

April 17. Proceeding two leagues we entered into the kingdom of Valencia, on a road cut through a mountain, which opens at once into one of the moſt fertile countries in Europe, the kingdom of Naples not excepted, abounding with olives, corn, figs, arbutus, and mulberry trees; and vines, which were already beginning to ſhoot, and the wheat to ear: this province alfo produces in palm or date trees, aloes, pomegranates, hemp, flax, rice, and the algarroba, garofero, carrobe, or locuſt tree: this laſt is an evergreen; the trunk is ufually from one to two feet in diameter, the leaves are of a dark green, ten on a twig, five on each fide; the fruit exactly refembles kidney-beans, and is an inch broad, and nine or ten inches long; they iſſue in cluſters from the branches and body of the tree in a very fingular man-

* The Portuguefe caleffeiro who travelled with me, was named Gaetano de Coimbra; and the Spaniard, Antonio de Gandia: each of thefe men was upwards of three months in my fervice, during which time they were very careful and honeſt; fo that they merit the mention that is now made of them.

ner; these pods are thick, mealy, and of a sweetish taste: when dry they are given to horses and cattle as provender. These trees are only found in this province, and those of Murcia, Granada, and Andalusìa\*. The following lines of Silius Italicus may with great propriety be applied to this country:

Nec Cereri terra indocilis, nec inhospite Baccho,
Nullaque Palladia sese magis arbore tollit.

We dined at the village of Moxent, which is five leagues from Almansa: the roads are sandy, and over hills. In the evening we proceeded four leagues farther to Xativa, the ancient Sætabis †.

---

\* In the second volume of Mr. James's History of Gibraltar, the author, describing the plains of Tetuan, says, " the next remarkable sort of wood " is the alcarobe, a tree of great curiosity, and merits much notice: the al- " carobe bears a cod in quantity and likeness much resembling the English " bean; the inner substance thereof is sweet, and lodgeth hard small kernels. " This fruit is eaten by the Moors of inferior condition, and by all at the " feast Ashorah; but it is chiefly preserved for their horses, to whom it is " both physic and repast; for the fruit of the alcarobe hath two excellent " properties, to drench and make their horses fat.

" Some have called the fruit locusta, and supposed it was the Baptist's " food in the wilderness, &c. &c. There is a great probability that the " fruit of the alcarobe is the same with the Prodigal's *ceratia*, or husks, for it " doth excellently accord with their description."

Mr. Armstrong, in his History of Minorca, p. 195, likewise mentions the opinion in regard to its having been the food of St. John, but he adds wild honey to it.

Miller calls it ceratonia, carouge, and St. John's bread.
Ceratonia Siliqua, Linn. Sp. pl. 1513.

† Celsa mittebat Sætabis arce,
Sætabis & telas Arabum sprevisse superba, &c.
Sil. Ital. lib. iii. v. 373.

This

This town was razed by Philip V. in 1714, for having fuſtained an obſtinate ſiege againſt him, but was rebuilt at the bottom of a hill, and by his order called San Phelipe. It has a ruined Mooriſh caſtle. The deteſted Borgia, who was afterwards pope Alexander VI. was born here. *

April 18. We travelled on a very good road, with ſmall canals of running water on each ſide, like thoſe in the plains of Lombardy, which render theſe plantations ſo uncommonly fertile. I ſaw here many rice-fields, which are always kept about three inches under water, above which the rice was juſt beginning to appear;. and mulberry trees were planted checquer-wiſe in theſe fields. We croſſed a branch of the river Xucar, on a narrow ſtone bridge of ſix arches. This delightful country is ſurrounded partly by high mountains (on the tops of which are many Mooriſh caſtles), and partly by the Mediterreanean ſea. We afterwards paſſed through the village of Alzira, and over another branch of the Xucar, on a ſtone bridge of two arches. The people were all employed in ſtripping the mulberry-trees of their leaves for food for the ſilk worms, which had been hatched a fortnight before.

There is a modern Spaniſh book in ſmall quarto, with four copper-plates, deſcribing the method of rearing mulberry-trees, and managing ſilk-worms, with the natural hiſtory of thoſe inſects :

* Catullus mentions this town in his twenty-fifth epigram.

the book is extremely well written. There is one paſſage in it which I know not whether the author meant in jeſt or in earneſt: he ſays, "many people waſh the ſilk-worm's eggs in the wa-
"ter of a fountain near the hermitage of our Lady de la Fuen
"Santa: if this waſhing cauſes them to thrive better, it is cer-
"tainly becauſe that great queen attends to their ſupplications;
"but as ſhe poſſibly may not attend to theſe ſupplications, the
"eggs may receive great hurt by theſe cold waſhings. I hold it
"to be better to waſh them with white wine, or with the urine
"of a healthy boy."

The lower claſs of men here wear linen-trowſers, which reach to the knees, much like the Highland fillebegs, and ſandals made of cord. The women have no caps, but plait their hair behind in a ſpiral figure, and faſten it with a large ſilver pin, in the ſame manner as thoſe of Bologna and Naples. We dined at Algemesì, and proceeded five leagues to Valencia, where we arrived in the evening, having travelled nine leagues this day; and put up at the Golden Croſs, which is a pretty good inn.

Valencia is one of the largeſt cities in Spain, and has an univerſity: its form is circular, and it is ſituated half a league from the ſea, 39° 34′ lat. and 22° long. from the iſle of Ferro, on a river called El Rio Blanco, or Turia, which does not however run through the city, but by the ſide of it. There are five handſome ſtone bridges built over this river, three of which have each ten arches, another has nine, and the laſt has thirteen.
Without

without the gates are the college of pope Pius V. and the palace of the viceroy, though this title is now altered to that of captain-general. The *alameda*, or mall, refembles our St. James's Park, but is much more beautiful, by reafon of the trees, which are palms, cyprefs', elms, and mulberry trees intermixed, of which there are four double rows, forming three walks or alleys. There are many agreeable walks along the river fide, which are faced with ftone, the better to refift the force of the water in winter. On one of the walls is a new ftone ftatue of St. Pedro Pafqual, but I could not learn who this faint was. In this wall was lately fixed a ftone, with part of a Roman fepulchral infcription, as follows:

SODALI CIV.
VERNARUM
COLENTE SIDIDE.

A plan of this city, in four fheets, was publifhed in 1705.

The day after my arrival was the feaft of St. Vincent Ferrer, the patron of this city, fo that I faw all the friars, and other idle drones, who *fruges confumere nati*, pafs in review, or proceffion:

"Monks, fide by fide with monks, went two by two."

As I fat in a bookfeller's fhop here, I picked up a book in fmall quarto, being a defcription of the city. Half of it is a relation of the " prodigious relics" contained in the " holy cathedral:"
they

they confift of fome of the Virgin's hair; a fhirt which fhe made for her fon, which is without feams; two grains of the myrrh offered by the holy kings; a bit of the fkin of St. Bartholomew; eight thorns from the crown of Chrift, " partly whole and partly broken;" three of St. George's fingers, with a piece of his banner; thefe ought certainly to be preferved in England; item, relics of the eleven thoufand virgins; fome *lignum crucis*, &c.. All which I neglected to fee. *

The thorns are probably like fome of thofe feen by Sir John Maundevile, in 1322, and of which he gives the following account:

" And o partie of the crowne of oure Lord, wherwith he was
" crowned, and many other relikes, ben in France in the kynges
" chapelle, and the crowne lythe in a veffelle of criftalle richely
" dyghte. For a kynge of Fraunce boughte theife relikes fom-
" tyme of the Jewes, to whom the emperour had leyde them to
" wedde, *(pledge)* for a gret fumme of fylvre. And zif alle
" be it fo that men feyn, that this croune is of thornes, zee
" fchulle undirftonde that it was of jonkes of the fee, that is to
" fey, rufhes of the fee, that prykken as fcharpely as thornes.

* Mr. Ap Rhys, p. 151, fays, " There is alfo an eye-tooth of the giant
" St. Chriftopher: there is a fellow to it at a town called Coria, in Caftile:
" and a German perfon of quality told Philip III. that he had feen part of
" the fkull of the fame faint that held three pecks. The authenticity of
" which precious relics being unqueftionable, they will be fo many ftanding
" evidences againft cardinal Baronius, who was fo rafh as to affert that St.
" Chriftopher was no giant."

"For I have feen and beholden many tymes that of Parys, and "that of Conftantynoble: for thei were bothe on made of "ruffches of the fee. But men han departed hem in two par- "ties: of the whiche o part is at Parys, and the other part is "at Conftantynoble; and I have on of tho precyoufe thornes, "that femeth licke a white thorn, and that was zoven to me "for gret fpecyaltee. For there are many of hem broken and "fallen into the veffells that the crowne lythe in: for thei breken "for dryeneffe, when men moven hem, to fchewen hem to "grete lordes that comen thidre."

This extract may ferve as a fpecimen of the ftyle of this curious book, of which I have an edition in Italian, printed at Milan in 1480, in Gothic characters: this edition is not mentioned in the preface to the Englifh one of 1725. It may not be amifs to obferve in this place, though foreign to the fubject, the great affinity which the Englifh language of that age bears to the prefent Dutch language: many of the expreffions ufed in this book are literally Dutch; for inftance, " waren fuftren; " hadden lever; fchipmannes; wanhope; zee wyten wel," &c. &c.

At the end of the above-mentioned Spanifh book, printed in 1738, are chronological tables, of which the following are extracts.

Anno
1250. The image of the Holy Chrift of Berito is found driving on the river againft the ftream.
1362. The great altar of St. John of the Market, burnt.
1372. The proceffions of the *Corpus* are reduced to a fingle one.
1384. Two holy wafers are found in the mouths of two fifhes.
1410. There are fuch fwarms of locufts that the city fends out fquadrons to kill them.
1416. The image of our *Lady of the Abandoned* is made.

In the fame year, on the 18th of June, the judges wear blue robes with gold fringes.
1418. *Tranfit*, or tranflation, of St. Vincent Ferrer.
1455. Canonization of ditto Saint, the city celebrates folemn feftivals, elects him for patron, and pope Urban VIII. approves of it.
1469. The great altar of the cathedral is burnt; fixteen thoufand two hundred and fixteen ounces of melted plate are afterwards recovered.
1549. Don Lewis Caftelvi invents the method of preferving fnow, and cooling water.
1605. The city orders a filver vafe to be made, to hold the relics of St. Vincent Ferrer.
1607. A boy fheds tears of blood at the foot of the gallows, becaufe he had murdered his father.
1609. The expulfion of the Moors out of this city, to the number of one thoufand five hundred.
1647. The body of St. Lewis Bertram is carried in proceffion to ftop the progrefs of the plague.

1651.

Anno
1651. The river overflows the city, and in the convent of the nuns of the moſt Holy Trinity, leaves a frog in a holy-water vaſe.

1731. This moſt illuſtrious city eſtabliſhes a houſe for the fabric of tallow candles.

1734. A capacious tennis-court is built.

1737. A fabric for tiles and earthen-ware erected.

In this year, on Monday the 11th of November, the profeſſed houſe of the company of Jeſus, celebrates with feſtive demonſtrations the canonization of St. Francis Regis, &c.

Theſe memorable events may make a pretty addition to a little book of chronological tables lately publiſhed.

The city is walled, and has five gates. The peaſants are dreſſed in white linen waiſtcoats and trowſers, with net hair-caps. The houſes are all numbered, and the names of the ſtreets are painted on tiles on the corner houſes. A great number of ſingle-horſe chaiſes ply in the ſtreets: the horſes have no bits in their mouths, but are governed by *caveçons*, or noſe-bands, in the ſame manner as they are at Naples.

The royal road intended to be carried on quite to Madrid, which is three hundred and twenty-two miles, was lately begun, and about ten miles of it are already finiſhed, very broad, level, and exactly in a ſtrait line, ſo that it ſurpaſſes the celebrated road

from

from Rivoli to Turin, which is nine miles in length. About a league from Valencia, the sea forms a lake of near three leagues long, and a league broad, called Albufera, inhabited by vast quantities of fish and water-fowl, among which are great numbers of flamingos.

Valencia is built on a spot of ground perfectly flat: the houses are very high, and the streets narrow and crooked: it contains fourteen parish churches, twenty-two convents of friars, and nineteen of nuns, with seven colleges. In the court of the Patriarchal college is a fountain, in the midst of which is a fine marble statue of a woman, the drapery especially is very beautiful. St. Mary de los Desamparados (of the Abandoned), is a new octangular chapel, with a cupola pretty well painted in fresco. The ceiling of the church of St. John del Mercao (of the Market) was painted in fresco by Palomino, in 1699. The church of Santa Caterina Nueva, is extremely elegant, the inside being entirely of the finest marble and gilt bronze. The church of St. Francis is equally beautiful and *riante*, being in the inside plain white stucco with gilt ornaments, in a very good taste, and not overdone. There is nothing remarkable in the cathedral: I ascended the steeple, and from thence had a fine prospect of the whole city, the adjacent country, and the sea.

The *dogana*, or custom-house, was built in 1760, and is a neat square, of seven windows on each side to every story. A temporary wooden edifice is erected for the bull-feasts.

The

The present silk-market was formerly a church. I made an excursion to el Grado, which is a small village on the sea-side: the shore is quite flat, and there is no harbour, so that only small fishing vessels can remain here in safety. I afterwards spent a day at Morviedro (Muriveteres), the ancient Saguntum, four leagues north from Valencia, which was situated on the top of a mountain, about a league from the sea, commanding an extensive prospect. Hannibal besieged it, and during nine months the inhabitants resisted all the forces of Carthage; and, at last, pressed by famine, preferred being buried in the ruins of their city to being taken by the besiegers: this happened in the year of Rome 535, one hundred and eighty-two years before the vulgar æra. The modern village is built at the foot of the mountain. The extensive walls of Saguntum, which are yet remaining, and are embattled, show that that city was very large: it is difficult to get over the heaps of ruins, and loose pieces of rock which are within these walls; and the difficulty is augmented by their being over-run with the Indian fig, or prickly pear, which forms impenetrable barriers:

"———— In shapeless ruin all,
And Indian figs o'er-top the mould'ring wall."

After much clambering, my guide conducted me to the ruins of the amphitheatre, which is a semicircle of two hundred and sixty-six English feet in diameter: it is situated on the slope of the mountain, and enough of it remains to distinguish the plan: it is built with a kind of flint; each stone is about nine inches square;

square; the cement is of morter. There are twenty-two rows of seats, and three rows of entrances *(vomitoria)*, nine in the uppermost, eleven in the middlemost, and six in the undermost. Near this lies a stone eight feet long, and two feet thick, sculptured on both sides with stars of six points. Over a doorway, which yet remains, is a white marble statue, without a head, about two feet high, the drapery of which is very fine: underneath is an inscription on a stone which has been taken out of the wall, and replaced with the letters upside down: an iron ring is seen in the door-case, which formerly received the hinge. At some distance, in a niche of the wall, is another mutilated statue of white marble, of the same size as the other. Here are also two other inscriptions; and in the wall, near a gate of the modern town, are inserted eight stones with as many more * : a French hermit has resided on this mountain many years: he was at that time in his eightieth year, but was still able to descend every day into the town, to procure provisions: he went by the name of Don Claudio, and told me that he was present at the battle of Almansa, in 1707. After we had emptied a bottle of wine together, I returned to Valentia.

During my stay in this city, I had the honour of dining with the captain-general, or viceroy, count de Sayve. That nobleman is a Frenchman, and was then near ninety years of age.

* All these inscriptions have been communicated to the Society of Antiquaries in London.

In the Latin work, entitled, *Eman. Martini Epistolarum*, is a plan of this amphitheatre.

## SPAIN.

Sir William Duncan * and his lady, and Mr. Boſwell (brother to the gentleman who has publiſhed an account of Corſica), who reſides here engaged in commerce, were of the party: his excellency regaled us with Engliſh porter and ale. In the evening we adjourned to Sir William's houſe, where we were entertained with a concert and a ball.

Valencia formerly had the privilege of coining copper money: the laſt pieces are dated 1710. I procured one of three *dineros*, and one of ſix: on one ſide are the arms of Spain, and on the reverſe the letter V under a royal crown.

There is a peculiar dialect uſed in this province, much reſembling the *Patois Limoſin*; I procured the only three pamphlets which have been printed in it: one of them contains ninety pages, and is intitled, " *Rondàlla de Rondàlles, a imitació del Cuento de Cuentos de Quevedo, y de la Hiſtoria de Hiſtories de Don Diego de Torres, compoſta y treta a llum per un curiès apaſſionat à la Lengua Llemoſina*, 1769: that is, " Story of Stories, in Imitation of the Tale of Tales of Quevedo, and of the Hiſtory of Hiſtories of Torres, compoſed and brought to the light by a curious Lover of the Limoſin language." I bought a book in Naples, written on the ſame plan, in the Neapolitan jargon, entitled, " *Lo Cunto de li Cunte*;" " Tale of Tales," by John Alexis Abattutis, 1728, five hundred and ten pages. The other

* This gentleman died at Naples in September 1774.

E e         two

two Valencian books are a description of the festival of the *Cor-pus* in measured prose, of which these are specimens.

| | |
|---|---|
| *Parroquies, convènts, mercat,* | Parishes, convents, market, |
| *Alameda, ermita, riù,* | Elm-walk, hermitage, river, |
| *Lo palau, dit del Real,* | The palace, called Royal, |
| *Los cinch ponts, ab ses arcades,* | The five bridges, with their arches, |
| *Y altres prodigs semetjants,* | And other similar prodigies, |
| *Admirantse de tos ells,* | Are all to be admired, |
| *Puix Valencia es un encant.* | For Valencia is an enchantment. |

i. e. appears as an enchanted place by reason of its beauty; and indeed the Spaniards always call it Valencia la Hermosa, the Beautiful.

| | |
|---|---|
| *La verge quen en la burrèta* | The Virgin who on the ass |
| *Và, en lo bon Jesus al braç* | Goes, with the good Jesus in her arms |
| *Sabran la fuyta es de Egypte* | You must know, is the flight into Egypt, |
| *Que Maria y Josep cast* | That Mary and chaste Joseph |
| *Feren, guardant à son fill* | Made, guarding their son |
| *De Herodes que era indignat.* | From Herod who was angry. |

The following words will be sufficient to show the affinity which this dialect bears to the French language.

*Dèu*

# SPAIN. 211

| | | | | | |
|---|---|---|---|---|---|
| *Deu* | God, | *paſſatemps* | pastimes, | *argent* | silver, |
| *el diable* | the devil, | *diverſions* | diversions, | *autumne* | autumn, |
| *lhome* | the man, | *gent* | people, | *clau* | key, |
| *vida* | life, | *interès* | interest, | *coll* | neck, |
| *mort* | death, | *decentment* | decently, | *dent* | tooth, |
| *anim* | soul, | *cel* | heaven, | *fam* | hunger, |
| *lamor* | love, | *terra* | earth, | *fil* | thread, |
| *martyr* | martyr, | *lì* | he, | *fum* | smoke, |
| *confeſſor* | confessor, | *ſol* | sun, | *joc* | joke, |
| *rector* | rector, | *lluna* | moon, | *l'um* | light, |
| *loncle* | the uncle, | *ulls* | eyes, | *nom* | name, |
| *Judio* | Jew, | *genolls* | knees, | *pa* | bread, |
| *any* | year, | *peus* | feet, | *vi* | wine, |
| *el mon* | the world, | *moli* | mill, | *porc* | hog, |
| *arbres* | trees, | *ſon pare* | his father, | *ſablo* | sand, |
| *paper* | paper, | *ſa mare* | his mother, | *torrent* | torrent, |
| *murmur* | murmur, | *ſon marit* | her husband, | *vernis* | varnish, |
| *paraules* | words, | *bon viatge* | good journey, | *vomit*, | vomit, |
| *os* | bone, | *vullch dir* | I will say, | | &c. |

The other book is intitled, " Praises of the Hebrew, Greek, " Latin, Castilian, and Valencian languages," in forty-four pages, written in 1574, and reprinted 1765. In this work the author *modeſtly* gives the preference to the Valencian dialect, quotes sixty of its words, which are pure Latin, and twice that number which vary but little from it. An oration of three

pages

pages in length is also inserted, which is Spanish and Latin, almost literally at the same time.

Most of the Valencians, in speaking Spanish, pronounce the *ci* like our English *th*, thus, *la thiudad de Valenthia*, and have a kind of lisp, which is not disagreeable, especially when it proceeds from the mouth of a pretty woman.

I was in hopes of seeing a play in this city, but, as it had not rained for some months, a stop was put to all public diversions; so that it is natural to suppose, that the Spaniards believe that prohibiting plays is a sure method of obtaining rain; indeed it is infallible at the long run, for supposing diversions were to be suspended for a year, there would most probably fall some showers in that time, and they would immediately be attributed to the merits of their self-denial, in abstaining from vain entertainments *.

On the 25th of April, I set out from Valencia early in the morning,

"while dewy drops hung trembling on the tree;"

* In the *Delices de l'Espagne*, vol. iv. I find that the church of St. Andrew's " principal ornament is the body of a saint of a fresh date, but " very powerful in works and in miracles; his name was Francis Jerom Simon, " and he died in 1612: it is said that during his life he concealed the pre‑ " cious talent he possessed of working miracles, but that he revealed it on " his death-bed. Five years after his death, his altar was seen hung with as " many shirts, and other presents, made by those whom he had cured, as any " altar of the most ancient and famous saints in Spain."

and after travelling five leagues, dined at Cullera, and then proceeded three long leagues to Gandìa, on a heavy fandy heath, producing pine-trees and aloes: this town is about a mile from the fea, and from the fhore the ifland of Yviça may be difcerned in clear weather.

April 26. We were this day near feven hours in going three leagues, to a fmall village called la Puebla, on a very bad ftony road. The chaife overfet, but we luckily efcaped any mifchief, and remained, as Mr. Pennant fays, after travelling on a fimilar road,

———— a wond'rous token
Of Heav'n's kind care, with necks unbroken.

The beauty of the country compenfated for the badnefs of the roads, which lie through forefts of palm, mulberry, garofero, and olive trees; fields of wheat and barley, bordered by pomegranate hedges, of which the fcarlet bloffoms formed a pleafing contraft to the variegated greens among which they grew. On each fide of the road are fmall canals, like thofe in the environs of Xativa. In the evening we travelled three leagues farther, to the village of Onteniente. The weather began to grow exceffively hot, fo that it was only poffible to travel in the morning and evening, the reft of the day being fpent within doors in eating, drinking, and fleeping. In thefe fouthern regions, at this feafon, the fun.

Darts

TRAVELS THROUGH

Darts on the head direct his forceful ray,
And fiercely sheds intolerable day.

The snakes began now to be seen basking in the sun on the roads: we shot several of them. Lizards of different sizes, from two inches to eighteen, swarmed among the stones and walls: the smaller sort are harmless, the larger are very fierce and dangerous. I have seen several, which being pursued by a little dog I had with me, would turn about and stand at bay, hissing violently: their mouth opens wide enough to admit a hen's egg; and their bite is so tenacious, that I have lifted them from the ground by putting a stick in their mouths: the tail easily breaks off from the body, and continues for a long time alive. Dr. Goldsmith, in the seventh volume of his History of Animated Nature, says, " Salt seems to be much more efficacious in de-" stroying these animals than the knife; for, upon being " sprinkled with it, the whole body emits a viscous liquor, and " the lizard dies in three minutes in great agonies." I was at that time ignorant of this particular, or I should have made the experiment, which I have tried on snails, and found it to have the same effect it is here said it will have on lizards, and which is not improbable. I shot many of them when they were running up the trunks of trees: they were very beautifully speckled with green, blue, and yellow, and were as cold as ice to the touch. The hot weather likewise hatched into life myriads of insects, of which the musquitos, or gnats, were the most troublesome.

—the

―― the air
Was peopled with the infect tribe that float
Upon the noontide beam ―.            MASON.

The walls were covered with them in the mornings; to thofe walls they had fixed themfelves, fatiated with our blood. An infinite variety of butterflies, formed the moft pleafing and beautiful clafs of thefe new-born infects, which

Ope'd their gay downs, and fpread their gold-dropp'd
 wings
Turn'd every beauty to the funny ray,
And winnow'd with foft wing their eafy way.
            HARTSON.

The fteeples of the churches we faw this day, are of very handfome architecture, and bear fome refemblance to that of the New-church in the Strand, in London.

April 27. This day, after a very high wind, fome fhowers of rain fell, which were the firft I had feen for upwards of two months. It is hardly poffible to exprefs how beautiful an appearance the country made afterwards; the trees were all revived, and the duft being wafhed off their leaves, gave them a verdure of an uncommon luftre. This province is termed the garden of Spain, and may very juftly be termed that of Europe. We dined at a venta, in the hogfty, as the fmoke in the parlour, which had no chimney, was infufferable. We paffed the night in the village of Villena, having travelled fix leagues over a

flat

flat country, producing pines, olives, and barley; and environed with high mountains. No oats grow in Spain: horses and mules are fed with chopped straw and barley, because oats would be of too heating a nature in these climates. Abundance of *escorzonero* grows in these parts.

April 28. We this day paffed by the town of Sax, which poffeffes a ruined Moorifh caftle (a view of which is inferted in one of the plates of this work), built on the fummit of a very high and craggy rock, both together forming a very romantic and remarkable view, to which Mr. Mafon's lines may be applied with propriety:

—— Time's gradual touch
Has moulder'd into beauty many a tow'r,
Which when it frown'd with all its battlements
Was only terrible.——

We dined at Monforte, and at night arrived at Alicante, having travelled near ten leagues: the road was tolerable, and partly over mountains covered with olive-trees. The diftance from Valencia to Alicante is about one hundred and fixty-four miles. This city is celebrated for the goodnefs of its harbour, which is quite open, but with fecure anchorage, and is ufually full of fhips loading wines, falt, and glafs-wort. The city is built on the flope of a high mountain, on the top of which the caftle is fituated. It contains twenty thoufand inhabitants, among whom are three or four Englifh families; three parifh churches, fix convents

convents of monks, and three of nuns: it has five gates; fifty-eight cannon are planted on three baſtions. The garriſon conſiſts of twelve hundred ſoldiers, and eight hundred militia-men. There is a ſmall inconſiderable theatre here.

Robert Wilkie, Eſq. his majeſty's conſul, was ſo obliging as to take me in his carriage to ſee *las huertas*, or the gardens, two leagues north from the town. I obſerved in the governor's garden, a ſilk-tree and ſome madder plants; and in that of el Señor Barnabeu, a very large garofero, or carrobe tree; it produces annually one hundred and thirty arrobes of fruit (each arrobe is twenty-ſix pounds), which are ſold for ſeventy dollars, about eleven pound fourteen ſhillings[*]. Almonds, pomegranates, double-leaved imperial myrtle, oranges, and lemons, are extremely plentiful in theſe gardens.

On our return home we paſſed through ſeveral fields of barilla, which is uſed in making glaſs. In Miller's Gardener's Dictionary is an account of this plant, of which here follows an extract:

"Salſola, Salicornia, Glaſs-wort, Soude.
"It is an annual plant which riſes about five or ſix inches "high, ſending out many ſide-branches from the bottom, which "ſpread on every ſide: the ſeed ripens in autumn, ſoon after

[*] This tree may ſerve as companion to the great orange-tree near Oporto.

"which

"which the plant decays. The manner of making the fal al-
"kali is as follows: having dug a trench, they lay laths acrofs
"it, on which they place the herb in heaps, and having made
"a fire below, the liquor which runs out of the herb drops to
"the bottom, which at length thickening becomes fal alkali,
"which is partly of a black and partly of an afh colour, very
"fharp and corrofive, and of a faltifh tafte. This, when
"thoroughly hardened, becomes like a ftone, and is called *foude*,
"or *barilla*; it is exported from Spain into other countries for
"making of glafs."

The leaves of this plant are long, narrow, flefhy, and full of juice, like thofe of famphire. The ftone likewife enters into the compofition of foap: it is ufually exported in maffes of feven or eight hundred weight. The beft is that which grows in the environs of Alicante.

The next day the conful's nephew was fo kind as to accompany me on an excurfion to a neighbouring ifle: we fet out early in the morning in a coach drawn by four mules, and after travelling four leagues arrived at the village of Santa Pola, near which I counted no lefs than fifty-three Dutch fhips that were loading falt. We had brought provifions with us, and as there was no inn, we dined in the houfe of one of the inhabitants, with two very agreeable Spanifh women. After dinner we embarked in a boat for the ifland of Nueva Tabarca, which is only a league off, and landed on it after an hour's failing.

This,

This island is about three miles in circumference, and is so barren, that there is not a tree to be found on it, nor a drop of water, except what is brought from the continent. It contains about four hundred inhabitants, who are all Spaniards, redeemed at the king's expence from the slavery in which they were in Barbary: there is a town built for them, and at that time the church was nearly finished: the streets are very regular, the houses small, and with flat roofs. These poor people live rent-free, and for the first year had each about nine pence a day allowed them by government: over the gate is an inscription in Latin and Spanish, importing, that the Count de Aranda caused this colony to be planted in the reign of Charles III. 1771. The inhabitants say that they are in a worse situation at present, than they were when under captivity: they are never suffered to land on the continent, and are often distressed for provisions and water, when tempestuous weather prevents the passage of boats to the island. They have contrived a manufactory of ropes, the profits of which barely keep them from starving. After a short stay here, we returned to our boat, landed in half an hour at Santa Pola, and then went back to Alicante.

On the third of May I set out for Murcia, and having gone four leagues, arrived at the large town of Elche, which is very agreeably situated in the midst of a forest of palm trees. The chief church, which was built in 1682, is of white stone, with an elegant cupola: the front is very handsomely carved: on each

each side of the principal entrance are three columns, one of which is plain, the next fluted, and the third twisted spirally: over these is represented the Assumption of the Virgin, environed by angels; and on the great altar is a tabernacle ornamented with eight neat marble columns.

I intended to have paid a visit here to the celebrated Don Jorge Juan, who, jointly with Don Antonio de Ullòa, published an account of America (in four volumes in small folio), which is translated into English; but being informed that he was confined to his bed through sickness, I did not chuse to trouble him. He died a few weeks after. In the afternoon we passed through the town of Albaterra, where there is a very neat church, with a cupola and two turrets; and then travelling between mountains on a good road, passed the night at Orihuela, which is a small town, situated on the river Segura, containing seven or eight churches. This day's journey was nine long leagues.

May 4. We this morning travelled four leagues, on a plain of wheat fields and mulberry trees; the road was very good, and arriving at the city of Murcia, we put up at an inn kept by gypsies: the first floor, which I occupied, was little better than a hog-sty; I agreed with a French *traiteur* that he should furnish me with provisions ready dressed, as our landlord and landlady could not supply us with any thing.

The horse which I had bought at Madrid being quite worn out with fatigue, grew so lame, that finding him utterly incapable of any future service, I made a present of him to a peasant before we arrived at Orihuela; who, in return, lent my servant an ass to convey him to Murcia, himself accompanying us on foot, to bring his ass back. The horse, which was literally a Rocinante, had cost me but five pounds, and had travelled near seven hundred miles with me. The name *Rocinante* is composed of two words, *rocin* an ordinary horse, and *ante* before.

The marquis de Clermont was arrived here with his lady: they were on their way to Lisbon: his excellency was appointed ambassador from the court of France to that of Portugal, and had taken the opportunity of travelling through Spain. I did myself the honour of waiting on them, and had the pleasure of conversing with the beautiful marchioness. They set out the next day for Madrid.

The first object of my attention in Murcia, after having delivered my letters of introduction, was the cathedral: it is built of white stone, and ornamented with much carving on the outside, executed in 1521; part of which represents large chains extremely well cut: they were then building a handsome square stone tower to this church. The city contains twenty thousand inhabitants: the streets are very narrow; but before the archbishop's palace is an ample piazza extending to the river Segura, which divides the city into two pretty equal parts, communicating

municating with each other by a very neat stone bridge of two arches. There is an agreeable walk along the river side, beginning from the large convent of St. Francis, and continued about a mile. The bull-feasts are kept in the great square, temporary seats being on those occasions erected for the spectators, some of whom hire places in the houses which environ those seats.

The *alameda*, or public walk, is planted with four rows of elms: at one end is a stone statue of the Virgin Mary, and at the other end those of the late king and queen of Spain, each statue is placed on the top of a high stone column. I do not recollect to have seen in any other place such bad statues as these are, in so conspicuous a situation. The public granary is a very large brick building. All the principal cities in Spain have a like edifice; when corn is plentiful and cheap, the granaries are filled at the expence of government, and if there should afterwards be a dearth, that corn is sold to the poor at an under price.

In every chief city in Spain is also a foundling hospital, into which all children whatever are admitted: there is a small wicket in the wall, near which is a bell; a child may be brought here at any time of the day or night, the bell is pulled, the wicket opens, and a person receives the infant, enquiring if it has been baptized. If the parents chuse afterwards to claim the child, they may have it again on describing it: not only natural children

dren are thus maintained, but many of the lower clafs of tradefmen who have larger families than they can bring up, place their new-born infants in thefe hofpitals for a few years; thus, from the convenience of thefe excellent inftitutions, there can poffibly be no temptation for a tender mother to deftroy her offspring; an unnatural crime that is too frequently committed in countries which arrogate the claim of being more civilized. Italy alfo contains many of the like hofpitals.

I faw the fmall theatre, which was at that time daily occupied by a troop of rope-dancers and tumblers, but they were foon to refign the ftage to a company of itinerant Italian fingers, who were juft arrived from Barcelona, and intended to perform a few operas here. During my fhort ftay in Murcia, I fpent every evening at the houfe of Doña Terefa Piña y Ruiz; that lady and her daughter were fo obliging as to affemble all their mufical acquaintance, themfelves finging tonadillas and feguedillas in a far fuperior manner than I had ever heard them fung before; the young lady had made a great progrefs in the ftudy of mufic, and accompanied herfelf with the harpfichord and guitar, as perfectly as a profeffed miftrefs of the fcience, fo that it was with the greateft regret that I parted from that amiable family, which I did on the 8th of May, and after travelling nine leagues, I arrived on the fame day at Carthagena. The firft league was among mulberry trees, and then paffing over a ridge of rocks, the remainder of the road is on a heath, with a few barley

fields

fields on each side. We dined at a venta, and in Carthagena put up at a French inn, the sign of the Golden Eagle.

The next day, Sunday, 9th of May, I waited on Daniel Bomeester, esq. his majesty's conful here: he accompanied me to the governor's, general Don Carlos Reggio: his excellency is a Sicilian, and a grand-crofs knight of the order of Charles III. In the evening I affifted at a concert in the houfe of Don Juan Manuel de Cargigal, who is colonel of the regiment del Principe, quartered here: at this entertainment were prefent a great number of ladies, and near a hundred and thirty officers.

Carthagena is one of the fineft ports in the Mediterranean, and one of the three royal marine departments; the other two are Cadiz and Ferrol. The town much refembles Plymouth: there are two dry-docks, which were conftructed by the late Don Jorge Juan. The arfenal is walled round: feveral fhips were at that time on the ftocks, and two thoufand flaves, being Moorifh prifoners and criminals, were employed in the loweft offices: I faw many of thefe wretches pumping water out of the docks quite naked, except a cloth wrapped round their waifts. In the harbour were three fmall gallies and four xebecs, which are a larger kind of gallies, and are ufed in cruizes made againft the Moors. The land at the entrance of the port is mountainous, and at that time a caftle was building on a hill to command the arfenal. There are two public walks;

that

that of the Alameda is very long, and planted with double rows of white elms; that of Santa Lucia is near the harbour. The town is chiefly inhabited by officers of the army and navy, who are always obliged to wear their uniform, and none under the degree of captains may carry a cane: their ranks are also distinguished by narrow gold or silver lace round the cuffs of their coats; a captain having a single lace, a lieutenant-colonel two, and a colonel three laces : a captain of a man of war also wears three laces. The marine uniform is a blue coat with red cuffs, red waistcoat and breeches, with a broad gold lace on the coat and waistcoat.

May 11. I dined at the governor's with thirty officers: they informed me, that the navy of Spain consisted at that time of about sixty-three men of war, which were,

One ship of one hundred and fourteen guns, and twelve hundred men, called the Most Holy Trinity.

Eight ships of eighty-four guns, and about eight hundred men each.

About fifty of seventy-four, and four of sixty guns.

Eight frigates of forty guns.

Twenty frigates of thirty guns, eight xebecs, and seven gallies, each of four guns, and one hundred and ten men; which are in all about one hundred and six vessels.

I have a list of the army, which was printed at Madrid, in 1773; according to which, I find that there are:

Troops of the Royal Houſhold.

Three companies of life guards.

A company of halberdier guards.

A regiment of Spaniſh infantry guards, and one of Walloon infantry: each regiment confiſting of ſix battalions.

And a brigade of four ſquadrons of Royal Carabineers.

Forty-ſix regiments of foot, of two battalions each, of which thirty-three are Spaniſh regiments; three are called thoſe of *Ireland, Hibernia & Ultonia*, of which all the officers are Iriſh Roman-Catholics; two Italian, four Walloon, and four Swiſs regiments.

Beſides theſe, there is a regiment of artillery of four battalions, and a regiment of engineers. The Royal Academy of Mathematics for the inſtruction of the officers and cadets of the artillery is in the caſtle of Segovia; and the academies for teaching the engineers are in Barcelona, and in Oran on the coaſt of Algiers.

There are alſo forty-two regiments of provincial militia, each of a ſingle battalion; forty-ſix companies of invalids, and one hundred and twenty-nine companies of city militia.

The cavalry conſiſts of fourteen regiments, of four ſquadrons each; and eight regiments of dragoons.

The Spaniards never use the method of recruiting to complete the complement of the men, but all those who are judged proper for service draw lots, and those on whom the lot fails, which are no more than five out of a hundred, are enlisted.

In the afternoon I saw the artillery exercised, by shooting at a blank, three hundred and thirteen toises distant, from six cannon and three mortars.

About six leagues east of Carthagena, the land advances into the sea by a point, which is called Cape Palos.

May 12. I set out early in the morning, dined at Puente Alamo, and passed the night at Totana, having travelled nine leagues on a good level heathy road. The low kind of wheat was already cut.

May 13. Proceeding four leagues we arrived at Lorca, which is a pretty large town, containing seven or eight churches. I waited on a colonel, to whom I had a letter: he accompanied me to a house where I saw a very fine picture, thought to be by Titian, representing St. Thomas feeling the wound in the side of Christ: the figures are half length, and as large as the life. The colonel ordered one of his soldiers, armed with a long gun and a sabre, to accompany us to Granada (which he did on foot, being near two hundred and thirty miles in five days), because this road is over mountains which are scarcely inhabited,

and

and where we frequently travelled thirty miles without seeing a human being, or a house; and sometimes troops of banditti, from twelve to thirty in a company attack travellers, whom they first murder and then rob, leaving the dead bodies with the carriages on the road, and carrying off the plunder upon the mules.. These banditti inhabit caverns among the mountains, and are armed each with a short blunderbuss, and half a dozen pistols stuck round their girdle; but as the whole province is alarmed when they make their excursions, we did not apprehend much danger, as we should of course be forewarned of their being in the neighbourhood: on those occasions travellers sometimes remain for a week, or more, in a town, waiting for the opportunity of being joined by other carriages and guards going the same way; so that there often arrives in Granada a suite of fourteen or fifteen chaises, composing a kind of caravan. With these precautions, and that of never being on the road before sun-rise, nor after sun-set, we arrived afterwards safe in Granada, having preferred suffering the trifling inconvenience of the heat to the danger of losing our lives. We several times saw two or three men armed with guns, lurking behind the mountains, then join us, walk a league or two, and afterwards having reconnoitred us, lag behind, and we saw no more of them: at such times I rode before on horseback, the servants walking on each side of the empty chaise, which was conducted by the calesseiro, and the soldier followed behind with the fire-arms in readiness. From Granada I took another soldier, who went with us to Cordova, after which I found it no longer necessary to have a guard, as

we

we were then entered into a more populous country. I paid these men a hard-dollar, or four shillings and six pence per day, besides maintaining them. These soldiers are likewise serviceable in procuring provisions and beds: they have passports from their colonels, which, on their return from having accompanied travellers, authorise them to demand provisions and lodging gratis, till they arrive at the place they set out from; without these passports they would be arrested as deserters: they sometimes abuse their authority, by extorting provisions from poor wretches who have none to spare, and by acts of violence. The first mentioned soldier when walking behind my chaise, met two peasants who had a very fine large dog with them, the dog barked at him, and, as he said, attempted to bite him, upon which, he immediately levelled his gun, and shot the dog dead, the peasants not daring to make the least expostulation; which instance of cruelty by no means raised his character with me; however, he was very faithful to us, especially as I allowed him as much tobacco as he chose to smoke. The day before we arrived at Granada he fell ill, occasioned by the very great fatigue of walking so far in such intense heats; so that I hired an ass for him to ride on.

In the afternoon we proceeded three leagues to the village of Lumbreras: the roads are very good, and are environed with high mountains, on the sides of which are some barley fields.

May 14. After travelling five leagues we entered into the kingdom of Granada, and rested at the village of Velez El Rubio:

bio: the road is carried in a serpentine form over barren mountains; and in this journey of seven hours, there is not a house, nor even a tree to be seen; all was still. We proceeded, after having *hecho la siesta*, that is, slept two hours after dinner, as usual,

> Along these lonely regions, where retired
> From little scenes of art, great nature dwells
> In awful solitude.————
>
> Where the green serpent, from his dark abode,
> Which ev'n imagination fears to tread,
> At noon forth issues.————       THOMPSON.

Our calesseiro this day shot a serpent of upwards of four feet in length. Having gone three leagues on a sandy road, lying between mountains, at the foot of which were some corn-fields and white elms, we got to Chiridel, where we passed the night on straw, in a venta kept by gypsies, " the doors and windows " of which were always open, by reason of their being none to " shut," as Taylor, the water-poet says, of a like hovel he was in, when he travelled through Bohemia. Our landlady, however, very obligingly danced a fandango with the soldier, to the sound of a *tambour de Basque & Castañetas*.

May 15. We went nine leagues, of which the first seven are over a barren hilly heath, on which I shot several larks of the large kind before mentioned *. We dined at Cullar, and in the evening arrived at the small town of Baza, where there is nothing remarkable, as the author of *les Delices de l' Espagne* says, "except the church of our Lady of Piety, which from time to time performs great miracles."

May 16. We continued our journey, and arrived at the town of Guadix, having travelled seven leagues over barren mountains, among which grow a few green oaks. Between Baza and Guadix are only two houses, one of which is the venta we dined at, and which might be called the Haunt of Meditation, as I imagine a more retired place can hardly be found in the deserts of Arabia. The immediate environs are very beautiful, being planted with elms and mulberry trees. To the left, at two leagues distance, we saw the Sierras Nevadas, behind which are the Alpuxarras mountains: they extend to about seventeen leagues in length, and eleven in breadth, and their summits are covered with snow, probably coeval with the mountains; they are so high, that from the top of some which are accessible, the Straits of Gibraltar, the coast of Barbary, and the cities of Tangier and Ceuta may be discovered.

May 17. We arrived this morning at a village called Purullena; its inhabitants have dug caves in the soft rock, which serve them for dwelling-places. We here hired an ass to carry one

* *Alauda Calandra Linn. Syst. Nat.* 283. In Edwards' Natural History, plate 268, is a coloured figure of this bird.

of the trunks up a mountain which we were to pass over, as the chaise was too much loaded to be dragged up such a long ascent, which took us an hour and a half: we afterwards dined in a venta, and then proceeded to Isnalloz, where we arrived after having travelled eight leagues, through a wild mountainous desart, melancholy, barren, and totally uninhabited: the roads were bad, and at times very dangerous, being along the edges of precipices. On one side the mountains rose almost perpendicularly, and on the other the fall was equally steep, and the road barely broad enough for the chaise to pass. In these places I always chose to walk. The descents are very rapid, and large stones which had fallen from the rocks frequently blocked up the passage; these stones we were obliged to remove, and tumble over the brink, which occasioned much delay, so that it was quite dark when we got to our night's lodging.

> Oft did the cliffs reverberate the sound,
> Of parted fragments tumbling from on high;
> And from the summit of the craggy mound,
> The perching eagle oft was heard to cry,
> Or on resounding wings to shoot athwart the sky.
> 
> BEATTIE's Minstrel, book ii.

The chaise had been once overturned, and much time and trouble was employed in setting it up again, as we had all the baggage to unload and reload. I was in it when it overset, but received no hurt.

May 18. It rained all this day: and having travelled five leagues, of which the laft two were over a fertile plain, producing corn, olives, flax, and hemp, and dined in a venta, we entered into the city of Granada, which is fifty-two leagues diftant from Carthagena. Thefe leagues were fo long, that on computing the time we had been travelling, which was feven days, or feventy-eight hours journey, at only three miles per hour, the diftance is at leaft two hundred 'and thirty-four Englifh miles, or thirty-three miles a day, performed by a fingle horfe drawing a chaife with two perfons in it, and two large trunks behind it; the caleffeiro and foldier having walked all the way, except now and then that I permitted them to ride on my horfe. Few of our Englifh poftilions or horfes would be able to undergo fuch fatigue, efpecially during that hot feafon. We put up at the inn kept by gypfies *, and procured a French *traiteur* to fupply us daily with provifions, ready dreffed.

May 19. After having delivered feveral letters of introduction, which I had brought from various places, one of the gentlemen to whom I was addreffed, accompanied me about the city. It is one of the largeft in Spain, and contains ninety thoufand inhabitants †; its form is circular, and it is fituated in a plain, three leagues from the foot of the Sierra Nevada moun-

* Thefe kind of inns are called *Mefones* by the Spaniards.
† A plan of this city is extant; it was publifhed in two fheets, towards the end of the laft century.

tains, whose snowy tops agreeably diversify the perpetual verdure of the environs. The small rivers Darro and Xenil run through the city. In the evening I attended several ladies to the play: the theatre is very mean and dark, and the acting was yet worse, consisting of low and ribald buffoonery; however, I was much entertained with the tonadillas and seguedillas which were sung, and with a fandango which was danced between the acts: the representation began at four, and lasted four hours. The ladies afterward took an airing in their chariots drawn by four and six mules, slowly driving backwards and forwards along the mall, or alameda, which is very pleasantly planted with trees on the side of the river Xenil: the gentlemen walked on foot, and from time to time got on the footstep of the carriages, placing their arm over the coach door, *cortejando las señoras*, *(cicisbeing* the ladies), which ceremony " I could not in con- " science" dispense with, as I had now acquired a sufficient knowledge of the language to be very sensible of the charms of these ladies' conversation. At nine we all adjourned to a coffee-house, and refreshed ourselves with ice-creams, as is customary every evening in all the southern climates of Europe.

May 20. I spent this day in viewing the chief edifices of the city. I went first to the cathedral, which is very large; the inside is within these ten years entirely encrusted with the finest marbles, highly polished, and enriched with ornaments of gilt bronze; but the whole is executed in so wretched and despicable a manner, that it only inspires contempt for the ignorance of the architects,

architects, sculptors, and masons who were employed in it, and for the persons who employed them. In the adjoining royal chapel are interred king Ferdinand and his queen, Isabel, who conquered Granada from the Moors in 1492, with their daughter, and her husband Philip I. father to Charles V. The church of *San Juan de Dios* (St. John of God), has a handsome stone front: the cloisters were painted in fresco in 1749, by Diego Sanchez y Saravia, who was yet living. I then went to the circular amphitheatre, which was erected for the bull-feasts in 1768-9: it is built of brick, but the seats are of wood; it has two rows of boxes, sixty-eight in each row: the inner area is one hundred and eighty-five feet in diameter: this edifice cost three hundred thousand reals, or about three thousand four hundred pounds; it is likewise made use of as a *manége*, where the gentlemen of the *Maestranza* exercise their horses. In the evening I rose on horseback with a Spanish gentleman to the *Sacro Monte*, or Holy Mountain, just without the city, where I was shewn a few caves, called *masmorras*, wherein the Moors formerly confined the Christians, and where they murdered ten holy bishops, who without doubt are " now happy." A church and convent is erected on this spot: the church possesses the relics of the bishops, and the friars possess a very capacious cellar filled with hogsheads of excellent wine, which made me pay more attention to the casks than to the bishop's bones. The worthy owners of the cellar cordially invited us to taste their liquor, which was readily agreed to, and having drank *quantum sufficit*, we remounted our horses, returned to town, and spent the evening

evening at the houfe of Don Jofeph Miguel de Cañaveral, whofe civilities to me claim this public acknowledgement: his daughter favoured us with finging feveral tonadillas, accompanied by a band of mufic which had purpofely been provided.

Granada is divided into four quarters, Granada, Alhambra, Albaycin, and Antequeruela; it has twelve gates, which are always open: it was formerly environed with a wall, on which were built one thoufand and thirty towers, not one of which now exifts. It is an archbifhoprick, an univerfity, and a royal chancery: it contains twenty-four parifh churches, and twenty-nine convents, (which have alfo each a church), eleven hofpitals, and four colleges. The ancient Illiberis was fituated near this city: many infcriptions have been difcovered among its ruins, and were lately publifhed, engraven on about fixty copper-plates. A copy of this work is depofited in the Britifh Mufeum. The editor is one Padre Juan Flores: he fhewed me his collection of medals; they are all Arabian, found in and about Granada: there are about fixty of gold, nine hundred of filver, and thirty of copper: he poffeffes likewife various Moorifh feals of gold, filver, copper, and bronze; fome talifmans, or amulets, and a great number of rings of the fame materials; feveral copper vafes with Arabian infcriptions; fome manufcript volumes on paper and parchment, various infcriptions engraven on copper, alabafter, and cornelians, and a few weapons ufed by the Moors who inhabited Granada three hundred years ago. I faw likewife at his houfe a very fine ftatue in bronze, a foot high, reprefent-

ing

ing an old man running; and feveral Roman and Grecian medals. He told me he would willingly fell the whole collection at once, but would not part with any fingle piece; neither did he chufe to mention the terms of purchafe. Moft of the filverfmiths ſhops contain Arabian medals, which are offered for fale. There is likewife a curious collection of Moorifh antiquities belonging to the city, of which I faw a defcription in manufcript.

The ftreets of Granada are very narrow, crooked, and badly paved; hardly a houfe is to be found in the whole city, to which the term of *palace* may be applied; and only three tolerable pictures are here to be met with; two of which, by Palomino, are in one of the chapels of the Carthufian church, which is fituated about a mile out of town: the altar there is of very fine marble, and the profpect from the library is extremely beautiful. The other picture is by Murillo, reprefenting Chrift when a child, and is in the nunnery del Angel. The marbles which are dug out of the quarries in this province are the moft beautiful in Spain: there is one ftreet in Granada confifting entirely of fhops, wherein marble fnuff and tobacco boxes, flabs, globes, ftones for ear-rings, bracelets, necklaces, and other toys are expofed to fale: I purchafed a couple of boxes, of which the marble is femi-tranfparent, and refembles agate. I had procured at Madrid fifty-two fpecimens of the different kinds of marble found in Spain, cut into pieces of about two inches fquare. The green marble is very plentiful here, and is much like the Italian *verde antico*. Moft of the houfes in Granada

have

have the rooms ornamented with some of these slabs, in gilt frames, and hung up in the manner of looking-glasses.

I spent this evening at the house of the marchioness of Casablanca, where we were entertained with a concert, and afterwards with cards: part of the company played at whist, part at piquêt, and the rest at various Spanish games with a peculiar kind of cards, much resembling those used in Switzerland, and known by the name of *cartes de taraut*. The backgammon tables which I saw used in Portugal and Spain are more simple than those we use in England, being without either points, or middle-piece, but are played on after the English manner. The Spaniards have many other games, such as *lotteries*, *biribis*, &c. the rules of which I am entirely ignorant of, as I always preferred conversation to such tedious and insipid, as well as expensive amusements. I lately mentioned the gentlemen of the *maestranza*, and it now remains to explain what that is. There are in Spain four confraternities, or brotherhoods, which are called *Real Maestranzas*, composed only of noblemen and gentlemen, whose number is unlimited: they are all under the protection of the king, and are instituted at Seville, Granada, Valencia, and Ronda: that of Granada was incorporated in 1686, and has taken for titular patroness, " the most holy " Mary, our lady, in the sovereign mystery of her immaculate " conception, under the invocation of our Lady of the Tri- " umph." Mars, Hercules, or even Hughes, who rides on two or three horses at a time, would be more eligible patrons; but the Spaniards do not think so.

The intent of thefe focieties is to breed, break, and manage horfes; the members of them wear an uniform, which is different in each of the four cities: that of Granada is blue, and that of Seville fcarlet, each with a broad filver lace, and a red cockade in their hats. The form of the oath adminiftered by the chaplain of the fociety to every candidate, previous to his admittance is fingular, and is as follows: "I N. N. fwear and "make a vow to God our Lord, into your holy hands, that I "will inwardly believe, outwardly confefs, and always main- "tain that the moft holy Mary, our lady, was conceived in "grace in the firft inftant of her moft pure natural being; and "for the greater facrifice to fuch a fovereign lady, I offer, by "every poffible means to affift, in order that the holy Roman "Catholic church may declare this facred myftery to be an article "of faith: and I promife to fulfill the engagements made by "this fociety, in order to facilitate this defirable event." \*

In the next page of the book of ftatutes and ordinances, from whence this is extracted, is, "and we agree, that when through "the divine mercy, the fortunate day fhall arrive, in which the "holy Roman Catholic church fhall declare this fovereign "myftery to be an article of faith, we will publifh it on horfeback "with the moft plaufible ceremonies, &c. &c. † The arms of

\* See *le Voyageur François*, vol. xvi. p. 34, on the fame fubject.
† An octavo book, printed in Barcelona, and intitled, "Graces of Grace, "falted acutenefles of the faints;" ends thus: "An infinite infinity of "times, by an infinite infinity of perfons, in an infinite infinity of places, "be praifed and adored the moft holy facrament of the altar, and the "conception.

these *Maestranzas* are, *or*, two horses bridled and running together, with this motto, *Pro republica est, dum ludere videmur.*

The royal palace of the Alhambra, is one of the most entire, as well as the most magnificent of any of the edifices which the Moors erected in Spain: it was built in 1280, by the second Moorish king of Granada; and, in 1492, in the reign of their eighteenth king, was taken by the Spaniards, commanded by Ferdinand, as was mentioned before. It is situated on a hill, which is ascended on a road bordered with hedges of double or imperial myrtles, and rows of elms. On this hill, within the walls of the Alhambra, the emperor Charles V. began a new palace in 1568, but which was never finished: the shell of it remains: it is built of yellow stone; the outside forms a square of one hundred and ninety feet: the inside is a grand circular court, with a portico of the Tuscan, and a gallery of the Doric order, each supported by thirty-two columns, made of as many single pieces of marble. The diameter of the area, which is without a roof, is ninety three feet: the covered portico is eighteen feet wide; consequently the whole diameter of the rotunda is one hundred and twenty-nine feet, which I measured myself. The palace has fifteen windows in front, and is two stories in height: between the windows are fourteen lions mouths and eagles beaks

---

" conception of Mary the most holy, without spot of sin in no one imagin-
" able instant."

*Finis coronat opus* indeed! The motto to this book is, " *Servite Dominum*
" *in lætitia.*"

alternately,

alternately, of bronze, and of very fine workmanship, each holding a large bronze ring: twenty-five of these are on the other sides of the edifice: on the frize is carved in large letters in stone, IMP. CÆS. CAROLO V. P.V. or *plus ultra:* and in several of the rooms the walls are covered with the same device in stucco, in French *plus oultre.* The grand entrance is ornamented with columns of jasper, on the pedestals of which are representations of battles in marble basso relievo. In the third volume of the *Delices de l' Espagne,* is a pretty accurate view of the interior part of this palace.

The Alhambra is a mass of many houses and towers, walled round, and built of large stones of different dimensions: the annexed plate will give a more distinct idea of its appearance and architecture, than the most elaborate description. There is a key in basso relievo over the great gate, which is represented in a corner of the plate. Almost all the rooms have stucco walls and ceilings, some carved, some painted, and some gilt, and all overloaded with various Arabian sentences, such as, " There is " no other God but God;" which is repeated thousands of times. All the floors are either marble or tiled; one in particular is paved with two slabs of white marble, each upwards of thirteen feet long, and about half as broad. Some of the walls are encrusted with a kind of coarse mosaic, composed of pieces of different coloured tiles, representing stars and foliages. The first cortile I entered, is an oblong square, with a fountain at each angle; and in the middle is a canal of running water, deep and wide

wide enough to fwim in. Round this cortile are feveral baths, the walls, floor, and ceiling of which are of white marble. In thofe parts of the Alhambra, where bricks have been employed in the building, the morter between the bricks is as thick as the bricks themfelves. Almoft all the columns are of white marble, and ufually eight times their diameter (which is of one foot,) in length. The capitals are much diverfified, as reprefented in the plate. La Torre de Comares is the largeft tower of the Alhambra. The fquare of the lions is paved with white marble, and has a portico quite round it, fuftained by one hundred and twenty-fix flender alabafter columns, which are placed by twos and threes: in the middle is a bafon, fupported on the backs of twelve lions, which are reprefented as large as the life, with their heads in front, though very clumfily fculptured: out of this bafon rifes a pedeftal which fuftains a fmaller bafon, containing a tube, from whence iffues a *jet d' eau*; the lions likewife fpout water out of their mouths: the whole of this fountain is of white marble. We next entered into the faloon *of Secrets*, which is a fmall octangular room; a whifper at one corner is diftinctly heard from the oppofite corner, but from no other place. The bathing room is entirely of marble and coloured tiles, and in the midft is a fountain, which formerly fupplied the baths with water: the niches in the wall contained the beds of the Moorifh kings. Here are befides a great number of fountains diftributed in the various rooms, and which ftill play.

In

In one of the rooms are two Roman ſtatues of two nymphs, of white marble, as large as the life, with cornucopias; and over a door is a very fine oval marble baſſo relievo, repreſenting Leda with the ſwan, whoſe neck is twiſted round hers, and is farther in a very indecent poſture; on each ſide is a ſatyr ſitting under a tree; this oval is three feet in its longeſt diameter, and eighteen inches in its ſhorteſt. This baſſo relievo, and the ſtatues, were placed here by Charles V.

We afterwards walked through the gardens, which abound with orange and lemon trees, pomegranates, myrtles, &c. At the end is another palace called Ginaraliph, ſituated on a more elevated ſtation than the Alhambra: from the balconies is one of the fineſt proſpects in Europe, over the whole fertile plain of Granada, bounded by the ſnowy mountains. Cloſe to the entrance of this palace are two exceeding large cypreſs trees, which are near five hundred years old, and are called the Cypreſſes of the Sultana-queen, as ſhe was diſcovered under them in familiar converſation with the Moor Abencerrage. In one room the walls are covered with the three following inſcriptions, repeated hundreds of times, in Arabic: " God alone conquers." " Glory " be to God." " God is my hope."

In the gardens I ſaw two jars, or pitchers, of blue and white earthen ware, each ſeven feet high, and five feet in diameter, with various inſcriptions. I brought a round tile away, taken

out of one of the rooms, the walls of which are entirely encrusted with the like *.

A Spanish book, in two quarto volumes, entitled, *Paseos de
Granada*, which is written in form of a dialogue, says, that the
city of Granada was built one hundred and fifty-one years after
the deluge. The querist asks if this account be certain; and the
answer is; " How, certain! it is an account approved by the
" church; a Franciscan account, that the virgin mother, Mary
" de Jesus de Agreda †, affirmed to have been revealed to her by
" God, and it ought to be taken for granted." Such co-
gent arguments indeed admit of no reply. In another part of
this book, is the following curious dialogue between a Granadine and a stranger, who are walking in a square, called del
Triunfo. " *Gran.* I imagine, sir, you do not know why this
" is the most chearful spot in Granada; at all times, in all sea-
" sons, in rain, sun-shine, wind, or snow, it is always plea-
" sant. *Stranger.* And for what other reason can it be so, ex-
" cept by its being large and eminent? *Gran.* Oh! sir, if
" you were a Granadine, your nature itself would indicate to you
" the cause of its splendor; the glad and tumultuous beatings of
" your heart would inform you. Do not you see that column
" that sustains all heaven? Do not you see that this spot is the

---

* A representation of it is inserted in the plate.

† This saint was born in 1602. In the third volume of Dr. Geddes's
Tracts is an account of her life.

" august

"august place of residence of the ever brilliant sun of heaven
" and earth? Do not you see, that *there* stands Mary, the most
" holy, our lady, represented in the adorable mystery of
" her immaculate conception? *Causa nostræ letitiæ,*" &c. &c.
&c. &c. &c. *

But to return to the Alhambra, I have only to add, that the before-mentioned Don Diego Sanchez, was at that time, by order of the Madrid Royal Academy of the three fine arts, assisted by several of its members, employed in taking exact plans, elevations, views, &c. both general and particular, of this palace, of which I saw some that were already engraven; one of which was a copy of a piece in fresco, said to be painted by the Moors; it represents three kings sitting; very stiff and bad, but the colouring is gay and brilliant, and intermixed with gold and silver. They are intended to be published in a folio volume, which will be an *unique* in its kind, as there is in no other part of Europe such a noble and well preserved specimen of the Moorish architecture, nor any modern palace in a more happy situation. By way of appendix to that work, the description and plates of Charles the Fifth's palace are intended to be added, though it is very uncertain when it will be published. I wanted to purchase copies of

---

* Dr. Geddes, in his first volume of Miscellaneous Tracts, first published in 1690, gives an account of part of a pocket-handkerchief found in the mountains of Valparayso in 1595, which the Granadines believe to have been used by the Virgin Mary to wipe her eyes with; the doctor's motto to this account is,

" *Parturiunt montes, nascitur ridiculus mus.*"

all the finished drawings, but Don Diego had positive orders from his majesty not to part with them, and it was with much difficulty, that I perfuaded him to confent to my copying the general view of the Alhambra.

I was difappointed in my intentions of waiting on his excellency Don Ricardo Wall, an Irifh gentleman, who is one of his Catholic majefty's privy-counfellors, and a lieutenant-general, refiding here, as he had, a few days before my arrival, fet out for Aranjuez to join the court.

On the 24th of May I fet out from Granada, taking a foldier as a guard, and traverfing the village of Santa-Fè, dined in a venta, and paffed the night in the town of Loxa, whofe environs are very agreeable. This day's journey, of eight leagues, was over a plain, producing corn, flax, hemp, beans, and faffron: we faw a great number of eagles; thefe birds fly exceeding high, and float upon the air in a circular motion, hardly ftirring their wings.

May 25. We paffed over two high mountains, and dined at a venta, no more than three leagues diftant from Loxa, but which had notwithstanding required feven hours to perform them in. We afterwards paffed over another mountain, having a diftant profpect of the city of Antequera; and, after four leagues journey, entered into the kingdom of Andalusia, and put up for the night at the village of Alamea, having traverfed a foreft of green

green-oaks. Large lizards, of the kind before mentioned, were very numerous, and the roads were covered with locusts, grafshoppers, crickets, and the beetle, known by the name of tumble-dung; this infect is very common in America. In the eighth volume of the History of Animated Nature, p. 137, is the following account of it, which is true in every respect.

"That beetle which the Americans call tumble-dung, particularly demands our attention; it is all over of a dusky black, rounder than those animals are generally found to be, and so strong, though not much larger than the common black beetle, that if one of them be put under a brass candlestick, it will cause it to move backwards and forwards, as if it were by an invisible hand, to the admiration of those who are not accustomed to the sight; but this strength is given it for much more useful purposes than those of exciting human curiosity, for there is no creature more laborious, either in seeking subsistence, or in providing a proper retreat for its young: they are endowed with sagacity to discover subsistence by their excellent smell, which directs them to excrements just fallen from man or beast, on which they instantly drop, and fall unanimously to work in forming round balls or pellets thereof, in the middle of which they lay an egg. These pellets they convey three feet deep into the earth, where they lie till the proper season, when the eggs are hatched, and burst their nests, and the insects find their way out of the earth. They work with indefatigable industry in rolling these globular pellets to the place where they are to be buried: this they are to perform.

"perform with the tail foremost, by raising up their hinder part, "and shoving along the ball with their hind-feet." The largest I saw was about the size of a walnut. These beetles quit their labour if any others come to their assistance, from whence is derived the Spanish proverb, " *La ayuda del escarabajo, que dexa* " *la carga quando le ayudan :*" the assistance of the beetle, which leaves its work when it is assisted *.

May 26. After travelling four leagues among olive-trees and green oaks, we dined at the village of Herrera, and at ten at night arrived at the city of Ecija, having passed the river Xenil over a stone bridge of three arches. During these last four leagues I observed nothing remarkable, except ten eagles flying circularly, and near each other : and that a few small stone crosses were placed on the sides of the road, to mark the spots where travellers had been murdered, but the ancient dates on these crosses quieted our apprehensions of meeting with the same fate.

> Y una cruz el parage determina
> De la tragica muerte repentina,
> En alguna inscripcion muy mal grabada,
> De las lluvias y el sol medio borrada.　　Observ. Rustico.

" And a cross shows the place of the tragical sudden death, with " a badly engraven inscription, half worn out by the sun and the " rains."

---

* Scarabeus Pilularis, Linn. Syst. Nat. 550. This is not the only species which employs itself in forming balls of dung.

May 27. I remained all this day at Ecija: this city is situated on the river Xenil, over which is a stone bridge of ten small arches. Near it is the *Alameda*, which was planted three years ago with young poplars: there are five stone columns, three at one end of this walk, and two at the other; on the tops are placed the statues in marble of the present king of Spain, the prince and princess of Asturias, Don Lewis, and my Lord St. Paul *(El Señor San Pablo)* all most execrably done.

Before the door of the stye where I resided, is an enormous gilt statue of Saint Christopher the Giant, probably by the same ingenious hand as the others. The theatre was lately built, and is of wood; it contains three rows of boxes, fifteen in each row: the boxes are ornamented with balustrades, and the first row is sustained by fifteen wooden pillars; underneath are benches, elevated gradually above each other: the seats in the pit are all appropriated to particular persons, who lock them up after the performance, and reserve the key. Here are six parish churches, twelve convents of friars, eight nunneries, and six hospitals. I waited on the marquis de Quintana, who accompanied me to see a cock-fight: the cocks had been procured from England; the battle and the betting were also after the English custom. The marquis de Peñaflor possesses the most conspicuous house in this city; it is very large, and contains fountains in almost every room of the ground-floor, rendering them very cool and refreshing in this climate, which is called the frying-pan of Spain. The chief square is large, and is surrounded by porticos.

May 28. Travelling three leagues on a plain, among corn-fields, olive-trees, and vines, the road bordered with hedges, aloës, and myrtle, we dined at the village of Carlotta, which was built at the king's expence, in the year 1769, and granted to German and Italian families, rent-free. All along this road are a number of small new-built houses, environed by cypress-trees, likewise inhabited by Germans, who make part of the colony, to the number of thirty thousand, procured from the Palatinate of the Rhine, for peopling the Sierra Morena, which is a chain of mountains separating Andalusia from New Castile, at least eighty leagues long, but of unequal breadth, and called *Morena*, from its brown colour. The inn in this village is kept by an Italian, and is the best I ever met with on the road in Spain. Arising from our *siesta*, we proceeded over hills, on a stony road, and passed over a brick bridge of five arches: on a church steeple I observed young storks in their nests. We afterwards descended a mountain, and passing the river Guadalquivir over a stone bridge of sixteen arches, immediately entered into the city of Cordova: we paid toll for the passage over this bridge, on the side of which is placed a bad statue of the angel Raphael, holding a shield, with this inscription: " *Yo te juro por Jesu Xpo, que soi Raphael angel,* " *aquië Dios tiene puesto por guarda de esta ciud.*" " I swear to " thee by Jesus Christ, that I am Raphael the angel, whom God " has placed as a guard to this city:" and in a square, near the end of the bridge, is a gilt statue of the same guard, perched on the top of a high marble column.

The

The weather was intensely hot this day, so that I was glad to remain within doors at the inn. The distance from Granada to Cordova is thirty-one leagues. I here dismissed my guard (not *Angel Raphael*), and never after had occasion for any other.

Cordova gave birth to the two Senecas, and to Lucan the poet.

> Duosque Senecas, unicumque Lucanum
> Facunda loquitur Corduba.     Mart.

And during the time of the Moorish empire, Avicenna and Averroes were likewise born here.

The great square is large and regular, and is surrounded by porticos. The bishop's palace is situated on the side of the river, and his gardens are open to the public. The cathedral was built by Abderamo, king of the Moors, in the year 787, and still retains the name of Mesquita; it is an *unique* in its kind; it is very large, the roof is flat and low, without any tower, though the Spaniards have built one near it: there are four or five Arabic inscriptions over the doors. The roof is sustained by a very great number of columns, placed in such an irregular manner, that I spent half a day in endeavouring to form some kind of a plan so as to be able to count them, but without any satisfactory success; however, I am certain, that their number surpasses five hundred and ninety; and in the cloisters, without the church, are upwards of forty more: these columns are each of a single piece, some of marble, some of jasper, of granite, of porphyry, of alabaster, of *verde antico*, &c. their height from the base to the capital is ten feet, and their diameter one and a half; the capitals much resemble those of the columns in the Alhambra at Granada, and had formerly been gilt, as the remains of the gilding are still to be seen on many of them\*: in various places the pavement has been so much raised as to cover the bases, so that the columns appear to grow out of the soil, much in the manner of those of the Doge's palace in Venice. Some of those in this church are plain, others are fluted, with one third of the fluting filled up, and others are fluted spirally. Some descriptions reckon twenty-nine naves, others nineteen, but the whole is such a scene of confusion, as renders it very difficult to be described so as to give any tolerable idea of this church. In an Italian essay on architecture, printed at Rome in 1768, is a short description of it, at the end of which the author says, " The " Christians, in order to build a chapel in the middle of the " church, have taken away a great number of those pillars, " which has partly spoiled the singular beauty of that fo-" rest of columns." This author says it was a temple of Janus before the time of the Moors; which is very probable, by reason of some of the columns having Corinthian capitals. The square before this church is very beautiful; being planted with eighty large orange-trees: in the midst is a pond, full of tench, and on each side is a fountain which continually plays; these are environed with cypress and palm-trees.

\* In the plate of the Alhambra, the last column represents one of those which are in this church.

Cordova,

Cordova is the greatest market for horses in all Spain; it is here that the so justly celebrated and beautiful Andalusian horses are to be seen, which it is death to export: they are all long-tailed and entire, very few geldings being found in Spain. Mares are only kept for breeding, and for treading out the corn: these are allowed to be exported. One would imagine Adonis's horse to have been an Andalusian one, from Shakespeare's description,

>   Round-hooft, short-jointed, fetlocks shag and long,
>   Broad breast, full eyes, small head, and nostril wide,
>   High crest, short ears, strait legs, and passing strong,
>   Thin mane, thick tail, broad buttock, tender hide.

They are fed with wheat-straw, which is preferable to hay, by reason of its juicy delicacy: sometimes barley is given to them. The mules and horses I made use of in travelling, were never during the journey suffered to lie down in the stable, but were tied with their heads close to the manger, so that they could sleep only standing: the bells which are tied about their heads and necks are never taken off; they make an exceeding disagreeable noise, but I never could prevail on any of the drivers to quit them; they are, however, useful in apprising chaises mutually of each other's approach in narrow roads, where there is not always room for two carriages to pass.

This city is the most agreeable of any in Spain for a place of residence: here are about thirty noble families, who alternately spend

spend the evenings at each other's houses. The night after my arrival I was at El Conde de Gabia's *tertulia*, where I had the pleasure of becoming at once acquainted with all these families: they live with great splendor; I never saw such magnificent equipages in any other part of Spain: here are fourteen or fifteen coaches, chariots, or phaetons, which were lately made in London, and as many more which were procured from Paris. I had an opportunity of seeing all these drawn by four and six beautiful long-tailed prancing stone-horses, as it was at that time Whitsuntide fair; the footmen were all in gold and silver laced liveries. One of the four evenings I remained in Cordova was spent at the house of the Marchioness de Villaseca: we were first entertained with a concert, and afterwards with a ball; the English country-dances consisted of near thirty couple: the refreshments were first chocolate, and afterwards lemonade, ice-creams, cakes, and various sorts of wines and *liqueurs*. The saloon we danced in is very large, hung with crimson damask, and enriched with several of the St. Ildefonso looking-glasses; the ceiling is of white stucco, with gilt foliages: the whole of these elegant decorations are executed in the French taste. There was much more freedom among the company than I ever observed at any assembly in England, and none of that obstinate shyness and reserve, which are so disagreeably peculiar to the English nation *in general*. We parted between two and three in the morning, and the next evening the Conde de Gabia gave a like entertainment at his house, to the same company, which was repeated on the evening following at another nobleman's house.

I observed

I observed that a great part of the furniture of these houses was English, such as mahogany chairs and tables, Wilton carpets, &c. I saw likewise three English hunters, which are the property of a nobleman here.

On the second of June I left this city, charmed with the politeness and sociableness of the gentry who inhabit it, and returned to Ecija, on the same road I came.

I observed several fields where cotton was growing: this plant is sown in March and April, and had just begun to appear above ground; it grows to about a yard in height, its flowers are yellow, with small red spots; from the midst of these issue balls like chestnuts, and of the size of a common nut; they burst in a triangle in September, and show their seed wrapt up in the cotton. Fifty pounds weight of the seed produces no more than eight pounds of cotton.

I here discharged my servant Baptiste, giving him ten pounds to defray his expences on his return to Lisbon, and the next day I continued my journey towards Malaga. We dined at a venta, and passed the night in the village of Cazeriche, nestling among the straw, after having travelled six leagues among olive-trees and corn-fields, through a violent rain which lasted the whole day, accompanied with thunder and lightning.

June

June 4. Passing over a woody heath, we re-entered the kingdom of Granada, and met two large wolves, which ran away as soon as they saw the chaise; these were the only wolves we found in Spain, as these animals are seldom seen by day: shortly after the chaise overset when I was in it, the axle-tree was broken, which prevented our proceeding, so that I left the chaise on the road to the care of my servant, the calessciro went to an adjacent village to procure wherewith to repair the damage, and I rode on horseback alone to Antequera, which was two leagues off. This city is situated on an eminence, and possesses the ruins of a Moorish castle: it contains four parish churches, eleven convents of monks, eight of nuns, and several hospitals. I have a concise Spanish account of this city, which says, that it is dominated by Mercury and Mars, from whose influences it participates in love of letters and of arms; how justly I cannot pretend to say. Its district produces wheat, barley, rye, beans, kidney-beans, vetches, *garbanzos* (which are a kind of pease), lentils, oil, and wine; pears, apples, pomegranates, quinces, melons, water-melons, nuts, plums, cherries, apricots, figs, *brebas* (which are early figs, for they come twice a year in Spain); the vegetables are, sallads, coleworts, pepper, of that kind known in England by the name of red or Guinea pepper, garlick, parsnips, purslain, *berengenas* (which are a kind of pumpion), gourds, turnips, radishes, endive, cucumbers, and *tomates*; these last are a sort of apple of a scarlet colour, and of a very tart flavour; they grow likewise in the southern parts of

Italy

Italy and France, where they are called *marignani* and *pommes d'amour* \*; but no oranges or lemons are produced here, as the climate is too cold in winter.

The inn is kept by a Frenchman, and is a pretty good one. The chaise arrived the next day at noon : I set out immediately, and travelling five leagues over high, barren, and craggy mountains, arrived at a venta, where I remained all night.

June 6. We dined at another venta †, and in the evening arrived at Malaga, having travelled seven leagues this day, and crossed a small and shallow river at least a dozen times : the road is good, and is bordered with very large aloës, Indian figs, and pomegranate hedges, intermixed with shrubs, such as rosemary, sage, *geranium*, thyme, &c. In the morning we passed near the town of Arola, adjacent to which is a ruined Moorish castle on a hill, and in the evening we went by an aqueduct, which had formerly consisted of fifty-five low arches, but the last eleven are broken. I this day observed a very great number of the beautiful birds, which the Spaniards call *avelucos*: they are found in no other part of Europe, excepting in Granada and Andalusia, but

\* Lycopersicon. Solanum. Wolves-peach.
† Over the door of this venta is inscribed,
   Vamos entrando
   Vamos bebiendo
   Vamos pagando
   Vamos saliendo.

are to be met with in the East Indies, where they are called bee-eaters. In the second volume of Brookes's Natural History is the following account of these birds : " The bee-eater is of the "size of a black-bird, and has a black bill, thick at the base, "bending downwards, and near two inches long; the eyes are "of a fine red, and there is a black streak on each side of the "head, which begins at the corner of the mouth, and runs be-"yond the eyes : the base of the upper chap, and under the "chin, are covered with bright pale blue feathers; the chin is "yellow, but the upper part of the back of the head is of a "dusky yellow, as well as the back and wings, only these last "are shaded pretty strongly with green, the tips of the quill-"feathers are brown, the breast and belly green, and the under "part near the vent of a pale yellow mixed with green ; the "outermost feathers of the tail are variegated with green and "yellow, and the two middlemost feathers are half an inch "longer than the rest, and terminate in sharpish points of a "brown colour ; the legs are black, and extremely short, the "feet have three claws forwards, and one backwards; the "tongue is slender, and rough towards the end, where it is "jagged."

To this description I add, that I engaged a peasant to get one of these birds alive for me, as shooting them would have spoiled the plumage, accordingly he brought me a cock, hen, nest, and eggs ; I could not distinguish the cock from the hen, as their colours, shapes, and sizes were exactly alike ; that which I supposed

posed to be the hen, was, at the time the nest was taken, sitting on her eggs, which were six in number; her eyes were quite closed, she seemed in a stupefied, and almost lifeless state, and I was informed that she sits on her eggs without intermission till they are hatched, being, during the time of incubation, fed by the cock: the eggs are of the size of those of a black-bird, and are totally white: these birds build their nests in holes in the banks of rivers; the holes are horizontal, and penetrate a yard or more into the earth. They feed on bees, wasps, and the like insects: they fly in flocks of twelve or fourteen, and make a whistling kind of noise; when flying they balance themselves with their wings extended and almost motionless; at such times, when the sun shines, their plumage is very brilliant. An officer at Gibraltar was afterwards so kind as to present me with one of these birds stuffed, which I yet preserve. The Museum belonging to the Royal Society in London, likewise possesses one of them\*.

But to return to Malaga, I first paid my respects to John Marsh, esq. his majesty's consul, and then having delivered my introductory letters, took a view of the city, which is situated at the foot of a high mountain, and was built by the Phenicians, eight hundred years before the vulgar æra: it is well fortified. The port is rendered safe and commodious by a mole near half

---

\* In the second volume of Albin's History of Birds, is a coloured print of this bird. Merops Apiaster. Linn. Syst. Nat 182.

a mile in length. The cathedral is a modern building, of white ſtone, and one of the handſomeſt and neateſt in Spain. There are twelve or fourteen Engliſh merchants eſtabliſhed here with their families; they trade chiefly in wine and ſalt. The only good picture in this city is in the poſſeſſion of Timothy Power, eſq. it repreſents the Virgin Mary and Child, St. John and St. Anne, whole lengths, and the figures are ſomewhat leſs than the life. I eſteem it to be one of Raphael's beſt paintings. I had the honour of dining at the houſe of the marquis del Bado: the gueſts were all ſerved in plate, and ſeveral pages were in waiting with fly-flaps, to prevent thoſe troubleſome inſects from ſettling on the diſhes. Mr. Power was ſo obliging as to give me an invitation to ſpend a few days at his country-houſe; accordingly his beautiful lady, and another *ſeñora*, mounted their *burros*, or jack aſſes, attended by Mr. Power, the conſul, two other gentlemen, and myſelf, on horſeback, and rode four leagues to the village of Alhaurin, on a road over mountains impaſſable for carriages, through a very fertile country, beautified with the moſt romantic proſpects, and with hedges of aloës, holly, and briar. His houſe is furniſhed in the Engliſh taſte, and his garden produces gooſeberries, blackberries, currants, &c. from plants procured from England; and theſe were the only plants of the kind I met with in Spain. We remained here four days, and were entertained with great hoſpitality and politeneſs, which rendered thoſe days ſome of the moſt agreeable I had paſſed in that kingdom. Before we returned to Malaga, we made a little excurſion to Cartama, which is about a league and a half diſtant from

from Alhaurin: it is a small village, where, in the year 1750, a temple was discovered about thirty feet under ground, with the remains of a stair-case: a marble hand, which represents a left hand, two feet and a half long, holding a kind of trumpet, eighteen inches long; the veins on the back of the hand, and the creases of the knuckles, are accurately expressed; the whole weighs about fifty pounds: ten very large white marble statues, though without heads or arms; eleven inscriptions on marble; a few medals; and a column of a single piece of reddish marble, twenty-four feet in height, and six in diameter. The hand was sent to Madrid, where it is now in the king's palace: the remnants of the statues were stuck in the ground at the corners of the streets, where they yet serve as posts to keep carriages from the houses; the column was erected on a pedestal before a church, and a cross placed on it; and, in 1756, the excavation was ordered to be discontinued, and the entrance closed. The temple was a square of about forty yards, and contains two other columns similar to that above mentioned; these were suffered to remain where they lay. On a very high hill, near this village, are the ruins of a Moorish castle. I procured a plan of the temple, and a copy of the eleven inscriptions: they are now in the possession of the Society of Antiquaries in London.

On my return to Malaga, I discharged the chaise which had brought me from Madrid, as I could have no farther use for it, because the roads from Malaga to Gibraltar, whither I intended to go, are impracticable for wheel carriages, so that there are no other

other means of going to Gibraltar but by sea, or on horseback. I agreed with a Spanish officer, who subsists by letting out horses, that he should furnish me with two horses, one for my servant, and one to carry the baggage, himself accompanying me on horseback, in his uniform, armed with pistols and a sabre, and procure a man to lead the baggage-horse on foot. We were to travel to Gibraltar by way of Ronda, in four days, and to rest one day between. I was to maintain him and his man.

Accordingly I set out on the 19th of June, at four in the morning, chusing to go by way of Ronda, because I had a desire to see that city, though this road is considerably longer and worse than that by Munda, on whose plains Pompey was defeated by Cæsar, of which battle a copious account is given in the thirteenth volume of the Universal History, and copied in Mr. James's History of Gibraltar. The distance from Malaga to Gibraltar, by the way I went, is twenty-three leagues, or about ninety two miles. We dined at the venta where I had before been, at four leagues from Malaga, and in five hours we travelled two leagues farther, which brought us to Casabonela, a village situated on the top of a mountain, and commanding a fine prospect of the sea. The inn here consisted of a single room, which served us for a kitchen and bed-chamber, so that our valorous Don Fernando and his man, with myself, my servant, the host, hostess, three children, and some foot-travellers, all slept on the straw together, with our cloaths on, which was very convenient, for, in the morning, having shaken off the straw, and put on our hats, we were ready dressed.

June 20. At four this morning we remounted, and after riding, or rather walking our horses during five hours and a half, in which time we had advanced only two leagues, we arrived safe at the village of Burgo, having passed over many steep and dangerous precipices, the road sometimes being carried over the edges of mountains not a yard wide, where the least false step would have hurled us to inevitable destruction : in these places I chose to walk, driving my horse before me, not daring to hold the bridle, lest, if the horse fell, he should pull me after him, indeed the beasts appeared to be as sensible of their danger as we were, carefully selecting places between the loose stones to procure a firm footing ; it was admirable to observe how sure-footed the baggage-horse was, though loaded on each side with a trunk of two hundred weight, and on the top of all a basket with provisions, and kitchen utensils. These deserts are only inhabited by vultures, eagles, wolves, and goats, which last animals clamber up the steepest places, and leap and run on the edges of rocks in an astonishing manner. At Burgo is a ruined Moorish castle.

After our *siesta*, we in seven hours proceeded three leagues farther to Ronda, travelling on the same kind of road : the vallies between the mountains producing green oaks and *almecinas*, or lote-trees, intermixed with cork-trees. The green oak resembles the common oak in its size, wood, and acorns, but the leaves are different, being somewhat like those of holly ; they are firm and prickly ; the upper-side of a deep green, the under-

under-side whitish, rather downy, and do not fall off in winter; the wood is very hard, and is used for making pivots, or axles to pullies: the acorns are almost as sweet as chestnuts.

The cork-tree much resembles the green oak, and likewise produces acorns: its bark is thick, light, spungy, of a grey colour, splits of itself, and parts from the tree, if care be not taken to gather it, which is done by splitting the trunk in its whole length, in order to get the bark off the more easily; it is then steeped in water to soften it, dried at a fire, and loaded with large stones to flatten it: this is the cork that is sent all over the world, and which is used for making of bottle-corks, buoys for fishing-nets, &c.

In these parts, as well as in many others in Spain, are found the trees which produce the kermes; these trees are called in Spanish *carrasca*, or *coscoja*, the berry-bearing *ilex*. In the eighth volume of the History of Animated Nature, is the following account of the kermes: " it is produced in the excrescence
" of the *ilex*, and appears at first wrapt up in a membranaceous
" bladder of the size of a pea, smooth and shining, of a brownish
" red colour, and covered with a very fine ash-coloured powder:
" this bag teems with a number of reddish eggs, or insects,
" which being rubbed with the fingers pour out a crimson li-
" quor: it is only met with in warm countries in the months
" of May and June. In the month of April this insect becomes
" of the size and shape of a pea, and its eggs some time after
" burst

"burſt from the womb, and ſoon turning worms, run about the branches and leaves of the tree: theſe are the females, but the males are very diſtinct from them, and are a ſet of ſmall flies like gnats, with ſix feet, of which the four forward are ſhort, and the two backward long, divided into four joints, and armed with three crooked nails; there are two feelers on the head, a line and a half long, which are moveable, ſtreaked, and articulated: the tail at the back part of the body is half a line long, and forked; the whole body is covered with two tranſparent wings, and they leap about in the manner of fleas." They are gathered before ſun-riſe, by women who purpoſely let their nails grow long to pick them off the leaves. Languedoc and Provence likewiſe produce theſe trees and inſects. They are uſed in dying and in medicine *.

June 21ſt. I remained all this day at Ronda †: this city is built on the edge of a mountain, which on one ſide is as ſteep as a wall, and ſaid to be upwards of nine hundred feet in height, and without any parapet or rail: I did not venture to look down, but deſcended the mountain on the other ſide to obſerve this ſingular precipice from below. The eagles

> "——that wing the midway air,
> Shew ſcarce ſo groſs as beetles."

\* Coccus Ilicis. Linn. Syſt. Nat. 740.
† A view of this town is inſerted in one of the plates in this work.

The body of a woman who fell from it, burst by the concussion of the air before it reached the ground, so that her bowels came out. The city is small, but has the honour of being the seat of a *Maestranza*, as was before mentioned. All the inns here are kept by gypsies. A new bridge, which joins the old to the new town, which is called *el Mercadillo*, was at that time nearly finished: it is built over a chasm formed by the mountain, and is to consist of three arches one above the other: besides this, there is another bridge of a single arch over a different part of this tremendous gap, at the bottom of which runs a small river. In the afternoon I rode on horseback about a league off, with a Spanish gentleman to see his gardens, which were only remarkable for the goodness of the fruit they produced, especially of the cherries, which were some of the finest I ever tasted.

June 22. We set out soon after three this morning, in the dark, and after sitting near eleven hours on horseback, we arrived at Alguzin, without having in the space of five leagues seen a single house. After sun-rise the weather was so hot, that it was with the utmost difficulty I could keep myself awake on my horse: I rode with an umbrella, and placed a sheet of white paper between my hat and head, which somewhat protected me from the intense heat of the sun's rays, which fell almost perpendicularly. Walking was too violent an exercise at such a season, and our horses only went a foot-pace, in order to keep with the baggage horse. A league beyond Ronda is a broken aqueduct, of which thirty-seven arches are yet entire. During the four first hours of this day's journey, the road was very beautifully diversified, having the little river of Ronda to the right, and on both sides high mountains covered with vines, olive and cork trees, and green-oaks. At two leagues from Ronda I observed a torrent pouring into the river, from a large cavern in the side of an opposite mountain. After dining, or supping, as this meal served for both, on an *olla-podrida* of salt *bacallào*, which is like the fish called poor-jack, fried in oil, with peafe, garlick, and red pepper, I turned into my straw nest at eight in the evening, and slept comfortably till two the next morning.

June 23. I was on horseback the moment after I awaked, for I had not undressed myself, and my horse had passed the night in the same apartment with me. After travelling six leagues we arrived at San Roque, having descended a mountain, which we did soon after leaving Alguzin; the road is tolerably level and good. I this day also rode eleven hours without stopping: as the road admitted it, I amused myself in galloping about a mile before, then dismounted, and lay in the shade of some tree or other till the baggage came up. I shot a butcher-bird, of which I saw great numbers, which I also did of a kind of black martins, which measured near twenty inches with their wings extended: these birds fly like swallows in flocks, and at a great height. It was one in the afternoon when we arrived at San Roque. I immediately went to sleep for two hours, and afterwards waited on the governor to obtain leave to pass the Spanish lines:

lines. But he would on no account permit my horse to pass them, unless I consented to have it returned to San Roque the same evening, fearing that I might export it from Gibraltar; which is strictly prohibited.; accordingly, I was obliged to conform, and agreed with the landlord of the inn, who is an Italian, that he should keep my horse in his stable till my return. We then set out and proceeded to Gibraltar, which is only one league from San Roque, but we were two hours in performing it, as the road is a deep and heavy sand. The country is quite barren. We then passed the Spanish lines, and shortly after the English lines; entered the town, and put up at a very bad inn, where the beds were full of bugs, which were the first I had yet felt in Spain. The next day I changed my inn, and went to the King's arms, which is a very good one, and contains the assembly-room. All the inns here are kept by British subjects. I waited on the governor, General Boyd, and had the honour of dining at his excellency's house, in company with admiral Sir Peter Dennis, whose ship was then in the bay.

The town of Gibraltar, which has been in possession of the English since the year 1706, is situated at the foot of the west side of a mountain, or rock, called Calpe by the ancients, which stands by itself, in 36° 8′ latitude. The length of this mountain is about two miles and three quarters from the north end, which rising abruptly out of the small isthmus, joins it to the continent: the most southern part is called Europa Point.

Its

Its perpendicular height above the level of the sea is one thousand three hundred and sixty feet, but Colonel James says one thousand four hundred and three. The eastern side is almost inaccessible, though several officers assured me they had clambered up to the summit by that side. Many apes and monkies inhabit its caverns and precipices, and are frequently shot: it is thought that these animals are not produced in any other part of Europe. The birds called *solitary sparrows* are also found here.

In the first volume of Edwards's Natural History of Birds, is a coloured figure of the solitary sparrow. The fourth volume of that work is dedicated to GOD; and at the end of that extraordinary dedication is as extraordinary a preface. The book was printed at London so lately as the year 1751. Mr. Edwards has surpassed in this respect any author I know of. A Spanish book, entitled, *Sayings and Deeds of King Don Philip II.* printed in Madrid in 1748, is dedicated to " the " most sacred Empress of Heaven and Earth, Mary, Mother of " God, Lady of the Universe, and Queen of the Angels." And the Italian book, entitled, *Embriologia Sacra,* by F. E. Cangiamila, of Palermo, Doctor of Divinity and of Laws, is dedicated to all the Guardian Angels. This book (quarto, Milan 1751, three hundred and twenty pages), treats about the duty of priests and physicians, who are to secure the eternal salvation of children shut up in the womb, by baptising them by means of

a spunge,

a fpunge, or a fyringe, as is defcribed in the firft volume of Triftram Shandy. A large copper-plate decorates this ingenious work, in which is reprefented a *fœtus* of fourteen different fizes, from the age of feven days to that of four months and a half; and the motto is from Matth. xviii. v. 10. " Take heed that ye defpife not one of thefe little " ones."

In blowing up the rock in various places, many pieces of bones, teeth, &c. are daily found, incorporated with the ftone; fome of thefe pieces have been fent to England and depofited in the Britifh Mufeum, &c. and in the Philofophical Tranfactions for 1770, is a circumftantial account of them. In the weft fide of this mountain is the cave called St. Michael's, eleven hundred and ten feet above the horizon. I entered it by the light of feveral torches, about two hundred paces: there are many pillars of various fizes, from the thicknefs of a goofe-quill to two feet in diameter, formed by the droppings of water, which have petrified in falling; the water perpetually drips from the roof, and forms an infinite number of *ftalactitæ* of a whitifh colour, compofed of feveral coats or crufts, and which, as well as the pillars, continually increafe in bulk, and will probably, in procefs of time fill the whole cavern. At the end of this cave is a hole of about fix feet in diameter, of which the depth is uncertain, and I had no inclination to explore it: bats abound here. One evening I afcended to the fummit of the

rock

rock in an hour, by the path called the Devil's-Gap, on a flight of two hundred stone steps, and then after having walked some time, went up four hundred more, which brought me to the signal-house built on the highest part of the mountain. The weather was very clear, so that I enjoyed the prospect of the town, the bay, the straits, Mount Abila, or Ape's-hill, on the African shore, the city of Ceuta, and great part of the Barbary coast; the towns of St. Roque and Algeziras, and the snowy Alpuxarra mountains. At night an infinitely greater number of stars,

" The life-infusing suns of other worlds,"

may be discovered from hence by the naked eye than from below, because in this elevated situation the atmosphere is much more pure and thin. I descended another way, passing by the remains of the Moorish castle. I was informed that there were at that time seven regiments in Gibraltar, and that about six hundred men were always on guard at a time: the discipline observed here is very strict, and the officers always appear in their regimentals. There are three hundred and forty guns mounted on the fortifications, and there is room for a hundred more: those of the grand battery are of bronze, the rest of iron: they are all fired in succession on the anniversary of his majesty's birth; the performance takes half an hour. At sunrise, sun-set, and at nine in the evening, a gun is daily fired.

The town confifts chiefly of one ftreet, which is tolerably broad and well paved; the other ftreets are crooked, narrow, and dirty: it contains an Englifh church, a Roman-Catholic one for the Spaniards and Portuguefe, who inhabit this town to the number of about three hundred, and are moftly fhopkeepers, and for about feven hundred Genoefe, chiefly mariners; and a fynagogue for the Jews, who amount nearly to the number of fix hundred: I conjecture that of the Englifh to be about two thoufand, exclufive of the military: befides thefe, there are a few hundred Moors who continually pafs and repafs to and from the Barbary coaft, trafficking in cattle, fowls, fifh, fruits, and other provifions, as nothing is to be had from Spain, which neither Jews nor Moors are ever fuffered to enter. The town has three gates; out of one of them I obferved fome officers playing at *golf* on the fands, in the fame manner as I had feen that game played on the Links, (a heath near Edinburgh,) Leith, &c.

There is a fmall theatre, where I had the pleafure of feeing *High Life Below Stairs*, and *Mifs in her Teens* extremely well performed: the actors were military gentlemen, who entertain themfelves weekly in this manner: the actreffes are fo by profeffion.

All European coins are current here, but confiderably under the value; a guinea paffes for no more than nineteen fhillings and fix pence; five Spanifh reals are only three here; a pefo duro,

which

which is here called a *cob*, is a dollar and a half of Gibraltar currency.

No person is allowed to go out of the English territory, either by land or sea, without a pass from the governor, who grants the inhabitants one annually. No vessels, nor even boats, coming from Gibraltar are suffered to land their people in any of the Spanish ports, till after they have performed a quarantine of three or four days. Here are taverns, coffee-houses, billiard-tables, shops, &c. as in England. The governor's garden is open to the public, and is much resorted to on Sunday evenings.

Since my return to England I obtained permission from the Board of Ordnance to see the model of Gibraltar, which is kept in the Tower; it is five feet in length, and is extremely accurate in regard to the dimensions of the rock, though many new fortifications have been added to Gibraltar since this model was made, which was thirty years ago.

I had a great inclination to make an excursion to Fez; accordingly I procured the necessary passes and letters, and agreed with the master of a small vessel that he should come to fetch me at Ceuta, from whence I intended to be landed on the shore of the river of Tetuan. I bought several pounds of green-tea, loaves of sugar, and silk handkerchiefs, to present to the Moorish governors, and hired a Moor who spoke English and Spanish extremely well, to accompany me. I set out on the 5th

5th of July, on a mule, and after riding four leagues along the shore, arrived at the village of Algeciras, which the English sailors call Old Gib. I here procured a bill of health, and the next morning, at four, embarked in the Spanish packet, which sails twice a week from hence to Ceuta, and crossing the Straits in seven hours, we landed at that city: the distance is about seven leagues. I immediately waited on the governor, who was so obliging as to order an officer to accompany me about the town, and in the evening I saw the Italian opera of *la Buona Figluola*, acted by a company of strolling players. Probably if I had travelled from Ceuta to Grand-Cairo, or to the Cape of Good-Hope, by land, I should not have seen another opera. This city belongs to the Spaniards; it is situated on the north side of a peninsula, of about three miles in length, and has no communication with the Barbary dominions, so that it can only be entered from the sea. The garrison consists of four regiments, or about three thousand men; and two hundred very fine and large bronze guns are planted on the fortifications. It is the place of exile as well for state criminals as for malefactors: these last are chained by the leg, and made to work. I observed a man with a small brass ladder fastened to the loop of his hat, in the manner of a cockade; I was informed he was the executioner. These men are not allowed to wear a cloak in any part of Spain. The only inn in this place, which is kept by an Italian, is insufferably bad; however, I only staid there one night, as the next day at noon, the vessel which I had hired at Gibraltar being arrived, I immediately embarked, and at seven in the evening we anchored in

the

the bay of Tetuan, which is seven leagues from Ceuta: the surf was so high that I could not land, and the wind became so violent, that at four the next morning we were obliged to weigh anchor and return to Gibraltar, where we landed at eleven, having in that time sailed thirteen leagues. In the evening of the same day the wind abated, so that I re-embarked at eight on board the same vessel, and at ten the next morning we landed on the Tetuan shore. We caught two large dog-fish, and gathered a great quantity of muscles from off the rocks.

I walked to the custom-house, or *marteen*, which is about two miles inland. A small village is built near it, and at that time a fair was held for mules, cattle, sheep, and fruit. Here I saw a great number of storks. Near this place is a small square fort with four guns; there is no other entrance but at the window, by means of a rope-ladder, which is afterwards drawn up. The Moors I saw here were in general tall handsome men, with long beards; their arms and legs are bare, they wear turbants on their heads, and yellow flippers on their feet. There is a dock here, in which were five small gallies on the stocks. Many of the men spoke English extremely well: some of them were playing at draughts. I did not see one Moorish woman, and probably should not if I had remained there till this time. I waited here four hours, at the end of which, the guide, who was to have travelled with me, returned from Tetuan whither I had sent him, which city is about four miles off, and is situated on the slope of a hill, as I could distinctly perceive from whence we were.

were. I knew that I could not enter into Tetuan, becaufe a Genoefe failor having a few months before accidentally fhot a Moorifh woman, the emperor had turned all the Chriftians out of that city, even the confuls, and would fuffer no ftrangers but Jews to enter it.

But to my very great forrow and difappointment, the guide informed me, that there was a new order fent to the governor, to fuffer no Chriftian, or European, to travel inland to any place whatfoever: this information at once blafted all my hopes of feeing the manners and cuftoms of thefe people, which was the more vexatious, as they totally differ from thofe of the Europeans, and that this was the only opportunity I ever had of travelling among them. All my fine fchemes of riding on camels, feeing the court of the emperor of Morocco, affociating with the Jewifh ladies, &c. were diffolved and vanifhed. However, as there was no poffibility of proceeding, I was obliged to fubmit patiently. I difmiffed my guide, and returned to the fhore. The veffel I came in remained to take in her loading, and very fortunately for me, there was another veffel ready to fail. Accordingly, twenty-two mules, twelve oxen, twelve thick-tailed fheep, and myfelf embarked in it at two in the afternoon, and at three the next morning we arrived again at Gibraltar; fo that in five days I made as many voyages, in three different veffels, in all fifty-fix leagues, employed my time and money in a fruitlefs and difagreeable manner; and after all, have only the idle fatisfaction of having barely fet my feet upon

the

the African continent. Several of the Moors whom I saw were on horseback; they ride with short stirrups, and their saddles are very high before and behind. Their money consists of *blanquillos*, which are small pieces of silver, stamped with Arabic characters, and of round bits of copper, with any impression: the Spanish coins are likewise current in Barbary *.

On the 16th of July I left Gibraltar, having hired a mule for my servant, another for my baggage, and a man to lead it on

---

* In 1771, was published a work, in two quarto volumes, entitled, "The History of the Straits of Gibraltar, including those ports of Spain and Barbary that lie contiguous thereto," by lieutenant-colonel Thomas James. This work contains the following eighteen plates, which are all very accurate and well engraven.

In the First Volume.

Chart of the Straits,            Plan of Cadiz.
Plan of Tangier,                 Chart of the Bay of Cadiz.

In the Second Volume.

Plan of the peninsula of Ceuta,  Plan of the parade,
Plan of part of a house in Tetuan, Two plates with the plan, elevation, and section of a fountain.
Plan of the north part of Gibraltar,
Three views of Gibraltar,        A small plan of a vault,
General plan of the peninsula of  And three Arabic inscriptions.
  Gibraltar,

The three views of Gibraltar were copied from four large plates, published in 1750, by J. Mace.

To this work I refer for a more particular account of Gibraltar; the author resided in that garrison from 1749 to 1755. His account of the currents is very curious, as well as that of Tetuan. Mentioning the Spanish priests in Gibraltar, he says, "Generally speaking, but one priest resides here at "a time; sometimes he has a visiting brother. They live very well, and "will drink freely, and enjoy the fair sex." Which customs I believe are followed by other ecclesiastics besides those of Spain.

foot;

foot, to go to Cadiz, in three days (the diftance is eighteen leagues, or about feventy-two miles), myfelf riding my own horfe, which had been twenty-three days in the ftable at San Roque. We did not fet out till noon, fo that we only travelled three leagues that day, to the village de los Barrios, where there is no inn nor venta, but I prevailed on an old fruit-woman to let me pafs the night on a large cheft in her fhop, having firft placed fome ftraw on it, and fupped on *gaf-pacho*. This is an excellent kind of *foupe-maigre*, than which nothing can be more cooling or refrefhing during the violent heats: it is made by putting a fufficient quantity of oil, vinegar, falt, and pepper, into a quart of cold water, and adding to it crufts of bread, garlick and onions fhred fmall. The bread all over Spain almoft rivals fnow in whitenefs, and is very delicious. Our hoftefs fupplied us with plenty of fruit, and then obligingly fmoked a *fegar* with me. The beafts remained all night in the yard.

July 17. At four this morning we proceeded on our journey, and after having travelled five leagues in near eight hours, on a mountainous road, through forefts of cork-trees, we arrived at a few huts of mud, which are dignified with the name of the village of Taivilla. After our *fiefta* we went to Vegel, which is three leagues off, traverfing a circular plain of about a league in diameter, fwarming with locufts and grafshoppers, and leaving a fmall lake, called La Jarda, which we faw, to the right. We paffed over a ftrong ftone bridge of four arches, one of which

which is very large, and immediately put up at the miserable venta at the foot of the mountain on which the town of Vegel is built. I observed very numerous herds of cattle grazing in the pasture lands.

July 18.

" Scarce had the sun dry'd up the dew of morn,"
when we again set out, and traversing a heath, and some olive-grounds, after three leagues journey, we arrived at the town of Chiclana : it is pretty large, and consists chiefly of houses built by the merchants of Cadiz for their summer retirement: these houses are plaistered and white-washed, the doors and shutters are painted green, and the roofs are flat. The inn where we dined is a very good one. In the afternoon we proceeded two leagues farther, on a very fine strait and level road, broad enough for four carriages abreast, having a forest of pine-trees on one side, and salt-marshes on the other. We passed over a strong stone bridge of five small arches, called *el Puente de Suazo*, with a fort at the end, then entered into the isle of Leon, and shortly after into the town of the same name, though it is usually termed La Ysla. This is a large new-built town, much resembling Chiclana; and the inn, which is kept by Italians, is an excellent one. It is but two leagues distant from Cadiz, so that it is much resorted to by the inhabitants of that city on parties of pleasure. I returned here four times, and shall afterwards give some farther account of this town.

July 19. At five in the morning I set out, and at seven arrived at Cadiz, travelling on a very fine road. I put up at an Irish inn, kept by one Latty, and met with very civil usage during the whole time of my stay. As his majesty's conful was in England, I waited on Mr. Dalrymple, the vice-conful, who was so kind as to accompany me to the governor's *el Conde de Gerena*. I afterwards delivered my introductory letters, and in the evening attended some ladies first to the Spanish theatre, and after the performance was ended, to the French theatre, which then opened. The Spanish one consists of three rows of boxes, nineteen in each row: these are all let to different families, so that strangers go into the pit, where the price of admittance is about a shilling, and from thence they can go from box to box to visit their acquaintances. A tragedy, translated from the French, called *Zayde*, was acted for the first time. The scenes were not changed during the whole piece: the actors were far from being excellent, so that my chief entertainment there was derived from the fandangos and tonadillas which were danced and sung between the acts. The French theatre is extremely grand, large, handsome, and well illuminated, and the actors, singers, dancers, and musicians, were all capital performers: I esteem it to be the most magnificent, and the best furnished with actors of any French theatre out of France. I had before seen those of the Hague, Amsterdam, Bruffels, Berlin, Dresden, and Vienna, all which are surpassed by this of Cadiz. The price of a pit ticket is about two shillings and three pence.

Besides

Besides these two, there is another theatre for the performance of Italian operas : it consists of four rows of boxes, sixteen in each row. The price of a ticket for the pit is the same as at the French theatre. I saw the comic opera of *la Locanda* represented here.

After these diversions end, which is usually about half past eleven, it is customary to walk in the *alameda*, or mall, till midnight. Here I saw

"—— Donne e Donzelle,
D' ogni età, d'ogni sorte, e brutte e belle."
Ariosto, Cant. xvii. v. 33.

Among the rest I observed several ladies who had fixed glow-worms by threads to their hair, which had a luminous and pleasing effect. In the book *de las Noticias Americanas*, published in 1772, by Don Antonio de Ulloa, page 143, I find that the Peruvian ladies likewise ornament their heads, necks, and arms, with strings of shining flies, the splendor of which gives them the appearance of coronets, necklaces, and bracelets of natural lights. This *alameda* is planted with double rows of white elms; seats of stone are fixed on each side : it is parted from the coach-road by iron rails, and commands a fine view of the ocean. It is as much resorted to by ladies of easy virtue as our St. James's Park, and is the only place in Spain where I found such barefaced licentiousness and libertinism. Masquerades are permitted during the carnival.

July 20. I spent this day in viewing the city: it is very small, and is situated on the extremity, or neck of a sandy island, or rather peninsula, joined to the continent by the before-mentioned bridge de Suazo. It is about sixteen miles long, and nine miles in the broadest part. The harbour is very capacious, being no less than nine miles in diameter, and the city is the most commercial in Spain, the first marine department, and the center of all the traffic to the West Indies. The author of *le Voyageur François*, in the sixteenth volume, gives a just and concise account of this trade, of which an extract is here inserted. " Cadiz is the place where the English, French, Dutch,
" and Italian merchants send their goods to be exported to
" America in Spanish vessels, which are divided into three
" classes; the fleet *(flota)*, the register ships, and the galleons.
" The *flota* consists of three men of war, and fourteen or fifteen
" merchant ships, whose burthen is from four hundred to a
" thousand tons. Those vessels are loaden with the best European
" productions; silks, stuffs, linen, velvet, ribbons, laces,
" glass, looking-glasses, paper, hard-ware, watches, clocks,
" shoes, stockings, books, prints, pictures, iron utensils,
" wine, fruit, &c. so that every nation is interested in the
" lading. Spain hardly contributes any thing but wine,
" which with the freight, brokerage, and taxes to the king,
" are all the advantage she derives from this commerce. The
" fleet sails from Cadiz to la Vera Cruz: the vessels which compose
" it are not allowed to part company, nor to put in, nor
" break bulk any where on the voyage. It takes in return.
" gold,

"gold, silver, jewels, cochineal, indigo, tobacco, sugar, cocoa, &c.

"The regifter fhips are equipped by, and fail for account of fome private merchants of Seville and Cadiz. When they think that the Americans are in want of certain goods, they prefent a petition to the council of the Indies, and defire leave to fend each of them a veffel of three hundred tons, for which leave they pay a certain fum; and, befides, are obliged to make confiderable prefents to different officers; and, though they only obtain leave to fend veffels of three hundred tons, there, neverthelefs, hardly ever fails any but fuch as are at leaft of double that burthen.

"The galleon fleet is compofed of eight fhips of the line, chiefly deftined to furnifh Peru with warlike ftores, but they are alfo filled with various merchandize for account of private perfons. Twelve other veffels fail under their convoy. This fleet may only trade on the coafts of the South Sea, and the other is limited to Mexico."

The houfes in Cadiz are very high, and the city is faid to contain eighty thoufand inhabitants.

In the evening I went to the Royal Obfervatory, which is well fupplied with telefcopes, microfcopes, air-pumps, electrical machines, and all kinds of mathematical inftruments, chiefly

chiefly made in London by Mr. Dollond and Mr. Bird. I had a small telescope with me, which I had bought of the first mentioned artist for thirty-five shillings, by the assistance of which, the astronomers observed distinctly the immersion of one of the satellites of Jupiter. I was here informed that the precise latitude of Cadiz is 36° 31′ 20″..

July 21: In the cathedral I saw a very good picture of St. Sebastian and an angel, by Murillo, whole length, and as large as the life; the back-ground is turned very black. I then went to the convent of Capuchin friars; over the great altar, in the church, is a picture twenty feet in height, and fourteen in breadth, painted by the same Murillo: it represents the espousals of St. Catherine. The figures are the Virgin Mary, the Child, St. Catherine, and several angels, all whole lengths, and as large as the life. This was the painter's last work, as he fell from the scaffold which was erected before it, broke his leg, and shortly after died. In the Sacristy are two other pictures by this artist, one of which represents the Assumption of the Virgin, which is a single figure, w. l. n. f. and the other, a half-length of Christ, bound and crowned with thorns. I afterwards went to the house of *el Marquès de Pedroso*, where I saw another picture painted by Murillo, and justly esteemed to be his best piece: it represents the child Jesus at about the age of five years, standing on a stone, on its left hand is Mary sitting, and on its right Joseph, who is represented as if going to kneel; they hold both the child's hands, each in their right hand: the Virgin's face

face is almoſt in profile; ſhe looks towards the child, and Joſeph towards the ſpectator; in his left hand he holds a branch of white lilies: the upper part of the picture repreſents *Dios y el Eſpiritu Santo*, under the ſhapes of an old man and a dove. I eſteem this to be the beſt picture I ever ſaw painted by a Spaniard. I could not learn that there were any other good paintings in Cadiz.

I purpoſely omit the ancient, true or fabulous, hiſtory of this city, and of the Egyptian Hercules, who is ſaid to have ſeparated the mountains Calpe and Abyla; the firſt of which is the rock of Gibraltar, and the other Ape's-hill in Barbary, by which means he opened a communication of the ocean with the Mediterranean; he then erected two pillars, as he thought, at the limits of the world; to which alludes

" —— a Gadibus uſque.
Ad Auroram & Gangen."

On them was engraven this well known inſcription: *Non plus ultra*. Charles V. eraſed the *non*, and preſerved the *plus ultra* for his own motto. I think it ſufficient to mention that Cadiz is the Gades of the ancients; it was firſt inhabited by the Phœnicians, then by the Carthaginians, and afterwards by the Romans, during which time I find it recorded in an old French book, " That their great riches had introduced ſuch luxury, " that the girls of Gades were ſought after in all public rejoic- " ings, as well for their ſkill in playing on divers inſtruments
" of.

"of music, *que pour leur humeur, qui avoit quelque chose de plus que de l'enjouement.*" This same book farther says, that "neither women nor hogs were permitted to enter into the temple which was dedicated to Hercules."

Dr. Veryard, who was here in 1685, says in page 278, of his Travels, which were published in 1701 : "In this temple was an altar dedicated to Poverty, and another to Arts and Sciences, intimating, that poverty was the mother of arts; though, by a strange change, science is now become the nurse of poverty."

The Reverend Mr. Clarke says, that " in one convent in this city, there is a *sarcophagus* with curious marble basso-relievos; it is now a cistern, and the good fathers have stuck two brass cocks into the bellies of two water-nymphs, who are henceforward condemned to a perpetual diabetes." I was ignorant of this elegant remark at the time I was in Cadiz, so that I saw neither the nymphs nor the cocks.

Father Labat, who was here in 1705, fills two hundred pages of his work with an account of Cadiz, part of which contains extracts from a Spanish history of that city, published in 1610, by a prebend of the *holy* church of Cadiz. This reverend writer assures us, that this city is the Tarsis whither Solomon and his friend king Hiram sent their ships, and that in the mines " *se hallaran en el coraçon de la piedra, granos de oro, a manera*
" de

"*de peçones de pechos de mugeres;*" i. e. " there were found in the heart of the ſtone, grains of gold, like the nipples of womens breaſts."

All the ſtreets in Cadiz are narrow, crooked, badly paved, and filthy. In 1722 a new church was begun, which is intended to be the cathedral: the building was afterwards diſcontinued, but is now reſumed, and, according to contract, is to be roofed within five years: it will be very magnificent, all that is hitherto finiſhed is of white marble, with very large fluted columns of the Corinthian order. Underneath are very ſpacious vaults for ſepulchres. According to a little book printed in Cadiz in 1770, there had already been ſpent in this building fourteen millions five hundred and eighty-ſix thouſand reals of vellon, about one hundred and ſixty-two thouſand pounds; and it will require as much again to complete it. Of theſe fourteen millions, about four were legacies and gifts, and the other ten were the produce of one-fourth per cent. on the commerce of Cadiz.

There are about thirty Engliſh merchants reſiding here, and a great number of French, Italians, Germans, Dutch, &c. but they aſſociate but little with the Spaniards; and in none of the Spaniſh houſes where I ſpent my evenings during near a month that I remained here, did I ever ſee any Engliſhman.

On Sunday the 25th of July, I crossed the bay, which is nine miles broad, in a boat, and after sailing an hour, I landed at the town of Port St. Mary, and had the satisfaction I had so long desired, of seeing a bull-fight, of which spectacle I had formed very erroneous ideas. As there has been no modern account of it published in the English language, excepting by Mr. Clarke and Mr. Baretti, and those accounts differ greatly from what I saw both in Port St. Mary and in Cadiz, I shall endeavour to describe them exactly as they were exhibited. Mr. Clarke had an opportunity of seeing a *fiesta de toros*, which I never had, this signifies *bull-feast*, and is only celebrated on extraordinary occasions, such as a coronation, the birth of an heir to the crown, the marriages of the royal family, &c. Those which I saw are termed *regocijos de toros*, *bull-rejoicings*. In Port St. Mary there are annually ten, in Cadiz twelve, in Seville four, in Granada four, and in Madrid and Aranjuez each six, on the Sundays of the months of June, July, and August, because the bulls will not fight except during the hot season.

The amphitheatre of Port St. Mary, as well as that of Cadiz, is entirely built of wood, and of no better architecture than the scaffoldings at Tyburn. Their form and dimensions are like those which have been before described [*]. At four in the afternoon I secured one of the best places, paying fifteen reals, or

---

[*] Usually about two hundred feet in diameter. See p. 157, 188, and 235 of this work.

three shillings and four pence. Those on the side which is exposed to the sun, are only ten reals, and the lowest places are six pence each. The amphitheatre was soon filled, the boxes with ladies and gentlemen full dressed, and the benches underneath with the mob: the *coup d'oeil* was very pleasing, especially by reason of its novelty. If women acted consistently, it were to be wondered at how those who would either faint, or feign to faint at the sight of a frog, a spider, &c. can delight in spectacles so barbarous as these are, where they are certain of seeing a number of bulls expire in agonies, horses with their bellies ripped open, men tossed on the beasts horns, or trampled to death, and every species of cruelty exhibited; but as they do not act consistently, the wonder ceases: the greater the barbarity, and the more the bloodshed, the greater enjoyment they testify, clapping their hands, waving their handkerchiefs, and hallooing, the more to enrage the bull. I have seen some women throw handfuls of nuts into the area of the combat, in hopes of causing the men who fight the bull on foot to fall over them. But as no general rule is without its exceptions, I own with pleasure, that I am acquainted with many Spanish ladies who never were present at a bull-fight, neither did they intend ever to see one \*. The governor of the city having seated himself in his box, the men who were to fight the bulls made him their obeisance; the area was then

---

\* The Reverend Mr. Clarke says, that he saw " ladies feasting with
" these bloody scenes those eyes which were intended only to be exercised
" in softer cruelties."

cleared of the mob, by a company of foldiers, who placed themfelves juft within the rails, which are breaft high. Ten bulls, which is the fixed number, were to be killed. Three men on horfeback were to encounter the bull; thefe are called *picadores*, jockeys: befides thefe, were four men who were to fight on foot, thefe they term *vanderilleros*, flag-bearers, and three *matadores*, flayers. Thefe are all butchers, cattle-drivers, &c. trained up from their youth to, and who gain their livelihood by this perilous profeffion: the firft are paid between three and four pounds each, every day on which they fight; the fecond have half that fum; but the laft, by being moft expofed to danger, and more dexterity being required of them, are allowed ten or twelve pounds each. Seventy or eighty horfes are kept in readinefs in an adjacent ftable: each of thefe beafts is of the value of about five or fix pounds; as they are often killed, and almoft always maimed, thefe anfwer the purpofe fufficiently. The faddles have a high peak before and behind, without which it would be impoffible to fit on the horfes, which are with great difficulty made to face the bull; fometimes they tremble with terror, rear up, kick, and are ungovernable: they are then obliged to have a handkerchief tied over their eyes, efpecially thofe which have been wounded in fome former combat. Their riders wear a kind of breeches and boots made of very thick buff leather, more impenetrable than even the *bottes fortes* of the French poftillions, but fupple; thefe are to prevent the bull's horns from goring the man fo eafily as they might otherwife do; ftrong fpurs are faftened to their heels. They are

dreffed

dressed in a waistcoat and short cloak, a broad brimmed hat on their heads, tied by a ribbon under their chins: their left hand manages the reins, and in their right they have a lance as thick as the wrist, and ten feet long, armed with a broad iron blade of a foot in length, but which is, by a thong twisted round it, prevented from entering more than a hand's-breadth into the bull's body. The foot-men wear light jackets and a long cloak; they have each a small dart in their hands, with a barbed point; the dart is ornamented with cut paper, like fly-traps: there are baskets full of these darts behind the balustrades, as the men frequently use half a dozen a piece to each bull, which, when dead, is dragged away with all the darts sticking in its body. The *matadores* are habited in the same manner as the last mentioned, and likewise amuse themselves by striking darts into the bulls. Their particular office will be explained hereafter.

Every thing being ready, the bulls remained to be driven across the area from the stables where they were, to a smaller stable behind the amphitheatre, where each was to be kept apart. The first stable was not far from the amphitheatre, and a wall of boards six feet high was put up the whole way the bulls were to pass. At a quarter past four the ten bulls were let into the area, in order to be put into the stables at the opposite door; a man on foot led a tame ox, which had been bred with the bulls, before, to decoy them into these: they followed the ox very quietly; but they do not always do so. The three horsemen placed themselves at some distance, one on each side of, and the other opposite to the door at which the bull was to enter: a trumpet was then sounded as a signal to let a bull in, and the man who opened the door got behind it immediately.

During this last quarter of an hour the bulls had been teased by pricking them in the backs: this is done by persons placed on the ceiling of the stables, which was low, and consisted only of a plank laid here and there, and between those planks was space enough to use any instrument for that purpose. The bulls were distinguished by a small knot of ribbon fixed to their shoulders, the different colours of which shew where they were bred, which is known by the advertisements.

The bull made at the first horseman, who received it on the point of the spear, held in the middle tight to his side, and passing under his arm-pit, which making a wide gash in the bull's shoulder, occasioned it to draw back, the blood running in torrents: the force with which the bull ran at the man was so great, that the shock had nearly overset him and his horse. It was then another man's turn to wound the bull, as only one is to cope with it at a time. They are never allowed to attack the bull, but must wait the animal's approach. The bull trotted into the middle of the area, and stared about, frighted by the clapping and hallooing of the multitude. The man on horseback always facing the beast, and turning when it turned: it then ran at the horse, and got another wound in the breast, and a third.

a third from the next horseman it attacked. It was now become mad with pain, the blood issuing from its mouth in streams, and faintness made it stagger, its eyes " flashed fury," it pawed up the ground, and lashed its sides with its tail; its breath was impetuously discharged like smoke from its nostrils; so that its head appeared as if in a mist. A trumpet then sounded, which was the signal for the horsemen to retire; and the men on foot began their attack, sticking barbed darts into every part of its body; the torture they inflicted made the bull leap from the ground, and run furiously at one of the men, who jumped aside; the bull then turned to another man, who had just stuck a dart into its back: this man took to his heels, and leaped over the rails, where he was safe: in this manner all the men continued tormenting the bull, who could hardly stand through loss of blood. The trumpet then sounded again, upon which the *matador* appeared, with a cloak extended on a short stick in his left hand, and in his right a two-edged sword, the blade of which was flat, four inches broad, and a yard long; he stood still, and at the moment the bull in the agonies of despair and death, made at him, he plunged the sword into the spine behind the beast's horns, which instantly made it drop down dead. If the *matador* misses his aim, and cannot defend himself with the cloak, he loses his life, as the bull exerts all its remaining strength with an almost inconceivable fury[*]. The

---

[*] When the *matador* succeeds in killing the bull by a single thrust, the populace throw money to him: I saw a Spanish nobleman fling a gold piece

dead bull was immediately dragged out of the area by three horses on a full gallop, whose traces were fastened to its horns. A quarter of an hour was elapsed, which is the time allowed for the murder of each bull, five minutes to the horsemen, five to the footmen, and five to the slayer.

Another bull was then let in: this was the wildest and most furious of any I ever saw. The horseman missed his aim, and the bull thrust its horns into the horse's belly, making the bowels hang out: the horse became ungovernable, so that the man was obliged to dismount and abandon it to the bull, who pursued it round the area, till at last the horse fell, and expired. Four other horses were successively killed by this bull, which, till then, had only received slight wounds, though one of the horses had kicked its jaw to pieces. One of the horsemen broke his spear in the bull's neck, and horse and rider fell to the ground; the rider broke his leg, and was carried off. The footmen then fell to work again, and afterwards the *matador* put an end to the life of this valiant animal, whose strength and courage were unavailing to save it. The third bull killed two horses, goring them under the belly, so that the intestines hung trailing on the ground. The seventh bull likewise killed two horses. In this manner were ten bulls massacred, and the whole concluded in two hours and a half. The bulls flesh was imme-

piece of three hundred reals, three pounds six shillings and eight pence, into the area for him, on one of these occasions.

diately

diately fold to the populace at ten quartos per pound, which is about three pence.

When the laſt bull had been ſufficiently wounded by the horſe‑men, the mob were allowed to enter the area; they attacked the bull on all ſides, and killed it with their knives and daggers. The bull ſometimes toſſes ſome of theſe fellows over its head.

The Spaniſh bulls are ſhaped like Engliſh oxen; their horns are very long, and they never bellow, or make the leaſt noiſe when they fight.

Dr. Goldſmith's remark is partly juſt; he ſays, " Thoſe wild " bulls, which the Spaniards pride themſelves ſo much in com‑ " bating, are very mean deſpicable little animals, and ſome‑ " what ſhaped like our cows, with nothing of that peculiar " ſternneſs of aſpect for which our bulls are remarkable." They are however, formidable enough.

The foot-combatants are not expoſed to much danger; their ſecurity depends upon their cloaks, which they fling on the bull's head when purſued by it, and by that means evade the animal, which always ſhuts its eyes before it puſhes. Much of their ſafety is likewiſe owing to their number; becauſe, when the bull runs at one man, another attacks it behind, and makes it turn. Some of theſe fellows will wait the bull's coming, and then purpoſely fall flat down, when the beaſt runs over them; and

and spends its fury in the air. Some cast their hats on the ground, which diverts the bull from the pursuit. Some bulls will not fight at all: but of those which do, each has its peculiar manner. I afterwards saw several of the former: the populace cried out, " *los perros, los perros,*" " the dogs, the dogs;" upon which three bull-dogs were let loose, and in a moment seized the bull by the nostrils, with a fierceness equal, if not superior to that of the English dogs; they pinned it to the ground, and then the *matador* killed it, by striking a small dagger into the spine behind the horns; the dogs could not be forced to quit their hold, even though the bull was dead, till their masters had almost strangled them by twisting ropes round their necks. These dogs are of the breed of those which the Spaniards carried with them when they conquered America, and by means of which they so barbarously caused the natives to be torn to pieces.

The bulls skins are generally pierced with so many holes, or wounds, that they might be compared to sieves. Sometimes a bull leaps over the rails among the people; but this unwelcome visitor is soon killed, being entangled between the benches. The horsemen always endeavour to place themselves fronting the bull, rather towards its left side, when they can, the better direct the lance which they have in their right hand. The next day being a festival, I saw another bull-fight, which was performed in the same manner, but the ten bulls were not so quiet when they crossed the amphitheatre before the combat began:

irritated

irritated by the noise of the multitude, they wreaked their vengeance on the man who led the tame ox: they tossed him on their horns from one to another for several minutes: the fellow however escaped with life, but terribly wounded. Nine of the bulls went at last into the stable, but the tenth attacking the horsemen, was dispatched in the usual way by all the combatants successively. The bulls sometimes halt, and smell at the blood which flows on the ground; and often when they have advanced half way in their career, they stop short, and survey the man on horseback calmly, whereupon they seem to collect courage, and then their fury redoubles. Sometimes the horse and the bull are both seen standing on their hind legs, leaning against each other, the cavalier's spear being in the bull's neck; but as this animal is the heaviest of the two, its weight always preponderates, so that the horse has no means of escaping but by flight, and the bull is so swift in pursuing, that it will follow a horse on full gallop three or four times round the area without losing ground, and with its horns touching the horse's buttocks. I observed that almost all the male spectators smoked *segars* during the whole time; they carried flints, steels, and a kind of tinder, called *yesca*, which consists of white filaments of a certain plant, to light their tobacco with *.

* Many Spaniards smoke tobacco shred fine and wrapt up in a small piece of paper, which they light: this method of smoking they call "*chupar tabaco en papel.*"

I afterwards faw a bull-fight in Cadiz. The advertifement, which was put into my hands concerning, it runs thus:

" Twelfth and laft *Corrido* (Courfe) this year.

" Punctual account of the bulls which are to be courfed in the " *plaza* (amphitheatre), of the very noble and loyal city of Cadiz, " on Sunday the 29th of Auguft, 1773, in the afternoon.

" Being deputies and perpetual governors,

Don N. N. and Don N. N.

" The ten bulls are the following : Six from the town of Al- " calà, bred by Don N. N. diftinguifhed by a fcarlet device. Three " from Chiclana, bred by Don N. N. with a white device. One " bull *para juguete,* for a play-thing."

The names of the *picadores, matadores,* and *vanderilleros,* are then fpecified, and as a poftfcript,

" To augment the diverfion, the picador N. N. is to fight a " bull on horfeback with darts, without a lance; he is then to " combat on foot, and afterwards kill it with the broad-fword. " The laft bull is to have wooden knobs on its horns; the valiant " negro N. N. is to fight with it, and give pleafure to the " public by his great valour and dexterity."

In Mr. Clarke's book are fome conjectures about the origin of thefe fpectacles, to which I refer *. According to the Spanifh hiftorians the firft bull-fight was exhibit in Spain in the year 1100..

* "——No corro fanguineo o ledo amante
" Vendo a formofa dama defejada,                      " O touro ,

## SPAIN.

On the 27th of July, I hired a single-horse chaise, and in three hours arrived at Xerez, which is two leagues from Port St. Mary. The road is sandy, and continues gradually rising, so that from the eminence on which Xerez is situated, I beheld a fine prospect over olive-grounds, intermixed with cottages white-washed, with a distant view of the bay of Cadiz. Xerez is a pretty large town, and is the mart for the wine known in England by the name of sherry: twenty thousand butts of this wine are annually exported; the price upon an average is fifty dollars per butt. I entered the town through a double Moorish gate, over which is an Arabic inscription. The streets are in general broad, but not paved. The great square has on one side a portico of twenty-two arches. Several noble families reside here. I waited on Mr. John Brickdale, who is the only English wine-merchant in this town: that gentleman was so obliging as to give me a letter to the superior of the celebrated Carthusian convent, which is a league distant from Xerez. On my arrival at this convent, which was between twelve and one, all the

> " O touro busca & pondose diante,
> " Salta, corre, sibila, acena & brada:
> " Mas o animal atroce nesse instante,
> " Com a fronte cornigera inclinada,
> " Bramando duro corre, & os olhos cerra
> " Derriba, fere, mata & poem por terra."
>
> Os Lusiadas, canto i. v. 88.

The joyful lover seeing his beautiful and desired lady, seeks for the bull in the bloody circus; he places himself before it, he leaps, runs, whistles, makes signs, and shouts; but the ferocious animal, in that instant inclining its horned front, runs loudly bellowing, with its eyes shut, overturns, wounds, kills, and throws to the ground.

holy fathers who inhabit it were afleep; and, as I would not difturb their repofe, and had no inclination to wait, I left it without having entered into it. On the gate is an infcription, purporting, that it was built by Andrès de Ribera (a private citizen of Cadiz), in 1571. I then walked over a bridge of eight arches, which is in fuch a ruinous condition, that people in carriages prefer fording the river, which at that time was fhallow, and proceeding three leagues, arrived at el Puerto Real, where I took a boat, and in an hour landed at la Yfla. We paffed by la Carraca, a fmall village, near which ten men-of-war were anchored, two of which were of eighty-four guns, and eight others broken up, being unfit for fervice.

At la Yfla, I faw a fmall elephant of feven feet high, which was juft arrived from the Philippine iflands, and was intended as a prefent for the king. The next morning I returned in a chaife to Cadiz.

On the third of Auguft I fet out for Sevilla, failing in the afternoon acrofs the bay to Port St. Mary, and there hired a one-horfe chaife to carry me to that capital.

Auguft 4. I paffed the night in Xerez: I there faw the body of a peafant who had juft been ftabbed, placed on a bier in the ftreet, with a box to receive alms for maffes to be celebrated for the good of his foul, and to defray the expences of his burial.

Auguft.

August 5. I set out by moon-light, at three in the morning, and after travelling five leagues, of which the first was sandy, but the others perfectly fine and level, among olive-trees and vineyards, rested at Lebrija. In the afternoon I proceeded six leagues farther, and passed the night in a venta. The road is quite flat, and not a house of any kind is seen between Lebrija and this venta. We had now approached the river Guadalquivir, on which many vessels were sailing: we saw several covies of partridges, and numerous flights of lapwings.

This afternoon we met a drove of ten bulls, which were to fight at Port St. Mary's. Three *picadores*, armed with lances, followed them; they environed the chaise, which put us under great apprehensions, but happily they were quiet, and passed on. We saw them coming at a distance, but there was neither house nor tree to retreat to.

August 6. We set out early in the morning, and after travelling four short leagues arrived at Sevilla, where I put up at the Cross of Malta: this inn is kept by an Italian, and is the best in Spain.

Sevilla is the largest city in the kingdom, and is situated in 37° 25′ latitude, in the middle of a plain, as level as any part of Holland. The river Guadalquivir divides it into two unequal parts; that on the south-side is called Triana: these parts are joined together by a mean and shabby bridge, consisting of planks laid on ten boats, forming the fegment of a circle, according as the tide runs. The city is nearly circular, fomething more than a mile and a half in diameter, and contains upwards of one hundred and twenty-thoufand inhabitants, though formerly it contained more than twice that number. A plan of this city was publifhed in 1771, in four large fheets.

The Spanifh proverb, " *Quien no ha vifto Sevilla, no ha vifto maravilla,*" is well known. This city is thought to have been founded by the Phœnicians, who called it Hifpalis, from whence the whole kingdom is called Hefperia: it is environed by an embattled wall, and has fifteen gates; it contains twenty-eight parifh churches, thirty-nine convents for men, and thirty-two nunneries, which have each a church; fourteen hofpitals, and fix colleges. The river Guadalquivir was anciently called Bætis: its prefent name is Arabic, and fignifies the Great River; it rifes in New Caftile, and falls into the ocean at San Lucar, after a courfe of feventeen leagues from Sevilla. The author of Telemachus gives a pleafing defcription of this river, in the eighth book of that work, beginning, " *Le fleuve Betis coule dans un païs fertile, & fous un ciel doux, qui eft toujours ferein, &c.*" This river is neither broad nor rapid, but very deep. There were at the time I was there fourteen Dutch veffels, of two or three hundred tons burthen, lying near the bridge, waiting for their cargoes of wool: which is a very dangerous commodity, for if proper care be not taken to air it frequently, by opening the hatches of the veffel, it

takes

takes fire; a Dutch veffel was by this means burnt down to the water's edge a fhort time before my arrival: this happened in the river, fo that the crew faved their lives, but if fuch an accident fhould happen at fea, the confequence is evident.

All the ftreets in Sevilla are narrow, crooked, and badly paved: the houfes are very high, which makes the ftreets fhady, and much cooler than they would otherwife be. There are more palaces, and other confpicuous buildings here, than in any other Spanifh city. Three or four Englifh merchants refide in it, but moft of the commerce is removed to Cadiz; fo that we have no conful here. The exchange, which formerly ferved for the merchants to affemble in, is at prefent fhut up, grafs grows within it as there does in the exchange at Antwerp. This at Sevilla, which is called *la Lonja*, is the handfomeft building here; its architect was Alonfo Berruguete: it is of the Tufcan order, of brick plaiftered over, and forms a fquare of one hundred and eighty feet, two ftories in height, eleven windows in breadth, and three doors to each fide; the principal ftair-cafe is very magnificent, a baluftrade furrounds the top. Near to this edifice is fituated the cathedral, which is the largeft Gothic building in Spain, or perhaps in Europe: the roof is fuftained by forty octangular columns, which form five naves: each of thefe columns is fixteen feet in diameter. The church, as well as the exchange, is environed by pieces of broken columns of granite and porphyry, linked to each other by chains to keep carriages off: a flight of feven fteps likewife encompaffes

thefe

these edifices. San Fernando is buried in the cathedral, and also the son of Christopher Columbus: on his grave-stone is engraven, *a Sevilla y Leon nuevo mendo diò Colon*; that is, Columbus gave a new world to Sevilla and Leon. I know not where Columbus himself was interred. At one end of the church is the famous *Torre de la Giralda*, or Tower of the Weathercock: it is three hundred and fifty feet in height, and exactly square, each side being fifty feet in breadth: the materials are stone to six feet from the ground, and all the rest are brick. At the height of two hundred and thirty feet, a smaller tower rises from it: the whole is crowned with a weather-cock, representing Faith under the figure of a woman, with a palm branch in one hand, and a flag in the other: this figure is fourteen feet in height. Near the middle of the little tower is painted round it, *turris fortissima nomen domini*, one of which words is on each side. The tower was built in the year 1000, as far as the belfrey, by Geber, one of the Moorish kings. The bells are five-and-twenty in number; the largest weighs one hundred and twenty-five quintals. In 1560 it was beautified, and built to the height it now is. I purchased a very large print of this curious fabric. I ascended it by thirty-six slopes, without steps; so that a horse can go up to the top, from whence there is a very fine prospect. This is not the only tower which is so constructed in the inside. I ascended St. Mark's tower, or *Campanile*, in Venice, which is three hundred and thirty-seven feet high, on thirty-seven of the like slopes; and the steeple of the church of St. Barbara, in Mantua, on twenty-five slopes. The town-house at Geneva

is

is acceffible as far as the fourth ſtory even in coaches, as the turnings are very broad, and paved.

The amphitheatre for the bull-fights is the largeſt in Spain, the inner area being two hundred and forty feet in diameter: in 1740 it was begun to be built of ſtone; thirty-five arches, or about one third of it, were finiſhed, when a ſtop was put to the building with that material, which was found too expenſive, and it was completed in wood, in which ſtate it now remains: under the boxes are eight rows of covered gradines, or ſeats, and nine of uncovered. Theſe amphitheatres ſerve ſometimes for the exhibitions of *juegos de cañas*, which are a kind of tournaments, wherein knights on horſeback caſt reeds at each other inſtead of lances.

The theatre confiſts of three rows of boxes, twenty in each row. I was there one evening: the actors were ſo extremely bad, that I could not get any perſon to accompany me thither, ſo that I ſoon quitted it, and repaired to the *alameda*, or mall, which is about three furlongs in length; five rows of trees divide it into four ſhady walks, or alleys: it is embelliſhed with ſix fountains and ſeveral ſtone benches, and ſmall canals of water run at the foot of each row of trees. At one end are two very high columns of granite, taken from a temple of Hercules which exiſted here in times of very remote antiquity; on the top of one is placed a ſtatue of Hercules, and on the other one of Julius Cæſar. At the other end of the mall are two modern columns, with a lion a lion on the top of each. Between the hours of six and eight in the evening the Spanish ladies refort hither in their carriages, and from ten to midnight they return hither again to walk, especially on Sundays, attended by their *cortejos*.

The royal tobacco fabric is fituated juft without the walls: it was built in 1757, wholly of white ftone, during the reign of the late king Ferdinand VI. It is a fquare of feven hundred and forty feet, and of two ftories in height: the chief front has twenty-nine windows in breadth, the back front twenty-five, and each of the two fides twenty-four: fifteen hundred men are conftantly employed in the manufacture of fegars and fnuff, and one hundred and ninety horfes alternately turn eighty mills for the fame purpofe. The whole fabric coft thirty-feven millions of reals, about four hundred and twelve thoufand pounds. I was informed that the neat revenue, cleared annually for the king, amounts to a million fterling : it is the only fabric in the whole kingdom. There is but one door by which it can be entered, to prevent the labourers from fmuggling the tobacco, which fome of them neverthelefs found means to do, by a very uncommon method, which was difcovered by their being obliged to be cured of the inflammation which happened to the part where they had concealed it. They are always fearched when they go home in the evening. The firft days they come to work the volatile parts of the tobacco and fnuff affect them fo as to caufe them to ftagger and reel as if they were intoxicated : I could only remain a few minutes among the fnuff-mills, and even then with a handkerchief applied to my mouth and nofe.

Near this place, without the walls, and not far from the river, is the royal college of Sant' Elmo, where one hundred and sixty boys are instructed in navigation, &c.

The hospital *de la Sangre*, for sick women, is also worthy of notice, on account of its size, having no less than thirty-three windows in front: it is not yet finished, though it was begun half a century ago.

The *alcazar*, or palace of the ancient kings, was built partly by the Moors, and partly by Don Pedro the Cruel. Several of the rooms have their walls covered with Arabic inscriptions; most of the ceilings are gilt; the floors are of small bits of marble, inlaid in various figures, in the same manner as the pavement of St. Mark's church in Venice: it is at present inhabited by El Señor Don Pablo de Olavide, intendant general of Andalusia, at whose table I frequently had the honour of dining: this gentleman is one of the richest Spanish subjects, and lives with the splendor of a prince. The modern part of this palace has the *plus ultra* inserted in every room, together with the Imperial Eagle. This was done during the reign of Charles V. who was as fond and vain of this motto as the gouty nobleman represented in one of Hogarth's prints was of coronets, which he even caused to be engraven on his crutches. There is a large garden behind the palace, planted with groves of orange and lemon trees, and embellished with fountains and terraces: its proprietor generously leaves it open to the public.

Being informed that the mint of Sevilla contained nothing but what is found in all others, I did not go to see it.

After having viewed the public edifices I went in search of pictures: Murillo, Velasquez, and de Valdes, three of the best Spanish painters, were born in or near Sevilla, so that I expected to find many of their pictures here, and I was not disappointed. I first waited on Don Francisco de Bruna, to whom I brought an introductory letter: that gentleman began by showing me his own collection of pictures, among which the following are worthy of notice.

A picture representing the Adoration of the Three Kings, who are painted as large as the life, together with Joseph, *la Virgen*, *el Niño*, and a servant: the child is in swaddling-clothes: the background is obscure, and the shadows are very strong, somewhat in the manner of Guido. This picture is one of Velasquez's best pieces.

An original portrait of Quevedo, with spectacles, by the same Velasquez. A fine engraving, by Carmona, of this picture is inserted in the fourth volume of the Spanish Parnassus.

Four small pieces by Teniers.

Two small Flemish landscapes.

Four correct drawings of the battles of Alexander: the figures are about four inches in size.

A book in folio, with drawings, by Murillo, de Valdes, and Cornelis Schut, done about the year 1680.

In the midst of this gentleman's library I observed a table made of a single plank of caoba, which is a sort of red wood resembling mahogany, brought from the West Indies, sixteen feet and a half long, and a yard broad.

In the palace of the duke of Alcalà, which is commonly called Pilate's House, as it is said to be built like that which Pilate inhabited, I saw a very fine picture by Leonard da Vinci, representing the Virgin Mary standing between Joseph and John, and holding the child, who stands on a table. The figures are whole lengths, and about four feet in proportion. At each of the four corners of the court-yard is placed a gigantic marble statue of Ceres, Pallas, &c. and under the porticos which surround it, are busts of the Cæsars, probably of Italian *antico-moderno* workmanship.

In the church of San Felipe Neri, I saw a *pietà*, by Van Dyke: the figures are as large as the life, and whole lengths.
In the church of la Caridad are,
Two large pictures called the Triumph of the Crofs, representing skeletons, deaths' heads, crowns, crosses, &c. by Juan de Valdes: these are esteemed to be his best works.
Eight very large pictures, in which the figures are all whole-lengths, and of the natural size, by Murillo. They represent
Lot and his three guests.
Moses striking the rock.

A faint

A Saint called San Juan de Dios, carrying a poor sick man on his back, an angel assists him, and lightens his burthen.

Saint Isabel, queen of Hungary, picking the scabs off the head of a leper. This picture is so naturally painted that it causes disgust.

The miraculous multiplication of five loaves and as many fishes.

St. Peter delivered out of prison by an angel.

Christ healing a sick man.

The return of the Prodigal Son.

Besides these, Murillo painted two small pieces, one representing the Annunciation, and the other the Virgin and Child, which are likewise preserved here.

In the church of St. Angel, I saw a picture by Rubens, representing Christ sitting on the clouds, at the right hand of the Father, whose feet rest on a globe, supported by three flying Cupids, which perhaps were intended for cherubims. At the bottom corners of this picture are St. John and St. Peter. All these figures are whole lengths, and nearly as large as the life.

In the Carthusian convent, are three small pictures by Albert Durer.

In the chapel of the Noviciado church are eleven small pictures by Tintoretto.

Besides these, Murillo painted the following pieces which I did not see, by reason that some are never uncovered but on particular

ticular days of the year, and that in the convents where I went to fee them, the friars were either afleep, or fo lazy that they would not give themfelves the trouble of fhewing them to me.

In the Capuchin convent, fixteen pictures over the altars in the church.

In Santa Marìa la Blanca, two.

In St. Auguftin, that over the great altar, one over another altar, and one in the facrifty.

In St. Francifco, all the paintings in the fmall cloifter, eleven in number.

In los Venerables, the Conception and St. Peter, and feveral in the refectory.

Six in the cathedral, which are placed in fuch a bad light, that they can hardly be perceived.

The other churches contain pictures, which are too tedious to mention, by fecond-rate painters, fuch as Pedro Campaña, Luis de Vargas, Francifco Zurbaran, Francifo Herrera el Viejo, Alonfo Cano, Francifco Pacheco, Pablo de Cefpede, Pablo Roelas, Pedro Villegas, Bafco Pereira, Francifco Varèla, Moralès, Alonfo Vafquez, Antonio Mohedano, Juan de Valdes, and Martin de Vos. And in the archbifhop's palace are a few by il Calabrefe.

I made an excurfion of about a league and a half on the other fide of the river, to fee the ruins of the amphitheatre of the ancient

cient Italicum, called Old Sevilla at prefent: it is fituated between two hills, and is of an oval form, whofe longeft inner diameter is two hundred and thirty-fix feet, and its fhorteft one hundred and fifty-two: fome of the arches yet remain; they are built of red bricks, each about a foot fquare, the reft is compofed of fmall irregular ftones and pebbles, with as much morter as ftone. By the ruins may be difcovered, that it had anciently two chief entrances, oppofite to each other in the longeft diameter, fourteen *vomitoria*, or entrances to the feats, or gradines, of which fourteen rows are ftill to be diftinguifhed. Emanuel Martini mentions this amphitheatre in the firft epiftle of the eighth book of his work, which was cited in the defcription of the amphitheatre of Saguntum.

On my return I obferved many ftorks nefts on the church of St. Ifidoro, and various fields planted with liquorice, the roots of which grow here to a very great fize.

During my ftay in Sevilla, I had the pleafure of being frequently with Don Antonio de Ullòa, who is well known in England by his defcription of America, which is the beft modern account of a voyage that has ever been publifhed in the Spanifh language*. He informed me, that in the library of the king of Denmark, at Copenhagen, he faw the beft collection of Spanifh books that is to be met with out of Spain, and that

---

\* It is tranflated into Englifh, in two octavo volumes.

all the editions of the various Spanish authors are the re preserved. His brother Don Martin de Ullòa likewise resided in Sevilla. They assured me, that four leagues from this city is a small tower called *la Torre de Quatro Abitas*, which may be shaken by a person who ascends it, to such a degree as to spill liquids out of a glass; and that all along the coasts of Spain are watch-towers, from mile to mile, with lights and guards at night; so that from Cadiz to Barcelona, and from Bilbao to Ferrol, the whole kingdom may by these means be successively alarmed in case of an invasion.

I cannot conclude my account of Sevilla, without mentioning my particular obligations to the governor the Marquis de Arco-Hermoso, and to the beautiful and accomplished marchioness de Malespina, at whose houses I spent my evenings in balls and musical parties.

Having sufficiently gratified my curiosity in this city, and fearing lest too long a stay might attach me too much to it, I reluctantly parted from my acquaintances, and on the 19th of August, at five in the morning, embarked in a four-oared boat, which I had hired to carry me to San Lucar, which is seventeen leagues, on the river Guadalquivir: the banks on both sides are quite flat, so that it appeared as if we were sailing on a Dutch canal. We met two large Dutch ships which were going to Sevilla for wool. The river was covered with water-fowl of various species, and the shores with lapwings, and innumerable flocks of buſtards, from four to twenty together: I fired at ſeveral of theſe birds, but, as the ſhot was too ſmall, it only wounded them ſlightly. I obſerved alſo two or three kingfiſhers hovering about the banks. I had filled my *boracho* with wine, and took proviſions from Sevilla. I paſſed the night on a bench in the boat, and the next morning at five landed at San Lucar de Barrameda, a ſmall town at the head of the bay, into which the river, now grown conſiderably wider, diſcharges itſelf. I waited on his majeſty's conſul, Wyndham Beawes, eſq. This gentleman is author of the *Lex Mercatoria Rediviva*, which was publiſhed ſome years ago, and intends to publiſh a hiſtorical account of Spain, in three folio volumes: he was ſo kind as to ſhew me part of the firſt volume, which is already printed; it contains Diſſertations on Solomon, on Tyre, on Cadiz, being the land of Ophir, &c. He informed me, that three leagues from San Lucar is a ſmall tower, which was looſened from its foundation by the earthquake in 1755, and thrown bottom upwards, in which poſition it now ſtands.

I here hired a ſingle-horſe chaiſe, which in five hours brought me to Port St. Mary. The diſtance is five leagues, and the road is very ſandy and heavy. Here I procured a paſſage in a boat, and after an hour and a half's ſailing landed in Cadiz.

About half-way acroſs the bay is a ſand-bank, which is very dangerous in bad weather; when the Spaniards ſail over it, they take off their hats, and ſay a Pater noſter and an Ave Maria for the

the souls of the passengers who have perished on that bank, and the master of the boat makes a collection of a few copper pieces, to pay for the masses to be celebrated to deliver those souls from purgatory. They have a similar custom in France, when criminals are executed: I saw a man broke alive on the wheel at Bourdeaux, and just before the executioner performed his part, the spectators prayed bare-headed.

On Sunday the 22d of August, I saw another bull-fight at Port St. Mary.

The next day I waited on the marquis de la Cañada, a gentleman of Irish extraction; his surname is Tyrry: he possesses a large and well-chosen library; among the books which compose it, are most of our English authors, ancient and modern.

Among his collection of pictures are the following:

The original small sketch, by Murillo, of the picture which he painted in the Capuchin church at Cadiz.

A small Madonna, Child, and St. John, by Murillo, copied from that which is in the royal collection in Paris: there are two different engravings of this picture.

An original piece by Ostade, boors smoking, of which the print is likewise engraven.

Two more small pictures, by Ostade. A small picture by Micris.

A Madonna by Cornelis Koet: and a Sea-piece.

I alfo faw here a marble *farcophagus* found at Medina Sidonia: it is eight feet in length, and three in height and breadth; its fides are in baffo relievo.

An urn of marble, found in the port of Cadiz foon after the earthquake in 1755.

A fmall bronze ftatue of Neptune, found in the ruins of the temple of Hercules in Cadiz, in 1639.

A fmall Venus of marble.

All thefe are engraven in the feventh volume of count Caylus's Antiquities. Father Florez, in his *Efpaña Sagrada*, and an old book, *de las Antiguedades del Reyno de Sevilla*, both mention this *farcophagus*.

On the 24th of Auguft I returned again to Cadiz.

Auguft 25. I rode on horfeback to la Yfla, and dined there at the houfe of admiral Don Andrès Reggio: this gentleman is a Sicilian, knight of the orders of Malta and St. January, and brother to the governor of Carthagena before mentioned. In the afternoon the admiral was fo obliging as to order his fixteen-oared fhaloop to convey me to el Puerto Real, where I faw a *loa*, or farce, reprefented in the theatre, which has no roof, and was only covered with a fail. At fun-fet the *Ave Maria* bell tolled, upon which the actors fufpended their fpeeches; and they, as well as the audience, who rofe from their feats, recited a fhort prayer, and then fell to fpouting again.

The next day I examined the admiral's pictures, which are depoſited in a houſe he has here, but found none worthy of obſervation, except one repreſenting the Madonna, Child, and St. John, nearly as large as the life, ſaid to be by Titian, which is not improbable, as it is a very fine piece; and ſixteen pictures of fowls and fiſhes, by one Felix Celi, which are painted in a peculiar ſtyle.

Soon after leaving this houſe, I took boat and landed at la Carraca, where I ſaw the armoury and arſenal, containing (as I was told) ſufficient arms and ammunition to equip forty men of war. This village is a place of baniſhment for criminals: about four hundred of theſe wretches work here, with chains about their legs and waiſts.

I then returned to la Yſla, and had again the honour of dining with the admiral, and a great number of officers: ſome of theſe accompanied me to the academy of *las guardias marinas*, the marine guards, where one hundred and ſixty young noblemen are educated at the king's expence: they are taught navigation, aſtronomy, mathematics, arithmetic, drawing, fencing, dancing, and the Engliſh and French languages. This academy was inſtituted in 1717, and contains ſeveral models and ſections of ſhips, globes, and other apparatus neceſſary for teaching the ſciences mentioned. In the evening I rode back to Cadiz.

In the account of the Travels of Meſſieurs Van Egmont and Heyman, publiſhed in 1759, it appears that they landed in Cadiz, while on their voyage to Conſtantinople: they ſay, " The exchange at Cadiz is only a ſtreet adjoining to the market, " called Calle Nueva, but it is a very diſagreeable place to " ſtand in, and generally very dirty. There is likewiſe no " ſettled hour for buſineſs, and on theſe accounts the moſt emi- " nent merchants are rather to be found in their counting- " houſes than on the exchange:" which is the caſe at preſent.

On Sunday the 29th of Auguſt, I ſaw a bull-fight in Cadiz: one of the bulls, which would not fight, was abandoned to the dogs, who pinned his noſe to the ground ſo immoveably, that the *matador* put an end to its life without the leaſt danger to himſelf.

September 1. I went in a coach, which the Spaniards call *galera*, drawn by four mules to la Yſla, where I again dined at the admiral's houſe: he had juſt received two ſhells, of the oyſter kind, from the Philippine iſlands; I meaſured them, and found the longeſt diameter of each to be three feet five inches and a quarter, and their ſhorteſt two feet and an inch, Engliſh meaſure. I ſaw in the anatomy chamber at Leyden, in Holland, two ſhells, the largeſt of which is two feet eight inches in its longeſt diameter, and twenty inches in its ſhorteſt; it weighs one hundred and fifty pounds. In the evening, having taken leave of my acquaintances in la Yſla, I returned to Cadiz.

I pur-

## SPAIN.

I purchased four live cameleons *, two of which I killed and preserved in spirits of wine, the other two I brought with me to England alive, where they died: the largest was near a foot in length, including the tail In vol. vii. p. 151, & *seq.* of the History of Animated Nature, is an accurate description of this animal. It is produced from an egg, and has two claws standing forward, and two others backwards to each foot: its creeping motion, when on level ground, is very slow. I preserved mine on a small tree, on which they would sit motionless for days together. I every day opened their mouths and fed them with eight or ten flies each, which they took a long time to swallow, and at last they died of hunger, as I could not procure any more flies I attempted to feed them with worms, spiders, &c. which they constantly rejected: the tongue is very thick and long: the animal is as helpless and defenceless as a toad. Since my return to England I procured two toads, in order to observe their method of feeding, which they did out of my hand, wherein I held some maggots, which had engendered in rotten meat: the toads darted out their tongues, with a motion as rapid as the flyer of of a jack, so that the eye could scarcely follow them, and swallowed the maggot which adhered to the glutinous part of the tongue. In the Appendix to the third volume of the British Zoology, Mr. Pennant has inserted a particular account of the toad, in which he fully proves that those reptiles are perfectly innoxious. But to return to the cameleon,

* Lacerta Chamæleon. Linn. Syst. Nat. 364.

it can blow itfelf up and contract itfelf, by a method fimilar to that in pigeons, whofe crops are fometimes greatly diftended with air. The cameleon is very cold to the touch ; the fkin refembles fhagreen, but very foft, becaufe every one of the little protuberances which compofe it, of about the fize of a pin's head, is as fmooth as if it were polifhed : its colour is generally of a whitifh green, rather yellow underneath the belly : in climbing, the animal ufes its tail as well as its legs, and proceeds with the utmoft caution, fearful of falling; the tail is twifted round a bough, and never loofened till all the feet have got a fecure hold. It fometimes defcended from the tree on which I kept it; in order to effectuate this, it hung fufpended by its tail to the extremity of the loweft branch, and from thence let itfelf gently fall to the ground. It changes its colour at pleafure, into various hues of white, yellow, blue, and green; fometimes it appears black, with bright yellow fpots. The conftruction of the eyes is very remarkable, " they are very " little, though they ftand out of the head ; they have a fingle " eye-lid like a cap with a hole in the middle, through which the " pupil appears, which is of a fhining brown, and round it is a " little circle of a gold colour, juft like that round a toad's eye: " the animal often moves one eye when the other is entirely at " reft, nay fometimes one eye will look forward while the other " looks backward, and one will look upwards while the " other regards the earth :" the fockets of the eyes move as if they were placed on pivots *.

\* Sir John Maundevile fays, he was in an ifland where he faw " many
" camles

I now agreed with the captain of an English vessel that he should admit myself and servant as passengers: the vessel was destined to London. The few days before my departure I spent in getting informations concerning things which I was desirous of knowing before I quitted the kingdom, the result of which I shall here place together.

I purchased several *snake-stones*, *piedras de serpiente*, and have had the honour of presenting one of them, together with a circumstantial account, to the Royal Society in London: they are made of burnt hartshorn, in oval pieces, about the size of a shilling, and half an inch thick; on being applied to wounds caused by the bite of a serpent, or other venomous animal, they adhere to them, and imbibe the poison, after which they fall off; being then put into milk or wine, they discharge the venom

"camles that is a lytille best as a goot, that is wylde, and he lyvethe be the eyr, and etethe nought ne drynkethe nought at no tyme. And he chaungethe his colour often tyme: for men seen him often seithes, now in o colour and now in another colour; and he may chaunge him into alle manner of coloures that him list, saf only into red and white."

In the Italian edition, printed in 1480, the above passage is as follows: "in questo paese sono molti camalioni li quali sono picolli amo: do che chyerong saluatici e vano tutavia con la golla aperta per prendere laire ipero che egli vineno sollamente de lapre e non mageno ne beueno alcuna cossa eli cambiano colloro spesse siate perche alcuna siate se vedeno de uno collore e una altra volta de uno altro elli se possono mutare de ogni collore che vogliono saluo che in rosso ne in bianche."

they had attracted, and are applied anew as long as they will stick to the part affected, and in the end, as it is said, effect a cure: they are sold at about a shilling a-piece.

After the account of Cintra (p. 21.), I omitted to mention, that the adjacent rocks produce the plant known by the name of fly-plant. I suppose it to be the *Ophrys insectifera, Linn. Sp. Pl.* 1343. probably either the variety marked ε, or that marked ζ. See the first Breynii centuria plant. tab. xlv. fig. 2.

In most parts of Spain crickets are kept in small wire cages, placed on the window ledges: they are each in a separate cage, with a bit of sallad, and keep continually chirping. I bought a vase of a kind of earthen ware, of a singular construction; it consists of two bottles joined together by the bellies, and a handle; on the top of one is an uncouth human figure, and on the other is a kind of spout, which is a whistle at the same time: this vase was brought from Perù. A figure of one, similar to it, is engraven in the second volume of the Spanish edition of Ulloa's History of America.

The elastic gum, or *caoutchouc*, is common both here and at Lisbon. In the Memoirs of the Royal Academy of Sciences at Paris, for the years 1763 and 1768, are copious accounts of this resin, which is since become well known in England. The following extracts from those Memoirs will suffice to explain its nature. " This resin, as it is called, has been brought from dif-
" ferent

"ferent parts of South America and Asia. Mr. de la Condamine, in the relation of his voyage down the river of Amazons, first entered into some detail concerning its origin, and the manner in which the Indians collect it, and form it by means of earthen moulds into various shapes. From his, and other accounts, it appears that it is a milky exudation, or a kind of natural emulsion, flowing from incisions made in a certain tree: while in this liquid state, it receives from them the particular form intended to be given to it. The liquor soon dries, and acquires a solid consistence; manifesting, at the same time, a most extraordinary degree of flexibility and elasticity." Its colour is a deep brown, somewhat transparent: a ring made of it to fit the finger, may with ease be extended so as to be drawn over the hand and arm, and on being slipped off, will instantly return to its former dimensions[*]. It is very efficacious in rubbing out lines made by a leaden-pencil, for which use much of it is sold in London. In the shops at Lisbon it is to be met with in many grotesque figures of birds, beasts, &c. and is there called *boracho*. The above-mentioned Memoirs, continue thus: "Its chemical properties are not less extraordinary, as this intractable substance had hitherto resisted every attempt that had been made to reduce it to its orginal fluid state: it was indissoluble in water, spirits of wine, oils, and camphire, but was at last dissolved in vitriolic æther. The uses to which this discovery is applicable appear to be various. The solidity,

[*] Priapi, et machinæ annuli Sinensium dictæ, ex hac resina conficiuntur.

"flexibility,

"flexibility, and elasticity of the *caoutchouc*, and its property of
"not being affected by aqueous, spirituous, saline, oily, or other
"common solvents, renders it a proper and valuable matter for
"the construction of tubes, catheters, and various other instru-
"ments in which these properties are wanted, &c." For a farther account I refer to the Memoirs, and to the Monthly Reviews
for September 1767, vol. xxxvii. and the Appendix to the
forty-sixth volume, published in June 1772.

In most parts of Spain, but especially in Cadiz, are sold vases
made of a kind of white earth: these at night are filled with
water, and a vessel placed under them, into which the next
morning the water will have filtrated through those vases perfectly purified. This earth is called *barro*: another kind of the
same name, but of a red colour, is brought from Mexico: the
Spaniards put pieces of it among their snuff, which it pre-
serves cool, giving it the smell of fresh earth, which odour is
likewise communicated to water put into jars of this material.

In 1492, the first comedy was acted; and, in 1546, the first
coach was made use of in Spain.

I was one evening much surprised at seeing a lady, with
whom I had the day before been in company, when she was
dressed in the height of coquetry, make her appearance in a
nun's black habit, with a leathern thong, to which hung knotted
cords, round her waist. She told me she had made a vow to wear

that.

that habit for six months, by way of penance, inflicted voluntarily on herself for some sins she said she had committed. On enquiry of one of her female friends, I found that it was only because her husband had forbid his house to her *cortejo* \*; so that the poor lady thus publicly testified her sorrow for her swain's discharge. Other ladies, in the like disconsolate situation, sometimes make a vow not to go to a play or an assembly for six months, or a year, according to the degree of their disappointment; but they always attribute these vows to some religious motive, such as the recovery from a fit of sickness, or from any dangerous accident: elderly ladies have been known to make such rash vows for the remainder of their lives, renouncing the follies and vanities of the world, because the world renounced them, and which vows they have always strictly kept, because no man thought it worth his while to tempt them to break them. Many Spaniards of both sexes leave orders that they shall after death be carried to the grave in the habit of some religious order:

> " ⸺ and to be sure of Paradise,
> Dying put on the weeds of Dominic,
> Or in Francisean think to pass disguis'd."
> 
> Parad. Lost, book iii..

Many of the images and statues of *santos* and *santas*, male and female saints, which are placed against the walls of the cor-

\* To express myself in the words of a celebrated French astronomer, " he did not like that his wife, her *cortejo*, and himself, should form an equilateral triangle."

ner houses of the streets throughout the cities in Spain, have *parasols & paraplúies* placed over their heads, which defend them from the sun and rain. A similar safe-guard is granted to the stone and wooden saints in the streets of Padua in Italy. It may not be improper here to admire the complaisance of the Venetians, who have, by their own authority, canonized several gentlemen, who have not been created saints by any other nation, witness St. Moses, St. Job, St. Samuel, St. David, St. Jeremiah, and St. Zachariah, each of which personages has a church in Venice dedicated to him.

The *bull of the crusade* is sold all over Spain; every individual is obliged to buy one annually, without which no one can either be married, confessed, or buried: the price for common people is about six pence; for *illustres* or private persons sixteen reals, about three shillings and seven pence; the nobility pay what they please above that sum. This brings in a neat revenue to the king of twenty-four millions of reals annually, or about two hundred and sixty-seven thousand pounds. I purchased one for myself: it is vilely printed, partly in Gothic characters, and in the Spanish language, on a sheet of very coarse paper.

The purport of it is as follows:

" 1773.
" Summary of the graces, indulgences, and faculties, that our
" most holy father pope Clement XIII. of happy memory, has
" deigned

"deigned to concede by the bull of the holy crufade to our lord
"the king, and to thofe faithful, who being in his king-
"dom of Spain, or other dominions of his Catholic majefty,
"help and ferve him in his wars againft the infidels for the
"year 1773.

"Our moſt holy father having confidered of what import-
"tance it is to the Catholic religion, that the faithful fhould
"affift our lord the Catholic king, in the war which he con-
"tinually maintains againſt the enemies of our holy faith,
"to defend and propagate it; and that they would concur
"the more gladly and chearfully to fuch a laudable and
"pious work, if they might thereby obtain fpiritual re-
"wards, his holinefs has condefcended to difpenfe the fol-
"lowing indulgences and graces with a liberal hand, &c.
"&c.

"Firft, To the king our lord, and to every faithful Chriftian
"who moved by faith, fhall fight againſt the infidels at his own
"expence, the fame indulgences are granted as to thofe who go
"to the conqueft of the Holy Land; and the fame to thofe who
"fend another perfon at their expence. The foldiers occupied
"in the faid war are excufed by his holinefs from votive fafts,
"and they are permitted to employ themfelves in war even
"on feftivals.

"Item, To thofe who contribute alms towards the faid expe-
"dition, his holinefs gives permiffion to have maffes celebrated,
"to receive the facraments, or to be chriftened, married, and
"buried:

" buried (provided they do not die excommunicated), an hour
" before fun-rife, and an hour after noon, during the whole
" year, except on Easter-day.

" Item, They may by the advice of their two phyficians,
" fpiritual and corporal, eat meat, even in Lent, and eggs and
" milk whenever they pleafe, of their own authority.

" However, during Lent, patriarchs, archbifhops, bifhops,
" and prelates, are not allowed to eat eggs or milk, if they are
" under fixty years of age.

" Item, They may obtain a plenary remiffion of all
" their fins, once during their life, and again in the article
" of death.

" A perfon who takes this *bull* twice in the fame year, en-
" joys all thefe indulgences, graces and privileges twice
" over, &c. &c. &c.

It concludes thus: " And whereas you Don R. T. have
" contributed the alms of twenty-one quartos (fix pence), which
" is the tax impofed by virtue of apoftolical authority, and
" that you have received this *bull* written in your name, and
" which you are to preferve, we declare that we grant to
" you, and that you may ufe and enjoy all the aforefaid graces,
" &c. during this year."

Underneath this is printed, " days on which a foul is drawn
" out of purgatory.

✝ Septuagint

" + Septuagint Sunday.

" + The Tuesday after the first Sunday in Lent.

" + The Saturday after the second Sunday in Lent.

" + The third and fourth Sundays in Lent.

" + The Friday and Saturday after the fifth Sunday in Lent.

" + The Wednesday of the octave of Easter.

" + The Thursday and Saturday of the octave of Whit-
" suntide."

These are the ten days which were before mentioned in the account of Madrid.

Capers are produced in many parts of Spain: they are the buds of the shrub called *alçaparro*, gathered before they expand, dried in the shade, and afterwards pickled for use. Sponges are thrown up by the sea on most of the Spanish coasts.

The method of raising water from the wells in the gardens, is by the Persian wheel; it is used all over Portugal, Spain, and the Levant. A wheel of five feet, or more, in diameter, is placed vertically over the well, sustained by an axis fixed on wooden posts; to this wheel is fastened a band, which reaches a foot or two below the surface of the water, a great number of earthen pitchers, each holding three or four pints, are fixed to this band by the neck, their mouths all turned the same way, a horizontal wheel is so fixed, that its pinions may fall in exactly with the cogs, or pins of the vertical one: on the top of the axis of the horizontal wheel is a pole, at the extremity of which

which another pole is inserted perpendicularly, and to this an ox, an afs, or a horfe is faftened, which turns the engine round: as the pitchers come to the top they empty themfelves into a ftone trough, from whence the water is conveyed by a canal into a ciftern, which ftands high enough for it to run freely to all parts of the garden. The water lies fome hours in the ciftern expofed to the rays of the fun, by which the chilnefs is removed, which would be very prejudicial to the tender plants. The foregoing defcription is partly extracted from the *Hiftory of Minorca*, in which ifland the like engines are ufed.

The eaftern method of treading out the corn is ftill ufed by the Portuguefe and Spaniards. Homer has defcribed it in the twentieth book of the Iliad.

" As with autumnal harvefts cover'd o'er,
" And thick beftrown, lies Ceres' facred floor.
" When round and round, with never weary'd pain,
" The trampling fteers beat out th' unnumber'd grain.

POPE.

Inftead of fteers, mares are ufed in thefe kingdoms for that purpofe, from ten to twenty at a time. Hand-mills, or *querns*, are common in Spain. Mr. Pennant, in his Tour in Scotland, p. 211, quarto edition, has defcribed one which he faw in that country: and in his Voyage to the Hebrides, p. 286, has inferted a plate reprefenting two women at work at the *quern*.

The habits of the Spanish gentry of both sexes, are entirely in the French fashion: the Macaroni ladies in Cadiz wear yellow powder in their hair, which to me appeared nauseous and unbecoming: they use neither paint nor patches. When women have occasion to walk the streets in Spain, they are covered with a black silk veil, and are then styled *tapadas*, i. e. shut up; in this disguise they much resemble one another, which is very convenient for intriguing. In the plate of the aqueduct of Segovia inserted in this work, are the figures of a Spanish *majo* and *maja*, or man and woman, in an undress; and likewise the representation of a carriage, to which six mules are put by long traces.

There are a great number of billiard-tables in Cadiz, as well as in most of the capital cities in Spain, and likewise many *trucos*, which are a peculiar kind of billiard tables, with twenty pockets, played on with very large balls, which are to pass through an iron arch fixed in a certain part of the table.—Horseshoes are beaten into the shape required, when the iron is cold, which makes them last much longer than they would otherwise do.

The beggars who swarm in every part of these kingdoms are as insufferably troublesome as they are in Italy: I have frequently been interrupted while conversing with acquaintances in the streets, by the vile paw of a disgusting old woman familiarly placed on my arm, and on turning to look at the object have started

started with horror at the shocking spectacle: these wretches even insolently intrude themselves into churches and coffee-houses, and expose their cadaverous and rotten limbs close under the nose of the affrighted spectator.

At all the fairs which I saw in Spain, I observed in the booths horns made of clay, painted, and of various dimensions; they are purchased, and presented by way of raillery to jealous husbands, &c.

In several houses in the sea-port towns in Spain, I observed paintings of the different coloured races of beings, which are produced by the Spaniards intermixing with the Indians in America, and under the paintings were inscribed the names of those races. I caused the inscriptions which are under sixteen pictures I saw in Malaga to be copied; they are as follows, though they may appear somewhat unintelligible, and it will be very difficult to prove the truth of what is therein advanced. The terminations in *a* are feminine, those in *o* masculine.

1. From a Spanish man and an Indian woman proceeds a Mestizo, or a Mestiza.
2. From a Spaniard and a Mestiza, a Castiza.
3. From a Spaniard and a Castiza, a Española.
4. From an Española and an Indio, a Mestindio.
5. From a Mestindio and a Castiza, a Coyota.
6. From an Indio and a Coyota, a Harnizo.

7. From a Spanish man and a Negro woman proceeds a Mulato.
8. From a Spaniard and a Mulata, a Morisco.
9. From a Morisco and a Spanish woman, an Alvino.
10. From an Alvino and a Spanish woman, the issue are perfect Negroes.
11. From a Negro and an Indian woman, a Lobo.
12. From an Indio and Loba, a Sambaigo.
13. From a Sambaigo and a Mulata, a Cambujo.
14. From a Cambujo and a Mulata, an Albaraffado.
15. From an Albaraffado and a Mulata, a Barzino.
16. From a Barzino and a Mulata, the issue is a Negro with smooth hair.

This remarkable circumstance of the children of almost white parents, as specified in the tenth and fixteenth races being quite black, was confirmed to me by Don Antonio de Ulloà at Sevilla, but as I cannot pretend to demonstrate it, I leave it as I found it.

The short cloak formerly worn by the Spaniards is now laid aside, as are also their spectacles, ruffs, and long swords, and the only mark of their former gravity consists in the deep brown colour of the habits of the common people.

Chocolate is the daily morning beverage of almost all ranks of Spaniards and Portuguese. The usual phrase made use of in the Spanish language on parting with a person is, *Vaya V. S. con Dios*, " May your worship go along with God," which is equivalent

equivalent to our Farewell, or Adieu. For, " I thank you," the Spaniards say, " *Viva V. S. mil años*. " May your worship live a " thousand years ;" to which the answer sometimes is, " *Poco* " *mas o menos*, a little more or less."

Gold or silver coin, even Spanish, is not allowed to be brought into, or carried out of any of the cities of Spain, more especially Cadiz, if it exceeds ten pounds, without paying four per cent. duty to the king. The ship in which I embarked brought one hundred and sixty bags, each containing a thousand hard dollars, to England, which amounted to near thirty-six thousand pounds. These dollars were of silver, of the value of about four shillings and six pence each, and chiefly coined in Mexico; every bag weighed sixty-one pounds and a half, and the freight was a half per cent.

The packets, which sail usually every week from Lisbon to Falmouth, frequently bring as large a sum, in gold pieces of thirty-six shillings, to England. There are no bank-notes in these kingdoms.

The chief products of Spain are corn, wine, oil, fruits, raisins\*, honey, cork, and salt, which last is so abundant, that

---

\* Raisins are of two sorts; those which are called sun raisins are made thus: when the grapes are almost ripe, the stalk is cut half through, so that the sap may not penetrate farther, but yet that the bunch of grapes may remain suspended by the stalk. The sun by darting on them candies them, and when they are dry they are packed up in boxes. The second sort is made

the kingdom of Murcia alone is able to supply all Spain with that commodity. In the province of Biscay are a great number of iron mines; in Andalusia are many mines of lead; and in Murcia much sulphur is made. Marble quarries abound all over the kingdom. The principal manufactures are of silk and wool. Silk, which has been cultivated in Spain ever since the year 1492, is chiefly produced in the kingdoms of Valencia and Murcia; and wool in the two Castiles. The other productions are hemp, flax, cotton, &c. much coral is fished out of the sea near the mouth of the river Ebro.

Tunny are caught in summer in great abundance near Conil, on the Andalusian coast. These fish are from seven to ten feet in length, and weigh about a hundred and a half. The duke of Medina-Sidonia is proprietor of this fishery, which brings him in annually upwards of ten thousand pounds. The fish is eaten fresh and salted: it is exported to Italy, where it serves for food to the equipage of the gallies which cruise in the Mediterranean: this fish is very firm and nourishing, and much resembles veal.

The whole kingdom is over-run with French knife-grinders, tinkers, and pedlars, who collect much money by exercising these mean trades, after which they return to their own country,

made after the following manner: when the vines are pruned, the tendrils are preserved till the time of vintage; a great fire is then made, wherein those tendrils are burnt, and in the lye made from their ashes, the newly gathered grapes are dipt, after which they are exposed to the sun to dry, which renders them fit for use.

leaving the Spanish dons weltering in their pride, lazinefs, and mifery.

All works intended to be printed in Spain muft undergo fuch a number of revifals and corrections, and muft be licenfed by fo many various tribunals, fuch as that of the inquifition, &c. that it is enough to difcourage any attempts towards putting the Spanifh literature on a better footing.

In the year 1764, the inhabitants of the kingdom of Spain, of the feven Canary iflands, of the ifland of Majorca, and of the cities of Oran and Ceuta, on the African coaft, which include all the Spanifh dominions in Europe and Africa, were numbered, and a printed lift of them publifhed, of which the following is an extract.

Cities, towns, and villages, 21221  
Cathedrals - - 108  
Monafteries - - 2052 containing 67777 monks.  
Nunneries - - 1028 containing 34651 nuns.  
Colleges - - 312  Total 102428 ufelefs beings.  
Hofpitals - - 2008  
*Ventas* - - 9930  

The number of fouls who are of age to receive the facraments is fix millions three hundred and fifty thoufand one hundred and ninety-fix, to which the afore-mentioned hundred and two thoufand four hundred and twenty-eight drones being added, compofe pose a total of six millions four hundred and fifty-two thousand six hundred and twenty-four adult persons: if the children were to be added, such an addition might probably double that number. Before the discovery of America, in 1492, it is said that the population of Spain amounted to twenty millions, but that discovery drained the kingdom of almost half its inhabitants, and the remaining half *wisely* expelled a million of Moors out of their country in the same year, and another million in 1610 and 1612. In the time of Cæsar, history assures us, that there were no less than fifty millions of souls in Spain.

On the 6th of September the captain of the vessel in which I intended to embark, acquainting me that he designed to sail the next morning, I went on board in the evening. This ship was of one hundred and eighty tuns burthen, mounted with several guns, and navigated by fifteen men. The cargo, besides the silver before mentioned, consisted of cochineal and indigo. On the 7th in the morning we set sail, and the next day were out of sight of land. On the 11th we had, by estimation, passed Cape St. Vincent, and by easterly winds were driven as far as eighteen degrees west from London. We had sometimes strong gales, which made the ship, though loaden, sail eight or nine knots in an hour. On the 24th we saw a vast number of porpoises playing about the ship. The next day, on sounding, ground was found at eighty fathom. On the 27th,

"As with a longing seaman's look I gaz'd,"

I had

I had the pleasure of seeing land, which proved to be the Start Point in Devonshire. The vessel was now environed with shoals of millions of pilchards. At last, on the 29th of September, being the twenty-third day of our voyage, I landed at Dover at four in the morning, perfectly satisfied with this tour, which had proved more agreeable and instructive to me than any other part of my travels, owing to the novelty of all the objects in kingdoms which are seldom visited by travellers, and to the kindness of the Portuguese and Spaniards in general, whose cordial and generous hospitality demand all the acknowledgments and thanks that are in my power to give. I shall always retain the greatest esteem for the Spanish nation in particular; and if, in various parts of this work, I have inserted a few pleasantries about their religion, I am certain that the candid Spaniards will join in the laugh, especially as the prejudices of their fore-fathers are daily losing ground, so that it is not improbable that in process of time Spain may become a seat of toleration and literature, equal to any other kingdom, and that it may be said with Gonzalo Argote de Molina.

" Levanta noble ESPAÑA,
" Tu coronada frente,
" Y alegrate de verte renascida
" Por todo quanto baña,
" Entorno la corriente
" Del uno y otro mar, con mejor vida."

APPENDIX.

# APPENDIX.

### Nº I.

### ITINERARY.

| | Leagues. |
|---|---|
| FROM LISBON to *Mafra* and back, is | 15 |
| ————— to *Cintra* and back | 7½ |
| ————————— to *St. Julian's* and back. | 7½ |
| | 30 |

From LISBON to OPORTO, by way of *Alcobaça*.

A Ferry.

| | | | Leagues, or Hours. | |
|---|---|---|---|---|
| First day | Alverca | | 4 | 6 |
| | Caſtanhera | | 4 | 3 |
| Second day | Otta | | 7 | 8 |
| | Tagara | | | |
| Third day | A venta | | 3 | 5 |
| | *Alcobaça* | | 3 | 4½ |
| Fourth day | *Batalha* | | 2 | 5 |
| | *Leyria* | | 2 | 3 |
| Fifth day | Pombal | | 5 | 6 |
| Sixth day | Pondès | | 5 | 6½ |
| | COIMBRA | | 2 | 3 |
| Seventh day | Amolhada | | 3 | 5 |
| Eighth day | Sardon | | 4 | 4 |
| | Ferry over the Vouga. | | | |
| | Albergaria | | 4 | 4 |
| | | | 48 | 63 |

APPENDIX.

|  |  | Leagues, | or Hours. |
|---|---|---:|---:|
| | Brought over - - - | 48 | 63 |
| Ninth day | { Sant' Antonio - - | 6 | 7¼ |
| | { A venta - - - | 1 | 2 |
| | Ferry over the Douro. | | |
| Tenth day | Oporto - - - | 5 | 7¼ |
| | | 60 | 80 |

From Oporto to *Almeida*.

Ferry over the Douro.

|  |  | | | |
|---|---|---:|---:|---:|
| First day | { A venta - - - | | 4 | 5½ |
| | { Sant' Antonio - - | | 2 | 4¼ |
| | { Albergaria - - - | | 0 | 7¼ |
| Second day | { Ferry over the Vouga - - | | 8 | 0 |
| | { Sardon - - - | | 0 | 4 |
| Third day | Barilhe - - - | | 5 | 8 |
| Fourth day | Cargal - - - | | 3 | 6 |
| Fifth day | { A venta - - - | | 4 | 7½ |
| | { Vinhosa; the worst road in Portugal | | 1 | 3 |
| Sixth day | { Celorico - - - | | 2 | 5 |
| | { Cavaçal - - - | | 2 | 3¼ |
| Seventh day | { A venta - - - | | 3 | 5 |
| | { *Almeida* - - - | | 4 | 6 |
| | | | 38 | 65½ |

From Oporto to Salamanca.

Enter Spain.

|  |  | | |
|---|---|---:|---:|
| First day | Obispo - - - | 1½ | 2 |
| Second day | *Ciudad-Rodrigo* - - | 5 | 6¼ |
| | | 6½ | 8¼ |

## APPENDIX.

|  |  | Leagues, | or Hours. |
|---|---|---|---|
| Brought over | | 6¼ | 8¼ |
| Third day {A venta / A venta} | | 9 | 11 |
| Fourth day {A venta / SALAMANCA} | | 3¾ / 4 | 7¼ |
| | | 22¼ | 26¼ |

### From SALAMANCA to VALLADOLID.

| First day | {A venta / A venta} | 7 | 6½ |
|---|---|---|---|
| Second day | Zamora | 6 | 6 |
| Third day | Toro | 6 | 8½ |
| Fourth day | Tordesillas | 6 | 7 |
| Fifth day | {Simancas / VALLADOLID} | 3 / 2 | 4 / 4 |
| | | 30 | 36 |

### From VALLADOLID to MADRID through SEGOVIA, St. Ildefonso, and the Escorial.

| First day | {Valdestillas / Olmedo} | 8 | 9¼ |
|---|---|---|---|
| Second day | {Coca / Santa Maria} | 7 | 8½ |
| Third day | SEGOVIA | 5 | 7 |
| Fourth day | St. Ildefonso | 2 | 2¼ |
| Fifth day | A venta | 3 | 5 |
| Sixth day | {Guadarama / The Escorial} | 4 / 2 | 8½ |
| Seventh day | MADRID | 6½ | 9 |
| | | 37½ | 50 |

# APPENDIX.

From MADRID to *Aranjuez* by way of TOLEDO.

|  |  | Leagues, | or Hours. |
|---|---|---|---|
| First day | Illescas | 6 | 9½ |
|  | Cabañas | 3 |  |
| Second day | Toledo | 3 | 3 |
| Third day | Aranjuez | 7 | 8¼ |
|  |  | 19 | 21 |

From *Aranjuez* to VALENCIA.

| First day | Ocaña | 2 | 3 |
|---|---|---|---|
|  | Coral | 5¼ | 8 |
| Second day | Quintañar | 3 | 5 |
|  | Pedronosa | 5 | 6 |
| Third day | Provençor | 3 | 4 |
|  | Minaya | 4 | 6 |
| Fourth day | La Roda | 3 | 3 |
|  | La Gineta | 3 | 3¼ |
| Fifth day | Albacete | 3 | 3¼ |
|  | Villar | 5 | 6 |
| Sixth day | Boncte | 3 | 3 |
|  | Almansa | 4 | 5 |
| Seventh day | Moxent | 5 | 6¼ |
|  | Xativa, or San Phelipe | 4 | 5¼ |
| Eighth day | Algemesì | 4 | 5 |
|  | VALENCIA | 5 | 7 |
|  |  | 61¼ | 80 |

From VALENCIA to *Morviedro* and back again is 8 leagues.

From

# APPENDIX. 343

From VALENCIA to *Carthagena*, by way of *Alicante* and *Murcìa*.

|  |  | Leagues, | or Hours. |
|---|---|---|---|
| First day { Cullera | - - - | 5 | 7 |
| Gandìa | - - - | 3 | 5½ |
| Second day { La Puebla | - - - | 3 | 6½ |
| Onteniente | - - - | 3 | 4½ |
| Third day { A venta | - - - | 3 | 5 |
| Villena | - - - | 3 | 4½ |
| Fourth day { Monforte | - - - | 5 | 8 |
| *Alicante* | - - - | 4 | 5½ |
| Fifth day { Elche | - - - | 4 | 4½ |
| Orihuela | - - - | 5 | 7 |
| Sixth day  *Murcìa* | - - - | 4 | 5½ |
| Seventh day { A venta | - - - | 5 | 7 |
| *Carthagena* | - - - | 4 | 4½ |
|  |  | 51 | 75 |

From *Carthagena* to GRANADA.

|  |  | | |
|---|---|---|---|
| First day { Puente Alamo | - - | 4 | 5½ |
| Totana | - - | 5 | 7 |
| Second day { *Lorca* | - - - - | 4 | 5 |
| Lumbreras | - - - | 3 | 4 |
| Third day { Velez el Rubio | - - | 5 | 7 |
| Chiridel | - - | 3 | 4 |
| Fourth day { Cullar | - - - | 4 | 7 |
| *Baza* | - - - | 4 | 6 |
| Fifth day { A venta | - - - | 4 | 6½ |
| *Guadix* | - - - | 3 | 4½ |
|  |  | 39 | 56½ |

## APPENDIX.

|  |  | Leagues, | or Hours. |
|---|---|---|---|
| Brought over | | 39 | 56¼ |
| Sixth day { A venta | | 3 | 5 |
| { Ifnalloz | | 5 | 7¼ |
| Seventh day { A venta | | } 5 | 8¼ |
| { GRANADA | | | |
| | | 52 | 77¼ |

### From GRANADA to CORDOVA.

| First day | { A venta | 4 | 5 |
| | { Loxa | 4 | 6 |
| Second day | { A venta | 3 | 7 |
| | { Alamea | 4 | 7 |
| Third day | { Herrera | 4 | 7 |
| | { Ecija | 4 | 7 |
| Fourth day | { La Carlota | 3 | 5 |
| | { CORDOVA | 5 | 7 |
| | | 31 | 51 |

### From CORDOVA to *Malaga*.

| First day | To *Ecija* | 8 | 12 |
| Second day | { A venta | 3 } | 9½ |
| | { Caferiche | 3 } | |
| Third day | *Antequera* | 6 | 9 |
| Fourth day | A venta | 5 | 8 |
| Fifth day | { A venta | 3 | 4¼ |
| | { *Malaga* | 4 | 5¼ |
| | | 32 | 48¼ |

From *Malaga* to Cartama and back is 6 Leagues.

From

# APPENDIX.

### From *Malaga* to *Gibraltar* by way of *Ronda*.

|  |  | Leagues. | or Hours. |
|---|---|---|---|
| First day | A venta | 4 | 5¼ |
|  | Casa Rabonela | 2 | 5 |
| Second day | Burgo | 2 | 5¼ |
|  | Ronda | 3 | 7 |
| Third day | Alguzin | 5 | 10½ |
| Fourth day | San Roque | 6 | 11 |
|  | Gibraltar | 1 | 2 |
|  |  | 23 | 46¼ |

### From *Gibraltar* to Cadiz.

|  |  |  |  |
|---|---|---|---|
| First day | San Roque | 1 | 2 |
|  | Los Barrios | 2 | 3 |
| Second day | A venta | 5 | 7½ |
|  | Vejel | 3 | 4¼ |
| Third day | Chiclana | 3 | 6½ |
|  | La Ysla de Leon | 2 | 3 |
| Fourth day | Cadiz | 2 | 2½ |
|  |  | 18 | 29 |

### From Cadiz to Sevilla.

|  |  |  |  |
|---|---|---|---|
|  | Cross the bay to *Port St. Mary* | 3 | 1 |
| First day | Xerez | 2 | 3 |
| Second day | Lebrija | 5 | 5¼ |
|  | Venta | 6 | 6 |
| Third day | Sevilla | 4 | 4 |
|  |  | 20 | 19¼ |

Y y                                    From

# APPENDIX.

From SEVILLA to San Lucar, on the river *Guadalquivir*, is 17 leagues, which I failed in 20 hours.

From *San Lucar* to Port St. Mary, is 4 leagues, or 5 hours.

With refpect to the fhort excurfions which I made, the diftances from the feveral towns are mentioned in the former part of this work.

From Malaga to Vejel, by way of Gibraltar, the roads are impaffable in carriages.

I have thought it neceffary to mention the number of hours I employed in travelling from place to place, becaufe the leagues being generally only computed diftances, convey no determined idea of the fpace from one place to another. The ufual rate of travelling is from three and a half to five Englifh miles per hour, according as the roads are mountainous or level. The total number of leagues which I travelled from Lifbon till my arrival in Cadiz (exclufive of the voyages crofs the Straits of Gibraltar), is 578, in which I employed 800 hours, fo that thofe leagues probably amount to about three thoufand Englifh miles [*].

[*] Mr. Clarke has inferted in his work the Itinerary from Bilbao to Madrid, and from thence to Lifbon: and Mr. Baretti has publifhed an Itinerary of the roads from Lifbon to Madrid, and from thence to Saragoffa and Barcelona, &c. &c.

SUMMARY.

# APPENDIX.

## N° II.

## SUMMARY of the HISTORY of PORTUGAL.

ABOUT the year 714 of our æra, the Moors invaded Portugal, and continued in poffeffion of the greateft part of that kingdom till about the year 1072: during which period the other part of Portugal was governed by a fucceffion of twenty-five kings. In the year 1080, Count Don Henry made himfelf mafter of moft of the territories then in fubjection to the Moors, and reigned over the whole kingdom upwards of twenty years, without ever accepting the title of king; fo that the firft king was

Don Alfonfo I. born 1109; died 1185; reigned 57 years: he is buried in a convent in Coimbra. A Portuguefe account of this king fays, "That God operates feveral prodigies by means "of his body, as may be feen in the tenth fection of the *Appa-* "*rato Hiftorico*, which was printed in Rome in 1728, for the "beatification of that venerable king." Twenty-feven Elogies are inferted in that work.

2. His fon, Don Sancho I. born 1154; died 1211; reigned 26 years; buried in Coimbra.

3. His fon, Don Alfonfo II. born 1185; died 1223; reigned 12 years; buried in Alcobaça.

4. Don Sancho II. born 1202; died 1248. After having reigned nineteen years, he oppreffed feveral ecclefiaftics,

who complained to the pope (Innocent IV.): the king received admonitions from Rome, to which he paid no attention; so that *his holiness* deposed him in year the 1242, placing his brother Don Alfonso on the throne in his stead. Don Sancho was obliged to quit the kingdom, and take refuge in Toledo, where he died, and is buried.

5. His brother, Don Alfonso III. born 1210; died 1279; reigned 32 years; interred in Alcobaça.

6. His son, Don Denis; born 1261; died 1325; reigned 46 years; buried in the convent of Odivelas.

7. His son, Don Alfonso IV. born 1291; died 1357; reigned 32 years; buried in Lisbon. This king caused the beautiful Dona Ignez de Castro to be barbarously murdered in 1355, because she had clandestinely espoused his son Don Pedro. One of the best tragedies in the Portuguese language is founded on this story; and a French author, named Lamotte, has imitated it *.

8. Don Peter I. born 1320; died 1367; reigned 10 years; buried in Alcobaça, close by his spouse Dona Ignez. He was called the Cruel, because, notwithstanding he had sworn to his father that he would forgive the murderers of Dona Ignez, yet he caused two of them to be put to death, tearing out their hearts from their breasts, and afterwards burning them. He had the meanness to strike one of these wretches on the face whilst he was under these tortures. The king then caused the skeleton of Dona Ignez to be taken out of its sepulchre, to be invested with the royal habits, and the crown to be placed on its

---

* There is a Spanish tragedy on the same subject, written in 1577.

head.;

head; he ordered the Portuguese to acknowledge their queen in those insensible remains. The hem of its garments was then kissed by the nobility; and that novel and singular ceremony was the cause of its being said, that Dona Ignez reigned after having lived, and that she arose out of the tomb to mount the throne. In the tragedy above mentioned, she likewise is placed on the throne after her death.

9. His son, Don Ferdinand, born 1345; died 1383; reigned 17 years; buried in Santarem.

10. His brother, Don John I. born 1357; died of the plague in 1433: reigned 48 years; buried in Batalha.

In 1415, the city of Ceuta, in Barbary, was conquered by the Portuguese navy, which consisted of 220 sail (probably *sails*), commanded by the king in person.

In 1420, the Madeira islands were discovered by Gonçalvez Vaco and Tristas Vaz.

11. His third son, Don Edward, born 1391; died of the plague in 1438; reigned 5 years; buried in Batalha.

12. His son, Don Alfonso V. born 1432; died 1481; reigned 43 years; buried in Batalha.

13. His son, Don John II. born 1455; died 1495; reigned 14 years; buried in Batalha. The Portuguese account says, "that his body remains still uncorrupted; which, according to "some persons is a sign of its being predestinated."

In 1492, he refused the offers of Christopher Columbus, who in the same year discovered the new world for king Ferdinand and queen Isabel of Spain.

14. Don Emanuel, duke of Beja, and grandson to king Edward, born 1469; died 1521; reigned 26 years; buried in Bellem.

In 1497, Vasquez de Gama was sent by this king to continue the discoveries made in the Indies. He returned to Portugal after two years absence, having landed at Mozambique and Calicut, and pushed his navigation almost as far as Goa. The following year the king, after having rewarded de Gama, sent a new fleet to the Indies, under the command of Peter Capral, who, after four-and-twenty days sailing, landed in the Brasils, from whence he continued his route, and made an alliance with the kings of Cochin and of Cananor. In 1502, Don Emanuel went in person in pilgrimage to Santiago de Compostella, from a principle of devotion.

15. His son, Don John III. born 1502; died 1557; reigned 35 years; buried in Bellem. The most memorable action that I find recorded of this monarch is, that as he knew that Saint Thomas preached and died in the East Indies, he ordered the viceroy to make enquiries concerning the place of his sepulture, and concerning the particulars of his life. The famous Don John de Castro lived during this reign: his life, written in the Portuguese language, by Jacinto Freyre de Andrada, is much esteemed. The inquisition was established in Portugal about this time.

In 1555, Alvarez Cabral returned to Goa, having on board the celebrated Don Lewis de Camoens, who, in his *Lusiadas*, has sung the conquests of the Portuguese in the Indies.

# APPENDIX.

In 1531, an earthquake deftroyed almoft the whole city of Lifbon; and, it is faid, that thirty thoufand inhabitants perifhed among the ruins.

16. His grandfon, Don Sebaftian, born 1554; died fighting againft the Moors near Tangier in Africa, in 1578, having reigned ever fince the age of three years. For a fable about this prince, fee *le Voyageur François*, vol. xv. p. 259.

17. Don Henry, cardinal, fon to king Emanuel, and uncle to the late king, born 1512; died 1580; reigned about a year and a half: he is interred at Bellem. The Portuguefe account of his death fays, " he died in Almeirim. There was a great " lunar eclipfe the fame night, and an univerfal forrow, becaufe " every body perceived that the whole kingdom was alfo eclipfed " by that death. In the year 1682, his body was tranfported " from Almeirim to Bellem, and a noble monument erected " over it by order of king Peter II. By this means his body was " feen entire after having been buried 102 years, fo that we " have reafon from thence to believe that it enjoys beatitude."

In the fame year Don Philip II. of Caftile, took poffeffion by force of the kingdom of Portugal: he died and was buried in 1598 in the Efcorial, which he had founded, having lived 71 years, of which he had reigned 43 in all in Spain, and 18 in Portugal *.

---

* In 1583, the celebrated Don Ferdinand de Toledo, duke of Alba, died in Lifbon. In 1588, the fleet known by the name of the Invincible Armada, was fent againft England: part of it perifhed by tempefts, and part was taken by admiral Sir Francis Drake, fo that Spain loft by that expedition a hundred veffels, about one hundred and twenty-five thoufand men, and near two millions fterling.

19. His son, Don Philip III. succeeded him (Philip II. of Portugal); he died in 1621, after having reigned 22 years; he is buried in the Escorial.

The twentieth king of Portugal was Don Philip IV. (III.) son of the preceding monarch. His viceroy was massacred in 1640, and Don John, eighth duke of Bragança, was proclaimed

21. King of Portugal, by the name of Don John IV. he was born in 1604, and died in 1656, after a reign of almost 16 years: he is interred in the convent of S. Vincente de Fora, in Lisbon *.

Thus the Portuguese shook off the Spanish yoke, which they had borne for sixty years.

22. His son, Alfonso VI. born 1643; died 1683; reigned 11 years; buried in Bellem. This king, who was of a very weak understanding, was deposed in 1667, and his brother, the Infante Don Pedro, placed on the throne in his stead as regent.

Alfonso's queen accused her husband of impotence, upon which she was divorced, and her marriage declared to be null: she, without quitting the title of queen, married the regent (her brother-in-law) by means of a dispensation from cardinal de Vendôme, legate *a latere* in France, and the pope confirmed that dispensation by a brief.

---

* The manner in which the count-duke of Olivares announced to Philip the IV. the loss of Portugal, shows how kings are flattered in their misfortunes, and how truths, which are unpleasing, are hidden from them. " I " come, said he, to acquaint you with a happy piece of news: your ma- " jesty has gained all the fortune of the duke of Bragança; he has thought " proper to cause himself to be proclaimed king, and by his crime his estates " are confiscated to your majesty."

APPENDIX.

In 1668, a treaty of peace was concluded between Spain and Portugal : the court of Madrid acknowledged Portugal to be free and independent, and cut off from her coat of arms that of the crown of Portugal. Spain retained only Ceuta, which city had not followed the revolution in 1640. Thus finifhed a bloody war, which had lafted twenty-fix years. After the death of Alfonfo VI. which happened in 1683, the regent was proclaimed

23. King, by the title of Don Peter II. He was born in 1648, and died in 1706, after a reign of 38 years: he is buried in the convent of St. Vincente de Fora, in Lifbon.

24. He was fucceeded by his fon, Don John V. born 1689: he died in 1750, after having reigned near 44 years, and was buried near his father. He was regretted by his fubjects, whom he had rendered happy by his wife and prudent government, and by his generous and patriotic virtues. In 1748, pope Benedict XIV. granted the title of *fideliffimo* (moft faithful) to him and to his fucceffors.

25. His prefent majefty, Don Jofeph fucceeded his father in 1750: he was born in 1714. In 1755, an earthquake nearly deftroyed Lifbon. In 1758, a blunderbufs was difcharged at his majefty as he was returning to his palace at Bellem by night, and the following year the delinquents were executed near the fpot. In 1762, the Spaniards and the French invaded Portugal, but peace was fhortly after concluded between the three kingdoms.

kingdoms. His majesty, in 1729, espoused Dona Maria, princess of Asturias, daughter to Philip V. of Spain *.

The Portuguese history, from which most of these particulars were extracted, concludes thus, " From the time that he has "mounted the throne and handled the sceptre, he has shewn, "not only by the majesty of his person, and the clemency of "his genius, but by the generosity of his actions, that in him "is re-produced into lively existence the magnanimous heart of "his memorable father; and every Portuguese heart will be a "shield to the life and glory of our august monarch, who "in military campaigns will terrify the the most distant climates "of the universe with the echo of his valour." !

* An account of the present royal family is given in p. 11. of this work.

# APPENDIX.

### N° III.

## SUMMARY of the History of SPAIN.

THE Phœnicians about 240 years before the vulgar æra, called the Carthaginians into Spain: these were conquered by the Romans, who were in their turn vanquished by the Goths. Their first king, Ataulfo, died by the year 421. To him succeeded thirty-two other kings; and during the reign of the thirty-fourth king, Rodrigo, in 712, the Saracens and Moors, to the number of twenty-four thousand, invaded Andalusia, put the king to flight, and conquered Algeziras, Sevilla, Cordova, and many other cities. They afterwards made themselves masters of the greatest part of the kingdom, and pushed their conquests to the Gothic Gaul. In the year 718, great numbers of Christian Goths and Spaniards, who had taken refuge among the mountains of the Asturias and Biscay, finding their enemies employed at such a distance, chose Pelayo for their chief: he gained several victories over the Moors, and in 737 died, after having reigned in the northern provinces of Spain [*]. He was succeeded by his son Favila, who was killed the following year by a bear when he was hunting. The 37th king was Alfonso I. surnamed the Catholic, son-in-law to Pelayo. During his reign

---

[*] About this time a king of Navarre was also elected.

a civil war broke out among the Moors, which gave Alfonso an opportunity of retaking many provinces. He died in 757. He was succeeded by his eldest son Don Fruela. In 761, he built the city of Oviedo, made it an episcopal see, and the capital of his dominions, from whence the ancient kings were styled kings of Oviedo. He was the first who introduced the title of *Don* in these kingdoms. The Moor Abderamo conquered Saragossa, and the provinces of Aragon and Catalonia. In 765, he entered into an alliance with Pepin king of France, with a view to ensure the peaceable possession of his dominions in Spain. About this time the Moorish gallantry, arms, and arts flourished; and they rendered Granada and Cordova two of the most beautiful cities in Europe: thus the Barbarians were become the civilized inhabitants of Spain, and the Spaniards were changed into Barbarians. In 767, Don Fruela murdered his brother, and the following year was assassinated himself, and another of his brothers, named Don Aurelio, placed on the throne. He died in 774, and was succeeded by Don Silo, who died 782. The 41st king was named Mauregato: he died in 789. About this time Abderamo built the famous mosque in Cordova, and died shortly after. The 42d king, Don Veremundo, or Bermudo I. abdicated the throne, and died four years after. He was succeeded by Don Alfonso II. surnamed the Chaste: the time when he began his reign is very uncertain; some historians place it in 762, others in 791: it is supposed that he died in 842, and his son Don Ramiro I. succeeded him. He gained a memorable victory over the Moors by the miraculous assistance of the apostle

St.

# APPENDIX.

St. James, patron of Spain, who appeared at the head of his army, according to the Spanish historians, and from thence forward a part of all military spoils have been allotted to the share of that saint and soldier *. Ramiro died in 850, and his son Don Ordoño I. reigned in his stead †, till 865, when he died, and was succeeded by his son Don Alfonso III. He abdicated, in 911, in favour of his son Don Garcia, who reigned only three years. His brother, Don Ordoño II. succeeded him, and died in 923. His brother, Don Fruela II. was then placed on the throne, which he filled thirteen months, and died detested by his subjects because of his tyranny. Don Alfonso IV. son of Don Ordoño II. was then proclaimed king of Leon and the Asturias. After reigning three years he abdicated in favour of his brother, Don Ramiro II. and turned monk in the monastery of Sahagun: soon after which he repented, and attempted to regain the throne, but his brother caused his eyes to be put out. Don Ramiro died in 950, after having declared his son Don Ordoño III his successor. He died in 955, and his son Don Ordoño IV. reigned one year, at the expiration of which he was murdered by his uncle Don Sancho I. surnamed the Fat, who placed himself on the throne. He was poisoned in 967, and the crown was given to his son Don Ramiro III. under the regency of his mother Doña Theresa, and Doña Elvira, sister to the late king, and a nun in a monastery in Leon. A French

* Clave Historial. p. 170.
† The streets of the city of Cordova were paved by the Moors in 853. A French author says, that those of Paris were not paved till 1183.

author makes the following reflections upon this event. "This is perhaps the only example we find in history of a turbulent and warlike people suffering themselves to be governed by a nun; and of two women, who being jointly entrusted with the government, had the common good in view in all their actions, without division, without quarrels, without rivalship, and without jealousy."

About this time the first king of Castile reigned, so that Spain was governed by four different kings, which were those of Leon and the Asturias, of Navarre, of Castile, and the Moorish king of Cordova. Don Ramiro died in 982, and was succeeded by his son Don Bermudo II. who died in 999. Don Alfonso V. then reigned till the year 1027, when he was killed by an arrow at the siege of Viseu in Portugal. His son, Don Bermudo III. then filled the throne. In 1037, Don Garcia IV. king of Navarre, aided by his brother Ferdinand I. king of Castile, gave battle to Don Bermudo, who was defeated and killed, and with him ended the male posterity of the Gothic kings descended from Pelayo. Ferdinand advanced towards the city of Leon, at the head of his victorious army, caused himself to be there crowned, and united that kingdom to Castile, by virtue of his marriage with Doña Sancha, sister to the late king Bermudo. A new king *sprung up* in Aragon about this time. Ferdinand divided his kingdom among his three sons, and died in 1065. The eldest son, Don Sancho, seized on the possessions of both his brothers, but he was prevented from enjoying them, being assassinated in 1072. He was succeeded by his brother, Don Alfonso VI. who

was

## APPENDIX. 359

was proclaimed, after having taken an oath that he was innocent of his brother's death, in prefence of the celebrated Rodrigo Diaz de Vivar, fo well known by the name of the *Cid* (which in the Morifco language fignifies *Lord.*) Alfonfo confined his younger brother, and took Galicia from him. In 1085, he conquered Toledo from the Moors. Nine years after which, the *Cid* conquered Valencia for the king his mafter: he died in 1099. A French author fays, that the tragedy by Peter Corneille, which is intitled after him, and which has been tranflated into almoft all the European languages, has given a greater luftre to his name than all his military exploits did. Alfonfo died in 1109; and the 62d king was Don Alfonfo VII. He was fucceeded, in 1126, by Don Alfonfo VIII. and he, by Don Sancho III. in 1157, who reigned only a year. Don Ferdinand II. afterwards reigned a very fhort time, during the minority of Don Alfonfo IX. who was the 66th king. Ferdinand died in 1188, and Alfonfo in 1214 after a reign of 56 years. His fon, Don Henry I. fucceeded him, and was killed the following year by the fall of a tile on his head. Don Ferdinand III. furnamed the Saint, was then proclaimed. He conquered Sevilla from the Moors in 1248: he died four years after; and, in 1671, was canonized by pope Clement X. who gracioufly permitted the Spaniards to celebrate the feftival of their new faint. He was fucceeded by Don Alfonfo X. furnamed the Wife. He was elected emperor at Franckfort in 1257; and, at the fame time, another party elected Richard earl of Cornwall, and brother to king Henry III. of England, emperor. Alfonfo went to Beaucaire, where he had an interview with pope Gregory X. who refused to confirm his title of emperor. He died in 1284: he composed Aftronomical Tables, and two books on the philofopher's ftone, which laft are faid to be yet preferved in the Royal Library at Madrid. His fon, Don Sancho IV. was then crowned; he was furnamed the Brave; died in 1295, and was fucceeded by his fon Don Ferdinand IV. The Spanifh hiftorians write, that this monarch having caufed two brothers to be thrown from a rock in the kingdom of Jaen, without any trial, they fummoned him to appear before God within thirty days, and that he accordingly died on the laft of thofe days, though in perfect health: this is faid to have happened in 1312. His fon, Don Alfonfo XI. then reigned. In 1342, he laid fiege to the town of Algeciras, which was in poffeffion of the Moors, who defended it with cannon againft the feeble machines of war then in ufe to batter down walls. This is the firft time we find artillery mentioned in hiftory: it was probably invented by the Moors, though gun-powder had before been invented in Germany. This fiege lafted two years, but at length the town capitulated by order of the kings of Morocco and Granada, upon condition of a truce of ten years taking place between them and the king of Caftile. Don Alfonfo died of the plague in 1350. He was fucceeded by his fon, Don Peter the Cruel, who was excommunicated by the pope in 1355; and, in 1369, after a reign, of which every day had been diftinguifhed by the moft barbarous executions, ftabbed by his brother Don Henry II. who was then proclaimed king: he died in 1379, and was

fucceeded

succeeded by his son, Don John I. This prince, in 1390, was killed by a fall from his horse. His son, Don Henry III. then reigned. The first clock which was seen in Spain was placed in the cathedral of Sevilla in 1400. In 1402, Don Henry received Ambassadors and magnificent presents from the famous Tamerlane. In 1405, Henry enacted laws by which he ordered Jews and concubines of ecclesiastics to wear a distinguishing mark on their clothes; and the following year he died. His son, Don John II. who was but fourteen months old, succeeded him, under the regency of his mother and his uncle: at the age of thirteen he took the reins of government into his own hands. In 1434, an ambassador was sent to him from Charles VII. king of France, requesting his assistance against the English: this ambassador was received by Don John sitting on a magnificent throne, with a tame lion at his feet, in allusion to his crown of Leon. He died in 1454, and was succeeded by his son, Don Henry IV. surnamed the Impotent, who died in 1474. It was suspected that he was poisoned by contrivance of Doña Isabel, daughter to John II. she married the king of Aragon, and they were jointly proclaimed sovereigns of Castile and Aragon, under the names of Don Ferdinand V. and Doña Isabel. During their reign the inquisition was established, and in the first *auto-de-fé*, in 1481, seven persons were burnt alive. They conquered upwards of seventy cities and towns, which were possessed by the Mahometans,. among which was the city of Granada, which put an end to the dominion of the Moors in Spain, after having lasted almost eight hundred years. In 1492, America was

was discovered by Christopher Columbus. In 1496, the title of *Catholic* was granted to the kings of Spain by pope Alexander VI. In 1504, queen Isabel died. In 1509, Oran, in Africa, was taken by the Spaniards ; and, in the same year, king Henry VIII. of England, espoused Doña Catherine of Aragon, daughter to Don Ferdinand, but afterwards Henry divorced her, and separated himself from the Romish church. In 1513, Peru, Chili, and Paraguay, in South America, were discovered, and the city of Panama founded. Don Ferdinand died in 1516, having first caused himself to be invested with the Dominican habit.

In the mean time, Don Philip I. reigned over Castile from 1504, till his death, which happened two years after. The 81st king of Spain was Don Charles I. of Luxemburg, (afterwards the emperor Charles V. in Germany): he was proclaimed in Valladolid in 1519. In the same year Ferdinand Cortez conquered Mexico. Charles was the first sovereign who assumed the title of *majesty*. He abdicated the throne at Brussels in 1555, in favour of his son, who was proclaimed by the title of Don Philip II. Charles had been nine times in Germany, six times in Spain, four times in France, seven times in Italy, ten times in the Netherlands, twice in England, as many times in Africa, and eleven times at sea. He died two years after his abdication, in the monastery of St. Just, whither he had retired after a reign of upwards of forty years. In 1559, Don Philip ordered two *autos-de-fé*, or religious executions, in Valladolid, at one of which himself was present; seventy unhappy wretches of both sexes were there burnt alive. This barbarous

barous monarch confined his own son in prison, where he languished and died: and, in 1568, sent the no less barbarous duke of Alva to massacre those inhabitants of the Netherlands who refused to embrace the Catholic Faith. In 1581, Philip was proclaimed king of Portugal after the death of Don Henry. In 1586, he finished the building of the Escorial: in 1588, sent the navy styled the *Invincible Armada*, against England; and, in 1598, he died, after a reign of near 43 years. He was succeeded by his son, Don Philip III. who died in 1621. His son, Don Philip IV. then filled the thrones of Spain and Portugal; but, in 1640, he lost the crown of the latter kingdom, which was seized by the duke of Bragança. In 1647, he renounced all pretensions to the seven United Provinces, and declared them free and independent. In 1653, he permitted the cruel tribunal of the inquisition to celebrate an *auto-de-fé*, in which of seventy-two Jews and heretics, some were burnt, and others whipped and banished. He died in 1665, after a reign of 44 years, and left his kingdom to his son Don Charles II. who was at that time an infant of four years of age, under the regency of his mother. She appointed her confessor, father Nitard, to be grand inquisitor, and placed him at the head of her council. This German Jesuit said one day to a grandee who spoke haughtily to him, " Remember, it is you that are to respect me, " who have every day your God in my hands, and your queen " at my feet." He was afterwards sent ambassador to Rome, and attained to the dignity of cardinal. At the age of fifteen Don Charles

Charles took the government into his own hands; and, in 1679, espoused, at Burgos, the princess Louisa of Orleans, niece to Lewis XIV. of France; and, by way of rejoicing at these nuptials, an *auto-de-fé* was ordered, in which twenty-two victims of the inquisition perished in flames, and sixty others were condemned to corporal punishment. Don Charles died in 1700: as he had no children, he, by his will, declared the duke of Anjou to be his successor, upon condition that he should never be capable of succeeding to the crown of France. The duke was second son to the Dauphin, nephew to Don Charles, and was proclaimed king at Madrid, under the name of Philip V. In 1724, he abdicated the crown in favour of his son Don Lewis, who died of the small-pox in the same year, having done nothing more remarkable, then causing five Jews to be burnt in an *auto-de-fé*. His father then resumed the government of the kingdom, and died in 1746, after a reign of 46 years. He was twice married; by his first marriage, which was with Doña Louisa of Savoy, he had three sons; the two first dying, the third succeeded to the crown by the name of Don Ferdinand VI. By his second marriage, which was with Doña Isabel Farnese princess of Parma, he had a son named Don Charles (the present king of Spain), who, in 1734, was declared king of Naples; two sons who died young, the late duke of Parma, and the infant Don Lewis who is yet living; the present queen of Portugal; the late dauphiness of France; and the present princess of Piedmont.

# APPENDIX.

Don Ferdinand VI. died in 1759\*, and was succeeded by his present majesty, Don Charles III. (89th king). Berni, the Spanish historian, in his book, mentioned in p. 177 of this work, and which is dedicated to the king, thus expresses himself: " Our actual monarch, whom God preserve, is the lord
" Don Charles III. of Bourbon: he succeeded his beloved bro-
" ther the lord Don Ferdinand VI. he espoused the lady Doña
" Maria-Amelia of Saxony, who is in glory (i. e. dead).

" Leaving his praises to better pens than mine, I shall only
" say, that through the mercy of God, we glory in a monarch
" happy in religion, justice, piety, together with arts, sciences,
" fabrics, and rewards to the deserving; and we are obliged to
" pray to God for the spiritual and temporal salvation of our
" Catholic monarch (and royal family), and to offer with all
" our hearts, our lives and our goods in defence of his royal
" person, and in obedience to his laws and decrees, with an
" especial precise obligation to know him, love him, fear him,
" honour him, and guard him. First, because in the temporal
" he holds the place of God, and is called the vicar of God.
" Secondly, because the authority of his laws is approved by
" the holy scripture, *By me kings reign, and princes decree justice:*
" *By me princes rule, and nobles, even all the judges of the earth.*
" Prov. viii. v. 15 and 16. Thirdly, because our sovereign, in
" the temporal, acknowledges no superior in this world, but on-
" ly the king of kings, who is God, our creator, redeemer, and

\* This monarch and his father, Philip V. are both said to have died insane.

" saviour.

" faviour. Fourthly, becaufe our monarch is head, heart, and
" foul of the people, and fuch a lover of his vaffals, and of the
" upright adminiftration of juftice, that he governs and com-
" mands us according to the fcientific laws of the kingdom,
" which are praifed by all the civilized nations in the world, as
" they teach us catholic, juridical, and oeconomical rules up-
" on all occafions, for the better fervice of God, of the king, and
" of the public good, and on the moft folid foundations explain
" to the Spaniards their obligations to their fovereign : fo that
" we muft ferve, fear, and love him with a fine affection, by the
" fight; by the hearing; by the fmell; by the tafte; by the
" feeling; by the tongue; by the underftanding; by the fancy;
" by the imagination; by the thinking; and by the remem-
" brance *."

\* See p. 167 for an account of the prefent royal family of Spain.

# APPENDIX.

## Nº IV.

### CATALOGUE of BOOKS which describe SPAIN and PORTUGAL.

#### ENGLISH.

*MEMOIRS of the Court of Spain*, 1679, 1 vol. 12mo. translated from the French, by *T. Brown*: political.

*The Lady's Travels in Spain*, 1679, 2 vols. translated from the French.

> A new incorrect edition of this romantic work was published in 1774.

*Miscellaneous Tracts*, by Dr. *Michael Geddes*, 4 vols. 8vo. 1690, on the inquisition, the expulsion of the Moors, &c.

*The History of the Conquest of Spain by the Moors*, translated from the Spanish, by *M. Taubman*, 1687, 1 vol. 8vo.

*A brief History of the Kings of Spain*, by *Captain John Stevens*, compiler of a Spanish and English Dictionary, 1701, 1 vol. 8vo.

*Travels in France, Spain*, &c. 1701, a small folio, by *E. Veryard*, M.D. Of this work only ten pages relate to Spain.

*The History of the Royal Genealogy of Spain*, translated from the French by *Thomas Richers*, 1718, 1 vol. 8vo.

*Brome's*

*Brome's Travels through Portugal, Spain, Italy,* &c. 1712, 1 vol. 8vo.

*An Account of Spain and Portugal,* by *Udal ap Rhys* (or *Price*), 1749, 1 vol. 8vo. a compilation.

*Letters concerning the Spanish Nation,* 1761, 1 vol. 4to. by the Reverend *Edward Clarke,* chaplain to the Earl of Bristol.

*Journey through Portugal and Spain,* by *Joseph Baretti,* 1760, 4 vols. 8vo. From Lisbon through Madrid to Barcelona.

*History of Minorca,* by *John Armstrong,* 1 vol. 8vo. with a map and four plates, 1756.

*History of the Straits of Gibraltar,* 2 vols. 4to, by *Lieutenant Colonel James,* with eighteen plates, 1771 *.

*A Description of the Escurial,* 1760, 1 vol. 4to. with twelve beautiful copper-plates: *Done* into English by *Geo. Thompson.*

*Berni's Genealogy of the Kings of Spain,* 1 vol. folio. I never could get a sight of this translation.

### FRENCH.

*Voyage d'Espagne, par C. de Sercy,* 1655, 1 vol. 4to.

*Lettres de Madame de Villars,* ambassadrice en Espagne en 1679, a small duodecimo, printed at Amsterdam in 1760.

*Voyage d'Espagne, par Bergeron,* 1690, 1 vol. 8vo.

*Relation du Voyage d'Espagne, par Madame Daunois,* 1679, 3 vols. 8vo. This is the original work which is translated, and entitled the *Lady's Travels.*

\* See p. 277, for a farther account of this work.

# APPENDIX.

*Voyage du Pere Labat en Espagne & en Italie*, 8 vols. 8vo.
The firſt volume gives an account of Cadiz and Sevilla, and where the author was in 1705; the other ſeven volumes contain a deſcription of Italy.

*L'Etat preſent de l'Espagne, par l'Abbé de Vayrac*, 3 vols. 1719.

*Delices de l'Espagne & du Portugal*, 6 vols. 12mo. 1730, with a great number of indifferent copper-plates.

*Annales d'Espagne & de Portugal*, 8 vols. 8vo. 1741: both theſe works are by *Don Juan Alvarez de Colmenar*, and are chiefly compilations. There is likewiſe a 4to. edition of the *Annales*, in 4 vols. with copper-plates.

*Deſcription de Liſbonne*, 1 vol. 8vo. 1730.

*Hiſtoire Abregée des Peintres Eſpagnols*, 1 vol. 8vo. 1740, tranſlated and abridged from *Don Antonio Palomino Velaſco*'s Spaniſh work.

*Abregé Chronologique de l'Hiſtoire d'Espagne, par M. Deſormeaux*, 5 vols. 8vo. 1758.

——————————————— *& de Portugal*, in two thick 8vo vols. 1765.
This is eſteemed to be the beſt hiſtory of the Peninſula.

*Voyage d'Espagne en 1755*, printed in 1772, 2 vols. 8vo. This is a very bad and imperfect tranſlation of *Father Caimo's* book, by *P. de Livoy*.

*Voyage de France, d'Espagne, de Portugal*, &c. *par M. S.* 4 vols. 12mo. 1770.
The two laſt volumes give a very conciſe account of the writer's Tour through Spain in 1729.

*Anecdotes Espagnoles & Portugaises*, 2 vols. thick octavo, 1773: historical.

*Histoire de l'Afrique & de l'Espagne sous la Domination des Arabes, par M. Cardonne*, 1765, 3 vols. 8vo.

There is at present a work carrying on in Paris, intitled, *Le Voyageur François*, compiled by the *Abbé de la Porte*. Eighteen volumes in 8vo. have already appeared: half of the fifteenth contains the description of Portugal, and the sixteenth that of Spain.

## ITALIAN.

*Lettere d'un Vago Italiano ad un suo Amico*, in 4 vols. 8vo. 1755, by Father *Norberto Caimo* *.

*Stato presente di tutti i Popoli del Mondo.*

This work, which is publishing in Venice, is to be comprised in 30 volumes, of which 27 have appeared: the 14th and 15th treat of Spain and Portugal, and have a great number of badly engraven copper-plates, chiefly copied from those in the *Delices de l'Espagne*, and some of them are mere works of fancy, especially the View of Madrid, where the engraver has represented ships sailing near the town; and that of Gibraltar, where there is the view of a city supposed to be situated on the top of the rock. The print of the Cortile *de los Leones*, in the Alhambra at Granada, is tolerably accurate.

* For a farther account of this work, see p. 96.

I know

# APPENDIX.

I know not of any German or Dutch book which defcribes thefe kingdoms, except the *Travels of Van Egmont*, where, in the fecond chapter of the firft volume, is fome account of Cadiz.

In 1738, were publifhed at Amfterdam, two quarto volumes, entitled, *Emanuelis Martini Ecclefiæ Alonenfis Decani, Epiftolarum, libri duodecim*, with a fine head of the author, and two other plates, one of which is a plan of the amphitheatre of Saguntum.

## PORTUGUESE.

*Mappa de Portugal, pelo Padre Joaõ Baut. de Caftro*, 3 vols. 4to. Lifbon, 1762, with bad maps.

*Monumento acro de Mafra, por Fr. do Prado*, one fmall folio, with three plates, 1751.

*Roteiro Terreftre de Portugal*: this is a duodecimo, copied from de Caftro's above mentioned work.

## SPANISH.

*La Efpaña Sagrada, del P. Florez*, 25 vols. in fmall 4to. with a few plates of infcriptions, &c. This work is chiefly ecclefiaftical hiftory.

*Medallas de las Colonias Municipios y Pueblos Antiguos de Efpaña*, by the fame Father *Florez*, 2 vols. 4to. Madrid, 1758, with 58 extremely well engraven plates of the medals. I believe there are two more volumes of this work publifhed lately.

APPENDIX.

*Hiſtoria de las Reynas de Eſpaña*, 2 vols. 4to. by the ſame author.

*Clave Hiſtorial*, by the ſame hand, 4to. Madrid, 1769. At the end of this work is inſerted a ſmall print, repreſenting one of the medals ſtruck in honour of admiral Vernon, after his having taken Puerto-Bello, in 1739; the author wilfully confounds this victory with the unſucceſsful expedition againſt Carthagena, in 1741, and ſays, " this medal will be a perpetual teſtimony " of the pride and levity of the Engliſh."

*Don Juan de Mariana* publiſhed a hiſtory of Spain in the laſt century, which was lately reprinted in Madrid, in three folio volumes.

*Compendio de la Hiſtoria de Eſpaña*, 2 vols. 12mo. Madrid, 1767. This is a very elegant and liberal tranſlation from the French of Father *du Cheſne*, by the celebrated Father *Joſeph de Iſla*, author of *Frey Gerundio*.

*Guerra de Granada por Don Felipe II. contra los Moriſcos, por Don Diego de Mendoza*, 8vo. 1766.

*Theatro univerſal de Eſpaña, por Don Franciſco de Garma y Salcedo*, 4 vols. 12mo. 1768: hiſtorical and political.

*Genealogìa de los Reyes de Eſpaña*, 1720, 12mo. Antwerp, with a few maps.

*Deſcripcion del Eſcorial, del P. Andres Ximenez*, a new edition in folio, with many copper-plates, Madrid, 1764.

*Deſcripcion de la Provincia de Madrid, por D. Thomas Lopez*, with a map of the environs of Madrid, 1763, 12mo.

*Deſcripcion*

# APPENDIX.

*Descripcion de Valencia, por Pasqual de Gillò,* 1738, 8vo. with a plan of the city.

*Descripcion del Reyno de Portugal, por D. Francisco Nipho,* 1762, 12mo.

*Coreo general de España.* This is a work of which the first volume in quarto was published in Madrid 1769, by the same Don Francisco Nipho: five volumes have already appeared, and it is yet continued, treating of agriculture, arts, and commerce, with a few wooden cuts.

*Noticia Geografica del Reyno y Caminos de Portugal, por Don Pedro Rodriguez Campomanès,* 1762, 8vo. dedicated to his excellency Don Richard Wall [*].

*Viage de España, por Don Antonio de la Puente.* There were two volumes of this work published in Madrid, 8vo. 1772 and 1774, and it is intended to be continued: it is pretty well written, but very diffuse, as these two volumes contain only the description of Toledo, Aranjuez, and the Escorial.

*Paseos por Granada,* two small quartos, 1764. In this work some information may be picked up from among a heap of nonsense. I was acquainted with the author in Granada.

To these may be added, *Creacion, Antiguedad, y Privilegios de los Titulos de Castilla, por D. Joseph Berni,* printed, Valencia, 1769, in a thick folio, dedicated to the present king. This book contains a list of the Spanish monarchs, and of all the nobility,

---

[*] Smollet's translation of Don Quixote is dedicated to this gentleman.

but many errors have unavoidably crept into it: it is ornamented with the heads of the sovereigns, though but badly engraven.

There are existing in Spain several folio histories of Toledo, Sevilla, Granada, Cordova, Madrid, Segovia, Salamanca, &c. all published a hundred years ago, and very uninteresting: for example, that of Segovia, which is in folio, makes not the least mention of the aqueduct of Trajan, but then it contains a particular account of relics, and the like rubbish.

From among all this heap of books (most of which I have been under the disagreeable necessity of reading), I recommend the following to the perusal of the intelligent reader.

The 15th and 16th volume of *Le Voyageur François*; Father Caimo's Italian work; La Ysla's Compendium of the History of Spain; and de la Puente's *Viage de España*. The plates in the *History of Gibraltar*, and in the *Description of the Escurial*, are worthy of inspection.

APPENDIX. 375

N° V.

Some Account of the SPANISH and PORTUGUESE
LITERATURE.

VOLTAIRE, in his Essay on Epic Poetry, having criti-
cised the *Lusiad* of *Camoens*, and the *Araucana* of *Ercilla
de Zuñiga*, which are the best epic poems of the two nations,
the first of which is written in the Portuguese, and the second in
the Spanish language; I shall begin with them, availing myself
of all his remarks, when I find them consonant with those of
the writers of their respective nations.

Lewis de Camoens was born in Lisbon, about the year 1523,
of an ancient Portuguese family, whilst John III. reigned in
Portugal. His successor, Don Emanuel, who was determined
to pursue the scheme which had so often proved abortive, of
opening a route to the East Indies, by way of the ocean, sent
Vasco de Gama, in 1497, with a fleet for that celebrated enterprize, which having succeeded, laid the foundation for the
commerce which Europe still carries on by sea with the Indies.
In 1553, Camoens went to the Indies; a vague desire for travelling and making his fortune; the danger to which his indis-
creet gallantries at Lisbon had exposed him; his discontented
situation at the court; and above all, that curiosity which most-

ly

ly attends a great genius, were the motives which concurred to induce him to leave his country. He first served as a volunteer on board a ship, and lost an eye in a naval combat in the Straits of Gibraltar. The Portuguese had already a viceroy in the Indies. Camoens, when at Goa, was exiled by that viceroy, because he had satirized some principal persons residing there, and languished several years in an obscure corner on the frontiers of China, where the Portuguese had a small factory, and where they had begun to build the town of Macao. There it was that he composed his poem on the discovery of the Indies, which he intitled the *Lusiada*, a title which is but little applicable to its subject, and which properly signifies *Portugada*. He obtained a small place in Macao, and returning from thence to Goa, he was shipwrecked on the coast of China, and is said to have saved his life by swimming with one hand, and holding his poem, which was his all, in the other. On his arrival at Goa he was cast into prison, from whence he was released only to undergo a greater misfortune, which was that of following a petty, proud, and avaricious governor to Sofala in Africa. He returned at last to Lisbon with his poem, which was his whole fortune: he printed it in 1572, and obtained a pension of about thirty pounds of our money, which was soon taken from him. He had then no other retreat than an hospital, where he passed the rest of his life; and, in 1579, died abandoned by all. He was scarcely dead, when many honourable epitaphs were made on him, and he was placed in the rank of great men. Several towns disputed the honour of having given birth to him: so

that

that he experienced Homer's fate in every thing: he travelled like Homer, he lived and died poor, and gained no reputation till after his death. These examples ought to teach men of genius, that it is not by genius that a man acquires a fortune and lives happily.

The subject of the *Lusiada* is neither a war, the quarrel of a hero, nor the world in arms for a woman, but only a new country discovered by the assistance of navigation. The poet sets off thus *:

" I sing the signalized men, who from the occidental coast of
" Lusitania, over seas never before navigated, passed even be-
" yond Taprobana (Ceylon), and in a remote country founded
" a new kingdom."

" Let the navigations of the sage Grecian, and of the
" Trojan be no more wondered at. Let the fame of the
" victories of Alexander and Trajan cease, for I sing the
" illustrious Lusitanian whom Neptune and Mars obeyed: let
" the ancient Muses be silent, for his valour surpasses all they
" have sung of others; and you, nymphs of the Tagus, if ever
" I celebrated in humble verse your beautiful river, grant me an
" elevated and flowing style, for Phoebus has ordained that your
" waters shall not envy those of Hypocrena, &c. &c."

* The French paragraphs which Voltaire has inserted in his above mentioned essay, and which he says were translated from the original Portuguese, are different from the following translated quotations, because I have given them as they really are.

APPENDIX.

The poet conducts the Portuguese fleet to the mouth of the Ganges, by way of the Cape of Good Hope: he describes the different nations inhabiting the coasts of Africa: he artfully intermixes the history of Portugal in that description. In the third canto, stanza 118, is the story of Dona Ignez de Castro: this part Voltaire esteems to be the most beautiful in the whole poem, and says, that there are few parts in Virgil more affecting or better written.

Voltaire thus continues: The simplicity of the poem is ennobled by fictions as novel as the subject. The following one, I venture to affirm, will be admired in all times, and by all nations.

"When the fleet is on the point of doubling the Cape of
"Good-Hope, at that time called the Promontory of Tempests,
"a formidable object is discovered: it is a phantom which rises
"out of the bottom of the sea; his head touches the clouds;
"tempests, winds, and thunders environ him; his arms extend
"over the whole surface of the waters: this monster, or this
"god, is the guardian of this ocean, of which the waves had
"never yet been ploughed by any vessel; he threatens the fleet,
"he complains of the audacity of the Portuguese, who are
"come to dispute the empire of those seas with him, and an-
"nounces all the calamities which they are to suffer in the pro-
"secution of their enterprise." Canto v. stanza 39.

The literal translation of part of the above passage is as follows:
"One

# APPENDIX.

"One night a cloud, which darkened the air, appeared over our heads, the tempeftuous fea roared horribly, fo that our hearts trembled; a phantom was then feen in the air, of an enormous ftature and deformed human fhape, his fize furpaff- ed that of the Coloffus of Rhodes, his beard was fqualid, his eyes funk in his head, his hair clotted with earth, his complexion pallid, his mouth black, and his teeth yellow; his horrid voice, which caufed our hair to ftand on end, feemed to iffue from the bottom of the fea, &c."

Another fiction in this poem is much admired by the Portuguefe, and conforms to the Italian genius: it is an enchanted ifland, which appears at fea, in order to refrefh Gama and his fleet*. This ifland is faid to have ferved as a model for the ifland of Armida, defcribed by Taffo a few years afterwards. There Venus, aided by the counfels of the Eternal Father, and, at the fame time, feconded by the arrows of Cupid, caufes the *Nereides* to fall in love with the Portuguefe; each of whom embraces a Nereid, and Vafco de Gama falls to the lot of Thetis. In the ninth canto, that goddefs tranfports him to the top of a high mountain, fituated in the moft delicious part of the ifland, from thence fhe fheweth him all the kingdoms of the world, and the glory of them: and in the tenth and laft, foretels the deftiny of Portugal.

\* *Os fermofos Limões, alli cheirando*
*Eſtaõ virgineas tetas imitando.*      Canto ix. Stanza 56.

The goodly lemons, with their button-caps,
Hang imitating virgin's fragrant paps.      FANSHAW.

                                 Camoens.

Camoens, after having abandoned himself without reserve to the voluptuous description of the island, and of the pleasures into which the Portuguese are plunged, thinks proper to inform the reader, that this whole fiction only implies the pleasure that an honest man feels in doing his duty.

The principal aim of the Portuguese, after the establishment of their commerce, is the propagation of the faith, and Venus takes the success of that enterprize upon herself. To speak seriously, such an absurd miracle disfigures the whole work in the eyes of a sensible reader; but the beauty of the style, and the imagination in the expression, have sustained the reputation of this poem. Thus the beauties of execution have classed Paul Veronese among the greater painters, though he has placed Benedictine monks and Swiss soldiers in subjects taken from the Old Testament. Camoens is perpetually guilty of the like absurdities; he quotes Ulysses and Æneas to the king of Melinda, as if an African barbarian understood Homer and Virgil. But of all the defects in this poem, the greatest is the little connection its parts have with each other; it resembles the voyage it describes. On the whole, the work contains many beauties, and has delighted the Portuguese nation for these last two hundred years [*].

In the 6th canto, (stanza 45 to 68), a tale is told *as how* twelve Portuguese knights went to England, towards the end of the four-

---
[*] Almost all the foregoing remarks are translated from Voltaire.

teenth century, and fought with, and vanquished twelve English knights, who had asperfed the fame of the like number of English ladies, and had

> " Said they would prove that such and such of them,
> " Had been too lavish of their honor's gem." FANSHAW.

The whole poem is comprised in ten cantos, and the total number of stanzas is 1102; each stanza consisting of eight lines.

There is an old Spanish translation of the Lusiad extant, but I never could meet with it.

In 1655, an English translation of the Lusiad was published by Richard Fanshaw. This is a thin folio, without any notes, but ornamented with the portraits of Camoens, Don Henry of Portugal, and Vasco de Gama. In p. 299 of the present work, I have inserted a stanza from Camoens, which is thus translated by Mr. Fanshaw:

So a brisk lover in the bloody place
(His beauteous mistress by, in a balcon)
Seeks out the bull, and (planted face to face)
Curvets, runs, whistles, waves, and toles him on;
But the stern bruite, ev'n in a moment's space
(His horned brow low'd to the earth) doth run
Bellowing about like mad; and (his eyes shut)
Dismounts, strikes, kills, and tramples under-foot.

As

As this translation is very difficult to be met with, I shall add another stanza, as a specimen of the author's versification.

### Canto ix. v. 83.

O what devouring kisses (multiply'd),
What pretty whimp'rings did the grove repeat!
What flatt'ring force! what anger which did chide
Itself, and laugh when it began to threat!
What more than this, the blushing morning spy'd,
And Venus, (adding her's to the noon's heat)
Is better try'd then guess'd, I must confess:
But those who cannot try it, let them guess.

The original runs thus:

*O que famintos beijos na floresta,*
*E que mimoso choro, que soáva,*
*Que afagos tão suaves, que ira honesta,*
*Que em risinhos alegres se tòrnava!*
*O que mais pasião na menhãa, & na sesta,*
*Que Venus com prazeres inflamáva,*
*Melhor he experimentálo, que julgálo,*
*Mas julgueo, que não pòde exprimentálo.*

In justice to Camoens and to Fanshaw, I beg leave to add part of Dona Ignez's pathetic supplication to her husband's father, who was determined to have her put to death.

*Para*

# APPENDIX.

*Para o cco criſtalino levantando*
*Com lagrimas os olhos piedoſos,*
*Os olhos, porque as mãos lhe eſtava atando*
*Hum dos duros miniſtros riguroſos :*
*E depois nos mininos atentando,*
*Que tão queridos tinha, & tão mimoſos,*
*Cuja orfandade como may temia,*
*Para o avò cruel aſſi dizia.*

*O' tu, que tens de humano o geſto, & peito,*
*(Se de humano he matar huma donzella*
*Fraca, & ſem força, ſó por ter ſugeito*
*O coração, a quem ſoube vencella)*
*A eſtas criancinhas tem reſpeito,*
*Pois o não tens a morte eſcura della,*
*Movate a piedade ſua, & minha,*
*Pois te não move a culpa, que não tinha.*

Thus tranſlated:

Lifting unto the azure firmament
Her eyes, which in a ſea of tears were drown'd ;
Her eyes, for one of thoſe malevolent
And bloody inſtruments, her hands had bound ;
And then, the ſame on her dear infant's bent,
Who them with ſmiling innocence ſurround,
By whom poor orphans they will ſtreight be made,
Unto their cruel grandfather thus ſaid :

O thou,

O thou, whose superscription speaks thee, man,
(That the contents were suited to the cover!
A feeble maid thou wouldst not murther than,
Onely for loving him, who first did love her)
Pity these babes *(the babes about him ran)*
In thy hard doom since I am spot all over,
Spare, for their sakes, their lives, and mine: and see
Whiteness in *them*, though thou wilt not in *me*.

I am informed that a Mr. Mickle of Oxford intends shortly to publish another translation of this poem.

A French translation (in prose) of the Lusiad, was published by Duperon de Castera, in three octavo volumes, with remarks. This is the most despicable translation that has ever disgraced any work, and I shall leave the reader to judge of the demerit of the notes and explanations, by quoting a few of them. " In " this poem, Venus represents the Christian religion; Bacchus, " the devil; Mercury, the angels, who are the messengers of " God, in our religion, as he was the messenger of Jupiter, in " that of the pagans.

" Mars represents Jesus Christ: the allusion is natural enough; " Jesus Christ has shed his blood, he has fought for us, and his " goodness has furnished us with arms to combat vice; we may, " without a crime, call him the god of war, especially after " what St. John says in the first chapter of the Revela-" tions: ' His voice was as the sound of many waters: and he
" had

"had in his right-hand seven stars; and out of his mouth went
"a sharp two-edged sword.' This description does not ill be-
"come a warrior. As to what Camoens adds about the ancient
"love of Mars to Venus, it must be understood of the love of
"Jesus Christ to the church. Cupid represents divine love,
"and ought always to accompany religion, which would with-
"out it be a mere lifeless beauty."

In the second canto, the story of Acteon is introduced, and our ingenious commentator says, " the myftical sense of this "fable, is, that if Acteon, and others who, like him, give a "loose to violent passions, were to discover the beauties of true "religion, they would be charmed with them. Mars, who is "Jesus Christ, feels his heart penetrated with tenderness on "beholding the beauties of his religion. Vulcan, who is a De- "mon as well as Bacchus, conceives a cruel jealousy on that ac- "count. All this is as it ought to be; and far from criticising "our author, ought we not rather to admire the delicacy "of his emblems, and the excellent use he makes of fabulous "history?"

In the notes on the ninth canto, after the description of the island where the Nereids amuse themselves with the Portuguese sailors, the explanator says, " Poetry has always had a right to "make use of corporal images, in order to teach us moral and "metaphysical knowledge; not only Grecian and Latin authors, "but even the Psalms of David, the Canticles of Solomon, &c. "abound in the like allegories, &c."

By this time I imagine the reader is sufficiently disgusted with this kind of remarks, so that I shall only add, that in one of the notes on the sixth canto, its worthy author has commemorated the names of the dozen knights who so valiantly fought for the English ladies; says he, " I thought I should have acted un-" justly by those great men, if I had passed over their names in " silence; so many personages are transmitted to posterity who " do not deserve to be remembered, and should we refuse a few " lines to the memory of those who ought to serve us for models?"

And this book was printed in Paris in 1768!.

The new Paris edition of the works of Camoens, in three duodecimo volumes, 1759 (in Portuguese), contains, in the first volume the *Lusiad*; and, in the two others, upwards of 300 sonnets. A poem in three cantos, entitled, Of the Creation and Composition of Man, in 201 stanzas. Two comedies in verse, each of a single act: the one entitled, King Seleucus, and the other, The Amphitrions; and several pieces of miscellaneous poetry.

TOWARDS the end of the sixteenth century, Spain produced an epic poem, celebrated for the singularity of the subject, as well as for some peculiar beauties, but more so for the character of the author.

Don Alonso de Ercilla y Zuñiga, knight of the order of Santiago, and one of the gentlemen of the bed-chamber to the

# APPENDIX.

The emperor Rodolf II. was born in Bifcay about the year 1540. He was brought up from his youth in the palace, and in the fervice of the emperor Charles V. he was afterwards page to king Philip II. and accompanied that prince in his travels through the Netherlands and Germany *.

Don Alonfo fought in the battle of St Quintin, and afterwards, " impelled by an infatiable avidity of acquiring true " knowledge, that is to fay, to know men and to fee the world," travelled through Spain, France, Italy, Germany, Hungary, Bohemia, and England. When he was in London, he heard that feveral provinces of Peru, and of Chili, had taken arms againft the Spaniards, their conquerors (this attempt of the Americans to recover their liberty, is treated as rebellion by the Spanifh authors); the paffion he had for glory, and the defire of feeing and undertaking extraordinary things, made him return to Spain, and embark for thofe parts of the new world. He landed in Chili with a few troops, and remained there during the whole time of the war.

On the fouthern frontiers of Chili is a little mountainous country, called Araucana, inhabited by a more ferocious and robuft race of men than is found in any other part of America. They fought in defence of their liberty longer, and with more

* In the folio edition of the book, entitled, *Viaje de el P. Incipe Don Phelippe, per Don Juan Chriftoval Calvete de Eftrella*, printed at Antwerp in 1552, Don Alonfo is frequently mentioned.

courage than the rest of the Americans, and they were the last that were subdued by the Spaniards. Don Alonso was exposed to many dangers during the prosecution of the war; he saw, and performed many surprising actions, of which the only reward was the honour of conquering rocks, and of reducing a few barren lands under the obedience of the king of Spain.

Don Alonso during the war conceived the design of immortalizing his enemies, by immortalizing himself: he was at the same time the conqueror and the poet, writing at night the actions of the day *, and was frequently obliged to lay down his pen and take up his sword; he fought in seven pitched battles, and returned to Spain with the first part of his *Araucana* finished, when he had not yet attained to the age of twenty-nine years. In 1577, he published the above-mentioned first part; and, in 1590, the entire poem. He was then about forty-three years old; after which there is no mention made of him in history, either regarding his station, his works, or the time and place of his death.

His poem is divided into three parts, containing 37 cantos, and the total number of stanzas is 2603, which is more than double the number of those of the Lusiad.

A continuation of the *Araucana*, by *Don Diego de Santistevan Osorio*, is usually bound with the original poem, in the Spanish editions. This continuation is comprised in 20 cantos, or about 2300 stanzas.

\* *Estando así una noche retirado,*
*Escribiendo el suceso de aquel dia.*        Canto xxiii. Stanza 61.

The

# APPENDIX.

The poem is called *Araucana*, from the country where the events happened which are commemorated in it *. It begins with a geographical description of Chili, and with an account of the manners and customs of the inhabitants. Such a beginning, which would be insupportable in any other poem, is necessary here, where the scene is laid beyond the other tropic, and where the heroes are savages, who would always have remained unknown to us, if they had not been conquered, and thus celebrated. The subject which is novel, gave rise to singular thoughts. I shall give the reader one example, as a spark of the noble fire which sometimes animated our author.

" The Araucanians, says he, were greatly astonished when
" they saw creatures like men, carrying fire in their hands, and
" mounted upon monsters, which fought under them; they at
" first thought them to be gods descended from heaven, armed
" with thunder, and followed by destruction, which made them
" submit, however reluctantly. But after a time, becoming fa-
" miliarised with their conquerors, they discovered their passions
" and their vices, and judged that they were men. Ashamed
" then of having crouched under mortals similar to themselves,
" they swore they would wash their error in the blood of those
" who were the cause of it, and to execute an exemplary, terrible,
" and memorable vengeance on them †."

\* Most of the following remarks on this poem are translated from Voltaire.
† Canto i. stanza 64. And, canto ii. stanza 7.

Voltaire

APPENDIX.

Voltaire has very juftly made a comparifon between Don Alonfo and Homer, in regard to a particular paffage in the works of each of thofe poets; and, in order to do juftice to the Spaniard, I fhall give an extract of the whole paffage, together with Voltaire's judgment on it.

Part of the fecond canto contains a fubject which much refembles the beginning of the Iliad, but by being treated in a different manner, deferves to be placed under the eye of the impartial reader. The firft action of the Araucana is a quarrel which arifes among the barbarian chiefs, as that between Achilles and Agamemnon in Homer. The difpute is not about a captive, but about the command of the army. Each of the favage generals vaunts his merit and his exploits, and the difpute grows fo warm, that they are ready to come to blows. Then one of the Caciques (named *Colocolo*) as old as Neftor, but lefs prejudiced in his own favour than the Grecian hero, makes the following harangue.

 "Caciques, illuftrious defenders of our country, it is not the
" ambitious defire of commanding which engages me to fpeak
" to you. I do not complain that you fhould fo warmly difpute
" an honour which would be perhaps due to my age, and which
" would adorn my decline. It is my tendernefs for you, it is the
" love that I owe to my country, which follicits me to demand
" your attention to my feeble voice. Alas! how can we have
" an opinion of ourfelves good enough to pretend to any grandeur, and to be ambitious of pompous titles; we who have
" been

"  been the unhappy subjects, and the slaves of the Spaniards.
"  Your anger, O Caciques, your fury, should they not be
"  rather exercised against our tyrants? Why do you turn against
"  yourselves those arms which might exterminate our enemies,
"  and revenge our country? Ah! if you will perish, seek a
"  death which will obtain glory. With one hand break the
"  shameful yoke, and with the other attack the Spaniards, and
"  do not spill in a sterile quarrel the precious remains of that
"  blood which the gods have left you to revenge yourselves.

"  I applaud, I own, the haughty emulation of your courage:
"  that same pride, which I condemn, augments the hopes
"  which I conceive. But, let not your blind valour combat
"  against itself, and let it not, itself, destroy the country it ought
"  to defend. If you are resolved not to cease your quarrels, plunge
"  your blades into my frozen blood. I have lived too long:
"  happy he who dies without seeing his country-men unhappy,
"  and unhappy by their own fault! Listen then to what I ven-
"  ture to propose to you: your valour, O Caciques, is equal;
"  you are all equally illustrious by your birth, by your power,
"  by your riches, by your exploits: your souls are equally
"  worthy of commanding, equally capable of subjugating the
"  universe. It is those celestial presents, which cause your
"  quarrels. You want a chief, and each of you deserves to be
"  it; thus, as there is no distinction between your courages,
"  let strength of body decide what the equality of your virtues
"  would never have decided, &c." The old man then pro-
poses an exercise worthy of a barbarian nation, to carry a large
and

and heavy beam, and to grant the honour of command to him who bears the weight of it longest.

As the best method of perfecting our taste, is to compare together things of a similar nature, let us oppose the discourse of *Nestor* to that of *Colocolo*, and renouncing that adoration which our justly prejudiced senses pay to the great name of *Homer*, let us weigh the two harangues in the balance of equity and reason.

After *Achilles*, instructed and inspired by *Minerva*, the goddess of Wisdom, has called *Agamemnon* a drunkard and a dog; the sage *Nestor* rises to calm the irritated spirits of those two heroes, and speaks thus:

" What a satisfaction will the *Trojans* have when they hear
" of your discords? Your youth ought to respect my years, and
" submit itself to my counsels. I have formerly seen heroes
" superior to you. No, my eyes will never more behold men
" similar to the invincible *Pirithoüs*, to the brave *Cineus*, to
" the divine *Theseus*, &c. I went to the wars with them, and
" though I was young, yet my persuasive eloquence had power
" over their minds. They listened to *Nestor*: hearken then,
" young warriors, to the advice which my age gives you.
" *Atrides*, you must not retain the slave of *Achilles*; son of
" *Thetis* you must not treat the chief of the army haughtily.
" *Achilles* is the greatest, the most courageous of warriors; *Aga-*
" *memnon* is the greatest of kings, &c."

His

His speech was infructuous; *Agamemnon* praised his eloquence, and despised his advice.

Let us consider on one side the art with which the barbarian *Colocolo* insinuates himself into the minds of the Caciques, the respectable sweetness with which he calms their animosity, the majestic tenderness of his words, how much the love of his country animates him; how much the sentiments of true glory penetrate his heart; with what prudence he praises their courage, while he represses their fury; with what skill he gives the superiority to no one: he is at once a dexterous censor and panegyrist, so that all submit to his reasonings, acknowledging the force of his eloquence, not by vain praises, but by speedy obedience. On the other side let us judge whether *Nestor* is wise in talking so much about his wisdom; whether to contemn the Grecian princes, and to place them below their ancestors, be a sure method of engaging their attention; whether the whole assembly with pleasure hears *Nestor* say, that *Achilles* is the most courageous of all the chiefs who are present. After having compared the presumptuous and unpolite babbling of *Nestor* with the modest and measured discourse of *Colocolo*, the odious difference which he puts between the rank of Agamemnon and the merit of Achilles, with the equal portion of grandeur and courage artfully attributed to all the Caciques, let the reader pronounce; and if there be a general in the world, who willingly suffers his inferior to be preferred to him in point of courage; if there be an assembly, the members of which will patiently endure an orator to talk of them contemptuously, and brag of their anceſtors at their expence, then *Homer* may be preferred to *Alonſo* in this particular caſe.

It is true, that if *Alonſo* in one only paſſage is ſuperior to *Homer*, he is in almoſt all the reſt of his poem inferior to the leaſt of poets: one is ſurpriſed to ſee him fall ſo low after having taken ſuch a high flight. There is, without doubt, much fire in his battles, but no invention, no plan, no variety in the deſcriptions, no unity in the deſign. His poem is more ſavage than the nations which are the ſubject of it. Towards the end of the work, the author, who is one of the principal heroes of the poem, performs a long and tedious march during the night, followed by a few ſoldiers, and, to paſs the time, he diſputes with them about *Virgil*, and principally on the epiſode of *Dido*. He takes this opportunity of entertaining his ſoldiers with an account of *Dido*'s death, as it is told by ancient hiſtorians; and, in order the better to give *Virgil* the lie, and reſtore the reputation of the queen of Carthage, he amuſes himſelf with diſcourſing upon this ſubject during the greateſt part of two cantos (32d and 33d).

There are no other works of *Don Alonſo* extant beſides the *Araucana*, except a ſmall Elegy of four ſtanzas, which is publiſhed in the ſecond volume of the *Spaniſh Parnaſſus*, together with a head of the author, engraven by *Carmina*.

# APPENDIX.

The *Araucana* has never (to the best of my knowledge) been translated.

As a specimen of the author's poetry, I shall insert the speech of Colocolo to the Caciques.

*Colocolo, el cacique mas anciano,*
*A' razonar asi, tomò la mano.*
　" *Caciques del Estado defensores,*
*Codicia de mandar no me convida*
*A' pesarme de veros pretensores*
*De cosa, que á mì tanto era debida;*
*Porque segun mi edad, yà veis, señores,*
*Que estoy al otro mundo de partida;*
*Mas el amor, que siempre os he mostrado,*
*A' bien aconsejaros me ha incitado.*
　" *Por qué cargos honrosos pretendemos,*
*Y ser en opinion grande tenidos,*
*Pues que negar al mundo no podemos*
*Haber sido sujetos, y vencidos?*
*Y en esto averiguarnos no queremos,*
*Estando aun de Españoles oprimidos:*
*Mejor fuera esta furia egecutalla.*
*Contra el fiero enemigo en la batalla.*
　" *Qué furor es el vuestro, ó Araucanos*
*Que á perdicion os lleva sin sentillo?*
*Contra vuestras entrañas teneis manos.*
*Y no contra el tirano en resistillo?*

*Teniendo*

Teniendo tan á golpe á los Christianos,
Volveis contra vosotros el cuchillo?
Si gana de morir os ha movido,
No sea en tan bajo estado, y abatido.

" Volved las armas, y animo furioso
A' los pechos de aquellos que os han puesto
En dura sujecion, con afrentoso
Partido, á todo el mundo manifiesto:
Lanzad de vos el yugo vergonzoso:
Mostrad vuestro valor y fuerza en esto:
No derrameis la sangre del Estado,
Que para redimir nos ha quedado.

" No me pesa de vér la lozanìa
De vuestro corazon, antes me esfuerza;
Mas temo que esta vuestra valentìa
Por mal gobierno, el buen camino tuerza:
Que vuelta entre nosotros la porfìa,
Degollais vuestra patria con su fuerza:
Cortad, pues, si ha de ser de esta manera,
Esta vieja garganta, la primera.

" Que esta flaca persona, atormentada
De golpes de fortuna, no procura
Sino el agudo filo de una espada,
Pues no la acaba tanta desventura:
Aquella vida es bien afortunada,
Que la temprana muerte la asegura;

# APPENDIX.

*Pero á nuestro bien público atendiendo,*
*Quiero decir en esto lo que entiendo.*

" *Pares sois en valor y fortaleza:*
*El cielo os igualó en el nacimiento:*
*De linage, de estado, y de riqueza*
*Hizo á todos igual repartimiento;*
*Y en singular por ánimo y grandeza*
*Podeis tener del mundo el regimiento:*
*Que este gracioso dón no agradecido,*
*Nos hà al presente tèrmino traido.*

" *En la virtud de vuestro brazo espero,*
*Que puede en breve tiempo remediarse;*
*Mas hà de haber un capitan primero,*
*Que todos por èl quieran gobernarse:*
*Este serà quien mas un gran madero*
*Sustentare en el hombro sin pararse;*
*Y pues que sois iguales en la suerte,*
*Procùre cada qual de ser mas fuerte.*"

*Ningun hombre dejò de estàr atento,*
*Oyendo del anciano las razones;*
*Y puesto yà silencio al parlamento,*
*Hubo entre ellos diversas opiniones:*
*Al fin, de general consentimiento,*
*Siguiendo las mejores intenciones,*
*Por todos los Caciques acordado*
*Lo propuesto del viejo fue aceptado.*

# APPENDIX.

The works of Cervantes, Quevedo, and Feijoo, are too well known in England to need any commemoration here.

Of the books of Phyfic, Law, and Divinity, which fwarm in the Spanifh and Portuguefe languages, as well as in others, I fhall fay nothing, becaufe I underftand them not.

In 1768, the firft volume, in octavo, of a work entitled *El Parnafo Efpañol*, was publifhed in Madrid. In 1770, three more volumes appeared, and a volume in each of the three fubfequent years. This work is a collection of the beft Spanifh poems, and fugitive poetical pieces, with fome account of the lives of the authors, and a fhort criticifm on each piece, very beautifully printed, and ornamented with twelve elegant copper-plates, all engraven by Carmona. I fhall give a fhort account of the contents of each volume, and prefent the reader with fome of the moft felect pieces, with the tranflations as literally as the two languages will permit. After a frontifpiece, reprefenting Apollo fitting among the Mufes, the work opens with a tranflation of Horace's Art of Poetry, by Vincent Efpinel.

Then follow twenty-two canzonets, felected from the forty-four, compofed by D. Efteban Manuel de Villegas, under the title of *Delicias*.

Several detached pieces.

A Madrigal, by Lewis Martin, as follows:

# APPENDIX.

*Iba cogiendo flores,*
*Y guardando en la falda*
*Mi ninfa, para hacer una guirnalda ;*
*Mas primero las toca*
*A' los rosados labios de su boca,*
*Y les dá de su aliento los olores ;*
*Y estaba (por su bien) entre una rosa*
*Una abeja escondida,*
*Su dulce humor hurtando ;*
*Y como en la hermosa*
*Flor de los labios se halló, atrevida,*
*La picó, sacò miel, fuese volando.*

"My nymph collected flowers into her lap, in order to make a garland; but she first applies them to her rosy lips, and with her breath gives them their odour. A bee (happily for it) was hidden within a rose, stealing its sweets; and when it approached the beautiful flower of her lips, it boldly stung them, extracted honey out of them, and flew away."

A SONNET by *Lupercio Leonardo de Argensola.*

*Tras importuna lluvias amanece*
*Coronando los montes el sol claro,*
*Alegre salta el Labrador avaro,*
*Que las horas ociosas aborrece.*

*La corva frente al duro yugo ofrece*
*Del animal, que à Europa fue tan caro,*
*Sale de su familia fuerte amparo,*
*Y los surcos solícito enriquece.*

*Vuelve de noche á su muger honesta,*
*Que lumbre, mesa, y lecho le apercibe,*
*Y el enjambre de hijos le rodéa.*

*Fáciles cosas cena con gran fiesta,*
*El sueño sin embidia le recibe.*
*O corte, ó confusion, quién te desea!*

"The bright sun rises, among importunate rains, crowning the mountains: the greedy labourer abhors idle hours,
and goes joyfully to work; he offers to the yoke the bent
neck of the animal, which was so dear to Europa; he is the
strong support of his family, and carefully enriches the fur-
rows; he returns at night to his honest wife, who prepares
fire, table, and bed for him, and his swarm of children environs him: he eats his light supper with great content, sleep
receives him without envy. O court, O confusion, who desires thee!"

A SONNET by *Christoval Suarez de Figueroa.*

*O bien feliz el que la vida pasa*
*Sin vèr del que gobierna el aposento,*
*Y mas quien deja el cortesano asiento*
*Por la humildad de la pajiza casa!*

# APPENDIX.

*Que nunca teme una fortuna escasa*
*De agena envidia el ponzoñoso aliento:*
*A' la planta mayor persigue el viento;*
*A' la torre mas alta el rayo abrasa.*
   *Contento estoy de mi mediana suerte:*
*El poderoso en su deidad resida:*
*Mayor felicidad yo no procuro:*
   *Pues la quietud sagrada al hombre advierte*
*Ser para el corto espacio de la vida*
*El mas humilde estado, mas seguro.*

"O happy is he who passes his life without entering into the dwelling of those who govern, and who abandons courts for the humility of a cottage! who never fears a scanty fortune, nor is tainted by the poisonous breath of envy. The tallest trees are most persecuted by the winds, and the highest towers are soonest struck by lightning. I am content with my middling station, let the powerful enjoy their grandeur, I desire no greater happiness. Because sacred quietude teaches, that for the short time we are allotted to live, the most humble station is the most secure."

Nine of Virgil's Eclogues by various hands.

The twentieth Epigram of the first book of Martial, beginning, *Si memini fuerant tibi quatuor, Ælia, dentes, &c.* thus translated by *Barthol. Leonardo de Argensola*.

*Quatro dientes te quedaron*
*(Si bien me acuerdo); mas dos,*
*Elia, de una tòs volaron,*
*Los otros dos de otro tòs.*
*Seguramente tosèr*
*Puedes yà todos los dias,*
*Pues no tiende en tus enc`ias.*
*La tercera tòs que hacer* \*.

The AMINTA of *Tasso*, translated into Spanish blank verse, by D. *Juan de Jauregui*, in 1607.

The following celebrated passage in the first scene of the first act:

*Forse, se tu gustassi anco una volta.*
*La millesima parte de le gioie,*
*Che gusta un cor amato riamando,*
*Diresti, ripentita, sospirando:*
*Perduto é tutto il tempo,*
*Che in amar non si spende;*
*O mia fuggita etate*
*Quante vedove notti,*

---

\* This has been translated into English, beginning,

    " When Gammer Gurton first I knew,
    " Four teeth in all she reckon'd, &c."

It is to be found in an old song-book, called *The Nightingale*.

*Quanti*

# APPENDIX.

*Quanti dì solitari*
*Hò consumato indarno,*
*Che si poteano impiegar in quest' uso,*
*Il qual più replicato, é più soave.*
*Cangia, cangia consiglio,*
*Pazzarella che sei:*
*Che 'l pentirsi da sezzo nulla giova.*

Is thus translated:

*Tù, por ventura, si una vez gustases*
*Qualquier mìnima parte del contento*
*Que goza un corazon amante, amado,*
*Dijeras suspirando arrepentida:*
*Todo el tiempo se pierde,*
*Que en amar no se gasta:*
*O' mis pasados años,*
*Quàntas prolijas noches,*
*Quàntos silvestres solitarios dias*
*Hè consumido en vano,*
*Que pudiere ocuparlos*
*En estos amorosos pasatiempos!*
*Muda, muda de intento,*
*Simplecilla de tì, que no te entiendes*
*Y arrepentirse tarde importa poco.*

" Perhaps if thou wert only once to taste the thousandth
" part of the happiness which is enjoyed by a heart loving and
" beloved;

" beloved; thou wouldſt ſay, repenting and ſighing, loſt is
" all that time which is not ſpent in loving! O my paſt years,
" how many widowed nights, how many ſolitary days have
" I not conſumed in vain? and which might have been employ-
" ed in amorous paſtimes, *which are the more ſweet the more
" often they are repeated\**. Change, O change thy opinion,
" ſimple girl as thou art, for repentance is of no ſervice when
" it is too late."

The ladies will not, I hope, be diſpleaſed at here finding this
ſame paſſage as verſified by William Ayre, eſpecially as the advice which is contained in it merits attention.

"  Could I to thy ſoul reveal,
"  But the leaſt, the thouſandth part,
"  Of thoſe pleaſures, lovers feel
"  In a mutual change of heart;
"  Then, repenting, wouldſt thou ſay,
"  Virgin fears from hence remove,
"  All the time is thrown away,
"  That we cannot ſpend in love.
"  Years are paſt, and took their flight,
"  Fooliſh days of coy diſdain
"  Oh! how many a widowed night!
"  Paſt alone and paſt in vain,

\* This line is in the Italian, but not in the Spaniſh.

" Hours

# APPENDIX.

"Hours that in love employ'd,
"Could with blifs the fenfes fill;
"Bliffes, that the more enjoy'd
"Greater grow, and fweeter ftill.
"Ah! change thy carriage, change thy heart,
"Late repentance caufes fmart;
"What a filly girl thou art!"

The fecond volume contains the portraits of Garcilafo de la Vega, and of Don Alonfo de Ercilla y Zuñiga. It begins with Eclogues by Garcilafo; then follows the difpute of Ajax and Ulyffes about the arms of Achilles.

Anacreon, tranflated in fixty monoftrophes, by D. Efteban Manuel de Villegas.

The Judgment of Paris, an epic fable, on occafion of the public entry which Don Ferdinand VI. made into Madrid in 1746, by D. Ignacio de Luzan.

The greateft part of the fecond canto of the *Araucana* before mentioned.

The Gatomachia, or Battle of the Cats, a burlefque epic poem, by Lope de Vega, under the fictitious name of Thome de Burguillos. This is a poem of ninety-feven pages in verfe, divided into feven *filvas*. Then follow a great number of fmaller poems.

The third volume contains the portraits of *Frey Lope Feliz de Vega Carpio*, and of *Dr. Barthol. Leonardo de Argenfola*.

About

About a third part of this volume confifts of poems by de Vega, among which are the following:

Amarillis, an Eclogue of fifty pages.

A fhort poem, entitled *the Flea*.

A Sonnet compofed of hard words, which concludes thus: "Underftand'ft thou, Fabio, what I am faying? How, fhould I not underftand it! Thou lieft Fabio, for I myfelf do not underftand it."

In the feventh volume, I find a fonnet by Pedro Efpinofa, which, after a deal of pompous nonfenfe, concludes thus: "Thou who read'ft this, do not be afraid if thou underftand'ft it not, becaufe even I who made it do not underftand it, fo help me God."

A Sonnet by *D. Manuel de Velafco.*

*Quieres fer gran Señor? ponte fevero:*
*Gufta de fabandijas: tèn enano:*
*Con los pìcaros fé muy cortefano,*
*Y con la gente honrada muy grofero:*
   *Monta de quando en quando por cochero:*
*Lleva á pafear tus mulas en verano:*
*Haz defear lo que penda de tu mano;*
*Y olvidate de que eres caballero.*
   *Si te pide el rendido, tuerce el gefto:*
*De agena bolfa no efcafees gafto:*
*Para las vanidades echa el refto.*

Solo

*Solo con tu muger serás muy casto:*
*Pide, debe, no pagues; que con esto,*
*Si no eres gran Señor, seras gran trasto.*

" Dost thou desire to be a great lord? be haughty; have a
" taste for butterflies; keep a dwarf; be very civil to rogues,
" and very rude to honest people: get upon the coach-box and
" drive thy own mules in summer-time: with-hold what is in
" thy power to bestow, and forget that thou art a gentleman.
" If a favour is begged of thee, turn thy face away: spare not
" another's purse, and squander every thing upon vanities.
" With thy wife alone be chaste; demand, owe, and pay not;
" and by these means, if thou art not a great lord, thou art a
" great rascal."

The Doctrine of Epictetus, seventy pages, translated by Don Francisco de Quevedo Villegas.

Phocilides, translated by the same hand, twenty pages.

The Fable of Apollo and Daphne, in burlesque verse, by Jacinto Polo de Medina.

Seven Epigrams by the same, one of which is

*Cavando un sepulcro un hombre*
*Sacò largo, corvo y grueso,*
*Entre otros muchos, un hueso,*
*Que tiene cuerno por nombre:*
   *Volvióle al sepulcro al punto;*
*Y viéndolo un cortesano,*

*Dijo:*

*Dijo: bien haceis, hermano,*
*Que es huefo de efe difunto.*

" A man who was digging in a grave, among many other bones found a large horn, which he buried carefully again. Another perfon feeing this, faid, Thou doeft well, brother, becaufe that is one of the bones of the perfon who was here interred."

After feveral detached poems, this volume concludes with a fong by the Licentiate Dueñas. The laft couplet contains a very falfe and unjuft fatire on the ladies.

——— *ya no te quejes de mugeres;*
*Y ſi quejarte quieres,*
*Forma de mì querellas,*
*Porque me fié de ellas:*
*Que entònces la muger es buena cierto*
*Quando es mala y perverſa al deſcubierto.*

" ——— Do not complain of women, but if thou wilt complain, complain of me who have trufted them; for a woman is moft certainly good when fhe is *openly* perverfe and wicked."

The fourth volume is decorated with the portraits of Don Diego Hurtado de Mendoza and Quevedo.

The most remarkable pieces it contains are the following:

A Sonnet by Don Diego, and another on the same subject by Lope de Vega. This last has been translated into English, and published in Dodsley's Collection of Poems, which I hope to be pardoned for inserting here after the Spanish originals.

SONNET by *Don Diego Hurtado de Mendoza.*

*Pedis, Reyna, un soneto, y ya le hago:*
*Ya el primer verso y el segundo es hecho:*
*Si el tercero me sale de provecho*
*Con otro verso el un quarteto os pago.*

*Ya llego al quinto: España! Santiago!*
*Fuera, que entro en el sesto: sus, buen pecho:*
*Si del setimo salgo, gran derecho*
*Tengo à salir con vida de este trago.*

*Ya tenemos à un cabo los quartetos:*
*Qué me decis, señora? no ando bravo?*
*Mas sabe Dios si temo los tercetos.*

*Y si con bien este soneto acabo,*
*Nunca en todo mi vida mas sonetos*
*Que de este, gloria à Dios, ya he visto el cabo.*

" You ask a sonnet, my queen, I am making it;
" The first and second verses are already made;
" If the third succeeds happily,
" I shall pay you with one couplet.

" I have

" I have now got to the fifth line; Spain! St. James!
" Softly, I enter into the sixth, courage:
" If I get through the seventh, it will be a great action,
" I must get out of this scrape with life.
" Now I have finished the quadruplets:
" What do you say, madam? do not I proceed finely?
" But God knows if I fear the triplets.
" And if I end this sonnet happily,
" No more sonnets during my life
" As I have, glory be to God, concluded this one.

### Sonnet by *Lope de Vega*.

*Un soneto me manda hacer violante,*
*Que en mi vida me he visto en tal aprieto:*
*Catorce verfos dicen que es soneto:*
*Burla burlando vàn los tres delante.*

*Yo penfè que no hallàra confonante,*
*Y eftoy à la mitad de otro quarteto;*
*Mas fi me veo en el primer terceto,*
*No hay cofa en los quartetos que me efpante.*

*Por el primer terceto voy entrando,*
*Y aun parece que entrè con pie derecho,*
*Pues fin con efte verfo le voy dando.*

*Ya eftoy en el fegundo, y aun fofpecho*
*Que voy los trece verfos acabando:*
*Contad fi fon catorce, y eftà hecho.*

Thus

Thus translated by Mr. Roderick.

" Capricious B . . . . a sonnet needs must have,
" I ne'er was so put to 't before:——a sonnet!
" Why fourteen verses must be spent upon it;
" 'Tis good howe'er t' have conquer'd the first stave.
   " Yet I shall ne'er find rhymes enough by half,
" Said I, and found myself i'th' midst o'the second.
" If twice four verses were but fairly reckon'd,
" I should turn back on th'hardest part and laugh.
   " Thus far with good success I think I've scribbled,
" And of the twice seven lines have clean got o'er ten.
" Courage! another 'll finish the first triplet.
   " Thanks to thee, Muse, my work begins to shorten,
" There's thirteen lines got through, driblet by driblet.
" 'Tis done! count how you will, I warr'nt there's fourteen."

SONNET by an unknown hand.

*El que tiene muger moza y hermosa*
*Qué busca en casa de muger agena?*
*La suya es menos blanca? es mas morena?*
*Es fria, floja, flaca? no hay tal cosa.*
   *Es desgraciada? no, sino graciosa.*
*Es mala? no por cierto, sino buena:*
*Es una Venus, una Sirena,*
*Un fresco lirio, y una blanca rosa.*

*Pues qué busca? dò và? de dònde viene?*
*Mejor que la que tiene piensa hallarla?*
*Ha de fer su buscar en infinito?*
  *No busca èl muger, que ya la tiene:*
*Busca el trabajo dulce de buscarla,*
*Que es el que enciende al hombre el apetito.*


" He who has got a young and beautiful wife, what does he
" seek in the house of another man's wife? is his own less fair?
" is she more brown? is she cold, idle, weak? No such thing.
" Is she deformed? No, she is graceful. Is she wicked? No
" certainly, she is virtuous; she is a Venus, a Syren, a fresh
" lily, and a white rose. What does he then seek? whither
" goes he? whence comes he? does he think to find a better
" than he has gotten? is his search to be endless? He does not
" seek a wife, for he has one already; he seeks the sweet la-
" bour of searching, which alone excites the appetite of man."

The two Odes of Sappho, translated by Don Ignacio de Luzan.

The first, which is the Hymn to Venus, is too long to have a place here. In the Spectator, N° 223, the English reader may see a translation of it.

The second is translated, as Mr. Addison, in the 229th N° of the Spectator, says of the Latin translation by Catullus, " With
" the same short turn of expression, which is so remarkable in
" the Greek, and so peculiar to the Sapphic Ode."

# APPENDIX.

*A los celestes dioses me parece*
*Igual aquel que junto à tì sentado*
*De cerca escucha como dulcemente*
   *Hablas, y como*
*Dulce te ries; lo que à mi del todo*
*Dentro del pecho el corazon me abrasa.*
*Mas ay! que al verte, en la garganta un nudo*
   *De habla me priva:*
*Se me entorpece la lengua, y por todo*
*El cuerpo un fuego ràpido discurre:*
*De los ojos no veo: los oidos*
   *Dentro me zumban::*
*Toda yo tiemblo: de sudor elado*
*Toda me cubro: al amarillo rostro*
*Poco faltando para ser de veras*
   *Muerta parezco.*

In the above mentioned *Spectator* is a French translation by Boileau, and likewise an English one, which are in every body's hands.

In Dodsley's collection\*, is an imitation from the Spanish poem of Quevedo, upon Orpheus and his wife, by the Reverend Dr. Lisle, beginning " When Orpheus went down to the regions below." The original (which consists of forty lines) is in the third volume of Quevedo's works, quarto edition. It ends

\* And likewise in those by Aikin and Donaldson.
(See Dodsley vol. 2. p. 230:)
         thus::

## APPENDIX.

thus: "Happy is the married man, who once becomes single, but superlatively happy is he who twice gets rid of one wife."

In the volume of *el Parnaso*, of which I am now giving an account, is a short poem on the same subject by the same hand.

> *Al Infierno el Tracio Orféo*
> *Su muger bajò à buscar,*
> *Que no pudo à peor lugar*
> *Llevarle tan mal deseo.*
>
> *Cantò, y al mayor tormento*
> *Puso suspension y espanto*
> *Mas que lo dulce del canto*
> *La novedad del intento.*
>
> *El dios adusto ofendido,*
> *Con un estraño rigor*
> *La pena que hallò mayor*
> *Fue volverle à ser marido.*
>
> *Y aunque su muger le diò*
> *Por pena de su pecado,*
> *Por premio de lo cantado*
> *Perderla facilitò.*

"The Thracian Orpheus descended into hell to seek his wife, as he could not go to a worse place on such a bad errand. He sung, and suspended the greatest torments, not so much by
"the

" the sweetnefs of his song, as by the novelty of his intention.
" The stern god was offended, and as the most rigorous punish-
" ment he could devise, permitted him again to become a huf-
" band. But though he gave him his wife again to punish him
" for his crime, yet to reward him for his music, he put him in
" the way of getting rid of her."

  SONNET by the same, never before published.

*Esta es la informacion, este el proceso*
*Del hombre que ha de ser canonizado,*
*En quien, si es que viò el mundo algun pecado,*
*Advirtiò penitencia con excess :*
 *Doce años en su suegra estuvo preso,*
*A' muger y fin sueldo condenado :*
*Viviò bajo el poder de su cuñado :*
*Tuvo un hijo no mas, tonto y travieso :*
 *Nunca rico se viò con oro ò cobre :*
*Viviò siempre contento, aunque desnudo :*
*No hay incomodidad que no le sobre :*
 *Viviò entre un herrador y un tartamudo :*
*Fue martir, porque fue casado y pobre :*
*Hizo un milagro y fue no ser cornudo.*

  " This is the information and process of the man who is to
" be canonized; and who, if ever he committed any sin, did
" superabundant penance for it. He was during twelve years
" dominated by his step-mother, was condemned to a wife,
           " without.

"without wages, lived under the power of a cousin, and had
"an only son, who was both foolish and disorderly. He
"never possessed either gold or copper; he lived always con-
"tentedly, though he was almost destitute of clothing, and
"overloaded with afflictions: he lived between a blacksmith and
"a stutterer; he was a martyr, because he was married and
"poor; and he performed one miracle, which was, that he
"never was a cuckold."

It appears rather extraordinary to meet with such a sonnet in a book licensed by the inquisition.

The next poem I find worthy of notice is a Treatise on Painting, by Pablo de Cespede, painter and poet\*: it contains seventy-six stanzas, each of eight lines. One of the finest passages in this poem is the description of the horse: the author has made great use of Job's sublime description of that noble animal, see Job, chap. xxxix.

### Sonnet by *Lupercio Leonardo de Argensola.*

*Quièn casamiento ha visto sin engaños,*
*Y mas si en dote cuentan la hermosura?*
*Cosa que hasta gozarla solo dura,*
*Y os deja al despertar con desengaños.*
  *O menos en la hacienda, ò mas los años:*
*Y al fin la que parece mas segura*

---

\* His name is mentioned in p. 311 of this work.

*No esta sin una punta de locura,*
*Y à veces con remiendos de otros daños.*
   *Mucho debes à Julia, Fabio amigo,.*
*Que de tantos peligros te ha librado*
*Con negarte la fè que te debia.*
   *Tù de que engaña al otro eres testigo,*
*Y lloras no haver sido el engañado?*
*Riete sino quieres que me ria.*


"Who has ever seen a marriage without fraud, more espe-
"cially if beauty be part of the portion? which lasts no longer
"than till it be enjoyed, and leaves one to wake undeceived.

"Either the years of the woman are more, or her estate is
"less; and even in the safest way marriage is a kind of folly,
"and only patches up the evils it wished to mend.

"Friend Fabius, thou owest much to Julia, who has per-
"mitted thee to escape so many perils, by denying thee her
"hand; and dost thou, who art witness to the deceit used to
"others, lament that thou art not the party deceived? Laugh,
"if thou wilt not have me laugh at thee."


A SONNET supposed to be written by *Don Diego de Mendoza.*

*No hoy cofa mas gastada, ni traida,*
*Que la saya de Inès, y el pobre manto:*
*Un cerrojo de carcel no lo es tanto,*
*Ni la playa del mar siempre batida:*

*No les dà hora de huelga la perdida.*
*En Pascua, ni Domingo, ni Disanto*
*Y tanto los aqueja, que me espanto*
*Como no dàn al traste con la vida.*

   *La rueda de Ixion, que no sosiega,*
*Y su pena infernal que no reposa*
*Respeto de este manto està parada.*

   *Pero la misma Inès tiene otra cosa*
*Que su persona y ella no lo niega,*
*Que està muy mas traida y mas gastada.*

" There is nothing more common, nor more worn than the
" cloak and petticoat of Agnes; a prison-bolt is not more used,
" nor yet the shores which are eternally beaten by the waves:
" their mistress never suffers them to rest either on Sundays or
" holidays, and uses them so much, that I wonder they are not
" fretted to pieces. The wheel of Ixion, which never rests,
" and the never-ceasing pain it inflicts, stand still in compari-
" son with this cloak. Nevertheless the same Agnes has another
" thing of which she is very liberal, and which is much more
" worn, and much more often used."

This sonnet is somewhat in the style of one of Shenstone's *Levities*, which begins

   " Let Sol his annual journies run."

# APPENDIX.

The fifth volume is ornamented with the portraits of Fr. Luis de Leon, and el Conde de Rebolledo, and contains nothing but what is called sacred poetry, being songs and sonnets addressed to Christ, to the Virgin Mary, to St. James, to the archangel St. Michael, to the most Holy Trinity, to the Samaritan Woman, to the most Holy Sacrament, part of the Lamentations of Jeremiah, &c. I have not read this volume, but I believe the English reader's curiosity will be gratified in being acquainted with the subjects of three or four of the sonnets: one of which runs thus:

" A clown asks Faith how the entire, real, and phy-
" sical body of God can be contained in the sacramental bread,
" and likewise in every one of its parts when broken? To which
" Faith answers, that as a looking-glass, though broken into
" thousands of pieces, still reflects an entire image, so," &c.
&c. &c.

In another sonnet, is a passage which says, " The iron of the
" lance of Longinus served him for a steel, Christ for a flint,
" and the Cross for tinder," &c. &c.

The sonnet, in p. 39, is extraordinary, but will not bear an English translation.

The last sonnet in the book is literally thus: " The so-
" vereign Pages of the most holy God, stand with white torches
" and white tapers in the empyrean palaces; a thousand sorts
" of Indian incenses and Syriac perfumes smoke upon carpets
" ornamented with foliages, between amaranths and silvered
" lilies. The Virgin arrived at the empyrean saloon, (a visit
" greatly

"greatly defired by heaven) with the fun for her mantle, and
"the moon for her pattens. The feraphims proftrated them-
"felves at her feet, the angels fung joyfully to her, and the
"Holy-Word placed her at his fide."

The fixth volume confifts wholly of dramatic pieces *. After a frontifpiece reprefenting tragedy, are the two Spanifh tragedies written in 1577 by F. Geronimo Bermudez; they are entitled *Nife to be pitied*, and *Nife crowned with laurels*, or the Hiftory of Doña Inès de Caftro princefs of Portugal †. They are each in five acts, and in blank verfe, with double choruffes, of which three are Sapphic.

Then follows *The Vengeance of Agamemnon*, a tragedy of a fingle act, in profe, with choruffes, tranflated from Sophocles by Fernan Perez de Oliva.

*The Sorrowful Hecuba*, a tragedy of one act, in profe, by the fame hand, from Euripides.

*Ifabela*, and *Alexandra*, two tragedies by Lupercio de Argenfola, each of three acts, in blank verfe.

Thefe two tragedies are praifed by Cervantes in the firft part of his Don Quixote. It cannot be expected that I fhould here give the plot of them, I have thought it fufficient to indicate where they are to be found.

---

* The name of the compiler of this collection of poems is now acknowledged to be Don Juan de Sedano.

† See pages 348 and 383 of this work.

# APPENDIX.

The seventh and last volume contains the portraits of Fernando de Herrera, and Don Luis de Gongora y Argote, and a great number of short miscellaneous poems, from which I shall select the following

Two Epigrams by *Baltasar del Alcazar.*

| | |
|---|---|
| *Magdalena me picò* | *Mostròme Ines por retrato* |
| *Con un alfiler un dedo:* | *De su belleza los pies,* |
| *Dijela: picado quedo,* | *Yo le dije: eso es Ines* |
| *Pero ya lo estaba yo.* | *Buscar cinco pies al gato.* |
| *Riòse, y con su cordura* | *Riòse, y como eran bellos,* |
| *Acudiò al remedio presto:* | *Y ella por estremo bella,* |
| *Chupòme el dedo, y con esto* | *Arremeti por cogella,* |
| *Sanè de la picadura.* | *Y escapòseme por ellos.* |

I conjecture these epigrams to be somewhat allegorical, and shall not translate them, for a reason which will be obvious to those who understand the Spanish language.

Eight Eclogues by *Quevedo,* entitled *La Bucolica de el Tajo.*

A Sonnet by King Charles II. of Spain, not worth inserting, with which I shall embellish and conclude the account of this collection, as the compositions of monarchs are not numerous: it was written about the year 1695.

*O rompa ya el silencio el dolor mio,*
*Y salga de este pecho desatado;*

# APPENDIX.

*Que sufrir los rigores de callado*
*No cabe en este pecho, aunque porfio.*

*De obedecerte, Anarda, desconfio,*
*Muero de confusion desesperado,*
*Ni quieres que sea tuyo mi cuidado,*
*Ni dejas que yo tenga mi alvedrio.*

*Mas ya tanto la pena me maltrata*
*Que vence al sufrimiento; ya no espero*
*Vivir alegre: el llanto se desata;*

*Y otra vez de la vida desespero:*
*Pues si me quejo tu rigor me mata,*
*Y si callo mi mal dos veces muero.*

" O let my sorrow break silence, and issue loose out of this
" breast; for to suffer the rigours of concealment this constant
" breast can no longer bear. I fear I cannot obey thee, *Anarda*,
" I die with despairing confusion, and thou wilt not that my
" cares shall become thine, nor wilt permit me to use my own
" free-will. But thy troubles so much ill-treat me, that they
" vanquish my sufferings; I no more hope to live happily; I
" must give way to my mourning; I again despair of life; be-
" cause if I complain, thy rigour kills me, and if I conceal my
" pain I die twice."

In 1772, Don Joseph Vasquez published two small books, entitled *Los Eruditos a la Violeta*, which implies the *Violet Literati*, for the use of those who pretend to know much, and study little.

APPENDIX. 423

little. These books contain the most celebrated passages of several ancient and modern authors in various languages, with a Spanish translation of every one of them, together with common-place remarks, to enable those who know nothing of the matter to talk learnedly upon subjects they do not understand. The two first pages of *Paradise Lost*, are quoted and translated in this work. The whole is an ingenious satire, and if translated might possibly be acceptable to English *Jessamine Literati*. The same author shortly after published a volume of lyric poems, entitled *Ocios de mi Juventud*, or *Productions of my youthful leisure Hours*. Of these I shall insert a specimen.

Satyrical Verses, in *Quevedo*'s style.

*Que dé la viuda un gemido*
*Por la muerte del marido, ya lo veo:*
*Pero que ella no se ria*
*Si otro se ofrece en el dia, no lo creo.*
  *Que Cloris me diga à mi,*
*Solo he de quererte à ti, ya lo veo:*
*Pero que, siquiera, à ciento*
*No haga el mismo cumplimiento, no lo creo.*
  *Que los maridos zelosos*
*Sean mas guardias, que esposos, ya lo veo:*
*Pero que están las malvadas*
*Por mas guardias mas guardadas, no lo creo.*
  *Que al ver de la boda el trage,*
*La doncella el rostro baxe, ya lo veo:*

*Pero*

*Pero que al mifmo momento*
*No levante el penfamiento, no lo creo.*

   *Que Celia tome el marido*
*Por fus padres efcogido, ya lo veo:*
*Pero que en el mifmo inftante*
*Ella no efcoja el amante, no lo creo.*

   *Que fe ponga con primor*
*Flora en el pecho una flor, ya lo veo::*
*Pero que aftucia no fea*
*Para que otra flor fe vea, no lo creo.*

   *Que en el templo de Cupido.*
*El incienfo es permitido, ya lo veo:*
*Pero que el incienfo bafte*
*Sin que algun oro fe gafte, no lo creo.*

   *Que el marido à fu muger*
*Permita todo placer, ya lo veo:*
*Pero que tan ciego fea,*
*Que lo que vemos no vea, no lo creo..*

   *Que al marido de fu madre*
*Todo niño llame padre, ya lo veo:*
*Pero que él por mas cariño*
*Pueda llamar hijo al niño,. no lo creo.*

   *Que Quevedo criticò*
*Con mas fatyra que yo, ya lo veo:*
*Pero que mi mufa calle,*
*Porque mas materia no halle, no lo creo.*

                                        " That

# APPENDIX.

"That the widow groans for the loss of her husband, I see; but that she would not laugh if another offered on the same day, I do not believe.

"That Chloris tells me, that she loves only me, I see; but that she would not, if necessary, pay the same compliment to a hundred others, I do not believe.

"That jealous husbands are more guardians than spouses, I see; but that their wives are the more virtuous because they are guarded, I do not believe.

"That the damsel should cast her eyes down, and be bashful when the preparations are making for her wedding, I see; but that at the same time she does not raise her thoughts, I do not believe.

"That Celia should accept the husband chosen for her by her parents, I see; but that at the same instant, she does not chuse a lover, I do not believe.

"That Flora places a beautiful flower in her breast, I see; but that it be not artfully to show another flower, I do not believe.

"That in the temple of Cupid, incense is permitted, I see; but that incense is sufficient, without spending any gold, I do not believe.

"That the husband permits his wife to partake of all diversions, I see; but that he should be so blind as not to see what we see, I do not believe.

"That the child should call its mother's husband father, I see; but that he can always call the child his own, I do not believe.

"That

"That Quevedo criticifed more fatyrically than I do, I be-
"lieve; but that my mufe is filent for want of more matter, I
"do not believe."

### EPITAPH.

*El que eftà aqui fepultado,*
*Porque no logrò cafarfe,*
*Muriò de pena acabado.*
*Otros mueren de acordarfe*
*De que ya los han cafado.*

"He who here lies buried, died for grief becaufe he was not
"fortunate enough to be married; others die for forrow that
"they are married."

I purchafed a fmall book in Madrid, which had juft been
publifhed, entitled *Los Literatos en Quarefma*. An affembly of
learned men are fuppofed to meet together every Sunday during
the fix weeks in Lent, and to pronounce a difcourfe, or fermon,
of which the text is to be taken from fome celebrated author.
Accordingly fix fubjects are felected, as follows. The firft,
how prejudicial it is to the advancement of literature, and of
every thing ufeful, to be oppofed by perfons who murmur at
all innovations: the text is, Καὶ ἄλλα πλειςα περὶ τῶν φίλων καὶ
οἰκείων κακὰ εἰπεῖν, καὶ περὶ τῶν τετελευτηκότων κακῶς λεγειν, out
of the laft chapter of the *Characters of Theophraftus*. "There
"are

# APPENDIX. 427

" are murmurers who not only speak evil of their friends and
" companions, but also even of the dead *."

The second, on the education of youth, the text from Cicero's oration in favour of M. Celio: *Hæc igitur est tua disciplina? sic
" tu instituis adolescentes? ob hanc causam tibi hunc puerum pa-
" rens commendavit & tradidit?"* " Is this thy teaching? dost
" thou thus instruct youth? was it for this that the father of
" this young man recommended him to thy care?"

The third, upon theatrical points, the text from the forty-eighth chapter of the second volume of Don Quixote: " *Habiendo de
" ser la comedia espejo de la vida humana, exemplo de las costum-
" bres, é imágen de la verdad; las que ahora se representan son espe-
" jos de disparates, exemplos de necedades, é imágenes de lascivia.*"
" Comedy ought to be a mirror of human life, an example
" of customs and manners, and an image of truth; whereas
" those comedies which are now represented are mirrors
" of absurdity, examples of folly, and images of lasci-
" viousness."

The fourth, upon the difficulties and obligations of a poet; the text from the second satire of Boileau.

* This translation is not exactly literal, a few words are added to complete the sense.

" Mau-

"  *Maudit soit le premier dont la verve insensée*
"  *Dans les bornes d'un vers renferma sa pensée:*
"  *Et donnant à ses mots une étroite prison*
"  *Voulut avec la rime enchaîner la raison.*"

" Cursed be the first who foolishly shut up his thoughts in
" the limits of verse; and who, by imprisoning his words,
" enchained reason in rhyme."

The fifth, upon the partiality of critics, the text from Pope's
Essay on Criticism.
"  *Some foreign writers, some our own despise,*
"  *The ancients only, or the moderns, prize.*

The sixth and last discourse, is to set forth the evils to which
mankind are subject, and to prove that the only way of alleviating them is by means of society, and decent communication between the two sexes: the text from Tasso's tragedy of Turismondo.

"  *La nostra umanitade è quasi un giogo*
"  *Gravoso che Natura e'l Ciel impone,*
"  *A cui la donna, o l'uom disgiunto e scevro*
"  *Per sostegno non basta.*

" Our humanity is almost a grievous yoke, which nature
" and heaven imposes on us, and which neither woman nor
" man, if they live disunited, is capable of bearing."

The

# APPENDIX.

The book contains no more than the three firſt diſcourſes, the laſt of which, upon theatrical points, is preceded by the following ſonnet addreſſed to a bad dramatic poet.

*El que de ſu quietud tanto ſe olvida,*
*Que entrega à bravo mar fràgil navìo ;*
*El que en la guerra, por moſtrar ſu brio,*
*Pone contra mil balas una vida ;*
   *Quien todo ſu caudal de un lance envida ;*
*Quien no eſgrime, y ſe arrieſga à un deſafìo ;*
*Quien ſe expone al capricho, ù al deſvìo*
*De una muger hermoſa y preſumida ;*
   *El que ſube á una càtedra ſin ciencia,*
*Y el que al pùlpito ſaca ſus ſermones*
*Fundando en ſu memoria ſu eloqüencia,*
   *Todos ellos de ti tomen lecciones*
*En materia de arrojo y de imprudencia ;*
*Pues al Teatro das compoſiciones.*

"He who forgets his quietude enough to truſt a frail veſſel to the tempeſtuous ſeas; he, who in war, to ſhow his courage, expoſes one life to a thouſand bullets; he who riſques his whole capital upon a ſingle adventure; he who cannot fence and ventures a challenge; he who expoſes himſelf to the caprice or ſhyneſs of a beautiful and preſumptuous woman; he who mounts a chair without ſcience, and who in the pulpit pulls out his ſermons, and truſts to memory for his eloquence:

430                    APPENDIX.

" quence: all thefe take leffons from thee in regard to rafhnefs
" and imprudence, for lo thou giveft thy compofitions to
" the theatre."

The author in this difcourfe, after having remarked how little
the unities of time and place are regarded in the Spanifh plays,
fays that " the Hiftory of the Life of *Chriftian Jacobfen Draken-*
" *berg*, who died at the age of one hundred and forty-fix years,
" would form a curious dramatic piece, if the fcenes were thus
" diftributed. Act I. Scene I. How the faid *Chriftian* was born
" in Norway in the year 1626. Scene II. how he ferved in the
" artillery at Copenhagen. Scene III. how at the age of one
" hundred and fix years he went to fetch his baptifmal certifi-
" cate. Act II. Scene I. How at the age of one hundred and
" eleven years he married a refpectable lady of fixty. Scene II.
" How he ufed to read the newfpapers without fpectacles, &c.
" Act III. Scene I. How he walked two leagues from a
" village where he was, to the city of Arrhus. Scene II. How
" he died in 1772. Laft fcene, His obfequies are celebrated, a
" funeral fermon preached, a proceffion paffes, and a monument
" is erected to his memory, with an epitaph in the Danifh
" language, &c. &c."

The author then gives a plot of a piece, wherein unity of
place is as little attended to as unity of time is in the foregoing piece. He fuppofes a play to be reprefented, of which the
principal action is the conqueft of New Spain. " The curtain
                                                      " draws

"draws up and shows us a sea-port town in perspective, supposed
"to be Santiago de Cuba. Hernan Cortès sets sail from thence
"with his navy; the scene shifts, and another sea-port town is
"seen, which is that of *Vera-Cruz*, where Cortès arrives, re-
"counting what had happened to him at the Havana, &c.
"Then is represented that most valorous and never-enough-to-
"be-applauded action of boring holes in the ships and sinking
"them; and Cortès declares his intention of proceeding to
"Mexico. The decoration changes, and we find ourselves in
"the identical city of Mexico, the court and place of residence
"of the powerful emperor Motezuma. Many memorable ac-
"tions are exhibited, the conquest is completed, and, when
"the audience least expects it, the port of Vera-Cruz is again
"discovered, from whence Cortès sets sail for Spain. We take
"it for granted, that all the spectators swim after Cortès to the
"town of Palos, and accompany him to Sevilla; and for the
"sake of eighty-two leagues more or less, it would not be rea-
"sonable to abandon him in his journey to Toledo. The scenes
"already represent that imperial city, and Cortès is received
"in it by the emperor Charles V. with demonstrations of sin-
"gular esteem."

"Thus, instead of saying, *we are going to the comedy, we
"are going to the tragedy*, we ought to say, *we are going
"to the chronicles, to the novel*, or *we are going to ramble,
"or to travel.*

"After

"After the unities of time and place, it is neceſſary to ob-
"ſerve the unity of action, otherwiſe we might repreſent in a
"ſingle piece the whole ſeries of the wars of Alexander, or all
"the adventures of Don Quixote.

"But ſuppoſing the three unities to be preſerved, it is not
"enough for perfection; there are many other things neceſſary,
"ſuch as artifice in the plot, probability in the adventures, na-
"tural thoughts, purity of ſtyle, variety in the dialogue, ve-
"hemence in the affections; and, generally ſpeaking, a certain
"importance in every thing that is ſaid and done, capable of
"intereſting and ſuſpending the paſſions of the audience, al-
"ways ſuppoſing the ſelection of a proper ſubject.

"Now even if a theatrical compoſition ſhould have all theſe
"neceſſary qualities, there only remains a ſingle trifle to inſure
"its ſucceſs, and that is, taſte; becauſe to pleaſe or diſpleaſe does
"not always depend on the merits or defects of the work. For
"example, we will ſuppoſe that in digging into the earth, a
"manuſcript tragedy is found in a leaden caſe, and that its au-
"thor is unknown (becauſe if he were known there would be
"partiality), and that in this tragedy all good qualities abound,
"and that not only it preſerves the unity of time, place, and
"action, but likewiſe a thouſand other things which end in *Y*,
"as propriety, clarity, piety, morality, novelty, majeſty, proba-
"bility, and above all a correct Caſtilian, without harſh or lame
"verſes, and without any mixture of Galliciſms, from which
"God

" God, of his mercy and love, deliver us: we muft then confider,
" that as the earth produces mufhrooms without any particular
" cultivation, at the fame time it creates from night to morning
" a dozen actors of both fexes, who befides having true theatrical
" figures, rehearfe without gefticulation, without a pulpit-like
" declamation, and without an ill-timed drawling or affected
" tone. Now, were thefe perfons to reprefent the aforefaid
" uncriticifable tragedy, it is poffible that it would not pleafe
" for various reafons; for inftance, one of the audience would
" expect tempefts, eclipfes, battles, horfes, lions, tigers, and all
" forts of monfters and wild beafts; another waits for poetical
" comparifons and fimilies, abounding in flowers, plants, rocks,
" fields, conftellations, birds, fifh, fands, pearls, coral, fhells,
" &c. they find nothing of this kind in the new tragedy, and
" fo they take a nap till the *tonadilla* awakens them. Another
" hears the play with difguft, becaufe every action in it is very
" poffible, and that it contains no magical reprefentations
" neither by dint of necromancy, chiromancy, hydromancy,
" acromancy, pyromancy, geomancy, cleomancy, &c. no caves
" nor enchanted palaces, no vifions, fpirits, nor phantoms, as
" in *Don John* or *Hamlet:* an old man in the pit difdains the
" play, becaufe night with a ftarry black velvet mantle, earth in
" green fattin, and fea in blue plufh, are not actreffes in it;
" another is difpleafed becaufe the part given to A, was not given
" to B," &c. &c. &c. Thus far may fuffice to enable the
reader to form a general idea of this book.

# APPENDIX.

In 1759, a book was printed in Barcelona, in quarto, entitled *Arte Poetica Española.* Half this book contains specimens and examples of every kind of Spanish verse, acrostics, anagrams, labyrinths, &c. the other half is a dictionary, in which all words with similar terminations are classed together *.

One of the Enigmas in this book is the following:

*Qual es el* uno *que es* tres,
*Y estos tres si los contàres,*
*Aunque son* nones, *son* pares?

" What is the *one*, which is *three*, and those *three* if you count them, although they are *odd*, are *even?* The solution of this Enigma is, God; because in God alone a divine essence and three persons are found, which by being three are called *odd*; and for the equality which they bear to each other, are termed *even.*" !

The works of Garcilaso de la Vega were reprinted in Madrid 1765, 8vo. 187 pages, and consist of three elegies, about forty sonnets, and a few other pieces: the elegies are too long, and the other poems too trite to insert here.

The works of Don Lewis de Gongora are contained in a quarto volume (650 pages): this author died in 1627, aged

* An English dictionary of this kind is just published by J. Walker.

seventy-

## APPENDIX.

seventy-five. They consist of about a hundred sonnets (chiefly nonsense), and various miscellaneous poems. One of these sonnets is written in four languages, which are Spanish, Latin, Italian, and Portuguese. Another, which is addressed to the bridge of Segovia, on the river Mançanares at Madrid, wishes that mules urine may supply that river with water. In another sonnet, the author says, " this river does not deserve half a " bridge, and this bridge may serve for thirty seas; an ass " drank it up yesterday, and to-day has voided it out again by " urine." Another gives an account of a boy's having tied a horn to the tail of a dog, and that a widow cried out that it was a shame to see a thing which had been emblematically worn by so many honourable personages, prostituted so far as to be fastened to a dog's tail. A poetical piece in this work, which is addressed to two gentlemen who had a great affection for nuns, says, " you are troubled with three hundred female saints, you " are either broken looking-glasses, or you have three hundred " faces: but you have much of the god-head in you *(teneis* " *mucho de Dios)*, for you are present every where."

In 1694, was published at Antwerp, a Spanish translation of Guarini's Pastor Fido, by Doña Isabel Correa.

The most striking passages in this pastoral drama, are part of the chorus at the end of the second act, and the fourth scene of the third. This drama was translated into English verse in 1647: this translation was reprinted in 1736, and in the preface I find it attributed to Mr. Fanshaw. Into French, much about the same time, and several times reprinted, though without the chorusses; and into Dutch verse by David de Potter, in 1695.

At the end of the Italian Grammar, by the Abbé Antonini, I find an elegant French translation of the above-mentioned scene; and in Jackson's Elegies it is parodied and set to music. I believe there are other translations extant, but they are very difficult to be met with.

The Spanish translation of part of the second chorus is as follows:

> Es bien suave cosa
> El beso que se coxe
> De la purpurea y delicada rosa,
> Que una mexilla virginal descoxe,
> Mas quien experto la verdad entiende,
> Otro nectar mayor dulce comprende.
> Como juzgais vosotros venturosos,
> Que los probais amantes deliciosos,
> Dirà ser beso muerto ciertamente,
> Aquel aquien al punto la besada
> Belleza no bolviere el beso ardiente.
> Mas los tiernos con dulzidos resabios
> Golpes de dos enamorados labios
> Quando à herirse se van boca con boca,
> En aquel punto toca
>
> *A batalla*

# APPENDIX.

*A batalla (el amor) altisonante,*
*Despuntando una y otra flecha amante*
*Que en suave venganza,*
*Un labio y otro reiterado alcanza.*
*Son verdaderos besos, besos donde,*
*Como en flores abeja, amor se esconde,*
*Con firmes voluntades que exercita,*
*Tanto à otro se dà, quanto se quita;*
*Bese boca que el ambar lisongea,*
*O frente, o pecho, o mano,*
*Jamas podrà dezirse en modo llano,*
*Sin que encuentre la duda que à atropella,*
*Que parte alguna bese en muger bella,*
*Que besadora sea,*
*Sino la boca, donde en dulze calma,*
*Acuden à besarse una y otra alma,*
*Y con despiertos siempre veladores,*
*Peregrinos espiritus da vida,*
*Al hermoso thesoro,*
*De rubis besadores*
*Assi que entre ellos hablan alternados*
*Aquellos eloquentes si animados*
*Vesos, en son pequeño, aunque canoro*
*Grandes cosas en lengua no aprendida*
*Dulcissimos secretos veramente*
*Manifiestos à ellos solamente,*
*Y à otros encubiertos;*

*Tal gozo amando prueba, antes tal vida,*
*Alma con alma unida*
*Y son como de amor sin desconciertos*
*Besos tiernos besados*
*Por modos elegantes*
*Los encuentros tambien de dos amantes*
*Corazones amados.*

The English translation is thus:

" Well may that kifs be fweet that's giv'n t' a fleek
" And fragrant rofe of a vermilion cheek;
" And underftanding taflers (as are true
" And happy lovers) will commend that too.
" 'Tis a dead kifs, fay I, and muft be poor,
" Which the place kift hath no means to reftore.
" But the fweet ecchoing, and the dove-like billing
" Of two encountring mouths, when both are willing;
" And when at once both loves advance their bows,
" Their fhafts drawn home, at once found at the loofe
" (How fweet is fuch revenge!) this is true kifling,
" Where there is one for t'other without mifling
" A minute of the time, or taking more
" Than that which in the taking they reftore;
" Where, by an interchange of amorous blifles,
" At the fame time they fow and gather kifles.
" Kifs a red fwelling lip, then kifs a wrift,
" A breaft, a fore-head, or what elfe thou lift,

" No

# APPENDIX.

" No part of a fair nymph so just will be,
" Except the lip, to pay this kiss to thee.
" Thither your souls come sallying forth, and they
" Kiss too, and by the wand'ring pow'rs convey
" Life into smacking rubies, and transfuse
" Into the live and sprightly kiss their use
" Of reason ; so that you discourse together
" In kisses, which with little noise deliver
" Much matter ; and sweet secrets, which he spells
" Who is a lover ; gibb'rish to all else.
 " Like life, like mutual joy they feel, where love
" With equal flames as with two wings doth move ;
" And as where lips kiss lips, is the best kiss :
" So where one's lov'd, to love, best loving is. *

The poetical works of Don Antonio de Mendoça were printed in a quarto volume, 460 pages, in 1690: they consist of five *Comedias Famosas*, and miscellaneous poems, one of which addressed to a beautiful lady, who had a beautiful daughter, is as follows :

   *O fue milagro ō ventura,*
   *Que una beldad prodigiosa*
   *Quedò hermosa, quando hermosa*
   *Parió la misma hermosura :*
   *Yo en novedad tan segura*
   *Mi admiracion no acomodo*

\* For more on this subject, see the translation from *Secundus* lately published, under the title of *Kisses*.

            *Solamente*

*Solamente admiro el modo*
*De arrojallo, y no perdello*
*Pues dando todo lo bello*
*Se supo quedar con todo.*

"It was either by a miracle, or through luck, that a prodi-
"gious beauty should remain handsome, while being hand-
"some, she brought forth beauty itself: I cannot refrain from
"admiring such a novelty, and am astonished how she could
"throw away so much beauty, and yet not lose any, and bestow-
"ing all that is beautiful, should still know how to preserve
"the whole."

*The Life of our Lady*, precedes the comedies, and consists of 800 verses, not worth reading.

The poetical works of Don Juan de Tarsis, were first published in quarto, 1680: they may be consigned to oblivion without detriment to Spanish literature.

There is a Spanish comedy, intitled *The Adventures of Perseus*, in which Neptune and Medusa are among the dramatis personæ [*].

Lope de Vega wrote a book entitled *la Dorotea*, in two octavo volumes: it is a kind of pastoral rhapsody, in prose and verse.

[*] In the third volume of Mr. Baretti's Journey through Spain, is a good account of the comedy called *the Devil Preacher*, and also a concise one of the Spanish literature.

Romances

# APPENDIX.

Romances and books of chivalry, of which the Spaniards have a great variety, are very difficult to procure: I purchased a few; one of these is entitled *Various Prodigies of Love*, 1665, in eleven novels, five of which are written each without one of the five vowels; these are comprised altogether in 130 quarto pages: the first novel is wholly without any A, the second without an E, &c. It may easily be imagined that the sense is sacrificed to the whim, and that these novels are not distinguished for any peculiar beauty of style. Another is called *La Picara Justina*; it was first printed in quarto in 1640, and reprinted in 1735. At the head of the fifty chapters, into which this romance is divided, are the like number of Spanish verses, in all varieties: the book itself is the Life of a Libertine Hostess, and contains a strange mixture of indecency, nonsense, and religious matters: at the end of every chapter is a moral, to inform the reader that he is to take what he has been reading in the direct contrary sense, which is, as if a child were first to be taught mischief and then forbid to practise it. The author concludes thus: " All that this book contains I subject to the correction
" of the holy Roman Catholic Church, and of the holy inquisi-
" tion; and I warn the reader, that as often as he finds any
" passage which appears to set a bad example, he is to take
" notice, that it is there placed to be burnt in effigy; and, in
" such a case, he is to have recourse to the moral at the end of
" the chapter, and by so doing he will extract utility from the
" description I have given of the vices which abound in the
" world. *Vale. Laus Deo.*"

# APPENDIX.

Excepting this work, there is no indecent book in either the Spanish or the Portuguese languages.

*El Diablo Coxuelo*, is the original romance by *Luis Perez de Guevara*, which was translated into French, with great improvements, by *le Sage*, under the title of *le Diable Boiteux*.

At the end of the Spanish book is a novel, entitled *the Invisible Cavalier*, composed entirely of quibbles and low conceits; and another in which the vowel A is omitted.

The same *le Sage* translated and imitated another Spanish romance, called the *Life and Deeds of Estevanillo Gonzalez*.

The Spanish romance of the Life of Guzman de Alfarache, 2 vols. 8vo. by Mateo Aleman, 1681, has likewise been translated into the French language.

Three small duodecimo volumes were published in Madrid in 1769, after the old edition 1618, with additions, containing jests and witty sayings, for the most part as stale and insipid as those with which the English language is enriched by means of our sixpenny jest-books.

Frey Gerundio is a work at present well known in England, from its translation by the Reverend Mr. Warner. It was written by Father Isla; and, in 1757, he published in Antwerp, a quarto of eighty pages, entitled, *Wisdom and Folly in the Pulpit.*

# APPENDIX.

pit of the Nuns, *(La Sabidurìa y la Locura, en el Pulpito de las Monjas.)* It contains several sermons, which were published with the licences of the inquisition, and Father Isla turns them very properly into ridicule; however, the whole work is uninteresting to an English reader, as none of our sermons that I know of are written in such unintelligible bombast.

In 1672, a work was published in octavo, by Geronimo Cortès, being a Treatise on Terrestrial and Volatile Animals: this is properly speaking a translation of Pliny.

Father Joseph Torrubio, in 1754, published the first volume of a book, in small folio (200 pages), entitled *Apparatus for the Natural History of Spain*, with fourteen plates of shells, fossils, petrifactions, &c. In this book the author thinks he has proved indubitably that there was an universal deluge, by giving a description of all the kinds of shells and petrifactions which have been found upon the tops of, and in the highest mountains in different parts of the world. Conjecture is often mistaken for demonstration, and it will ever necessarily be so with regard to points which are morally impossible to be proved.

Torrubio's work seems to be known in England, as I find it cited in the third part of Edward's Gleanings of Natural History. See plate 336 of that book.

The only Spanish book on natural history which I have been able to find, besides the two above mentioned, is a work published in Madrid, 1762, 4 vols. small folio, with badly engraven copper-plates, entitled *Hiſtoria de las Plantas que ſe crian en Eſpaña, por Joſeph Quer.*

I have a quarto Spanish book, entitled, An Historical Relation of the *Auto-de-fé,* which was celebrated in Madrid, 1680, in presence of king Charles II. his queen, and the queen-mother: it contains a copper plate; the sermon (of fifty pages) which was preached before the execution of the criminals, the text from Psalm lxxiv. v. 22. *Ariſe, O God, plead thine own cauſe;* and a catalogue of the nineteen unhappy persons who were burnt alive, of the thirty-two who were burnt in effigy, and of the seven who were whipped, together with an account of their crimes, and of the sixty who were condemned, some to temporary, and some to perpetual imprisonment, some to banishment, and some to the gallies. Their majesties were present during the whole time the sentences were pronouncing, which was from eight in the morning till half past nine in the evening, when they retired, without having tasted any refreshment during the whole day; neither had the inquisitors nor judges. At half past nine fire was put to the scaffold, which was sixty feet square, and seven feet high, and the nineteen martyrs were burnt; six of these were women, and twelve men, who were condemned for Judaizing, and one renegade Spanish pirate, because he would not abjure

his

# APPENDIX.

his faith in Mahomet: they confifted of three rag-merchants, a flop-feller, an inn-keeper, a foldier, two fnuff-dealers, a pedlar, a ftrolling filverfmith, and three vagabonds; the women were all of the like refpectable profeffions. All their goods were confifcated, and the Spanifh account fays that ten of them had none.

The formula obferved by the holy tribunal of the inquifition in delivering the criminals out of its cuftody is thus: " We " muft, and hereby do furrender, the body of N. N. to juftice " and to the fecular power, more efpecially to M. M. chief ma-" giftrate of this city, and to his affiftants, whom we charge, " and affectionately pray (as much as lies in their power) to pro-" ceed with pity and tendernefs."

" The criminals were burnt alive, fhewing no fmall figns of " impatience, rage, and defpair;" and by about nine next morning *all* was reduced to afhes.

The crimes of thofe who were banifhed, or corporally punifhed, were bigamy: witchcraft: officiating in an ecclefiaftical character without having been ordained: and marrying, being a prieft.

The Defcription of America by *Don Jorge Juan* and *Don Antonio de Ulloa*, is well known in England by the tranflation [*].

In 1772, the above mentioned *Don Antonio de Ulloa*, publifhed a quarto volume of 400 pages, dedicated to the king, entitled, *Noticias Americanas*, or Phyfico-Hiftorical Difcourfes

---

[*] A fine portrait of *Don Jorge*, was lately publifhed in Madrid, engraven by *Caftro* and *Carmona*.

upon South America, and the eastern part of North America; it contains a general comparison of the soils, climates, and productions in animals, vegetables, and minerals, with an account of the petrifactions of marine bodies there found; of the customs and manners of the natives, and of the antiquities, with a discourse on the language, and of the manner by which the country was first peopled. This work well deserves an English translation, as a supplement to that of the former one, it being written with great candour and veracity, without any mixture of credulity.

In 1604, a work was published in two volumes folio, by the *Inca Garcilaso de la Vega*, entitled, *History of Perù*. It was reprinted in 1723: the first volume, dedicated to king Philip V. contains " Royal Commentaries, which treat of the origin of " the Incas, kings of Perù, of their idolatry, laws, and govern- " ment; of their lives and conquests before the arrival of the " Spaniards among them. The second, dedicated " to the most " glorious Virgin Mary, daughter, mother, and virginal spouse " of her Creator, and supreme princess of creatures," contains an " account of the discovery of Perù, of its being conquered by " the Spaniards; of the civil wars between the followers of *Pi-* " *zarro* and those of *Almagro* about dividing the lands."

At the same time, another folio volume was published by the same author, dedicated to Philip V's queen, and entitled *History of Florida*, with a continuation down to the year 1722: it

# APPENDIX.

is chiefly historical, and contains an account of the conquest of Florida by Hernando de Soto, &c.

With these three volumes, the Spanish booksellers usually sell a fourth, of the same size as the others, entitled, Chronological Essay towards a General History of Florida, from 1512, when it was discovered by Juan Ponce de Leon, till 1722, written by Don Gabriel de Cardenas, and dedicated to Lewis prince of Asturias, son of Philip V.

A similar work is, The History of the Conquest of Mexico, written by *Don Antonio de Solis y Ribadeneyra*: it is sufficient merely to mention it, as it has been translated into English. Several different editions have been published in the Spanish language; the last was printed in two large octavo volumes in Barcelona, 1771, with bad copper-plates. The author dedicated his work to king Charles II.

A work was lately published weekly in Madrid, 6 vols. 12mo. upon the model of the *Spectator*, entitled *El Pensador* (the Thinker). Among these periodical papers, I find a translation of Swift's letter to a young lady; this (and several essays contained in this work) is attributed to Don Ricardo Wall.

In imitation of *the Thinker*, a weekly paper was published in Cadiz in 1763, price one real de vellon (about three pence), entitled *La Pensadora Gaditana* (the Female Thinker of Cadiz): the whole

whole is comprised in fifty-two numbers, or four duodecimo volumes, each of about 400 pages. These two works merit being translated into the English language, the subjects are mostly novel; for instance, some of these papers are on *Marcialidad*, or the masculine behaviour of women; on effeminacy in men; on veiled women; on festivals; on the facility with which voyages to the East Indies are undertaken; on true modesty in women; on the want of friends in need; on the little attention fathers pay to marry their daughters advantageously; on the utility of critical papers to the public; on the choice of god-fathers and god-mothers; on step-mothers; on the multitude of ungrateful people in the world; on the choice of friends; on the abuses of processions, and the holy week; on pedantic phrases; and lastly, on death.

A small octavo book, printed in Madrid, 1747, is called *los Claros Varones de España, y Treinta y dos Cartas de Fernando de Pulgar:* it contain anecdotes of twenty five celebrated Spanish personages, and thirty-two letters of *Pulgar*, first published in 1632.

In 1626, an octavo book was printed, and a new edition published in 1748, entitled Sayings and Actions of Don Philip II. it is divided into eighteen chapters, which contain an account of his person, gravity, valour, magnanimity, equality of temper, clemency, piety, humility, devotion, religion, faith, modesty, benignity, temperance, prudence, wisdom, capacity, justice,

justice, rectitude, fortitude, patience, constancy, perseverance, liberality, magnificence, obedience, power, grandeur, zeal, confidence, and wit; here are thirty good qualities, or virtues, enumerated, which have probably never been attributed to any single personage but this monarch.

The work which has been mentioned, p. 239 of this book, entitled *Graces of Grace*, contains many melancholy proofs of the *Egaremens de l'Esprit humain*.

There is at present published monthly in Madrid, a *Mercurio Historico y Politico*, in the nature of the French *Mercures*. There is also a Spanish weekly Gazette.

A little pamphlet, of seventy pages, called *The Life of Lazarillo de Tormes, a Sharper*, is written with some humour: it was reprinted in Valencia, 1769.

In 1755, a small Spanish book was printed at Lions, in France, entitled Letters of Don Nicolas Antonio, and of Don Antonio de Solis (author of the History of Mexico before mentioned), published by Don Gregorio Mayans y Sifcar, a gentleman who is still living in Valencia. At the end of this book is an oration upon the Spanish eloquence by Don Gregorio.

In 1762, two small volumes were published, containing an account of various antiquities lately dug out of the earth in Granada.

# APPENDIX.

nada. The author's device is an eye and a pen, with this motto: "I came, I faw, and I wrote." He might have faved himfelf the trouble of writing, as his book is unintelligible.

When I was at Loretto, I purchafed a Spanifh book printed there, entitled, Defcription of the Holy Houfe, &c. and a catalogue of the treafure and jewels preferved in Loretto: it is embellifhed with four wooden cuts, and a large copper-plate map of the travels of that fame houfe from the Holy Land to where it now ftands: it will never travel any more, becaufe the Italians have built a chapel and a church over it.

A fmall book is extant, containing fourteen dialogues, and a fhort vocabulary, in the Spanifh and French languages, and the Bafque, or Bifcayan dialect, printed at Bayonne.

A fingle line may fuffice for a fpecimen of this jargon:

*Beguis icuftendena, gogos cineztendut.*

"He who fees with the eye, believes with the heart."

There is alfo an old book, entitled *Letters and Aphorifms of Antonio Perez, Secretary of State to Don Philip II.*

In 1774, the infante Don Gabriel, the king's fourth fon, publifhed a magnificent edition of Saluft, tranflated into Spanifh by himfelf: it is in one folio volume of about three hundred pages, and is embellifhed with a map of Numidia, a head of Saluft,

# APPENDIX.

Saluft, three large hiftorical plates, and eight vignettes, by Carmona, and other eminent engravers. At the end is placed a Differtation (forty pages) on the Alphabet and Language of the Phœnicians and of their colonies, by the prince's preceptor. Several plates, on which are engraven thirty-feven medals, and various infcriptions, illuftrate this differtation. A copy of this book is depofited in the Britifh Mufeum, and the prince prefented another to each of our univerfities.

Befides the tranflations of Spanifh books occafionally mentioned in the courfe of this work, we poffefs various tranflations of Don Quixote[*], Cervantes' Novels, Father Feijoo's Defence of Women (with additions), Quevedo's Vifions by Sir Roger l'Eftrange, and Quevedo's Comical Works, by Captain John Stevens.

That there are no more good Spanifh books in print is eafily to be accounted for, as authors dare not publifh any of their works without permitting their manufcripts to be perufed by the inquifitors; fo that till the inquifition is totally abolifhed, literature

---

[*] In 1738, Don Quixote was neatly printed in London in the original language, in four quarto volumes, with fine copper-plates.

In 1711, Edward Ward publifhed Don Quixote, " merrily tranflated in-
" to Hudibraftic verfe;" it is in two octavo volumes, and concludes after the Don " had forfaken his obftinate penance between the ftarving moun-
" tains."

can never flourish in Spain or Portugal. I have heard of many valuable manuscripts, and have, especially in Valencia and Sevilla seen some, which would do honour to the nation, if they were published, but which for the present must necessarily remain in obscurity.

---

THE Portuguese possess very few books that are worth perusing, though they abound in books of physic, law, and divinity. Besides those which I have already cited, I know of no more than the following.

*Rimas de João Xavier de Matos*, 8vo, *Oporto*, 1773 : it contains about a hundred sonnets, and several odes, songs, &c. At the end of the book is a protestation of the author, wherein he says, " The words fate, destiny, deity, &c. employed only " to express poetical fiction, have nothing in common with the " interior sentiments of the author, who, as an obedient son of " the church, submits himself to her determinations in every " thing." Mr. Addison, in p. 235, of his *Remarks on Italy*, quotes a similar protestation of an Italian poet. One of our poet's songs in praise of the Virgin Mary, begins with a translation of the first part of Horace's ode, " *Longe barbaro vulgo!* " *fugi, fugi de mim*, &c." I shall here insert two or three of the best sonnets.

*Huns.*

# APPENDIX.

*Huns graciofos olhos matadores,*
*Que ás vezes por mortaes ficão mais bellos.;*
*Huns dourados finiſsimos cabellos,*
*Das madeixas do Sol defprezadores :*
 *Huma face, de donde as proprias cores*
*Da matutina luz tirão modellos ;*
*Huns agrados tão doces, fem fazellos,*
*Que por elles amor morre de amores ;*
 *Hum rifo t$^a$o parcial da honeſtidade,*
*Que no infenfivel caufarà deſtroço*
*Quanto mais na razão, e na vontade :*
 *Eſta he a minha : oh timido alvoroço !*
*Eu tomo de dizello a liberdade :*
*Eſta he a minha . . . . a minha . . . . mas não poſſo.*

"Two graceful killing eyes, which by being mortal, are
"fometimes the more beautiful : fine golden treſſes which
"defpife the rays of the fun ; a face from which the colours
"of the morning light draw their models ; fuch fweet and un-
"affected graces, that love dies for love of them ; a fmile fo
"full of honeſty, that it would caufe an emotion even in the
"moſt infenfible, how much more in thofe who are maſters
"of their own reafon and will ! This is my . . . . oh timid
"embarraſſment ! I take the liberty of telling it : this is
"my . . . . . my . . . . . more I cannot."

*Eu.*

## APPENDIX.

*Eu vi huma paſtora em certo dia*
*Pelas praias do Tejo andar brinçando,*
*Os redondos feixinhos apanhando,*
*Que no puro regaço recolhia.*

*Eu vi nella tal graça, que faria*
*Inveja a quantas ha; e o geſto brando,*
*Com que o ſereno roſto levantando,*
*Parece namorava quanto via.*

*Eu vi o paſſo airoſo, a compoſtura,*
*Com que depois me pareceo mais bella,*
*Guiando os cordeirinhos na eſpeſſura.*

*Eu o digo de todo; vi a Eſtèlla:*
*De graça, de candor, de formoſura*
*Só poderei ver mais tornando a vella.*

" On a certain day I saw a shepherdess diverting herself on
" the banks of the Tagus, by collecting round pebbles into
" her lap: I saw in her such grace, as would cause envy in
" every woman; she was so delicate in her gestures, and
" shewed such a serene countenance, that she enamoured all
" who saw her. I observed her airy motion, and whole de-
" portment, which appeared more beautiful to me, as she
" guided her lambs among the woods, and I say that I saw
" a star: of grace, of candour, of beauty, I can only see
" more, by seeing her again."

# APPENDIX.

*Poz-se o sol; como jà na sombra fea,*
*Do dia pouco a pouco a luz desmaia:*
*E a parda mão da noite, antes que caia,*
*De grossas nuvens todo o ar femea.*

*Apenas jà diviso a minha aldea;*
*Jà do cypreste não distingo a faia:*
*Tudo em silencio està: sò là na praia*
*Se ouvem quebrar as ondas pela area.*

*Co' a mão na face a vista ao ceo levanto,*
*E cheio de mortal melancolia,*
*Nos tristo olhos mal sustenho o pranto:*

*E se ainda algum alivio ter podia,*
*Era ver esta noite durar tanto,*
*Que nunca mais amanhecesse o dia.*

" The sun sets; day-light vanishes by little and little, and
" turns into dismal obscurity, and the grey hand of night co-
" vers the skies with thick clouds. I can scarcely from my vil-
" lage distinguish the tops of the cypresses; all is silent; only
" the waves are heard breaking on the sands of the neighbour-
" ing shore. With my head reclining on my hand, I lift up
" my eyes to heaven, and I am lost in mortal melancholy,
" my sorrowful eyes are bathed in tears; and, if it were possible
" to obtain any alleviation, I would wish the night to endure so
" long, that day-break should never return *."

\* This translation is not exactly literal.

*Obras*

# APPENDIX.

*Obras Poeticas de Domingo dos Reis Quita*, Lisbon 1766, two small octavo volumes, containing thirty-five sonnets, various eclogues, &c. *Hermione*, a tragedy in five acts, in verse. *Castro*, a tragedy of three acts, in verse, founded on the story of *Dona Ignez*; and *Licore*, a pastoral drama, of three acts, in verse. There are no less than ten different licences at the end of this work. Another tragedy called *Dona Ignez de Castro*, written by S. Sylveira, was published at Lisbon in 1764. Mr. Mallet's tragedy of *Elvira* is on the same subject, and it has likewise been translated into the German language.

*Athalia, tragedia de Monsieur Racine*, *Lisboa* 1762. This is translated into Portuguese blank verse, and printed together with the original French text: at the end are various notes, which are very little to the purpose.

*O Peão Fidaigo*, *Lisboa* 1769. This is a translation of Moliere's comedy, *Le Bourgeois Gentilhomme*, in five acts in prose, by Captain *Manoel de Sousa*, who has likewise published a prose translation of *Moliere's Tartuffe*.

Two of *Goldoni*'s Italian comedies, called *la Serva Amorosa*, and *la Bottega del Cafè* *, were translated into prose, and acted at Lisbon in 1771.

* In 1757, two of *Goldoni*'s comedies were published in the English language, entitled *The Father of a Family*, and *Pamela*. This author has published upwards of a hundred dramatic pieces.

In

# APPENDIX.

In 1769, a Portuguese translation, in three acts, in prose, was published, of Ben Johnson's *Epicoene*: it was acted at Lisbon, though miserably disfigured.

There are a great number of Portuguese theatrical pieces, and among them it is probable there are some not totally despicable. In the piece entitled *Auto de Santa Catharina*, the dramatis personæ are St. Catherine, her Mamma, a Hermit, Jesus Christ, the Virgin Mary, an Emperor, an Empress, a Page, three Doctors, and four Angels. St. Catherine is married to Christ by the Virgin Mary upon the stage, and at last she is beheaded, and four angels enter singing, and carry off her body. But to the credit of the two nations, I inform the reader, that this kind of absurd and disgusting stage performances is at present prohibited by royal authority both in Spain and in Portugal.

A new edition of the *Life of Don John de Castro, fourth viceroy of India*, was published in the Portuguese language, Paris 1769, 8vo. (450 pages): it was written by *Jacinto Freyre de Andrada*. This work is divided into four books; in the first we are entertained with an account of a marble cross found at Goa, which had been made by Saint Thomas, and how, on a particular day, it first sweated blood, then became pale, afterwards black, then again of a splendid blue; and, lastly, returned to its original colour. In the second book we are informed, that, during a battle against the barbarian inhabitants of the Molucca islands, it rained ashes upon the enemies heads, and by that means

means they were vanquished by the Portuguese. In the third book is the copy of a letter which Don John wrote from Diù, in 1546, to the city of Goa, to borrow money, with a few hairs of his beard inclosed by way of pledge. The inhabitants of Goa lent him the money, and sent his hairs back to him, and they are still preserved by his descendants in a crystal vase set in silver. Don John died in Goa in 1548, aged forty-eight, having governed that city three years: he was afterwards interred in the convent of Bemfica, near Lisbon.

In 1741, were published at Amsterdam, two octavo volumes in the Portuguese language, of familiar, historical, political, and critical letters, written from Vienna in 1736 and 1737, by Don Francisco Xavier de Oliveyra; and, at the same time, another volume was published, entitled Travels of Don F. X. Oliveyra, in 1734: the author set sail from Lisbon, and landed at the Texel near Amsterdam, from thence he proceeded through Hanover, Leipsic, and Prague to Vienna. At the beginning of this work is the following protestation. " As a true, and at
" the same time unworthy son of the holy Roman Catholic
" apostolical mother-church, I subject all my writings to the said
" holy mother-church, protesting that I have not the least in-
" tention of recounting or saying any thing against her laws,
" &c. In the same manner I subject the said writings to the
" tribunals of the holy office, and to all other ecclesiastical and
" political tribunals of the kingdom of Portugal, &c. &c. &c.
" &c. Amsterdam 1740."

In

## APPENDIX. 459

In p. 16, of this Journal, the author says, " and as we had
" been for a week past expofed to continual tempefts &c. I took
" a refolution to avail myfelf of my reliques. I do not recount
" miracles, but I only tell this event as I would any other. At
" nine at night I flung into the fea feveral that I had with me,
" judging that the moft proper method for a finner to obtain
" favours from God, is to have recourfe to thofe patrons who
" glorioufly enjoy the prefence of that fame God : one of the
" principal reliques was of our Lady of Loreto, another of Saint
" Therefa, and another of pope Innocent XI. whom I venerate
" greatly. At four the next morning we difcovered the Scilly
" ifles, &c. &c."

I have the pleafure of being acquainted with the author: he
was born in 1702, and came to London in 1744 : two years after which he abjured the Roman Catholic religion, and, in confequence had the honour of being burnt in effigy at Lifbon in
1762.

Don Diego Bernardes, Don Claudio Manuel da Cofta, and
another Don, under the fictitious name of Melizen Cylenio,
each publifhed a volume of poems lately. I have not yet received them from Lifbon.

In 1761, a new edition of a work, in two quarto volumes, was
publifhed, dedicated to the late king John V. entitled *Colleccaõ
Politica de Apothegmas de Pedro Jofé Suppico.*

A Col-

A Collection of Voyages by the Portuguese is also extant in one quarto volume. I have not been able to procure either of these works, so that I can only indicate their titles.

In 1738, a single octavo volume was published in Paris, entitled *Theatre Espagnol*, by the *Du Perron de Castera* before mentioned; it contains extracts from ten Spanish plays, with reflections at the end of each, as pertinent as the notes to the French Lusiad; and, in 1770, four more volumes were published under the same title, by L\*\*\*, containing translations of fifteen plays, and five interludes.

An English book is extant, entitled *The Portugal History, or a Relation of the Troubles that happened in the Court of Portugal in 1667, and 1668*, in octavo, London, 1677, by S. P. Esq. in which king Alphonso VI. is characterised as one of the most wicked princes that ever existed.

In 1740, was published an octavo volume, entitled *The History of the Revolutions of Portugal, with Letters of Sir Robert Southwell during his Embassy there in 1667*.

It may not be thought improper to point out the few prints and maps engraven in Spain and Portugal, or relative to those kingdoms, because they cannot be purchased without being enquired

quired for, as no Spanish nor Portuguese bookseller will acquaint the curious traveller with their existence. Besides those which have been mentioned in the course of this work, I procured the following:

A large chart of the bay of Cadiz, published in Paris, 1762, by *le Sieur Bellin*.

A large chart of the Straits of Gibraltar, with a plan of the town and fortifications, and tables of the tides, Paris, 1761, Bellin. These two charts were published by order of the duke of Choiseul for the use of the king's ships.

A large and exact map of Portugal, Paris 1762, by Rizzi Zannoni.

Topo-hydrographical plan of the bay of Gibraltar, Paris.

A topographical map of the Streights of Gibraltar, with tide tables.

Geometrical plan of Gibraltar, with the new fortifications. These were both published in Madrid, 1762, by Lopez.

Seven whole-sheet views in Sevilla: these were engraven in 1738. They are badly executed, but the representations are exact. They consist of a general view, with the bridge of boats; the outside of the cathedral, with the tower; the exchange, with a procession of children redeemed from slavery; the town-house, with the procession on *Corpus Christi* day; the magnificent church of the Jesuits, built near the spot where St. Ignatius de Loyola was born; the royal seminary of Sant' Elmo, and the Hospital de la Sangre.

A set.

APPENDIX.

A set of eight prints was published in Madrid 1757, tolerably well engraven; they are, general view of the aqueduct of Segovia; view of the six middle arches of the aqueduct, on a larger scale; view of another part of the aqueduct; front view of the royal palace of Aranjuez; another view of the same palace; the Toledo bridge in Madrid, with elevations of the center arch, and other parts, on a larger scale; a monastery, and a church in Madrid.

A whole sheet coloured print, entitled *Estado Militar de España*, being the figures of a soldier from every regiment, cavalry and infantry, in the proper uniform.

A sheet with the figures of thirty founders of religious orders which exist in Spain, in their proper habits.

Four very large prints were published in London in 1756, dedicated to his majesty (then prince of Wales); they are so extremely well executed, that they merit particular mention: they were all drawn by C. Lempriere, and painted by R. Paton.

1. General view of Lisbon as before the earthquake, engraven by Anthony Walker.

2. View from the Tagus of the country between Alcantara and Bellem, by P. C. Canot.

3. View of Bellem, by P. Foudrinier.

4. View of the country westward of Bellem, by J. Mason.

There is a small view of the city of Oporto published in London, by J. and C. Bowles.

Several

## APPENDIX. 463

Several prints have been publifhed in Madrid by Carmona, Fabregat, and other engravers, reprefenting landfcapes, and other mifcellaneous pieces.

If I were to travel again in Spain, I fhould purfue the following route, which would nearly complete the tour of that kingdom: fuppofing I were at Bayonne, I would crofs the Pyrenean mountains at Fuenterabia, or Pampeluna in Navarre, vifit Bilbaô, in the lordfhip of Bifcay, Orduña, Santillana, and Oviedo in the Afturias; Ferrol, which is one of the three marine departments, Coruña, from which place to Falmouth Englifh packets formerly failed and returned; Santiago de Compoftella, a celebrated refort of pilgrims, all in Galicia; then to Leon, the capital of the kingdom of the fame name, through Palencia to Burgos; to Soria, near which place are the ruins of Numancia; to Saragoffa, capital of Aragon, fituated on the river Ebro; to Tortofa, near the mouth of that river, and then along the coaft to Barcelona; the environs of which city, and indeed the whole principality of Cataluña, are faid to be as well cultivated, and as fertile as the kingdoms of Valencia, Naples, or any part of Europe, and the inhabitants as numerous and as induftrious as thofe of Holland. Near Barcelona is the convent and hermitage of Monferrat; fituated on the fummit of a high mountain *; and from thence through Girona, crofs the Pyrenean

---
* In a German book in folio, publifhed in 1735, at Leipzig, entitled *Hiftorifcher Schauplatz, in welchen die Merkwürdigften Brücken der Welt*,

mountains to Perpignan: it would scarcely be worth going down to Alcantara, to see the bridge built over the Tagus by Trajan, nor to Badajoz, where there is a bridge of thirty arches over the river Guadiana.

My design was to have travelled from Oporto to Santiago de Compostella, but the roads are impassable in carriages, and the season would not admit of travelling on horseback, so that in order to arrive at Salamanca, I was obliged to return half-way to Coimbra: it is easy to trace an intended route, but very difficult to put it in practice in these kingdoms. I travelled the direct road from Aranjuez to Valencia, and by the track on the map may be seen how much it deviated from a strait line. If I had gone from Madrid to Saragossa and Barcelona, it would have made a difference in point of time of at least three months, so that by reason of the advanced season, I should have lost the opportunity of embarking at Cadiz.

Mr. Garrick has been so kind as to favour me with his imitation of the Spanish Madrigal, inserted in p. 399, with which I shall conclude this Appendix.

*in prospecten vergestellet und beschrieben werden, von Carl Christian Schramm,* or Description of the most remarkable Bridges in the World, with eighty-seven very large Copper-plates; one of the plates represents a very extraordinary bridge between Barcelona and Monserrat, with a prospect of that mountain.

For

## APPENDIX.

For me my fair a wreath has wove,
Where rival flow'rs in union meet;
As oft she kifs'd this gift of love,
Her breath gave fweetnefs to the fweet.

A bee within a damafk rofe
Had crept, the nectar'd dew to fip;
But leffer fweets the thief foregoes,
And fixes on Louifa's lip.

There, tafting all the bloom of fpring,
Wak'd by the rip'ning breath of May,
Th' ungrateful fpoiler left his fting,
And with the honey fled away.

# INDEX.

## A

AQUEDUCT at Lisbon, p. 7.
——— Coimbra, 46.
——— Segovia, 83.
*Aranjuez*, 187.
*Alcobaça*, 39.
*Almansa*, 195.
*Alicante*, 216.
*Almeida*, 55.
*Antequera*, 456.
*Alcaçar*, at *Segovia*, 83.
——— *Toledo*, 184.
——— *Sevilla*, 307.
Amphitheatre for the bull-fights at *Lisbon*, 32
——————— *Madrid*, 157.
——————— *Aranjuez*, 188.
——————— *Granada*, 235.
——————— *Cadiz*, 288, 318.
——————— *Port St. Mary*, 288.
——————— *Sevilla*, 305.
Amphitheatre, Roman, of *Saguntum*, 207.
——————— *Italica*, 312.
Anthony, St. generalissimo, 31.
Aloe work-bags, 36.
Ass, price of one, 64.
Archives of Spain, 65.
Apes and monkies, 269.
Armoury and arsenal, 317.
Arabic curiosities, 236.
Assassin's body exposed, 66.
*Aveluco* bird, or bee-eater, 257.

Appendix, 338.
*Araucana*, poem, 386.
Academy at *la Ysla*, 317.
*Auto-de fé*, book of an, 444.
Army, Portuguese, 22.
——— Spanish, 226.

## B

*Batalha*, 43.
*Bellem*, 10.
*Buen-retiro*, 151.
Basso relievo of a musical instrument, 65.
——————— of Leda, 243.
——————— at *St. Ildefonso*, 92.
Baboons cleansing heads, 22.
Bull-fight, 288.
Bull of the crusada, 326.
*Barilla* plant, 217.
Bee-eater, 257.
Beetle, the tumble-dung, 247.
Buffaloes, 188.
Black and white beings, 332.
Bones found in the rock of Gibraltar, 270.
Books, catalogue of, 367.
Book, dedicated to God, 269.
Bridge on boats, 302.

## C

*Cintra*, 18.
*Caluz*, 21.

*Coimbra,*

# INDEX.

*Coimbra*, 46.
*Ciudad Rodrigo*, 57.
*Coca*, 71.
*Carthagena*, 223.
*Cordova*, 250.
*Cartama*, 261.
*Ceuta*, in *Africa*, 274.
*Chiclana*, 279.
*Cadiz*, 280.
Coins, Portuguese, 24.
——— Spanish, 84.
Cities, number of, in Spain, 336.
Convents, ditto, ditto, ibid.
Criminals chained, 51.
Charles V. 67, and
Chancery, royal, at *Valladolid*, 69.
Clothes, old, 84.
Court of Spain, where pass the year, 88.
Crucifix by Cellini, 102.
Comedy, plot of a Spanish, 160.
Camels, 188.
Cameleons, 319.
Carrobe-tree, 197, 217.
Cork-tree, 264.
Cotton-fields, 255.
Cock-fight, 249.
Carriages, four-wheeled, 196.
Chronological tables, 204.
Colony of Germans, 250.
Catalogue of books, 367.
Castles, Moorish, of *Alcobaça*, 39.
————————— *Almansa*, 195.
————————— *Sax*, 216.
*Cortejo*, or *Cicisbeo*, 17, 234, 325.
Caimo, father, 96.

## D

Dress, 28, 33, 231.
Days of deliverance from purgatory, 172, 328.

## E

Entrance into Spain, 56.
*Escorial*, the, 98.
*Elche*, 220.
*Ecija*, 248.
Echo at *Toledo*, 185.
Elephants, 13, 300.
Elastic gum, 322.
*Embriologia Sacra*, 269.
English and Scotch colleges, 66.
——— nunnery at Lisbon, 32.
——— carriages and furniture, 254
——— theatre at Gibraltar, 272.
——— book dedicated to God, 269.

## F

*Fandango*, 17, 156.
Female knights, 62.
Fountains at *St. Ildefonso*, 88.
————— *Aranjuez*, 189.
————— *Ocaña*, 192.
French theatre at Cadiz, 280.
————— *gavachos*, 140.
Farce, plot of a Spanish, 164.
Fielding, buried at *Lisbon* in 1756, 27.
Foundling hospitals, 222.

## G

*Granada*, 233.
*Gibraltar*, 268.
———— model of, 273.
*Guadarama*, pass of, 98.
*Guadalquivir* river, 314.
Glow-worms, ladies decorated with, 282.
Gum, elastic, 322.
Green-oaks, 264.
*Gaspacho*, or *Soupe*, 278.
Grandees, 176.

Gypsies,

# INDEX.

Gypsies, 179.
Gardens of *St. Ildefonso*, 88.
——— *Aranjuez*, 189.

## H

History of Portugal, 347.
——— Spain, 355.
Horses, 253.

## I

*Julian*, *St.* castle of, 14.
*Ildefonso*, *St.* 86.
Island of Santa Pola, 218.
*Jorge Juan*, Don, 220.
Inquisition, 33.
Irish nunnery at *Bellem*, 32.
——— college at *Salamanca*, 58.
——— regiments, three. 226.
*Italian* opera at Lisbon, 2.
——————— Bellem, 10.
——————— Oporto, 48.
——————— Ceuta, 274.
——————— Cadiz, 281.
Itinerary, 338.

## K

King of Portugal, 11.
——— Spain, 167.
Knighthood, orders of, in Portugal, 23.
——————————— Spain, 177.
——————————— female, 62.
*Kermes*, trees which produce the, 264.

## L

*Lisbon*, 1.
*Leyria*, 45.
*Lorca*, 227.
*La Ysla*, 300.

Ladies, 9, 32, 36, 62, 144, 282, 313, 324.
Liquorice, 312.
Larks, 63.
*Lusiad*, poem, 375.
Liquefaction of blood, 173.

## M

*Mafra*, 15.
*Madrid*, 139.
*Mejorada*, 169.
*Morviedro*, 207.
*Murcia*, 220.
*Malaga*, 259.
*Michael's*, *St.* cave, 270.
*May*, Mrs. 9.
Monkies at *Gibraltar*, 273.
*Madder* plants, 158.
Model of *Gibraltar*, 273.
Marbles, 237.
Moorish palace, 240.
——— castles, 39, 195, 216, &c.
*Mesquita*, in *Cordova*, 251.
Mills, 32, 84, 306.
*Maestranzas*, societies, 238.
Mosaic at Lisbon, 3.
——— Madrid, 151.
Menagerie at Bellem, 13.
Music, 9.
Man burnt alive, 34.
Mint at Segovia, 84.
Manufactory of sword-blades, 186.
——————— plate-glass, 87.
——————— knives, 195.
Mountains, *Sierra Nevada*, 231.
——— *Alpuxarra*, ibid.
——— *Sierra de Estrella*, 52.
——— *Sierra Morena*, 250.

## N

*Naples*, annual miracle at, 174.
Navy of Portugal, 22.

# INDEX.

Navy of Spain, 225.
Navigation of rivers, 29.

## O

Odivelas, convent of, 36.
Oporto, 48.
Olmedo, 71.
Ocana, 192.
Operas, see Italian.
Orders, see Knighthood.
Old clothes, 84.
Orange-tree, 50.
Observatory in Cadiz, 283.

## P

Porto, 48.
Portuguese, theatres 2, 48.
——— royal family, 11.
——— coins, 24.
——— history, 347.
——— books, 375, 452.
Production of Portugal, 28.
——— Spain, 256, 334.
Population of Lisbon, 26.
——— Spain, 336.
Port St. Mary, 288, 315.
Port Royal, 316.
Pardo, the, 169.
Pruning of trees, 30.
Pigeon-houses, 41.
Pantheon, 108.
Pass of Guadarama, 98.
Plot of a comedy, 160.
——— an interlude, 164.
Purgatory, 173, 328.
Prayers for drowned persons, 314.
——— at a Lao, 316.
Penitent ladies, 324.

Palaces, at Bellem, 12.
——— Caluz, 21.
——— Valladolid, 67.
——— Segovia, 83.
——— St. Ildefonso, 86.
——— new ditto, 97.
——— the Escorial, 98.
——— Madrid, 140.
——— el Pardo, 169.
——— el Buen retiro, 151.
——— Toledo, 184.
——— Aranjuez, 189.
——— Granada, 240.
——— ditto Alhambra, ibid.
——— Sevilla, 307.
Pictures at Lisbon, 12.
——— Caluz, 21.
——— Salamanca, 58.
——— Valladolid, 66.
——— St. Ildefonso, 190.
——— the Escorial, 111.
——— Madrid, 143.
——— el Buen-retiro, 151.
——— Loeches, 171.
——— Lorca, 227.
——— Granada, 237.
——— Malaga, 260
——— Cadiz, 282.
——— Sevilla, 308.
——— Port St. Mary, 315.
——— Port Royal, 317.

## R.

Ronda, 265.
Roque, cape, 14.
——— San, 267.
Rabbit-warren, 41.
Roads, dangerous, 263, &c. &c.
——— itinerary of the, 338.
Reliques, 105, 202.

Rains,

# INDEX.

Rains, heavy, 35.
Raisins, 334.

*Spanish* books, 386.
Sea-voyage, 336.

## S

*Salamanca*, 58.
*Simanca*, 65.
*Segovia*, 72.
*Sax*, 216.
*Sevilla*, 301.
*St. Antbony*, 31.
— *Raphael*, 250.
— *Cecilia*, 9.
— *Roque*, 267.
— *Pola*, 218.
— *Julian*, 14.
— *Michael*, 270.
— *Philip*, 198.
— *Ildefonso*, 86.
Santiago, female knights of, 62.
Saints, Venetian, 326.
Stones in strange positions, 55.
Storks, 57.
Scotch college, 66.
Sheep, management of, 72
Silk-worms, 199.
Statues at Bellem, 13.
———— St. Ildefonso, 92.
Souls delivered, 173, 328.
Soldiers, hired, 228.
Shells, large, 321.
Snake-stone, 321.
Salmon, 5.
*Spain*, history of, 355.
——— royal family of, 167.
——— population of, 336.
*Spanish* theatre at Madrid, 159.
—————— Cadiz, 280.
—————— Sevilla, 305.
——— army, 226.
——— navy, 225.

## T

*Toro*, 64.
*Tordesillas*, 65.
*Toledo*, 180.
*Tobofo, el,* 194.
*Tetuan*, 275.
Toads, 319.
Tumble-dung beetle, 247.
Thunny-fish, 335.
Tobacco prohibited, 31.
———— fabric, 306.
Travelling, method of, 37, 196.
Trade to America, 282.
——— wine, 50.
Tower at Sevilla, 314.
———— shaking, 313.
———— topsyturvy, 314.
Towers, watch, 313.

## V

*Valladolid*, 65.
*Valencia*, 200.
*Venta*, a, described, 39.
Virgin Mary, 239, 244.
Voyage at sea, 336.
——— on a river, 314.
*Venetian* saints, 326.
Ulloa, Don Antonio de, 312.

## W

Women and hogs, 286.
Water-nymphs, 286.
Wind-mills, 32.

Wheels.

# INDEX.

Wheels to raife water, 329.
Wine trade at Oporto, 50.
——— Xerez, 299.
Wild-boars, 187.
Wolves, 256.

## X

Xativa, 198.

Xerez de la Frontera, 299.

## Z

Zamora, 63.
Zebras, 13.

# FINIS.

## ERRATA.

Page 14. line 6. *for* erafed, *read* rafed; p. 33. l. 12. *for* autos da fé, *read* autos de fé; p. 49. l. 4. *for* of, *read* to; p. 65. for *creci dos*, read *crecidos*; p. 74. l. 11. *for* fheep *read* ewes; p. 99. l. 21. *after* martyrdom, *read* except the crofs; p. 100. l. 7. *for* bread, *read* beard: p. 141. l. 5. *for* one the top, *read* on the top; p. 145. for *pernice*, read *pernici*; p. 152. l. 20. *for* whole a, *read* a whole; p. 174. for *fjour*, read *fejour*; p. 175. l. 17. *for* winter, *read* fpring; p. 197. l. 16. *after* produces, *dele* in; p. 268. *for* 1706, *read* 1704; p. 277. l. 5. *for* with, *read* without; p. 298. *laſt line*, *for* exhibit, *read* exhibited; p. 318. l. 12. *for* his, *read* its; p. 348. l. 3. *for* year the, *read* the year; p. 369 l. 3. *dele* and; p. 371. l. 13. for *acro*, read *facro*; p. 410. firſt line of the Spaniſh fonnet, for *violante*, read *Violante*.

www.ingramcontent.com/pod-product-compliance
Lightning Source LLC
Chambersburg PA
CBHW051844300426
44117CB00006B/263